kyles + 1 hr Aava

CLYDE CRUISING CLUB

SAILING DIRECTIONS

AND

ANCHORAGES

WEST COAST OF SCOTLAND
(TENTH EDITION)

Reprinted 1978

PUBLISHED BY

GILMOUR & LAWRENCE LTD.

CLYDEWAY INDUSTRIAL CENTRE

8 ELLIOT PLACE

GLASGOW G3 8EL

1974

CLYDE CRUISING CLUB

Commodore

G. Victor Dare, Esq.

Vice-Commodore

A. Donald Findlay, Esq.

Rear-Commodore

Peter Houston, Esq.

Hon. Secretary and Treasurer

A. G. Taggart, Esq.
S.V. Carrick,
Clyde Street, Glasgow G1 4LN
Tel: 041-552 2183

Hon. Editor

G. B. Vinycomb, Esq.

9th May, 1974

The Club would like to acknowledge the considerable assistance given by Commander R. G. Mowat, R.N. (Rtd.), in Proof Reading, Indexing, etc., in this the 10th Edition of Sailing Directions.

CLYDE CRUISING CLUB

SAILING DIRECTIONS

AND

ANCHORAGES
WEST COAST OF SCOTLAND
(TENTH EDITION)
Reprinted 1978

PUBLISHED BY

GILMOUR & LAWRENCE LTD.

CLYDEWAY INDUSTRIAL CENTRE

8 ELLIOT PLACE

GLASGOW G3 8EL

CLYDE CRUISING CLUB

Commodore

G. VICTOR DARE, Esq.

Vice-Commodore

A. DONALD FINDLAY, Esq.

Rear-Commodore

PETER HOUSTON, Esq.

Hon. Secretary and Treasurer

A. G. TAGGART, Esq.
S.V. Carrick,
Clyde Street, Glasgow G1 4LN
Tel: 041-552 2183

Hon. Editor

G. B. VINYCOMB, Esq.

9th May, 1974

The Club would like to acknowledge the considerable assistance given by Commander R. G. MOWAT, R.N. (Rtd.), in Proof Reading, Indexing, etc., in this the 10th Edition of Sailing Directions.

CONTENTS

LIST OF PLATES

CLYDE CRUISING CLUB

The ever-increasing popularity of yacht-cruising on our West Coast told its tale and, as early as spring 1965, this seventh edition was entirely sold out, so the eighth edition was put in hand and published in 1966.

With the formation of a 'Cruising Committee' a lot of new information came to hand and the annual supplements assumed massive proportions.

By late 1969 this edition was sold out and this, the ninth, was prepared and published in 1971.

The size of this edition was increased to correspond with the Admiralty Pilot.

The popularity of cruising on our west coast continued at an ever increasing acceleration, particularly among Irish, English and foreign yachtsmen, and, as early at late 1973, the ninth edition was sold out and this the tenth was put in hand for publication in 1974.

In compiling these Sailing Directions, it has been our aim to publish nothing that has not been verified by the personal observation of our members or friends.

Any new first-hand facts about anchorages on the West Coast, Isle of Man, the North-East Irish Coast, and also any corrections or additions to the information now published, will either be included in a supplement or filed for future use.

ADDITIONS AND CORRECTIONS

Information should be sent to: The Hon. Editor, c/o the Hon. Secretary, A. G. Taggart, Esq., S.V. Carrick, Clyde Street, Glasgow G1, through whom the Club will be pleased to give the latest information it possesses about any part of the coasts described to any cruiser wishing to visit these waters.

Note—The publishers while using every means in their power to ensure accuracy in verifying all details, cannot hold themselves responsible for any errors.

To encourage members to extend their cruising the Club has various Log Competitions:

The "Coats" Challenge Cup, presented by the late Sir Thomas Glen Coats, Bart., is for the best cruise of the season and is open to Sailing Yachts and Auxiliaries of all sizes, with no time restriction.

The "Ogg" Challenge Cup, presented by the late Wm. A. Ogg, Esq., is for the best cruise not exceeding 21 days, and is open to Sailing Yachts and Auxiliaries of all sizes.

The "Murray Blair Memorial" Challenge Cup, presented by the late Frank R. Blair, Esq., is for the best cruise of the season for Sailing and Auxiliary Yachts up to 8 tons T.M. in the Western Highlands not exceeding 14 days. No credit will be given for distance made under power. The committee have power to modify the conditions of the award.

The "Gibson" Challenge Cup, presented by the late Com. and Mrs. Robert Gibson, for the best cruise of the season, is open to Motor Boats only, and is restricted to 21 days.

The "John Dobie" Memorial Trophy awarded for a combination of cruising and racing.

The "Cruising Award" for a points competition where points are awarded for places visited, passages made, etc.

There is a series of social functions and lectures held throughout each winter season, which keeps the members in touch with one another and fosters that mutual friendship which is such an asset during the sailing months.

Although the Club is a Clyde organisation, its information and its hospitality are at the disposal of all fellow-cruisers from kindred clubs elsewhere who may visit the West Coast of Scotland.

To numerous members and friends we owe our acknowledgement and thanks for their whole-hearted co-operation and help.

G. B. VINYCOMB,
Hon. Editor.

INTRODUCTION

THE Sailing Directions which follow are divided into sections, each embracing a customary part of the cruising ground, as shown on the general chart which will be found a convenient form of reference.

The aim has not been to give detailed directions for open waters, where, with ordinary precautions, dangers may be avoided, but rather to call attention to places where experience has shown that there is a possibility of coming to grief.

Owners of Motor Yachts and Auxiliaries should bear in mind that these Directions are written primarily for Sailing Craft and that, under power, little difficulty will be experienced in making any of the anchorages.

Note—mark in a cable between Coll and Tiree.

It is difficult to say exactly what charts are necessary for the navigation of the Lochs and Channels dealt with, as those that some might think essential may seem superfluous to the more experienced. The lists of Admiralty charts given at the beginning of each part are divided into three groups. Group I are those charts which cover the whole area, are useful for approaching and navigation in open waters and for planning a cruise. Group II are on a larger scale and generally suitable for pilotage. Group III are on a still larger scale and being much more detailed are useful for those who intend to explore the recesses of the lochs. The plans for the anchorages, which are mostly taken from the Admiralty charts, are intended to illustrate the text, and when possible the chart should be referred to in conjunction with them.

Lists of charts available are given in the Catalogue of Admiralty Charts—Home Edition. A useful chart is 2635 which covers the whole West Coast from the Clyde to C. Wrath.

Across many of the lochs and channels on the West Coast submarine power and telephone cables have been laid (see sketch). The presence of these is indicated by shore marker boards. The North of Scotland Hydro Electric Board urges yachtsmen to avoid anchoring anywhere near cables and to remember that the cables do not necessarily lie in a straight line on the sea bed between markers. Damage to cables can result in very heavy claims against yachtsmen and adequate Third Party cover should be taken out. If a cable is inadvertently fouled the anchor cable should be slipped immediately to avoid damage and buoyed (if possible). The Hydro Board who have undertaken to recover anchors and cables free of charge should be notified as soon as possible.

Yachtsmen who launch and haul out their own yachts and sailing dinghies are further warned to take extreme care when in the vicinity of overhead power cables and masts should be lowered. There have been a number of serious accidents involving injury to yachtsmen and damage to yachts.

A few notes regarding tides, lights and buoys may not be out of place for the information of those who are coming new to the ground.

Owing to the offshore islands and the Mull of Kintyre, which act as baffles against the tidal undulations coming across the Atlantic, the directions of the streams vary very considerably in the area between the islands and the mainland and, to a lesser degree, in the waters east of the Mull (see sketch of Flood Tides).

A flood comes eastward along the north coast of Ireland and, when it reaches the North Channel, part is turned southwards into the Irish Sea and the Solway Firth, part carries on to the east into an area roughly south of Ailsa Craig where it divides one section turning south to fill up Loch Ryan then run south along the Wigtown coast to round the Mull of Galloway and so into the Solway Firth. The other section of this east-going stream turns north into the Clyde Estuary and its lochs passing both east and west of Arran, Holy Isle, Bute, Inchmarnoch and the Cumbraes. In the channel between the Cumbraes (The Tan) the flood runs North-East of Little Cumbrae into Millport Bay then flows East and West outwards. The ebb runs from West to East. In the Kyles of Bute one flood runs up the West Kyle into Loch Riddon and eastwards through the Narrows to meet, at about the church in the East Kyle, the flood that has come up east of Bute, turns west into Rothesay and Port Bannatyne Bays, filled up Loch Striven and entered the East Kyle.

Part of the flood coming from east, north of Ireland, is diverted by the Mull of Kintyre. A section of this turns southwards from about Machrihanish and, rounding the Mull, joins the flood running up Kilbrannan Sound and the main Clyde Channel; another section turns north up the Kintyre coast, passing east and west of Gigha, and so into the Sound of Jura and on into the Firth of Lorne filling all the lochs as it goes; a third part is turned back westwards along the south coast of Islay then northwards up that island's west coast to join the main flood coming in from the west and moving north-east. A branch of this stream passes north through the Sound of Islay to rejoin its parent stream south-west of Colonsay. The whole moves eastwards along the south coast of Mull and is united with the waters coming up the Sound of Jura.

A=HW—Hrs. after Dover   B=HW—Hrs. before Dover.

In the Dorus Mor, the Coirebhreacain, the Little Coirebhreacain (Grey Dogs) and Easdale Sound the flood runs **West** to join the flood coming north-east east and west of Colonsay.

The main flood coming from the west moves generally in a north-easterly direction as far north as the Little Minch. The stream runs north through Iona and Ulva Sounds and up the west coast of Mull; into Lochs Scridain and Lathaich and Loch na Keal and east in Loch Tuadh north of Ulva; north-west up the Sound of Mull and east into Loch Sunart; north-west through Gunna Sound and between Muck and Eigg; north in the Sound of Sleat and Kyle Rhea; west in Loch Alsh and through the Kyle of Loch Alsh then along the Skye coast as far as the Narrows of Raasay; north-west through Scalpay Sound and south through Caol Mor; north up the mainland coast north of Kyle of Loch Alsh to about the Crowlins and east into Lochs Carron and Kishorn.

Up the west coast of Skye the flood runs from Sleat Point to the Little Minch approximately north-west but in Soay Sound the tides (both ebb and flow) run west practically all the time.

In Barra Sound the flood enters from both east and west and the peculiarities of the Sound of Harris are described in the text under "Sound of Harris".

At about the level of Neist Point the stream swings north-east along the north-west coast of Skye then turns southwards down Raasay Sound and the Inner Sound to meet the above described north-running stream at the Narrows of Raasay and the Crowlins respectively (south through the Crowlins) and running south-east through Rona Sound.

There is very little stream west of the Outer Isles but, rounding the Butt of Lewis, one stream carries on eastward to Cape Wrath and along the north coast of Scotland and another turns south down the east coast of Lewis then swings eastwards about the level of Ru Re then northwards up the mainland coast to rejoin the east-going flow at Cape Wrath.

The flood flows into all lochs and bays except Tobermory Bay and the north entrances to Oban and Lamlash Bays where it flows **outwards.**

To all intents and purposes the direction of the ebb run is the reverse of the above.

In places there are eddies running in the opposite direction which can occasionally be made use of for short distances, but as a rule they are close inshore, and caution must be exercised in using them, on account of the rugged nature of the coast. In all cases where the wind is against the tide, the seas will be steep, and this should be considered before setting out, as in places where the seas have a long carry against a rapid adverse tide they may be so bad at times as to make it even dangerous for small craft to attempt making a passage through them.

Note—So complicated and varying are the tidal streams, the purchase of the small Abridged Tidal Atlas for the West Coast of Scotland and North Coast of Ireland is strongly advised.

Where the tidal stream attains a velocity of over 5 knots, it is almost impossible to make headway against it, even with a fair wind, thus it is always advisable to time the departure so as to have the tide favourable. The method of finding the time of high and low water is described below. In tide rips, the water swirls and boils, and the noise makes them seem much worse than they really are; but still, care must be exercised in going through such channels, especially if there are any rocks about, as the swirling affects the steering.

The highest and lowest tides occur at the times of the full moon and new moon (1½ days after on the West Coast of Scotland), the range between high water and low water being the greatest. These are Spring Tides. The Neap Tides occur at the alternate weeks between full and new moon, and the range of the tide is less than at Springs. The velocity of the Tidal Streams is greatest at Springs and least at Neaps.

The tidal constants shown in the Directions are referred to Dover as the standard port. This practice is not recommended by the Hydrographic Dept. for accurate predictions and so an Appendix is included showing time and height differences with references to a number of standard ports. The daily predictions for these are shown in Admiralty Tide Tables, Vol. I, most nautical almanacs and pocket tide tables. Variations in tidal heights are mainly caused by strong or prolonged winds and by unusually high or low barometric pressure. Differences between predicted and actual times of high and low water are caused mainly by winds.

The characteristics of lights are as follows:

FIXED   -   -   A continuous steady light.

FLASHING   -   Showing a single flash, eclipse greatest.

OCCULTING   -   A steady light, with, at intervals, one sudden and total eclipse. The period of light being greater than the period of darkness.

ISOPHASE   -   A light in which periods of light and darkness are equal.

GROUP FLASHING and GROUP OCCULTING are lights showing groups or flashes or groups of eclipses respectively.

REVOLVING   -   Light gradually increasing to full effect, then decreasing to eclipse.

ALTERNATING -   A light, showing alternately two or more different colours.

The system of Buoyage on the West Coast is the "Uniform System".

Going in from seaward or with the *main flood* stream, leave all black marks on the starboard hand and all red marks on the port hand. Staff and cone or diamond buoys are starboard hand, and staff and can or T port hand marks.

Striped buoys mark the ends of middle grounds, and green buoys mark wrecks and temporary obstructions.

The lights and buoys are corrected to the date of publication, but as these are liable to alteration at any time, reference should be made to a current nautical almanac. Many of the local marks, perches, and poles, etc., are under the jurisdiction of no public body, and are liable to be carried away and not replaced, which may be confusing at times. They are dependent on the local proprietor or inhabitants.

Distances are given in nautical miles of 6,080 ft.

The Weather Forecast Areas covering these Directions are as follows:

IRISH SEA   -   In Irish Sea all S. of a line running W. from Corsewell Point.

MALIN   -   -   Clyde Estuary, N. Coast of Ireland, and W. Coast of Scotland S. of Ardnamurchan.

HEBRIDES   -   W. Coast of Scotland N. of Ardnamurchan including the Outer Isles.

FAIR ISLE   -   N. Coast of Scotland including Orkneys and Shetlands.

ROCKALL   -   Approximately W. of Malin.

BAILEY -   -   Approximately W. of Hebrides.

Local Weather Forecasts from Glasgow Weather Centre (041–248 3451) and Belfast Airport Weather Centre (Crumlin 339).

The Sailing Directions are not intended for large craft, but are written for yachts of moderate draft.

Warning—Drinking water should not be drawn from burns when these burns flow through cultivated or grazing land as toxic sprays may have been in use. Nor should it be drawn from burns flowing **below** houses in isolated areas as the sewage from these houses may have been discharged into them.

CORRECTIONS AND ADDITIONS

If a stamped addressed envelope is sent to the Hon. Editor, C.C.C. Sailing Directions, c/o the Hon. Secretary, the Editor will supply all information (corrections and additions) that has come to hand since date of publication. To save unnecessary work any application other than a first should give the date of the previous application.

ABBREVIATIONS USED

Const.	Tidal constant of port
H.W.	High Water
L.W.	Low Water
O.S.	Ordinary Spring Tides
Sp.	Spring rise of tide from L.W.O.S.
Np.	Neap rise of tide from L.W.O.S.
Dover	Time of H.W. at Dover
P.O.	Post Office
Tel.	Telegraph Office or Telephone
Pt.	Point
Lt. or lt.	Light
Ev. or ev.	Every
fix.	Fixed
fl.	Flashing
occ.	Occulting
Iso.	Isophase
rev.	Revolving
alt.	Alternating
gp.	Group
wht.	White
blk.	Black
gn.	Green
hr.	Hour
m.	Minute
sec.	Seconds
fath.	Fathom
1 Cable	100 fathoms or 200 yards
G.M.T.	Greenwich Mean Time
con.	Conical
sph.	Spherical
horiz.	Horizontal
vert.	Vertical
C.C.C.S.C.	Clyde Cruising Club Sketch Chart

CHART MARKS

L.W.O.S.	Low water at ordinary spring tides.
	Rock, awash at L.W.O.S.
	Rock, usually with less than 6 ft. of water over it at L.W.O.S.
	Rock, 2 ft. below surface at L.W.O.S.
	Rock, 2 ft. above surface (dries 2 ft.) at L.W.O.S.
	Rocks, with limiting danger line.
	Shoal with 4 fath. of water over it at L.W.O.S. Shoals are often surrounded by 5 or 10 fath. lines also.
	Anchorage for large and small vessels.
	Direction of flood stream and speed in knots at spring tides.
	Direction of ebb stream.
	Overfalls and tide rips.
	Eddies.
	Black conical buoy (starboard hand).
	Red can buoy (port hand).

DOCTORS ON WEST COAST AND IN THE ISLANDS

Medical practitioners are to be found in all towns and in most villages in the Clyde Estuary and in Loch Fyne and in the towns in the Western Highlands and Islands.

Medical attention is also obtainable in the places shown below. This list is not a complete roll of practitioners nor is it guaranteed that the doctors in the places mentioned are in practice.

Achiltibuie	Connel	Mallaig	Skye—
Arisaig	Drimmin	Muasdale	Dunvegan
Aros	Gairloch, Ross	Tigharry, N. Uist	Staffin
Aultbea	Glenelg	Port Appin	Armadale
Ballachulish	Iona	Port Askaig	Portree
Balmacara	Kinlochleven	Port Ellen	Carbost
Balvicar, Seil	Kyle Akin	Salen, Sunart	Edinbane
Benbecula	Lairg	Scourie	Broadford
Borve	Ledaig	Tarbert, Harris	Kyle
Bunessan	Loch Carron	Taynuilt	Skeabost Bridge
Castlebay	Loch Inver	Tayvallich	Duisdale
Coll	Loch Maddy	Tiree	
Colonsay	Loch Aline	Ullapool	

PASSAGE MAKING

Should a coastal passage be contemplated and Coastguard surveillance wanted, application by letter or telephone should be made to H.M. Coastguard District Headquarters (Portpatrick—Tel. Portpatrick 209) for Form C.G.66.

On this form details of the intended passage and a description of the yacht is entered and C.G. stations along the route will be alerted.

There is no charge for this service but arrival at destination or any change in route **must** be immediately notified to nearest Coastguard station

PART I

FIRTH OF CLYDE

AND ADJACENT LOCHS

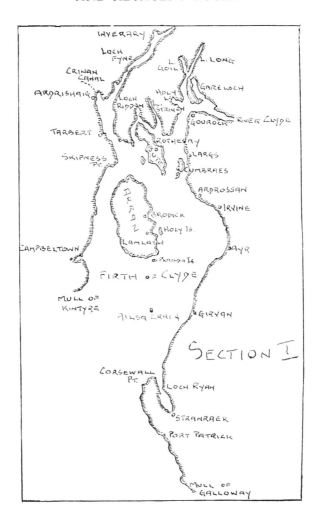

ADMIRALTY CHARTS

GROUP I

NUMBER	TITLE
2724	Approaches to the Firth of Clyde

GROUP II

2164	Bennane Hd. to Largs Channel
2144	Kilbrannan Sd. and approaches
2198	North Channel Southern part
2199	North Channel Northern part
2131	Firth of Clyde and L. Fyne

GROUP III

2007	Glasgow to Dumbarton
2006	Dumbarton to Gourock
1994	Port Glasgow to Dunoon
2000	Gareloch
3739	Upper part of L. Long
3746	Lower part of L. Long
1907	Cloch Pt. to Little Cumbrae, incl. L. Striven
1906	Kyles of Bute and Inchmarnock water
2382	Upper L. Fyne
2381	Lower L. Fyne
2472	Millport, L. Gilp, E. Loch Tarbert, L. Crinan
1864	Campbeltown, Lamlash, Brodick
2494	Ardrossan to Ayr
1403	L. Ryan

CLYDE CRUISING CLUB SKETCH CHARTS

1	Firth of Clyde, Kyles of Bute, approaches to Fairlie
2	Loch Gilp and Loch Gair, Minard and Otter Narrows
41	Firth of Clyde to Belfast and I.O.M.
42	Loch Ryan

CLYDE PORT AUTHORITY

"A Child's Guide to Clyde Approaches, Clyde Port Authority and Recommended Channels" is obtainable from the Club Secretary.

The Upper Reaches of the Firth of Clyde and adjacent lochs N. of a line drawn E. and W. through S. end of Little Cumbrae to the Ayrshire and Kintyre coasts come under the jurisdiction of the Clyde Port Authority who are responsible for administration of all aspects of navigation within the area.

The Gareloch, Loch Long and Holy Loch come under Statutory Instruments:

> The Clyde Dockyard Port of the Holy Loch Order No. 1140 of 1967.

> The Clyde Dockyard Port of Gareloch and Loch Long Order No. 1141 of 1967.

Owners expecting to sail or moor in these lochs are advised to obtain a copy of these orders from H.M. Stationery Office, price 5p and 8p respectively.

In these orders certain areas in all three lochs are scheduled as "Restricted Areas or Channels" and in Loch Long there are also two "Prohibited Areas".

Speed Limit—There is a speed limit of 12 knots throughout the whole of the Dockyard Port.

Restricted Area or Channel—No vessel shall enter, or moor or anchor therein when the signals described below are being displayed. Any vessel in the area when signal is shown must forthwith leave and keep clear. Maximum speed in these areas—7 knots.

Prohibited Area—Every vessel must keep clear of a Prohibited Area at all times.

Holy Loch Restricted Area—Waters 500 ft. on either side of a line joining the following 3 positions:

(a) 272° Strone Church Spire 3830 ft.
(b) 277°   ,,   ,,   ,,   6040 ft.
(c) 284°   ,,   ,,   ,,   8620 ft.

When restrictions are in force International Code Pennant nine will be exhibited by day, or 3 green lights (vertical) by night, in a conspicuous position, on the Floating Dock or by any vessel at the naval moorings and by any patrol craft present.

GARELOCH (see Sketch)

Rhu Narrows Restricted Channel—The area of water bounded by lines joining the following points as measured from Ardencaple Tower:

(i) 180°   7250 ft.
(ii) 163°   7600 ft.
(iii) 176° 4200 ft.
(iv) 182°   4500 ft.

then continuing, the water extending 250 ft. on either side of a line joining the following positions:

(a) 178° Ardencaple Tower   4350 ft.
(b) 059° Castle Light Pt.   1350 ft.
(c) 208° Rhu Church Tower   3900 ft.
(d) 305° Rhu Church Tower   4400 ft.

When restrictions are in force there is exhibited, by day, a red flag with a wht. diagonal bar and, by night, a red lt. above 2 green lts. (vertical), from

(a) At Faslane on Floating Dock or other conspicuous position.
(b) Rosneath Pier.
(c) Helensburgh Pier.
(d) Navy Buildings, Greenock.
(e) Patrol craft in Rhu Narrows.

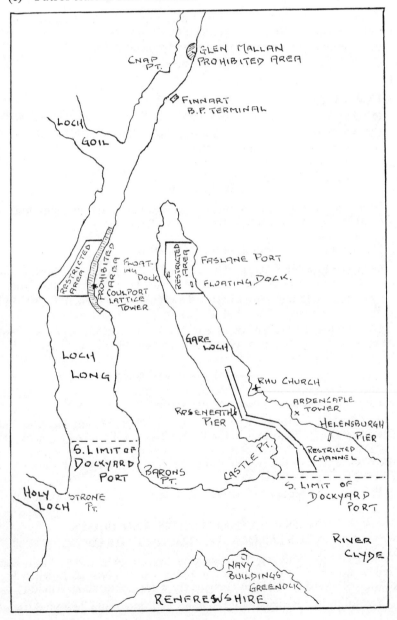

Faslane Restricted Area—Area bounded by:

(a) On the N. side by a line drawn along the parallel of latitude—56° 04' 00" N.

(b) On the S. side by a line drawn along the parallel of latitude—56° 03' 00" N.

(c) On the W. side by a line joining—
   (i) 56° 04' 00" N.   4° 50' 08·5" W.
   (ii) 56° 03' 21·3" N.   4° 50' 08·5" W.
   (iii) 56° 03' 00" N.   4° 49' 46·8" W.

When restrictions are in force International Code Pennant nine is hoisted by day or 3 green lts. (vertical) by night from—

(a) Faslane Floating Dock or other conspicuous position.

(b) Tugs or patrol craft in vicinity of area.

LOCH LONG (see Sketch)

Coulport Restricted Area—Area bounded by:

(a) On N. side by a line drawn along parallel of latitude 56° 04' 00" N.

(b) On S. side by a line drawn along parallel of latitude 56° 02' 54" N.

(c) On the W. side by a line joining—
   (i) 56° 04' 00" N.   4° 53' 04" W.
   (ii) 56° 03' 06" N.   4° 54' 00" W.
   (iii) 56° 02' 54" N.   4° 54' 00" W.

When restrictions are in force International Code Pennant nine is hoisted by day or, by night, 3 green lts. (vertical) from—

(a) Coulport Jetty.

(b) Tugs or patrol craft at N. and S. limits of area.

Coulport Prohibited Area—The area of water on the E. shore of the loch to a distance of 500 ft. from H.W. mark between the points lying—

   (i) 019½°, 1·15 miles from Lattice Tower (56° 03' 09" N., 4° 03' 45" W.).
   (ii) 152°, 0·53 miles from Lattice Tower.

Glen Mallan Prohibited Area—Area of water bounded by a line drawn from H.W. marks N. and S. of jetty and passing 500 ft. from jetty.

FIRTH OF CLYDE

The navigation of the Firth of Clyde presents little difficulty, as practically all the dangers are well marked by lights or buoys.

At Gareloch Narrows, Kyles of Bute Narrows, Minard Narrows and Otter Spit, Loch Fyne, and in the River Clyde itself above Greenock, the tides run rapidly, and must be studied; but as far as cruising is concerned, the velocity of the tidal streams elsewhere is so slight that, for all practical purposes, it may be neglected.

The average Spring rise is about 10 ft. and the Neap rise about 8 ft.

MAIN CHANNEL LIGHTS AND BUOYS
GREENOCK TO GARROCH HEAD

Detailed directions for the Main Channel are unnecessary, but it is as well to give the Cowal shore from about a mile north of Innellan Pier down to Toward a moderate offing as there are several shoal patches.

The following particulars of the lights and buoys may be found useful.

Mooring Buoys

Throughout the area there are many lit and unlit heavy mooring buoys laid in navigable waters and therefore dangerous after dark.

A large number of unlit ones are sited in "Tail of the Bank" anchorage S.S.E. of entrance to the Gareloch. There are 2 unlit ones in Cove Bay at entrance to Loch Long, E. side, and one unlit and one lit (fl. wht. lt. ev. 3 sec.) are in the centre of entrance to the Holy Loch. Midway between Kepoch and Cloch Pts. is one unlit and in Inverkip Bay one lit (fl. wht. lt. ev. 2½ sec.) with inshore of it and to south of it 5 unlit ones. About 5 cables N. of Skelmorlie Bank a lit one shows a red fl. lt. ev. 2½ sec. One lit (fl. wht. lt. ev. 2½ sec.) off Knock Castle N. of Largs. One lit (fl. wht. lt. ev. 2½ sec.) with 3 unlit to S. of it lie between Largs and Fairlie. Off E. shore of Great Cumbrae there are unlit trots just S. of Tomont End and in Ballochmartin Bay and 2 unlit buoys opposite Fairlie. Off E. shore of Bute about 8 cables off Ascog there is one lit (wht. fl. lt. ev. 2½ sec) and, inshore of this, a line of 6 unlit.

Buoyed Channels

From Garroch Head to the Gareloch Recommended Buoyed Channels have been laid down (see Plan).

Channel 1 (Firth of Clyde Channel) is a two-way channel, the outward bound traffic keeping W. and N. of a line of R. and W. vertical striped buoys, the inward to the E. and S. of it. The centre line begins midway between Cumbrae Lt. Ho. and Runnaneun Pt. Bn. From there it runs 011° through three of the above-mentioned buoys (approx. 3½ and 4½ miles between buoys) which exhibit from S. to N.: Mountstuart Buoy Gp. fl. (2) 10 sec.; Skelmorlie Buoy Gp. fl. (3) 15 sec.; Cowal Buoy Gp. fl. (2) 10 sec. and passes close W. of Warden Bank Buoy. At the Cowal Buoy the channel turns to 048° and passing midway between the Cloch Lt. Ho. and Dunoon Bank Buoy, reaches, after approx. 3 miles another R.W. striped buoy—Ashton Gp. fl. (3) 15 sec. Here it turns to 90° to Whiteforeland Buoy R.W. pillar Gp. fl. (2) 10 sec., passing S. of Rosneath Patch S. Buoy No. 27 fl. R. 2 sec. and then on into dredged channel.

About a mile S. of first of above-mentioned R. and W. vertical striped buoys there is, on E. side of channel, a B. and W. spherical buoy showing a wht. fl. ev. sec. This marks the N. point of entry to **Channel 2** (Skelmorlie Channel) which is intended primarily for **very large tankers.** It is marked by port and starboard lit buoys. At the bend in the channel N. of Great Cumbrae the port hand buoy shows a fl. red lt. ev. 4 sec. and the starboard hand one a wht. fl. lt. ev. 3 sec. All other port hand buoys show a fl. red lt. ev. 2 sec. and the starboard hand ones a fl. wht. lt. ev. 5 sec. This channel rejoins Channel 1 just S. of Warden Bank buoy.

No. 3 Channel (Loch Long Channel) branches off from No. 1 Channel N. of the Cloch Lt. Ho. and runs 000° to a gp. (3) fl. wht. lt. R. and W. vertical striped buoy W. of Barons Pt. buoy and, from thence into Loch Long. Ships bound for Holy Loch leave this channel when that loch is fully open.

No. 5 Channel (Ardmore Channel) is entered from No. 1 Channel at R. and W. sph. buoy, Ard 1 mentioned above, leaving it to starboard and, running E.N.E. passes first between Ard 2 buoy, a R. and W. sph. buoy (gp. (2) fl. wht. lt. ev. 10 sec.) to port and a starboard hand buoy (wht. fl. lt. ev. 5 sec.) then N. of Rosneath Patch. Thereafter the channel is marked by port hand buoys (fl. red lt. ev. 2 sec.) and starboard hand buoys (fl. wht. lt. ev. 5 sec.) until it turns into the Gareloch to pass E. of buoy marking Perch Rock (see under Gareloch).

No. 4 Channel (Kilcreggan Channel) is for traffic between the Gareloch and Loch Long (Naval Craft principally). It branches westwards from No. 5 Channel at the R. and W. sph. buoy (Ard 2 mentioned above) leaving it to port then follows the coast round passing between a starboard hand buoy (fl. wht. lt. ev. 5 sec.) and a port hand buoy (fl. red lt. ev. 2 sec.) and then, rounding Barons Pt. buoy, enters Loch Long.

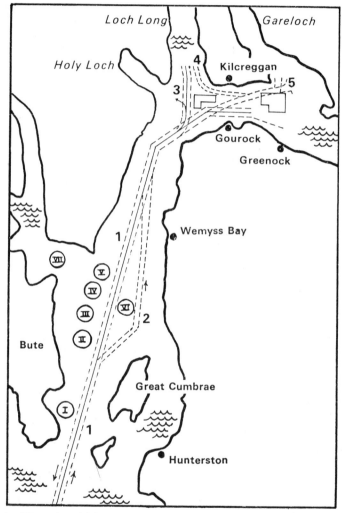

In the Plan the circles with Roman numerals are anchorages for very large tankers and the right-angled areas off Kilcreggan are anchorage areas.

Note—All vessels using these channels or crossing them come within the "Narrow Channel" Rule of the Road. Vessels using the channels will, by day, fly Pennant 1 in Channel 1, Pennant 2 in Channel 2, Pennant 5 in Channel 3, Pennant 7 in Channel 4, and Pennant 4 in Channel 5.

Container Terminal, Greenock. N.W. extremity marked by three lights in form of triangle. Top light FG; base lights FW.

Rosneath Patch, which lies between Gourock and Rosneath Pt., is marked by a structure which shows a gp. (3) fl. wht. lt. ev. 10 sec. The N. end of the patch is also marked by a blk. buoy (Ard 5—misprinted as Ard 3 in Chart No. 1994) showing a wht. fl. lt. ev. 5 sec. and the S. end by a red buoy (No. 27) showing a fl. red. lt. ev. 2 sec.

There is only 5–8 ft. at L.W. between the buoys.

Cloch Lighthouse, opposite Dunoon. Two recognition lights in vertical line 3m apart; upper FR, lower FG. Automatic fog signal 2 blasts every 30 seconds.

Cloch Speaking Beacon for boats with Wireless Receiving Sets. Wavelength—974 metres (308 kc/s). The listener hears (1) through the air, the 2 blasts from the siren; (2) on the radio ev. 50 sec.: "Cloch Point Lighthouse speaking". At the instant when you hear through the air the **commencement** of the **second** blast of this fog signal, your distance in **cables** from this lighthouse is stated on the radio. One, two, three, four . . ." and so on up to "thirty".

Inverkip—A red buoy, surmounted by a cross, moored here in summertime, is a yacht-racing mark; and the yellow and black con. buoy off Ardgowan Pt. marks a sewer outfall.

Warden Bank—A B. and W. Con. Chequered buoy, showing a fl. wht. lt. ev. 2 sec., lies to E. of mid-channel N. of Inverkip, marking the Warden Bank (min. depth 5½ fath.).

Skelmorlie Bank lies off the Ayrshire shore, between Wemyss Bay and Largs. It has 16 ft. on it at L.W. and is marked on its W. side by a blk. buoy showing a fl. red lt. ev. 2 sec. About 5 cables N. of Bank there is a mooring buoy exhibiting a red fl. lt. ev. 2½ sec. Buoy "J" in Skelmorlie Channel is to E. of Bank.

There are white posts on shore here, marking a measured mile, Courses 000° and 180°.

Gantock Rocks, off Dunoon. The S. end of this patch is marked by a wht. beacon showing a fl. R. ev. 2½ sec., and its N. end by a red buoy. Give these rocks a wide berth.

Off the Gantocks a green wreck buoy lies W. of a wreck and to the E. of that is a red can buoy showing a fl. red lt. ev. 6 sec. marking the Dunoon Bank (min. depth 11 fath.).

Innellan Beacon—A red and wht. chequers beacon between Innellan and Toward marks the outer end of the Bridges Reef which runs out from shore.

Toward Point—At the E. side of the entrance to Rothesay Sound. The lighthouse shows a wht. fl. lt. ev. 10 sec. The foghorn gives 1 blast of 3 sec every 20 sec. A red perch, and a red buoy well off-shore, mark the inner and outer ends of a rocky ledge running out from the Point.

Toward Bank lies between Toward Pt. and Bogany Pt. on Bute. It is marked by a blk. buoy (Barnhilt) showing a wht. fl. lt. ev. 3 sec. There is 13½ ft. on the bank at L.W.

Bogany Point—The westerly point of the entrance to Rothesay Sound. A red buoy marks the outer end of shoal water off this Point.

Garroch Head—On Runnaneun Point at the S. end of Bute, a wht. beacon shows a red fl. lt. ev. 6 sec.

Outside, off the Garroch Head, there is a tide rip which is bad in strong winds. **Const.** + 0 hr. 50 min. Dover.

Cumbrae Lighthouse—On the W. side of the Little Cumbrae. It shows a wht. fl. lt. 1 quick fl. ev. 3 sec. Fog signal gives 3 short blasts and 2 short blasts every 70 sec.

RIVER CLYDE—GREENOCK TO BOWLING
Charts 2006 and 2007

From Princes Pier, Greenock, where the river is entered, to Bowling, the channel is narrow, and should be attempted only when the tide is fair. **Const.** + 1 hr. 17 min. Dover. It is, however, very well marked and lighted by buoys and beacons, those to starboard being blk. or B. and W. chequers and those to port red, R. and W. chequers, or red with white superstructure, and no difficulty attends its navigation, provided the marked channel, the sides of which are steep-to, is rigidly followed. After passing the shipbuilding yards at Greenock, a good anchorage for yachts waiting for the tide is to be found at Greenock Great Harbour. Two fix. red lts. on east wall.

Note—When passing up the river, yachts should keep to the starboard side when passing other ships.

All pleasure craft wishing to enter an area E. of a line drawn from Clydeport Container Terminal (old Princes Pier) on S. shore to S. point of Ardmore Peninsula on N. shore (the River Channel Area) must get clearance from Port Control (Tel. 0475 22244) before doing so.

If proceeding up the River Leven it is best to time your arrival at Greenock for low water as, for the first hour or two of the flood, the river is usually clear of big ships.

If coming from Rhu do not be tempted to attempt to cut the corner as there is grave risk of going aground on the "Tail of the Bank".

Head straight for Princes Pier, Greenock, from where it is plain sailing up the river which is clearly marked by numerous channel buoys (see above).

Keep to the starboard side of the channel until the Leven opens out just to the west of Dumbarton Rock.

Leave the prominent Red Channel Beacon (the one nearest to, and S.W. of, Dumbarton Rock) to **starboard** and pass between the small unlit buoys marking the channel, red to port and black to starboard.

If proceeding to McAllister's Yard

Give "Sandpoint", the N.E. of McAllister's Yard, a wide berth and veer towards the shipyard on the E. bank before turning to port.

If laying up at McAllister's Yard, secure fore and aft between mooring buoys in river opposite yard.

It may be possible to secure alongside the pontoons to port, which makes unloading easier, but permission should be sought from the yard before tying up.

Even after 2 hours of flood tide the water is still fresh from the river rather than salt. This is useful for running main and outboard engines to clear them of salt water before laying up for the winter.

Caution 1   Do not go outwith main channel buoys.

Caution 2   Remember "Sail" has no right of way over big ships in the
                channel. Keep clear.

GARELOCH
Charts 2131, 2000 and 2006

The Gareloch is situated opposite Greenock. The eastern side off Helensburgh is shallow and the shore should not be approached too closely. At the S. end of Rhu Bay, off Cairndhu Pt., there is a blk. con. buoy (Cairndhu Buoy) exhibiting a wht. fl. lt. ev. $2\frac{1}{2}$ sec. marking outside edge of shoal water.

Off Rosneath Pt., on W. side of entrance, is a red can buoy exhibiting a fl. red lt. ev. 5 sec. and inside the buoy are the Perch Rocks which dry 6 and 2 ft. and the Green Isle (5 ft. high) which is joined to the mainland at L.W. A fl. wht. lt. (10 sec.) is exhibited from a red mast on Castle Pt. on the W. side and about ½ mile N. of Perch Rocks and E. of Perch Rocks blk. and wht. chequered buoys lit (fl. green ev. 10 sec.) and unlit mark D.G. Ranges.

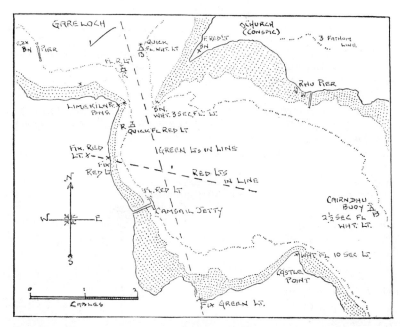

About ¾ of a mile above Castle Pt. the channel is narrowed to under ¾ of a cable by a spit, which covers at H.W., running out from Rhu Pt. which has on it a beacon showing a fix. red lt. visible over shoal water in Rhu Bay. The outer end of the spit is marked by a beacon showing a fl. all round wht. lt. ev. 3 sec. and further through the outer edge of the shoal water on the E. side is marked by a blk. con. buoy showing a quick fl. wht. lt. On the Rosneath side there is, on S. shore of Rosneath Bay, 2 fixed green lts. which, kept in line, lead through the centre of Narrows and, on Camsail Jetty on W. side of Bay, there is a fixed red lt. and, 1 cable N. of Jetty, 2 fixed red lts. which, kept in line, lead through centre of approach channel N. of Castle Pt. Just S. of Narrows there is a red can buoy showing a quick fl. red lt. and further through another red can buoy showing a red fl. lt. ev. 5 sec. The tide sets through the Narrows at 5 knots Sps. **Const.** + 1 hr. 17 min. Dover.

In Rhu Bay and on both sides of the loch N. of the Narrows are many mooring buoys (some of which are lit) of all sorts and sizes.

If working against the ebb, advantage may be taken of an eddy on the Rosneath side, and if against the flood, the Rhu side should be taken. At H.W. the tide sets right across the spit, and care must be taken to keep in the main stream through the channel. Inside the Narrows, the loch extends for 4 miles. About **3** mile N. of Narrows a blk. con. buoy showing a wht. fl. lt. ev. 2½ sec. lies in deep water just E. of mid-loch and, again in mid-loch and deep water there is, about 2 miles from head of loch, a lit mooring buoy showing a fl. red lt. ev. 6 sec. Both its shores are free from unmarked dangers but unlit mooring boys are a source of danger right to its head, if making a passage after dark. In the loch are many laid-up ships and 2 floating docks (one each side) lie off the Naval Base at Faslane. The loch dries out about a cable from its head. For "Restricted Area and Channel" see "Clyde Port Authority".

Anchorages

Helensburgh—Anchorages can be had in 2 to 3 fath. about 2 cables straight off the pier. A fix. red lt. is shown at the outer end of the pier, and a fix. green lt. at the inner end. Inside the anchorage it becomes very shallow. Much exposed to the S.

Stores—Shops. P.O. Tel. Hotels. Half-holiday—Wednesdays. Calor Gas. **Water**—Hydrant at pier. Sp. 10 ft., Np., 8 ft. Train connections.

Rhu Bay—Anchorage can be had on either side of the pier, but the N. side must be used with caution, as it is very shoal. Fuelling and watering float at pier with 8 ft. at L.W.

Stores—Shops. P.O. Hotel. **Water**—Hydrant on pier. Bus and train connections.

Mill Bay or **Rosneath Bay**—Sheltered anchorage 3 to 5 fath. to S. of Rosneath Pier. The best place is off a fence which runs down on to the foreshore. The strong eddies in the bay are apt to cause a foul anchor.

Stores—At village. Hotel. **Water**—At stables at pier-head. Ferry to Rhu.

Clynder—On the W. side of the loch above the Narrows. Anchor well off-shore in 4 fath., opposite boat-yard. The shore shelves rapidly. Strule Bay, just below the red perch marking a rock a little to the S. of Clynder, is a better anchorage if leaving a yacht for a period. Anchor fairly well off-shore, taking position from the moorings here.

Stores—Shops. P.O. Tel. **Water**—At pump well, and pipe at Strule Bay. Calor Gas.

Shandon—On the E. side of the loch. Anchor N. of the pier, opposite to the Hydro, well in-shore.

Stores—Shop. **Water**—Pipe on shore. Bus and train connections.

Faslane Bay—On the E. side of the loch, near the head. Anchor in 3 to 5 fath. anywhere in the bay. A deep water wharf and a lighter wharf have been constructed here, with depths of 33 ft. and 9 ft. respectively alongside.

Stores—At Garelochhead. **Water**—At burn. Bus and train connections at Garelochhead.

Garelochhead—At the head of the loch. Anchor in 3 to 4 fath., well off-shore, to the S. of the pier. Beware of many moorings in this area.

Stores—Shops. P.O. Tel. Hotel. Half-holiday—Wednesdays. **Water**—At pier, or tap at boat-hirer's slip. Train and bus connections.

LOCH LONG
Charts 2131, 3739, and 3746

It should be noted that very large tankers proceeding to the Oil Terminal at Finnart and nuclear submarines going to their base at Coulport lose much of their manoeuvrability when proceeding up the restricted waters of Loch Long at low speeds. Yachts **must** keep well clear of these vessels at all times and most particularly when ships are berthing.

It should also be noted that the authorities are still experimenting to find the best arrangement for buoyage of the loch and the navigational aids listed below may be altered, withdrawn or increased in number before the final establishment is settled. For prohibited and restricted areas see "Clyde Port Authority".

Loch Long is about 15 miles in length, and lies 3 miles W. of Rosneath Pt. A blk. con. buoy showing a wht. fl. ev. 5 sec. off Baron's Pt. marks the E. side of the entrance, and a R. and W. sph. buoy showing a fl. red lt. ev. 4 sec., marks the end of a spit off Strone Pt. on the W.

Four wht. pillars showing lights as indicated below are established on the W. shore.

(1) At the Raven Rock about $\frac{1}{2}$ mile S. of Ardentinny; fl. wht. lt. ev. 4 sec. Also a sectored G.W. and R. fixed and alternating lt.

(2) At Portdornaige about $1\frac{1}{2}$ miles N. of Ardentinny; fl. wht. lt. ev. 6 sec.

(3) At the Dog Rock at the N. side of entry to Loch Goil; fl. wht. lt. ev. 2 sec.

(4) At Knap Pt. about 2 miles N. of the Dog Rock; fl. wht. lt. ev. $1\frac{1}{4}$ sec. Also at Knap Pt. a lattice tower with orange day mark exhibiting a fix. wht. lt. These two lts. forming lts. in line leading up loch 031°.

North of Coulport on E. side there is a long jetty with a fix. orange lt. at S. end and a fix. red lt. at N. end.

Just N. of the Dog Rock off the E. shore there is Portincaple Buoy B.W. chequered fl. 3 sec.

At Finnart Oil Terminal there are a number of piers and dolphins all with fix. and fl. red, wht. and green lts. and opposite them, off W. shore, there are 3 red can buoys showing fl. red lts. About a mile further N. on E. side there is another with 2 fix. red lts. and a fl. wht. lt. just to S. of it and, a little further up the loch on W. side, there is a mooring buoy showing a quick fl. red lt. and, a mile to the N. in mid-loch, a mooring buoy shows a fl. wht. lt.

A line of 9 unlit mooring buoys are sited off E. shore from about $1\frac{1}{2}$ miles N. of Baron's Pt. buoy to about opposite the Raven Rock lt. and there are 5 unlit at S. end and one at N. end of Finnart Bay N. of Ardentinny (W. side).

There is no difficulty in the navigation of this loch, the shores being fairly clean.

There are a number of rocks on the E. side between Cove and Coulport, and also one **uncharted rock** on the W. side, just S. of Ardentinny, but they are close in-shore and are easily avoided. The winds, however, are usually erratic and baffling and, at times, the squalls are extremely fierce.

A torpedo-testing range is established in the upper reaches of the loch, but warning is given when it is being used. A red flag is shown on the rafts, and a siren is blown when torpedoes are running. The unlit rafts down centre of loch constitute a danger if coming in after dark.

About a mile from the head on the W. side a shoal runs out halfway across the loch from Ardgartan Point. It is marked by a red beacon on its outermost point.

Anchorages

Cove—On the E. side of the loch, just past Baron's Pt., anchor in 3 to 4 fath. to the N. of public convenience.

Stores—Shops. Tel. Half-holiday—Thursday. **Water**—Hydrant at pier. Steamer connection.

Coulport—About 3 miles N. of Cove. Anchor in 2 to 4 fath. to the S. of the pier. There is a sunken rock to be guarded against in-shore S. of pier, and bay is shoal. Two green fix. lts. arranged vertically are shown from pierhead, and a blk. con. buoy exhibiting a fl. wht. lt. ev. 10 sec. lies ½ cable off pier.

Stores—Cove nearest. **Water**—At burn to W. of pier.

Portincaple—About 5 miles N. of Coulport, on the same side. This bay shelves rapidly, and has an extensive L.W. mark. Anchor in 4 faths. off the centre of the bay, just past the small jetty.

Stores—Shop. P.O. Tel. Hotel at Whistlefield, above the bay. Half-holiday—Wednesday. **Water**—At burn to S.W. of bay. Train connection at Whistlefield.

Arrochar—At the head of the loch. Anchor in 2 to 4 fath., a little to the N. of the pier. The other side of the loch, opposite the pier, affords good anchorage in 3 to 5 fath.

Stores—Shops. P.O. Tel. Hotels. **Water**—At a tea-shop. **Const.** + 0 hr. 53 min. Dover. Sp. 12 ft., Np. 9 ft. Train connection. Calor Gas.

Blairmore—On the W. side of the loch, just N. of Strone Pt. Anchorage can be had in moderate depths all along this shore to the N. of the pier. Uncomfortable in S. winds.

Stores—Shops. P.O. Tel. Yacht slip. **Water**—At pier. Steamer connection.

Ardentinny—About 3 miles N. of Blairmore. Anchor well off-shore, just S. of the point here, in 2 to 3 fath., below the houses.

There is an uncharted rock lying well in-shore on the S. side of this bay to be guarded against.

Stores—Shop. P.O. Tel. Tea-room. Hotel specially catering for yachtsmen with moorings available for visitors.

Finnart Bay is too deep for convenient anchorage. Close in-shore, just above the pier, anchorage can be had in 6 fath.

Knap Bay and **Bute Hole**—These are two small bays between Finnart Bay and Loch Goil, which afford temporary anchorage in moderate depths, but otherwise the shores of the loch are steep-to, and the soundings very deep.

Coilessan—On the W. shore of the loch, between Dog Rock, at the mouth of Loch Goil, and Arrochar. Anchorage in 5 fath. off the house on shore.

LOCH GOIL
Chart 3739

The entrance to Loch Goil is about 7 miles up from the mouth of Loch Long, on its W. side. At the N. side of the entrance lies Dog Rock, a small islet connected with the shore at L.W. by submerged rocks and boulders. On this rock there is a 17-ft. high wht. pillar showing a fl. wht. lt. ev. 2 sec.

In Corran Bay, above the islet, there is an unmarked rock about the centre, but otherwise the shores of the loch are clean except for a shoal marked by a wooden tripod bn. This bn. is sited on most shallow point—**not** at its end. It lies about 2 cables off-shore and about 4 cables beyond Carrick Castle pier. Erratic squalls may be expected and, at times, they are fierce.

By Admiralty orders Loch Goil is, at certain times, closed to all traffic.

Flag signals will be flown at Ardentinny or Coulport when loch is closed. Vessels must keep clear of Douglas pier at all times. (See below under "Douglas Pier" under "Anchorages".)

Anchorages

Swine's Hole—The second bay on the port hand on entering the loch. Give both points of the bay a fair berth, and anchor in 3 to 4 fath., off a fence running down the shoreshore.

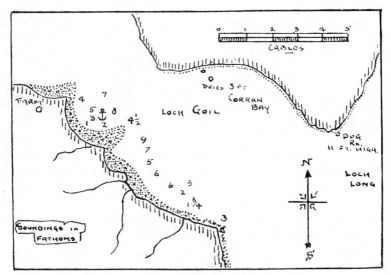

SWINE'S HOLE LOCH GOIL

Stores—Shop at Carrick Castle. **Water**—At burn.

Carrick Castle—On the W. side of the loch, about 2 miles from the entrance. Anchor on either side of the pier, well in-shore, in 3 to 5 fath. The N. side is the better.

Also, in N'ly winds, off a clump of houses (one white stone and others cedarwood) about halfway between Carrick Castle and Douglas piers. See caution about shoal N. of Carrick Castle given above.

Stores—Shop. P.O. Tel. Hotel. **Water**—Stand-pipe near shop. Bus connection.

Corrow Bay—Good anchorage in 4 to 6 fath. just N. of mouth of the Mayburn. A gravel pit marks the S. point of bay and a caravan park and chalet site is on the N. side.

Loch Goil Head—Anchorage can be obtained on the E. side ½ cable below the site of demolished pier but the soundings are deep even close in-shore. Available space is restricted as many local boats have moorings laid in the area. The best place is straight out from the pier in 3 fath.

The head of the loch dries out for some distance at L.W.

Stores—Shop. P.O. Tel. Hotel. **Water**—At pierhead (behind garage). **Const.** + 1 hr. 07 min. Dover. Sp. 10 ft., Np. 8 ft. Calor Gas.

Douglas Pier—Yachts should **not** anchor in vicinity of this Ministry of Defence pier (though there are some local boats moored there) as the bottom is fouled by cables laid down by Ministry for experimental purposes and by abandoned moorings.

There are no feasible anchoring places on the starboard hand on entering as soundings are very deep close in-shore.

Two unlit mooring buoys are laid in Corran Bay.

HOLY LOCH
Charts 2131, 1994, and 3746 and C.C.C.S.C. No. 1

Immediately to the W. of Loch Long lies Holy Loch.

It is about 2 miles in length and, excepting the spit which runs out from Strone Point to the E. of the entrance, it is free from dangers. This spit is marked on its outer end by a red and wht. sph. buoy showing a fl. red lt. ev. 4 sec. Off Lazaretto Pt. a red can buoy exhibits a fl. red lt. ev. 2 sec. and opposite, on N. shore off Graham's Pt., a blk. buoy showing a fl. wht. lt. ev. 3 sec. In the centre of the entrance there are 2 mooring buoys, the outer one of which shows a fl. wht. lt. ev. 3 sec. The head of the loch dries out for a considerable distance at L.W. and it is not advisable to go much further up than the pier at Robertson's Yacht Slip at Sandbank, on the W. side.

For Restricted Area, see under "Clyde Port Authority".

Anchorages

Hunter's Quay—At the W. side of the entrance. Good anchorage in 2 to 4 fath. just above the pier, taking position from the moorings lying here. The point just past the stone boathouse on shore is shoal. On pier are two fixed lts. R. and W. verticle.

Stores—Shops. P.O. Tel. Hotel. **Water**—Hydrants on shore and taps on slip below hotel. Steamer connection.

Ardnadam—On the W. side of the loch, round Whitefarlane or Lazaretto Pt., which is 1 mile above Hunter's Quay. This Pt. has a Memorial Tower on it. Anchor about 1 cable S.E. of the pier in 3 to 4 fath., or just past the pier well off-shore.

Stores—Shop. Hotel. **Water**—Tap behind grocer's shop. Motor services.

Sandbank—At the head of the loch. Be careful not to go beyond the yacht-yard here, as the loch shoals for about 4 cables at the head. Anchor well off-shore, S.E. of the pier, at the yacht-slip.

Stores—Shops. P.O. Tel. Yacht Slips. Sailmaker. **Water**—On pier or yacht-yards. Calor Gas.

Kilmun—Opposite Ardnadam. Anchor to the N.W. of pier in 3 to 4 fath.

Stores—Shop. P.O. Tel. **Water**—At pier. Steamer connection.

Strone—At the mouth of the loch, on the E. side. Anchor to the N.W. of the pier, clear of the steamer's track, in 2 to 3 fath., fairly well off-shore. Exposed anchorage.

Stores—Shops. P.O. Tel. Hotel. **Water**—At pier, Steamer connection. Calor Gas.

FIRTH OF CLYDE
Charts 2724, 2131, 1994, and 1907. C.C.C.S.C. No. 1
Gourock to Cumbrae Light
Anchorages

Gourock Bay—The best anchorage is on the S.W. side of the bay. The E. side is shoal. Yachts should be careful in anchoring as the bottom is very foul with lost ground tackle. Exposed to E. and N.E. winds. At the end of the railway pier, two green lts. vertical are shown, and a fog bell is struck every 6 sec. **Const.** + 1 hr. 17 min. Dover.

Stores—Shops. P.O. Tel. Hotels. Boat-yards, sailmakers and all yacht stores. Half-holiday—Wednesday. **Water**—Hydrants on the esplanade and at yards. Train and steamer connections.

Portkil Bay—Opposite Gourock. Anchor in 2 to 4 fath., well off-shore. Very exposed and dirty bottom.

Kilcreggan—½ mile W. of Portkil. Anchor in 3 to 4 fath., to the E. of the pier. Exposed to S'ly winds.

Stores—Shops. P.O. Tel. Boat-yard. Half-holiday—Thursday. **Water**—Tap at boat-yard.

Ashton—The south side of Gourock. It is very deep here, and the best place is just off the N. end of the esplanade.

This is the headquarters of the Royal Gourock Yacht Club and there is a jetty and club-house here for the use of members.

Stores—At Gourock. **Water**—Hydrants on shore.

Inverkip Bay—2¼ miles S. of Cloch Lighthouse. Temporary anchorage a little to the S. of the jetty, in 4 to 6 fath. Going in, give the mouth of Inverkip Bay a wide berth, as a shifting bank lies about 30 yd. off-shore. Exposed from N.W. through W. to S.W. The red buoy moored in this bay in summer is merely a mark for yacht racing. Yacht Marina with all facilities. Much industrial work in progress.

Stores—Shops. P.O. Tel. Hotels at village. **Water**—At Marina.

Wemyss Bay—Temporary anchorage to the N. of the pier. Pier shows 2 fix. red lts. vertical, 5 ft. apart. The anchorage is much exposed to W. and S.

Stores—Shops. P.O. Tel. Hotel. Half-holiday—Wednesday. **Water**—Hydrant at pier. Train and steamer connections.

Kirn—One mile S. of Hunter's Quay. Anchorage can be had in moderate depths all along the shore, but the best place is N. of the pier, clear of the steamer's track, in 2 to 3 fath. A fix. wht. lt. is shown at the end of the pier. Exposed to southward.

Stores—Shops. P.O. Tel. Hotel. Half-holiday—Wednesdays. **Water**—At point W. of pier. Steamer connection.

Dunoon—1½ mile S. of Kirn. The E. bay is very shoal, and is not recommended. The anchorage in the W. bay is off the boat-hiring stations, about 2 cables W. of the pier, 1½ cables off-shore, in 2 to 3 fath. The extreme W. of the bay is shoal. In entering West Bay give the Gantock Rocks a wide berth. A fix. wht. lt. is shown at the end of the pier, and in fog a bell is sounded when steamers are expected. Exposed to S'ly winds.

Stores—Shops. P.O. Tel. Hotels. Half-holiday—Wednesdays. **Water**—Pipe near centre of West Bay promenade. Steamer connection. Calor Gas.

Innellan—3 miles S. of Dunoon. The anchorage is about 2 cables S. of the pier, in 2 fath. Exposed N.E. through S. to S.W. The depths are irregular and must be noted. Beware of bank which stretches some way off-shore to N. of pier.

Stores—Shops. P.O. Tel. Hotels. Half-holiday—Wednesday. **Water**—Hydrants at head of steps on pier. Steamer connection.

Toward—The anchorage at Toward Pt. is in the bay just to the N. of point, in 2 fath. To the N. side of the bay a bad shoal runs out. Exposed N.E. through E. to S.W. winds.

Stores—Shop. P.O. Tel. **Water**—Hydrants ashore.

LARGS CHANNEL AND FAIRLIE ROADS
Charts 2131, 2164, and 1907. C.C.C.S.C. No. 1

This channel lies between the Cumbrae Islands and the Ayrshire shore. The shore between Largs and Fairlie is very shoal, and for 3 miles S. of Fairlie there is an extensive flat, Hunterston and Southannan Sands, which dry at L.W. The outer edge of this shoal is marked by Hunterston blk. perch and a blk. buoy off Fence Bay, and a blk. buoy off Brigurd Pt., and between these two, off Brigurd Spit a blk. buoy showing a wht. fl. lt. ev. 3 sec. ½ mile S.W. of Fairlie Pier, and about the same distance off-shore, lies Fairlie Patch, which is marked by a blk. buoy showing a fl. wht. lt. ev. 3 sec. on its outer edge. A blk. sph. buoy is moored near the seaward edge of Southannan Sands about 7 cables N.E. of Hunterston perch. Off Hunterston Power Station a blk. painted conical-shaped day mark has been established. In-shore of this mark there are underwater obstructions.

On the other side of the channel the Great Cumbrae shore is clean, and any unseen dangers off the Little Cumbrae are fairly well in-shore.

Large industrial projects in Hunterston area are being considered.

FAIRLIE ROADS

Anchorages

Largs—5 miles S. Wemyss Bay. Temporary anchorage in 5 fath., about ½ cable N. of the pier, opposite the Royal Hotel; beyond this the bay is very shoal. The soundings in the bay are deep. Exposed to winds from N. to W. and also to S. winds.

Stores—Shops. P.O. Tel. Hotels. Half-holiday—Wednesday. **Water**—At hydrant at pier. Train and steamer connections. Calor Gas.

Fairlie—2½ miles S. of Largs. The anchorage is in 4 to 6 fath., between Fairlie Patch and the pier, keeping off-shore. Much exposed to S. Close S. of pier there is a landing slip.

Stores—Shops. P.O. Tel. Hotel. Yacht-yard. **Water**—Hydrant at pier and at slip. Train connection.

Balloch Bay—On the Great Cumbrae, between Largs and Fairlie. On the charts it is named Ballochmartin Bay, and it is much the best anchorage about this part of the coast. There is a house on the shore, and the anchorage is any where opposite this spot, fairly well in-shore, in 4 fath.

Stores—Nearest at Millport, about 4 miles. **Water**—At house.

MILLPORT
Chart 2472 (see Plan). C.C.S.C. No. 1

At the S. end of the Great Cumbrae. The Eileans, locally known as the "Allans", two small islets, lie in the centre of the bay, and the best anchorage is close in to the E. side of the inner of the two in 2 fath. The rest of the bay to the E. of this affords anchorage in moderate depths, well off-shore, but is much exposed to S.W. winds. There are a number of cables across the Cumbrae Pass and Millport Bay. One of these lies parallel to and about a cable off the E. shore of the bay. If the wind is in S.W., or with a falling glass, it is better to avoid this anchorage altogether, and bring up in Balloch Bay or the Little Cumbrae, as the swell setting in from the S.W. makes the anchorage untenable. In winds from other quarters it is a splendid anchorage. Entering from the Fairlie Roads, give Farland (or Keppel) Pt. a fair berth.

If coming from the W., the Tan Spit, marked on its outer end by a blk. buoy, runs out from the S. end of the island for 2 cables and must be left to port. The Clash Rock lies beyond this buoy, in the entrance to the W. bay, and must also be left to port, and also the beacon with fl. red lt. ev. sec. on the outermost of the Allans. The W. bay should not be used by yachts.

Stores—Shops. P.O. Tel. Hotels. Half-holiday—Wednesday. Yacht-slip. **Water**—At hydrants. Steamer connection. Calor Gas.

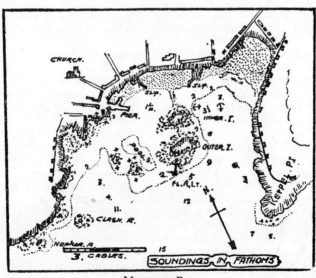

MILLPORT BAY

Little Cumbrae—There is a splendid anchorage in 2 fath. on the E. side of the Little Cumbrae, just inside the N. of the islet on which the old castle stands. Well sheltered from S. and W. winds. **Const.** + 0 hr. 51 min. Dover. Sp. 10 ft., Np. 6 ft.

This anchorage is restricted owing to the jetty extending further than expected, by boats on permanent moorings, and by 2 telegraph cables crossing the most sheltered part. A tripping line is recommended. In strong S'lies and in E'lies the anchorage can be uncomfortable. Under these conditions it is better to move to the N. end of the bay beyond the two islets. There is about 6 ft. at L.W. in channel between the islets and 10 ft. in channel N. of outer islet.

EASTERN BUTE SHORE
Charts 2131 and 1907
Anchorages

Glen Callum Bay or **Callum's Hole**—A small bay at the S. end of Bute, marked on its N. point by a wht. beacon, showing a red fl. lt. ev. 6 sec.

Care must be taken to avoid the rocks which lie about the centre of the bay, rather to the N. side. They cover at H.W. Temporary anchorage in 2 to 3 fath., about half-way up this bay, at swinging distance off the S.W. shore. Exposed to S'ly winds.

Stores—None. **Water**—At burn at head of bay.

Kilchattan Bay—2½ miles N. of Garroch Head. The head of the bay shoals badly, and this should be carefully noted, as it is very deceptive at H.W. The anchorage is at the S.W. side of the bay, between the new pier and the hotel, in 3 to 4 fath.

Exposed S.E. to N.E.

Stores—Shops. P.O. Tel. Hotel. **Water**—Tap at pier. Bus to Rothesay.

ROTHESAY BAY
Chart 1906, 1907. C.C.C.S.C. No. 1

Entering the bay from the E., round Bogany buoy, give the shore on this side a fair berth. Toward Bank, with 13½ ft. over it at L.W., lies out in the fairway, and is marked by a blk. buoy (Barnhilt) showing a wht. fl. lt. ev. 3 sec. and an unlit mooring buoy lies about 5 cables N.W. of it.

The bay is free of dangers except for the steamers' large mooring buoys (the innermost one of which shows a quick fl. wht. lt.), which must be looked out for if coming into the bay in darkness. The best anchorage is in 3 to 4 fath. off the old bathing place, which are about ⅓ mile N. of the steamer piers. This anchorage can be picked out at night by a noticeable gap in the window lights of the houses on shore, as behind the anchorage is the Skeoch Wood. If coming from the Kyles, give the shore between Ardbeg Pt. and the anchorage a wide berth, as it shoals out in places. A mast with fix. red lt. stands on the point but it is misleading in that it stands some way back from the H.W. mark. The steamer pier in the S.W. corner of the bay shows the following lights, but owing to the numerous shore lights they are not easily picked out: on the North Quay 2 fix. lts. red at the E. end, green at the W.; on Albert Quay 1 fix. red lt. A bell is sounded in fog when steamers are expected.

The many steamers passing through the bay make this anchorage uncomfortable for small yachts.

Exposed to E. and N.E. winds when it is very uncomfortable.

Stores—Shops. P.O. Tel. Hotels. Half-holiday—Wednesday. **Water**—Hydrants at boatmen's slips. Steamer connection. **Const.** + 0 hr. 58 min. Dover. Calor Gas.

Kirkmanfindlay or **Achavoulin Bay**—On the Toward shore, opposite Rothesay. The anchorage is W. of the jetty, and slightly E. of burn, in line between Toward Pt. and either Ardyne or the jetty point, in $3\frac{1}{2}$ fath., well off-shore. The shores shelves rapidly. A convenient shelter in E'ly winds. A blk. con. buoy showing a fl. wht. lt. lies off Ardyne Pt.

An unlit mooring buoy lies off centre of bay.

Port Bannatyne or **Kames Bay**—2 miles N. of Rothesay. Approaching from the S., give Ardbeg Pt. a wide berth, as it is very foul. A red can buoy off Ardbeg Pt. shows a red fl. ev. 2 sec. If coming into the bay from the Kyles, give the shore between Ardmaleish Pt. and the anchorage a wide berth. The anchorage is in 4 fath., between the disused steamer pier and yacht-slip. To the W. of the yacht-slip the bay is very shoal. There are a number of steamers' large mooring buoys in the bay.

Stores—Shops. P.O. Tel. Hotels. Yacht-yards. Showers are available at "The Tavern" during business hours. **Water**—Tap at Stewart's slip available to members and visiting yachtsmen. Bus to Rothesay. Calor Gas.

LOCH STRIVEN
Charts 2131 and 1907

Loch Striven is 7 miles in length and lies opposite Port Bannatyne. The entrance is between Ardyne Pt. on the E. and Strone Pt. on the W. The loch is free from outlying dangers to the head, which shoals for fully 2 cables, but the winds are baffling and, at times, the squalls are very fierce and erratic. An unlit mooring buoy lies N.W. of Ardyne Pt. about 4 cables, and a blk. con. buoy showing a fl. wht. lt. lies off Ardyne Pt.

There are one or two places, on each side, where temporary anchorage can be had in moderate depths, but mostly the soundings are deep right up to the shore. Kilchoan, on the E. side about 2 miles up from Strone Pt., S. of the church, has anchorage in moderate depths.

The Admiralty close Loch Striven to traffic at certain periods. A boat patrols the entrance at these times. At times buoys, some of which may be lit (white, green or red) are laid in the entrance.

Anchorage

Lochhead—Anchor just past the point on the E. side, near the nead of the loch, keeping well off-shore, in 4 fath. **Const.** + 0 hr. 56 min. Dover. Sp. 6 ft.

KYLES OF BUTE
Charts 2131 and 1906. C.C.C.S.C. No. 1

The eastern entrance to the Kyles of Bute is between Strone Pt., at the mouth of Loch Striven, and Ardmaleish Pt., on Bute. The outer end of the shoal water off Ardmaleish Pt. is marked by a blk. buoy showing a wht. fl. ev. 3 sec. From here for $3\frac{1}{2}$ miles to Colintraive the navigation presents no difficulty if the shores on either hand are given a fair berth, but, on approaching the site of Colintraive Pier, both shores shoal badly. A bank, which dries for about $1\frac{1}{2}$ cables off-shore stretches from the dismantled pier for about 4 cables E. and do not go E. of the point on which pier used to stand. Rudha Bodach, the point on the Bute shore opposite, shoals out for about 1 cable and is marked by a blk. con. buoy showing a wht. fl. lt. ev. 3 sec. There is a navigable channel $2\frac{1}{4}$ cables wide. Both sides of Rudha Bodach have an extensive L.W. mark. Past Colintraive the Burnt Islands divide the East Kyle into the Northern and Southern Passages (see Plan). The N. passage is marked on the shore side by a red can buoy which shows a red occ. lt. ev. 6 sec., and a red and wht.

chequers beacon; and on the Burnt Islands side by a blk. con. buoy off
the northern end of Eiln. More and by a blk. con. lit buoy off Eiln. Fraoich
showing a fl. wht. lt. ev. 3 sec. Inside the line of these 2 blk. buoys there
used to be two beacons (the more E'ly one being about 50 ft. W. of the
first buoy and the other about half-way between the N. ends of Eils. More
and Fraoich. Though they have been removed their plinths remain and
are only a foot or two below L.W. level. The position of the W'ly one is
shown on the Sketch Plan by a shaded square). The tide sets through the
Narrows at 3 to 4 knots Sp. **Const.** + 0 hr. 52 min. Dover. The ebb sets
westwards and the flood eastward. The flood continues past Colintraive
and on to Southall, just W. of Strone Pt., where it meets the flood stream
which comes up the Firth and enters the Kyles by Rothesay Sound.

The S. passage between Burnt Islands and Bute is winding, but is well
buoyed. Entering the S. passage, Rudha Bodach should be given a wide
berth. The channel is between the blk. buoy on Wood Farm Rock and

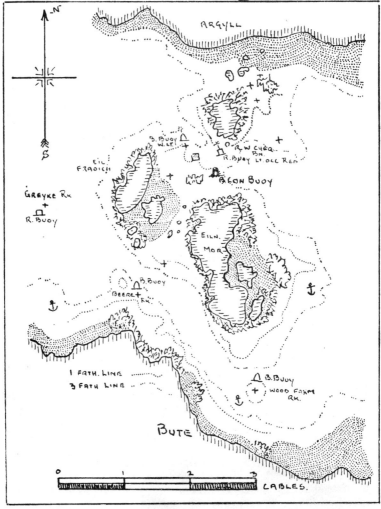

KYLES OF BUTE. BURNT ISLES NARROWS

Eilean More. The S. end of this islet should be given a moderate berth. A blk. buoy lies off Channel Pt., and must be left to port going westward. There is a submerged rock with 4 ft. on it at L.W.O.S. almost in the centre of the inlet between the islets opposite Channel Pt., and about on the line of the H.W. marks of the S. ends of the islets, and on a line joining the red and wht. beacon and Channel Pt. buoy. A red can buoy further through marks Greyke Rock, an isolated rock with 9 ft. on it at L.W.

When rounding the Buttock of Bute, give it a reasonable berth as there are some outlying boulders close-to, particularly on its W. side.

There is a detail plan of the Narrows on Chart Sheet 1906, which ought to be consulted if navigating these channels for the first time. The S. passage is the better if beating against a foul tide.

Through the Narrows, Loch Riddon branches off to the N. and the Kyle turns to the westward at right angles round the Buttock of Bute.

From here, for 1¼ miles to Tighnabruaich, the winds are usually very fluky. Rudha Ban, the point E. of Tighnabruaich, must be given a wide berth, as it shoals out. A red lt. buoy, showing a red fl. lt. ev. 4 sec. is moored off the point. There are no real dangers on this side for 4 miles further down the W., or Kerry Kyle, when Carry Rock buoy lies off shoal water on the mainland side. When first sighted from the N. this buoy appears to be well over on the Bute side of the channel. This buoy is red and shows a fl. red lt. ev. 4 sec. On the Bute side there is a shoal patch off Rudha Glas, the E. point of Blackfarland Bay, opposite Tighnabruaich. From the patch one can see straight up the steep road to the W. of the first house W. of the yacht-yard. This patch must be guarded against if beating across the Kyle. Round the next point further S., Rudha Dubh, there is a convenient anchorage from E'ly winds.

There are no other dangers in the Kerry Kyle until Ardlamont Pt. is reached. This point must be given a wide berth, as a bid spit runs out from it. It is marked on its outer end by a red buoy showing a fl. red lt. ev. 4 sec.

Two miles S. of Ardlamont, Inchmarnock Island lies off Bute. The passage between this island and the shore is ½ mile wide. Give both N. and S. ends of the island a fair berth. In the centre of the southern entrance to this channel lies Shearwater Rock, with 8 ft. on it at L.W. This rock must be guarded against, particularly if there is a heavy S'ly swell coming in. (See Anchorages in West Kyle.)

Anchorages in East Kyle

Colintraive—In the bay E. of the Narrows in 3 to 5 fath. just W. of the ferry slip. **Caution:** Keep well clear of the cable laid just W. of the slip. If making the anchorage after dark it is safer to keep well to the W., off the monument. The shore is, however, steep too at this end and care must be taken in strong E. winds as the gusts can be severe.

Stores—Shops. P.O. Tel. Hotel. **Water**—Behind P.O. and at spring on foreshore below above-mentioned monument. Ferry and bus connections to Rothesay. Sp. 10 ft., Np. 8 ft.

Anchorages at Narrows

There are three good anchorages at the Narrows: one about 50 yd. off the S.E. end of Eilean Mor, in 4 fath.; one inside and to the westward of Wood Farm buoy; and a third in the little bay on the E. side of the Buttock of Bute, keeping inside of a line between the point and the buoy off Channel Pt. (Wreck Bay).

Stores—At Colintraive. **Water**—At burns.

LOCH RIDDON

Loch Riddon branches off to the northward, just through the Narrow of the Kyles of Bute. It is about 3 miles in length, but only about half of it is navigable, as the head dries out at L.W. for fully $1\frac{1}{2}$ miles from Glendaruel at the top. Off the E. side, about $\frac{1}{2}$ mile from the entrance, lies Eiln. Dearg or One Tree Island, leaving a narrow channel between it and the E. shore, which is only navigable towards H.W. There are no hidden dangers in the loch, except the shoal water referred to at the head.

Anchorages

Fearnach Bay—On the E. side, at the entrance to Loch Riddon. A clean bay, with good anchorage in 2 fath. towards the N. side of it.

Ormidale—On the W. side of the loch, about $1\frac{1}{4}$ miles from the entrance. The anchorage is just beyond the pier, well in-shore, in 3 fath. Beyond this anchorage there is a point with a burn running down it, and above that the loch dries out. This is very deceptive at H.W.

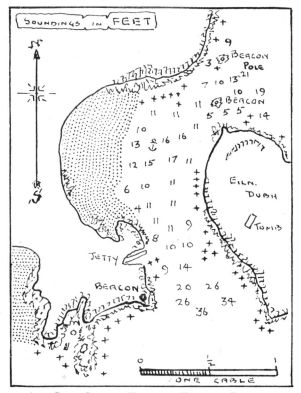

GLEN CALADH HARBOUR, KYLES OF BUTE

There is also good anchorage on the E. side of the loch, opposite Ormidale, in 2 fath. The same caution is necessary to avoid going too far up. Ormidale Pier should not bear much S. of W. from the anchorage. Do not go as far up as the long wall on the foreshore here.

Stores—Farms only. **Water**—At burns. Pipe at roadside beside pier. Calor Gas.

Glen Caladh—Behind Eiln. Dubh, at the W. point of the entrance to Loch Riddon.

The bottom was foul with chains from discarded moorings but they are reported now as well sunk in the mud.

The N. entrance is about 70 ft. wide, with a depth of 7 ft., the S. entrance is about ¼ cable wide and has 10 ft. in the fairway.

A wht. beacon on the mainland marks the W. point of the S. passage. In the N. passage leading into Loch Riddon, there is an islet marked by a wht. beacon, and a rock marked by a pole, lying in the channel between Eiln. Dubh and the shore, and the best passage is between these two. There is also a shallower passage between the S. beacon and the island.

Anchorages in West Kyle

Blackfarland Bay—On Bute, opposite Tighnabruaich. Good anchorage in 2 to 4 fath. in the centre of the bay. Coming down to this anchorage from the Narrows, Rudha Glas, the point before entering the bay, must be given a wide berth, as a bad shoal, which has only 3 ft. at L.W., lies off it. Part of it dries. A rock is reported close in-shore in the centre of the bay and care must be taken to avoid swinging over it if anchoring during an on-shore breeze.

Stores—At Tighnabruaich. **Water**—At burn.

Tighnabruaich—The water here is very deep, and the shore shelves rapidly, but good anchorage can be had in 6 to 8 fath., well in-shore, between the jetty to the W. of Rudha Ban and the pier, keeping well clear of any mooring buoys or pick-ups as chains may run to the shore. Exposed in S'ly winds, when Blackfarland Bay is much to be preferred.

Stores—Shops. P.O. Tel. Hotel. Yacht-yard. Half-holiday—Wednesday. **Water**—Tap on shore side of road beside yard. Steamer connection. Calor Gas.

Auchenlochan and **Kames**—Anchorage can be had anywhere off the mainland between Tighnabruaich and Kames piers, but about 3 cables S. of Kames pier there is a bad spit to be watched and another close N. of Kames pier.

Exposed to S'ly winds.

Shoal water extends fully a cable out at Tighnabruaich village.

Stores—Shops. P.O. Tel. Hotel. Half-holiday—Wednesday. **Water**—At burn or at houses. Steamer connection from Tighnabruaich.

Blindman Bay—1 mile N. of Ardlamont Pt. The anchorage is in 3 to 4 fath., to the southern side of the bay, off the houses ashore. Well off-shore, as it is shoal here. The holding ground is not good in certain parts of the bay. Anchor should be let go just before W. point of Inchmarnock closes H.W. mark of S. point of bay.

Water—At burn.

Ettrick Bay—On Bute, opposite Ardlamont Pt. The bay is very shoal and dries out for fully 2 cables at L.W. Anchor well off-shore, about the centre of the bay, in 3 to 4 fath. Exposed to S.W.

Stores—Rothesay nearest. **Water**—At burn. Buses to Rothesay.

Inchmarnock—There is good sheltering anchorage in 3 fath. on the E. side of Inchmarnock Island, off Mid Park Farm.

Stores—Farm only. **Water**—At burn.

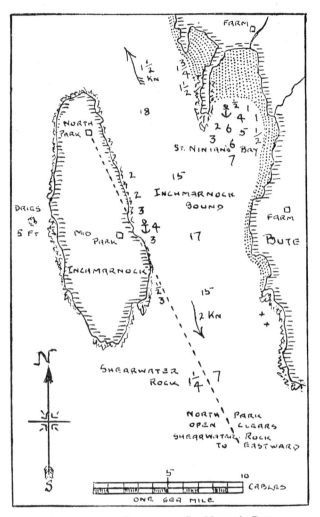

INCHMARNOCK SOUND AND ST. NINIAN'S BAY

St. Ninian's Bay—On Bute, opposite Inchmarnock. The anchorage is just inside St. Ninian's Pt., in 4 fath. This point should be given a very wide berth on entering, as there is a bad spit running out from it. The head of the bay dries out for about 3 cables. Exposed to S.W.

Shearwater Rock (see Kyles of Bute)—The house (North Park), on the eastern side of the island about 2½ cables from the N. end just open to the E. of the E. extreme of island leads close E. of this rock.

Stores—Small shops. **Water**—Well on spit, or at cottages.

Scalpsie Bay—This bay lies just S. of Inchmarnock. It is exposed to S'ly winds and is foul, and should only be used as a very temporary anchorage in off-shore winds. It must be entered with caution, anchoring near the centre and well off-shore. If standing into this bay when turning to windward along this shore, keep well off, as the shoal water extends much further out from both points than one would imagine.

LOCH FYNE
Charts 2381 and 2382, C.C.C.S.C. No. 2

Loch Fyne is about 35 miles long from Ardlamont Pt. to the head of the loch at Cairndhu. The entrance is between Ardlamont Pt. on the E. and Skipness Pt. on the W.

Skipness Pt. is foul, and a red buoy showing a red fl. lt. ev. 4 sec. marks the outer end of the rocks. A lt. fl. red ev. 10 sec. is exhibited from a beacon on the point.

The W. side of the loch is free from outlying dangers from this point up to Barmore Peninsula (see Anchorages on W. side, Loch Fyne) and from there to 3 miles below Ardrishaig, where there is Big Rock, lying about ½ mile off the centre of Strondoir Bay, and about 7¼ cables N.N.E. of Maol Dubh Pt. This rock has 7 ft. on it at L.W. High Rock and McLarty Rock, about 1 mile E. and E.N.E. of Big Rock, have 5 fath. on them and can be disregarded by small craft. In the bay N. of Barmore the Admiralty carry out diving tests and buoys are sometimes laid down about 4 cables off-shore. One or more of these buoys may be lit.

On the E. side there are several places to be watched.

Coming from the W., or Kerry Kyle, there is a long rocky ledge running out from Ardlamont Pt. The outer end is marked by a red buoy showing a red fl. lt. ev. 4 sec. The shore beyond the buoy should be given a wide berth, as it is foul.

From here, for 15 miles to Otter Spit, the navigation presents no difficulty if the eastern shores are given a fair berth.

Skate Island, marked by a beacon on its outer side, showing one wht. fl. ev. 3 sec., lies off the Ardlamont shore, 4 miles up from the point.

The islet can be passed on the inner side, but if using this passage, care must be taken to avoid a rock, which dries at two-thirds ebb, lying about 1 cable E.S.E. of the islet.

Off the mouth of Loch Gilp, 10 miles further up lies a blk. con. buoy marking the Sgeir Sgalag Rocks, 4½ cables S.S.E. of Ardrishaig lighthouse, with 2 ft. on them at L.W.

Southward of this buoy a red buoy showing a red fl. lt. ev. 4 sec., marks an isolated rock about 6 cables S.S.E. of the lighthouse with 4 ft. at L.W. and a 12 ft. shoal close eastward of it. Pass E. of red buoy and W. of blk. buoy.

A fl. lt. ev. 6 sec. on the end of Ardrishaig break-water shows wht. from N. 8° W. to N. over the channel, red from N. 58° W. to N. 8° W., and green from N. to N. 50° E. Not visible elsewhere (bearings magnetic from seaward).

To the N.E. of the blk. buoy, a blk. perch marks the outer end of foul ground off Dunchoan Islets, and there is a passage between the buoy and this perch which can be used with care, keeping well clear of both marks.

At Ardrishaig, in Loch Gilp, is the entrance to the Crinan Canal, the "high road" for small yachts making for the West Highlands. This canal saves a passage round the Mull of Cantyre, which is often very bad for small craft, and also saves a distance of roughly 80 miles.

The loch turns to the E.N.E. at this point, and the channel is narrowed to about 4 cables by Otter Spit, which runs out from the **eastern** shore for almost a mile. The outer end of this spit is marked by a blk. beacon, showing a wht. fl. lt. ev. 3 sec. A rock with less than 6 ft. on it lies about 8 cables S.W. of this light. Glas Eilean off the W. shore bounds the channel on the other side. It is marked by a fl. R. 5 sec. light on a grey pillar over a red gas tank.

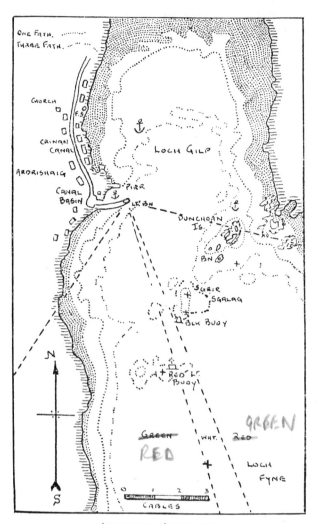

ARDRISHAIG APPROACHES

The spit dries at L.W. and extends fully $\frac{1}{2}$ cable W. by S. from the beacon, which **must be left to starboard going up the loch.** The ebb sets through the Narrows at $5\frac{1}{2}$ knots Sps., and the flood at 3 knots. **Const.** + 1 hr. 03 min. Dover, ebb commencing 1 hr. before H.W. and running for 7 hr., and the flood commencing at L.W. by the shore and running 5 hr.

$1\frac{1}{2}$ miles past the Narrows a rock, Carraig Geur, covering at half tide lies about 1 cable off the western shore, and if making for Loch Gair **this must be guarded against,** as one is inclined to hug this side rather closely. Its position is abreast the place where rock and heather give way to rough grass. About 300 yd. N. of it a long wall runs down to the beach

Loch Gair opens off to the westward, 3 miles above the Narrows,

7 miles above Otter Spit, the channel is obstructed by rocks and islets off Minard (see Sketch Plan).

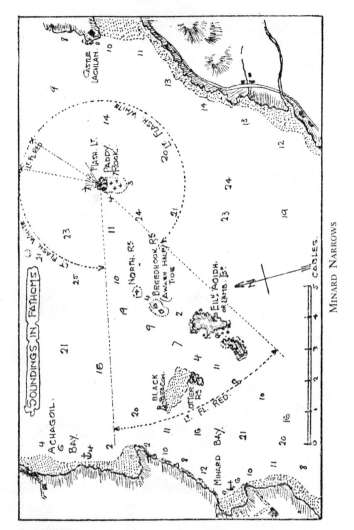

The lines of soundings show the channels through. The passages on either side of Otter Rock, and beacon are each 1½ cables wide, the Minard side being recommended, and the passages on either side of Paddy Rock are each 4 cables wide. Paddy Rock has a beacon with B. and W. vert. stripes showing a fl. lt. ev. 3 sec., red and wht. sectors as indicated on the Sketch Plan. Red from N. 59° E. to S. 78° E., wht. to S. 27° W., red to S. 45° W., wht. to N. 59° E. (bearings magnetic from seaward). The S.W. end of this rock is foul, and should be given a fair berth. At Minard Narrows the ebb sets through at 4 knots Sps., and the flood at 3½ knots.

There is no difficulty in the navigation from here to the head of the loch; but, if making for Inverary, the Upper Otter Spit, which lies ½ mile to the W. of the pier, must be noted. A tubular beacon at seaward end of tipped rock mound at Furnace shows a fl. R. and G. (vertical) lt.

The head of the loch dries out for ¾ mile at L.W.

Anchorages on East Side

Kilbride Bay—A wide bight, 2 miles up from Ardlamont Pt. Temporary anchorage in off-shore winds, in 3 to 4 fath., in the centre of the bay. The head of the bay dries out, and should not be approached nearer than 3 cables. Exposed from S.E. through S. to W.

Skate Hole and **Ascog Bay**—Behind Skate Island, just N. of Kilbride Bay. Going in, be careful to avoid the rock which covers at H.W., lying 1 cable E.S.E. of Skate Island. Anchorage can be had in Ascog Bay, but the head dries out for fully a cable. In Skate Hole the anchorage is in 2 fath., just inside the points of this little bay, which branches off to the N. of Ascog Bay. The greater part of it dries out. Exposed to S.W. (see inset plan in Sketch).

Stores—None. **Water**—At spring covered by wooden lid on right-hand side Skate Hole.

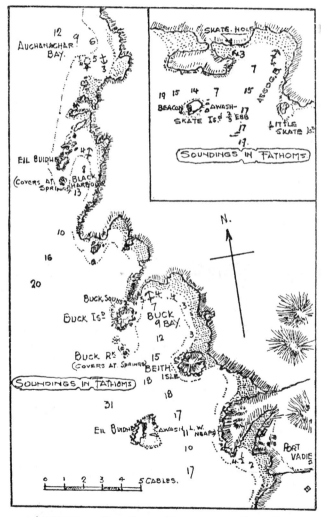

ACHANACHAR BAY, BLACK HARBOUR, AND BUCK BAY
SKATE HOLE (Inset)

Buck Bay—2 miles N. of Skate Island, and opposite East Loch Tarbert (see plan). Entering, give Buck Rock, which only covers at H.W. Sps., a wide berth, and anchor well off-shore in 3 to 4 fath. The bay can be entered through Buck Sound, the narrow channel between Buck Island and the shore, but there is under 2 fath. at L.W. in it. Exposed to S.W.

Stores—None. **Water**—At burns.

Black Harbour—1 mile N. of Buck Bay (see plan). Entering, give the rock which lies off the S. end of Buidhe Islet a wide berth. It only covers at H.W. Sps. Anchor in 3 to 4 fath. where marked on the plan. Exposed to S.W.

Stores—None. **Water**—At burns.

Achanachar Bay—$\frac{1}{2}$ mile N. of Black Harbour (see plan). Anchor well off-shore, inside the rock which lies in the centre of the bay, giving it a wide berth, as it shoals on its N. end. Exposed to W. to N.W.

Stores—None. **Water**—At burn.

NOTE—The foregoing three anchorages should be entered with great caution, as the approaches are very similar and one might readily be mistaken for another.

Otter Ferry—On the N.E. side of Otter Spit. Anchor well off the ferry pier, in 4 fath. An eddy sets round the bay, which makes the anchorage uncomfortable at times. Exposed to N.

A fix. red lt. is shown on the ferry pier.

Newton Bay—About 3 miles above Minard Narrows. Entering, a rock which lies off the W. point of the bay, must be guarded against. Anchorage in 4 fath., well off-shore.

Stores—Butcher's and baker's cart daily from Strachur. **Water**—At village.

Strachur Bay—3 miles E. of Newton Bay. The anchorage is in the S.W. side of the bay. The N.E. side shoals badly.

Stores—Shop. P.O. Tel. Calor Gas.

Cairndhu—Near the head of the loch. The anchorage is to the S. of the point below Cairndhu, opposite Kinglass House, well off-shore, in 3 fath. The shore is very shoal above this, and the whole bay off Cairndhu dries out at L.W., but there is good anchorage opposite the War Memorial, about a mile past Kinglass House.

Stores—Shop. P.O. Hotel.

Anchorages on West Side

East Loch Tarbert. Chart 2472—6 miles N. of Skipness Pt. and 8 miles N.W. from Ardlamont Pt. A perfect natural harbour, but is now very crowded and the entrances are very narrow (see plan). Only yachts which are handy in stays should enter the harbour. Cock Island and a rocky patch behind it lie in the channel and divide the harbour into the Deuchlands (or Buteman's Hole) and the main harbour. Entering the Deuchlands, a blk. con. buoy lies to starboard. Give this buoy a clear berth, as it is sometimes a few yards clear of the rock which it marks.

Cock Island is steep-to on this side, and should be kept well aboard until past the buoy; then turn into the Deuchlands immediately when clear, as there is foul ground off the island, a little further in. A rock, which covers at H.W. lies towards the head of the Deuchlands, and beyond this the bay shoals. Anchor in 3 fath., mud, anywhere in the bay, at swinging distance from the shore. Heavy permanent moorings and lost chains foul this anchorage badly, and anchor should have buoy and tripping line attached.

There is a passage between the Deuchlands and the main harbour by the N. of Cock Island.

A red buoy and a red perch mark the edge of the shoal water behind the island.

Entering the main harbour, a red perch showing a $\frac{1}{2}$ sec. fl. ev. 2 sec. red lt., marks the outer end of a spit, and the channel is between this perch and Cock Island. Two blk. poles, the more E'ly of which shows a wht. fl. lt. ev. sec., further in mark rocks off Cock Island and the patch behind it, and must be left well to starboard on entering. Anchorage can be had off the old pier, or off the old boat-yard in 2 to 4 fath., or in the Deuchlands (see above). Give the shoal patch behind Cock Island a fair berth. A $\frac{1}{2}$ sec. fl. green lt. ev. $4\frac{1}{2}$ sec. is shown from the dolphin at head of loch.

Sheltered from all winds.

For large yachts, or yachts slow in stays, an alternative, though more exposed, anchorage is off the Columba Hotel, W. of the steamboat pier, in 3 to 5 fath., or in the E. side of the bay opposite the perch, exhibiting red fl. lt., in 3 to 5 fath.

Stores—Shops. P.O. Tel. Hotels. Sailmaker. Half-holiday—Wednesday. **Water**—Hydrant at old pier. Steamer connection, Buses to Glasgow. Calor Gas.

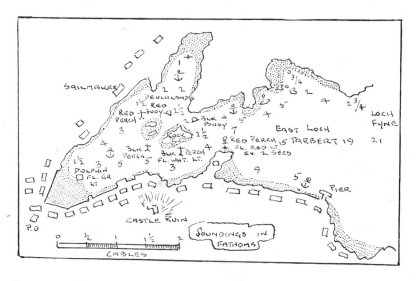

Barmore—About $1\frac{1}{2}$ miles N. of Tarbert, on either side of Barmore Peninsula. Entering, care must be taken to clear 2 rocks which cover, lying about $1\frac{1}{4}$ cables off the middle and N. end respectively of the peninsula. The N. anchorage is clean, but the S. bay dries out fully half-way at L.W.

Stores—At Tarbert. Hotel. **Water**—At burn.

Ardrishaig—Chart 2472. C.C.C.S.C. No. 2—In Loch Gilp. Entering Loch Gilp leave the red lit buoy to port and the blk. buoy to starboard (see sketch of Ardrishaig Approaches).

The anchorage is in 2 fath., just past the pier, opposite the Anchor Hotel, and well off-shore. From $\frac{1}{2}$ mile above the breakwater, Loch Gilp dries out at L.W. right to the head.

The entrance to the canal which leads through to Crinan, on the W. coast, is behind the breakwater (see Crinan Canal). The anchorage is exposed to S'ly winds, but shelter can then be had behind the breakwater or by going into the canal basin.

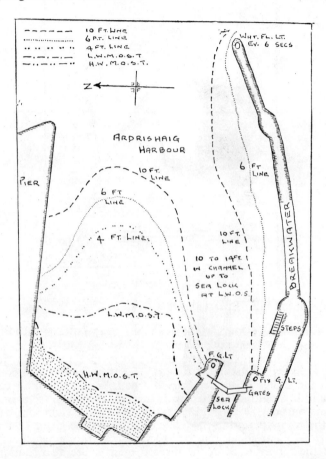

The beacon at the end of the breakwater shows a fl. lt. ev. 6 sec., wht. over the channel between the red and the blk. buoy leading into Loch Gilp, green to the westward, and red to the eastward (see sketch of Ardrishaig Approaches). A fix. green lt. is shown on each side of the entrance lock, and red fix. lts. on the pierhead and centre of entrance lock. **Const.** + 1 hr. 03 min. Dover. Sp. 9 ft., Np. $7\frac{1}{2}$ ft.

Stores—Shops. P.O. Tel. Hotels. Half-holiday—Wednesday. **Water**— At pier or on S. side of canal basin. Bus connections. Calor Gas.

Lagn a hulen Bay (Port Ann)—Opposite Otter Spit. Part of the bay, on the N. side dries out at L.W., but good anchorage can be had in moderate depths along the shore. Glas Eilean upon which a square Bn. shows a red fl. ev. 5 sec. lies in the mouth of the bay, and the channel to the N. of it has 5 fath., but both the island and the shore must be given a good berth if using this passage.

D

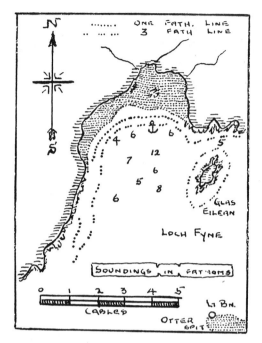

LAGN A HULEN BAY (PORT ANN)

Note—A Bn. on Glas Eilean shows a R. fl. ex. 5 sec.

Loch Gair—Chart 2382. C.C.C.S.C. No. 2—3 miles N. of Otter Spit. Entering this loch keep towards the W. point, on which stands a square tower, and anchor in the centre of the loch, in 2 to 3 fath., just past Colman Rock, which lies to starboard. This is perfectly sheltered anchorage; but the shores of the loch dry out at L.W. for about 1½ cables all round, and it should be entered with caution. Going N. from Loch Gair the points outside the loch (particularly that to the right and below the "S" of the compass rose in the Sketch Plan) must be given a wide berth. The more W'ly one shoals out for 1½ to 2 cables from a prominent yellow rock on the foreshore S. of the disused quarry. See also caution under Loch Fyne.

Stores—Occasional vans. Tel. Hotel. **Water**—At burn.

Minard—Anchorage can be had in Minard Bay, keeping well off-shore, in 2 fath. Also in Achagoil Bay, a little further up, well off-shore, in 4 fath. (see plan of Minard Narrows).

Stores—Shop. **Water**—At hydrant below village. Calor Gas.

Inverary—Good anchorage can be had off the mouth of the burn, just N. of the pier, well off-shore, in 5 to 6 fath. Two red lts. are shown on the pierhead. Coming from the S., the Upper Otter Spit which runs off-shore, about ½ mile below the pier, must be guarded against.

A large Admiralty mooring buoy is sometimes laid in the centre of bay and must be guarded against if coming in after dark.

Stores—Shops. P.O. Tel. Hotels. Half-holiday—Wednesday. **Water**—Hydrant in small box on pier. Bus connections. **Const.** + 1 hr. 98 min. Dover. Sp. 10 ft. Calor Gas.

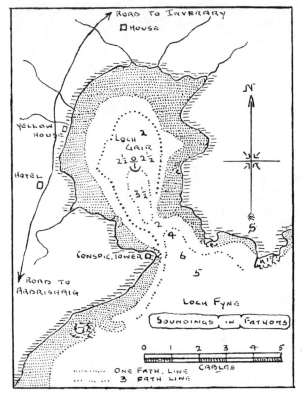

LOCH GAIR

KILBRENNAN SOUND
Charts 2144 and 2131

Kilbrennan Sound is the channel between the island of Arran and the Cantyre shore. It is a clear stretch of water extending for 20 miles from Skipness Pt. to Campbeltown Loch. The tide runs about 2 knots Sps., and in strong S.W. winds there is a bad tide rip over the Erin Bank, which lies in mid-channel 10 miles S.W. of Skipness.

Abnormal magnetic variation has been reported in the Sound, from a deflection of 5° eastward off Loch Ranza decreasing to normal off Kildonald Pt. on Cantyre.

Anchorages

Skipness Bay—Entering the bay, Skipness Pt. must be given a wide berth, as there are a number of bad rocks lying off it. A red buoy showing a fl. red lt. ev. 4 sec. marks the outer end of these rocks. A lt. fl. red ev. 10 sec. is exhibited from a steel framework column on Skipness Pt. The rocks lie inside and W. of a line between the buoy and Skipness Pt. Temporary anchorage in 2 to 4 fath., in N'ly winds, to the S. of the point, keeping well off-shore, as it is very shoal opposite the houses.

Stores—Shops. P.O. Tel. **Water**—Hydrant at P.O. **Const.** + 0 hr. 52 min. Dover. Sp. 9 ft., Np. 6 ft. Ferry to Arran (L. Ranza) with bus connection to Brodick and steamer to mainland.

Carradale Bay—12 miles S. of Skipness Pt. Good anchorage in 4 fath., just off Torrisdale Castle, in the S.W. corner of the bay. S'ly swell sets in here, and better shelter can be had in S. winds, to the N. of Carradale Pt. in Port Cranaig. Off Carradale Pt. a red buoy showing gp. (2) wht. fl. lt. ev. 12 sec., marks the outer end of foul ground. A combined breakwater and pier has turned part of the bay into a harbour, giving all-round shelter. During the week there is considerable activity of the fishing fleet throughout the night.

Stores—Shop. P.O. Tel. Calor Gas.

Saddell Bay—2½ miles S. of Carradale. Temporary anchorage in 2 to 4 fath., in centre of bay. Exposed from S.E. round to S.W. For boats drawing not more than 6½ ft. there is better shelter clear of the squalls coming out of the glen in 2 fath., about ½ cable off the more N'ly of two houses on the shore W. of Pluck Pt. and off an outcrop of rock on which there are rings to which a warp can be run if required.

Stores—Vans only. **Water**—At burn (see warning in Introduction).

Ross Bay—3 miles S. of Saddell. Temporary anchorage in 3 fath., sheltered from S'ly winds, behind Ross Island which lies to the S. of the bay.

Stores—Shop. P.O. Tel. **Water**—At burn.

Campbeltown Loch—Chart 1864—4 miles S. of Ross Bay. Coming S. from Ross Bay, Otterard Rock with a least depth of 10 ft. over it lies well off-shore, and there are a number of dangers inside it. The rock is marked on its S.E. side by a R. and W. sph. bell buoy, showing a wht. fl. lt. ev. 6 sec., and in-shore a red can buoy marks Long Rock (dries 5 ft.) and Smerby Rocks.

The passage between Otterard and Long Rocks has a least breadth of 3¾ cables and depths of over 5 fath.

At the entrance to Campbeltown Loch, there is a lighthouse on Davaar Island, showing a wht. fl. lt. ev. 20 sec. Fog siren, one blast of 3 sec. ev. 20 sec. The entrance to the loch is marked on the N. side by Millbeg Bank blk. con. buoy exhibiting a wht. fl. lt. ev. 2 sec. and on the S. side by Millmore red can buoy exhibiting a fl. red lt. ev. 10 sec. and by Millmore Bn. marking the outer margin of the Doirlinn Bank. About 3 cables W.S.W. of bn. there is a R.W. and blk. sph. buoy showing a gp. (2) fl. lt. ev. 10 sec. marking the Methe Bank (5 fath.).

About 4 cables W. of Millbeg Bank buoy there is a bn. marking the S. limit of Trench Flat on the N. shore and about 1½ cables W.S.W. of this bn. off Trench Pt. there is a blk. con. buoy (wht. fl. ev. 6 sec.).

On S. shore of loch there are 2 orange leading lts. which lead through the entrance channel between the Millbeg Bank and Millmore buoys and just N. of Methe Bank buoy. In the S.E. corner of the loch there is a pier with outlying dolphins. At the end of the pier there are 2 quick fl. green lts. (see sketch).

The beacon on New Quay has a fix. W. and G. sector lt. (G. to seaward) and that on Old Quay has a fix. R. and W. sector lt. (R. to seaward). At the head of the loch is a beacon showing a fix. wht. lt.

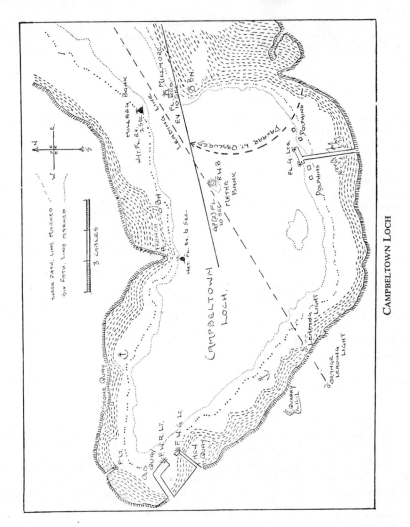

Anchorages

Well off the former lifeboat house, which stands in a play-park with swings on the S. side of the loch or in a bay to the E. of leading beacons off a row of houses.

Off-shore to eastward of a stone pier further up the loch on the N. side.

The first two are the more pleasant and are more sheltered in the prevailing wind but the holding ground is not so good in the first and, as the water is shoal, care must be taken not to go too close in-shore. Sp. 9 ft., Np. 6 ft.

Stores—Shops. P.O. at Cross. Tel. Hotels. Half-holiday—Wednesday. Steamer, bus, and air connections. **Const.** + 0 hr. 48 min. Dover. Calor Gas.

Kildalloig Bay—On the S. side of Davaar Island. Anchor in 3 fath., off Doirlinn Shoal, which connects Davaar Island with the mainland. Temporary anchorage in N.W. winds.

Stores—At Campbeltown.

ARRAN ISLAND
Charts 2144, 2131, and 1864

The island is about 17 miles long, and the total distance round about 60 miles. Coming from Loch Ranza, on the nothern end, round by the Cock of Arran and down the E. side, there are no outlying dangers, but the squalls off the N. end of the island are exceptionally fierce in strong winds. This caution should be specially noted.

By keeping a reasonable distance off-shore, there are no dangers down to Pladda Island, at the S. end. There are poles marking two consecutive measured miles between Sannox and Corrie. Course 322° or 142°.

Holy Island lies off Lamlash Bay, 13 miles S. of the Cock of Arran. On the S.E. end of it, there is a lighthouse called Pillar Rock, showing an alt. fl. lt. red and wht. ev. 30 sec. Fog siren gives 2 low blasts of 4 sec. each, in quick succession every $1\frac{1}{2}$ min.

On the S.W. end of Holy Island, there is a lighthouse, showing a fl. red lt. ev. 3 sec.

At the S. end of Arran lies Pladda Island, with a channel studded with rocks between it and the shore, a passage which should not be attempted without local knowledge. The lighthouse here shows a gp. fl. lt., 3 quick fl. during 7 sec. ev. 30 sec. Fog siren gives a $2\frac{1}{2}$ sec. blast ev. 20 sec.

Off Pladda there is a tide rip which is bad in strong winds.

7 miles W. of Pladda, the Iron Ledges extend off-shore for more than a mile. The outer end of this ledge is marked by a blk. buoy, which shows a fl. lt. ev. 6 sec. To clear this dangerous reef, Pladda Island should be kept in view until Imachar Pt. is open of Drumadune Pt. There is a 6 ft. rock 8 cables S.E. of Drumadune Pt.

From here to the N. end of the island, there are no outlying dangers, but a bad tide rip is sometimes experienced on the Erin Bank, which lies off Imachar Pt.

Anchorages

Sannox Bay—5 miles S. of the Cock of Arran. Temporary anchorage off the old stone pier, in 3 to 6 fath. There is an 8 ft. rock lying about the centre of the bay to be guarded against. Much exposed from N.E. to S.E.

Stores—Cafe open in summer months. Van also calls from Corrie. Tel. and P.O. **Water**—At burns, which should be drawn off **above** inhabited houses.

Corrie—1 mile S. of Sannox. Only a temporary anchorage in off-shore winds, in 6 to 8 fath., off the ferry jetty.

Stores—Shop. P.O. Tel. Hotel. **Water**—At burns. Motor to Brodick.

Brodick Bay—**Chart 838**—4 miles S. of Corrie. Good anchorage can be had in 4 to 6 fath., just N. of the pier, well off-shore and clear of the steamers' tracks. Anchorage can also be had off the jetty below the castle, or near Merkland Pt., in moderate depths. The bay is much exposed to E'ly winds. Two fix. red lts. mark the seawardmost projection of pier.

Stores—Shops. P.O. Tel. Hotels. **Water**—At pierhead. Steamer connection. Calor Gas. Garage at pier. Self-drive cars. Baths at Ormidale Hotel.

Lamlash Bay—**Chart 1864**—A splendid natural harbour lying between Holy Island and the shore. In working the N. entrance, the Hamilton Rock, which is above water, lies off Clauchland Pt., and should be taken on the outside. A red lt. buoy, fl. red ev. 6 sec., is moored in deep water between Hamilton Rock and Holy Isle.

Coming in from the S. there is a lighthouse on the S.W. end of Holy Isle showing a fl. red lt. ev. 3 sec. Fullarton Rock, lying about $\frac{3}{4}$ cable E.N.E. of Kingscross Pt., has a least depth of 8 ft. on it. A red can buoy, showing a gp. (2) fl. wht. lt. ev. 12 sec., marks this rock and should be left to port on entering.

A bad bank lies off Cordon, a little S. of stone pier, caused by the two rivers which flow into bay at that point.

Good anchorage can be found off the stone pier in 3 to 4 fath. (sandy bottom). This anchorage is exposed in N.E. winds and good shelter can then be found in 4 fath. well in-shore off the farmhouse on Holy Isle, opposite Lamlash, the best spot being off a stone erection on the beach (sandy bottom but considerable amount of weed). There is a wrecked assault landing craft close inshore S.W. of the jetty which is awash, lying in about 1 fath. The jetty should be used to land as the shore is rocky. Both these anchorages are reported as being subject to swell. Owners of Holy Isle discourage landing thereon.

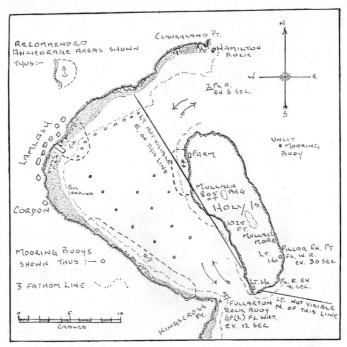

Good shelter in winds from W. through S. to S.E. in 6 fath. close in-shore off the Arran shore from below Cordon to near Kingscross Pt. In a S'ly gale this anchorage affords the best shelter.

There are many unlit mooring buoys in the bay (see sketch). Six off the N. shore on the line North Channel buoy and stone pier and three on outside limit of stone pier anchorage are laid on a long bottom trot and care must be taken not to anchor close to nor between them nor should yachts go between the six buoys and the N. shore. There are 3 further rows of buoys (6, 4 and 2) in centre of bay. Four cables E.S.E. of N. end of Holy Isle there is an unlit mooring buoy. The positions of mooring buoys may be altered when they are serviced.

Stores—Shops. P.O. Tel. Hotels. Shop. P.O. Tel. at Kingscross. **Water**—Lamlash—at the public conveniences 30 yd. W. of head of the quay. Bus to Brodick for steamer connection. **Const.** + 0 hr. 50 min. Dover. Sp. 10 ft., Np. 7 ft.

Whiting Bay—Temporary anchorage well off-shore in 2 to 3 fath. Much exposed from S. to N.E.

Stores—Shops. P.O. Tel. Hotels. **Water**—At pier.

Kildonan—On the N. side of Pladda Island immediately off lighthouse landing slip. Temporary anchorage in off-shore winds, in 3 to 5 fath., N. of the castle. (See caution about passage between Pladda and Arran.)

Stores—Shop. P.O. Tel. Hotel (Temperance). **Water**—At burns. Bus to Whiting Bay. Calor Gas.

Anchorages on West Side

The anchorages on the W. side of Arran, excepting Loch Ranza, are all much exposed, and are tenable only in off-shore winds.

Loch Ranza—Chart 2131—At the N. end of island (see plan). On entering give the N.E. point of the bay a wide berth to avoid the Cairn, an unmarked rock which lies off this shore. The best anchorage is at the head of the loch, below the castle, and slightly to the E. of it, in 3 to 4 fath. The W. side of the loch, above the pier, shoals badly and the bank dries at L.W. A fix. red lt. is shown on the pier. Moorings have been laid for visiting yachtsmen. Donations from users are requested to be left at the hotel.

In strong S'ly winds, the gusts from the glen are very fierce, and it is advisable to lay out a kedge at such times. Exposed to N'ly winds.

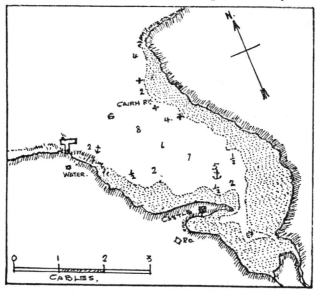

LOCH RANZA (Sounding in fathoms)

Behind the spit on which the castle stands, there is a very small pool with 5 ft. at L.W., which can be entered at H.W. There is no swinging room, and this pool should only be used by small craft in emergency.

Stores—Shops. P.O. Tel. **Water**—At tap on wall at pierhead. Ferry to Skipness. Hotel. Calor Gas. Bus to Brodick.

Catacol Bay—2 miles S. of Loch Ranza. Temporary anchorage to the S. of the bay, in 6 to 7 fath. Exposed from N.E. to W.

Stores—Farms only. Baker's van daily from Loch Ranza. **Water**—At burns.

Whitefarland Bay—4 miles S. of Catacol Bay. Temporary anchorage in 3 to 6 fath. Exposed from N. to S.W.

Machrie Bay—5 miles S. of Whitefarland Bay. Temporary anchorage in 3 to 4 fath., anywhere in the bay, but give the mouth of Machrie Burn a wide berth, as the shore shoals out there. Exposed from S.W. to N.W.

Stores—Shop. P.O. **Water**—At burn.

FIRTH OF CLYDE
Garroch Head to Mull of Galloway
Charts 2164

The navigation of the Firth from Garroch Head to Corsewell Pt. presents no difficulty, as all dangers are marked. The flood tide sets approximately N.N.E. and the ebb S.S.W., at 2 to 3 knots Sps.

Ailsa Craig lies in the fairway, 10 miles S. (true) of Pladda Isle, at the S. end of Arran. It has a lighthouse on its E. side which shows a gp. fl. lt., 3 fl. in quick succession during 13 sec. and eclipsed 17 sec. ev. 30 sec. A Tyfon fog signal giving 3 blasts each of 3 sec. duration ev. 45 sec. is sounded from a position close S.E. of lighthouse.

The lights on Holy Island and Pladda, on the Arran side, are described under "Arran Island", and those down the Ayrshire side will be described with the anchorages and coast in the pages which follow.

THE AYRSHIRE COAST
Charts 2494, and 2164

The Ayrshire coast, from the Cumbraes to Loch Ryan, a distance of about 50 miles, is not an attractive cruising ground, as it has no natural harbours, and is an exposed lee shore in the prevailing W'ly winds.

Farland Head to Troon—The coastline trends S.S.E. for $4\frac{1}{2}$ miles to Ardrossan, and has a sandy beach, shoaling gradually. Anchorage may be had anywhere in off-shore winds in 3 to 4 fath., but keeping well off-shore, as there are numerous outlying boulders. South of Ardrossan and Saltcoats comes the long sweep of Irvine Bay, with shallow sandy beach for about 9 miles to Troon, with Irvine mid-way, the only outlying dangers being the Lappoch Rock, $1\frac{1}{2}$ miles N. of Troon, marked by a dark cement beacon with red barrel on top, and the Mill Rock $\frac{1}{2}$ mile N.E. of Troon, well in-shore and marked by a red buoy. Temporary anchorage anywhere in E'ly winds, well off-shore especially between Irvine and Troon, at Gailes and Barassie, where the shoal water extends well out.

Anchorages

Ardrossan—Harbour Plan 1404—Off Ardrossan, to the N., lies Horse Island, a low rocky islet, about 3 cables long, with a grey stone beacon on its S. end and an iron cage beacon on an outlying spur. This stone beacon forms a good sea mark for picking up the harbour. South of Horse Island is the harbour entrance, the pier on the S. side having a lt. occ. ev. 4 sec. showing red when bearing N. 29° W. through northerly bearings to N. 49° E., and white elsewhere, when not cut out by land. (Bearings magnetic from seaward.) To avoid the Campbell Rock, a small conical rock to the S. of the harbour entrance, keep in the wht. lt. range when entering the harbour at night. Fog horn gives 1 blast of 10 sec. ev. minute. Opposite the pier and $\frac{1}{2}$ cable distant is the breakwater, inside Horse Island, with wht. lt. and red sector bn. on its S. end, red from N. 55° E. through easterly bearings to S. 40° E.; white elsewhere. (Bearings magnetic from seaward.) The Grinan Rock, marked by a red barrel buoy, lies between Horse Island and the breakwater, and should be left on port hand when entering. Two fix. green lts. are placed vertically on a mast at the N. end of Winton Pier. Two red vertical lts. are shown near the Pilot House and from Montgomerie Pier (2 blk. balls by day) when vessels are not to enter the harbour.

When inside the entrance, turn sharp to port and anchor behind the breakwater, in 2 to 4 fath., within comfortable swinging distance. The harbour shoals in-shore of this. There are landing steps inside the pier at the Pilot House, and at the mouth of the Inner Harbour at E. end of Winton Pier. If beating out of the harbour, the Campbell Rock to the S. is steep close to, as is also the Horse Island to the N. The ground between Horse Island and the breakwater is rocky, and yachts should keep S. of the Grinan Rock red buoy.

Stores—Shops. P.O. Tel. Hotels. Half-holiday—Wednesday. **Water**—At Pilot House. Train connections and steamers to Arran. **Const.** + 0 hr. 49 min. Dover. Sp. 10 ft., Np. 8 ft.

Saltcoats Harbour and Breakwater—The ground is shoal and rocky, and yachts should anchor outside.

Irvine—Lies about ½ mile up the River Irvine, and has a difficult entrance, over the bar, which is very shoal and must not be used near low water. Tidal signals are made from a tower on the S. side of the entrance—for each blk. ball showing add 1 ft. to the basic 7 ft. at L.W.O.S. at the bar.

The river is very narrow, and the channel marked by perches on each side, and a lt. each side of the entrance, 1 violet fl. ev. 6 sec. to starboard and 1 wht. fl. ev. 10 sec. to port. Fixed leading lts. (front green, rear red) are shown from wht. masts on the S. side of the river. In line when bearing E. by N. ½ N., they lead over the bar into the entrance between the violet and wht. lts. mentioned above. Once inside the entrance, the perches mark the channel up to the wharves. Two vertical red lts. (2 blk. balls by day) at the Pilot House indicate the harbour is closed.

A leading wind is required to enter or leave, except with local knowledge. Anchorage in the stream off the beach N. of the quay, taking position from the boats moored there. Another anchorage is in 2 fath., in a pool at the mouth of the River Garnock on its left bank, where it falls into the Irvine, about ¼ mile from the entrance.

Stores—Shops. P.O. Tel. Hotels. Half-holiday—Wednesday. Train connections. **Water**—From standpipes every 100 yd. on quay.

Const. + 0 hr. 49 min. Dover. Sp. 10 ft., Np. 8 ft.

Troon—See Plan on Chart 2494—Troon harbour pier is built on a rocky point extending N., and has a breakwater to the E. The Mill Rock marked by a red buoy lies ½ mile N.E. of the entrance, and the shoal ground to the westward is marked by a blk. buoy ¼ mile N.W., which must be left on starboard hand when entering. Making for Troon from the southward, this blk. buoy **must** be passed on starboard hand. The Crab Rock, a dangerous shoal which dries only at L.W.O.S., lies about midway between the buoy and the pier-end, and only intimate local knowledge permits navigation in this area. The ground to the S. of the entrance is shoal and rocky, and to the N. shoal and sandy, and the harbour should be entered on a bearing from S. to S.E. There is a wht. lt. on end of pier showing red over the rocks to the westward and a green and wht. light on the dolphin E. of pier-end. Also a red lt. on end of breakwater, obscured over the shoal water to the eastward. Siren in fog gives 1 blast of 4 sec. ev. 30 sec. Steer well up the harbour and anchor in 7 to 10 ft. of water off the Ailsa Shipyard as convenient, keeping clear of the water off the Ailsa Shipyard building berths and dry docks. In S'ly and W'ly winds keep the sheets well in hand as many flukes and shifts of wind will be experienced in working up the harbour.

Stores—Shops. Half-holiday—Wednesday. P.O. Tel. Hotels. Train connections. **Water**—At end of pier and at Pilot House. Troon town is ½ mile from the harbour, and the railway station 1 mile. **Const.** +0 hr. 50 min. Dover. Sp. 9 ft., Np. 7 ft.

Troon to Turnberry—Lady Isle, a small rocky island, lies 2 miles W.S.W. of Troon, and has two towers, the larger showing a wht. gp. fl. lt., 4 fl. ev. 30 sec. There are sunken rocks all round, and the island should not be approached too closely.

From Troon the coast tends S. for 5½ miles to Ayr, with a sandy beach, but with numerous sunken rocks and rocky spits, none of which is marked, and some extend well off-shore. The coast line is similar S. of Ayr for 4 miles to the Heads of Ayr, a bold rocky headland about 150 ft. high, with cliffs dropping sheer into the sea and forming a good landmark. The whole of Ayr Bay from Troon to the Heads of Ayr is studded with rocky patches, and should be navigated with great care, keeping well off-shore. Ayr Harbour should be approached on a bearing between E. and S.E. by E.

South of the Heads the coast is high and rocky for 2 miles to Dunure Harbour, and a further 4 miles to the S. end of Culzean Bay. South of this is Maidens, a sandy bay and fishing village, 1 mile N. of Turnberry Pt., which is low lying, with a lighthouse on its outer end showing a wht. lt. fl. ev. 12 sec.

Anchorages

Ayr—See Plan on Chart 2494—Ayr Harbour is formed by the mouth of the river Ayr, and has a difficult entrance for larger yachts, although smaller yachts can tack up the harbour entrance. Of the entrance are two starboard hand buoys, which if left to starboard when entering the harbour keep yachts clear of the St. Nicholas Rock and sands. The outer St. Nicholas buoy is a blk. conical buoy showing a wht. fl. ev. 2 sec. The inner St. Nicholas is a blk. conical unlit buoy. The leading lights on N. quay in line give the bearing for entering, 098° T. The S. pier has a wht. lt. occ. ev. 10 sec. (visible from 012° through E'ly bearings to 161°) and a fix. red lt. (from 012° to 066° over St. Nicholas Rock), and the breakwater to the N. a lt. fl. red ev. 6 sec., visibility 1 mile. For 2 cables inside the entrance, a solid concrete pier extends on the S. side and wooden piles on the N. side. Approach Pilot House on E. side of dock basin entrance and the Pilot will give instructions as to where to tie up. After heavy rains the river rises in spate and many tree trunks are liable to be carried down by the strong current. The main harbour is subject to swell

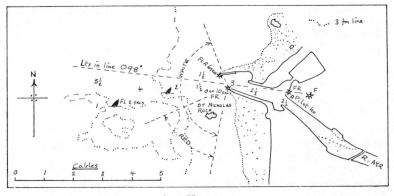

AYR HARBOUR

in W'ly winds and shelter might then be found in the dock. Two red vertical lts. (2 blk. balls by day) are shown from the Pilot House when the harbour is closed. One green lt. on Pilot House mast is displayed when ships are to enter the dock (cargo ships only).

Stores—Shops. P.O. Tel. Hotel. Chandler on N. quay. Half-holiday—Wednesday. Train connections. Water—At tap on Pilot's tower on N. quay and at fish market on S. quay. Const. + 0 hr. 50 min. Dover. Sp. 10 ft., Np. 8 ft. Calor Gas.

Dunure Harbour—A small harbour 2 miles W.S.W. of Heads of Ayr, dries almost out and is only suitable for vessels which can take the ground. A ruined castle on a knoll to the S. of the harbour forms a good landmark. Dunure is a fishing village, and the harbour has a good fleet of fishing boats. The entrance is narrow and requires local knowledge.

Stores—Small shop. P.O. Tel. Bus connection. Water—From well, 100 yd. from harbour, to the southward at end of row of fishermen's cottages.

Culzean Bay—3 miles S.W. of Dunure, in an open bay where anchorage may be had in 4 fath. in suitable winds. It provides a certain amount of shelter when the wind is to the southward of S.W.

Maidens Bay—A sandy bay 1 mile N.E. of Turnberry, has a breakwater on its S. side and a line of rocks across the mouth of the bay. The entrance is at the N. end, but requires local knowledge as there are numerous sunken rocks and sandbanks. The bay dries out at L.W. Maidens is a fishing village and has a large fleet of fishing boats. A scheme is under way to make this harbour an all-tide harbour and fish-landing port.

Stores—Small shop. P.O. Tel. Bus connections. Calor Gas.

Turnberry to Loch Ryan—The coast from Turnberry to Loch Ryan, a distance of about 20 miles, is principally high and trends S.W. with no outlying dangers of any note, except the Brest Rocks in the bay 1 mile S.W. of Turnberry. These are about ½ mile off-shore and are marked by a red iron cage beacon. The whole coast is studded with rocks close inshore, and if anchoring in off-shore winds this should be kept in mind. 5 miles S. of Turnberry is Girvan harbour at the mouth of the River Girvan. Bennan Head, 8 miles S. of Girvan, is a bold headland easily recognised. 2½ miles S. of Bennan Head is Ballantrae, a fishing village, and for the remaining 8 miles to the mouth of Loch Ryan the coast is high and steep-to.

Girvan Harbour—The approach from seaward is shoal for about ½ mile out. The entrance is narrow and difficult for sailing craft, between the S. pier and the ruins of the N. breakwater. Red lt. on S. pier. At low water there is 7 ft. on the bar (reported in 1964 as silted up to only 3 ft.). About 2 cables inside the entrance the S. bank bends sharply southward and beyond this between the S. bank and the new screen and jetty there is a good harbour with a minimum depth of 7 ft. at L.W. Along the N. face of the screen there is a 30 ft. wide channel dredged to a minimum of 9 ft. at M.L.W.S.T. which leads to a pool at the bend N. of the river where there is a minimum of 9 ft. at L.W.S.T. When coming in through the entrance keep the S. shore well aboard.

Stores—Shops. P.O. Hotels. Boatbuilder. Half-holiday—Wednesday. Train connections. Calor Gas.

Ballantrae—There is good anchorage in the roads in 4 to 5 fath. off the village, in off-shore winds (just N. of village lights if coming in after dark), but the place is quite open and exposed. A red stone breakwater on shore gives shelter from S.W. winds, but the harbour dries out at L.W.
    Motor service.

Loch Ryan. Plan 1403. C.C.C.S.C. 42—This loch, which is about 7 miles long and 1 to 2 miles wide, lies in a N. and S. direction, with a long sandy spit, "The Scar", running out from the W. side about half-way up. The Corsewall Lighthouse, 2 miles W. of the entrance, stands on a rocky point. It shows an alt. fl. lt. wht. fl. of 11 sec. eclipse 26 sec., red fl. 11 sec., eclipse 26 sec., during 74 sec. This is the principal leading light into the Firth of Clyde for ships coming from the southward. Off Milleur Pt., on the W. side of the entrance to Loch Ryan, is a blk. lt. buoy having a wht. gp. (3) fl. lt. ev. 15 sec. and a fog bell. This should be left to starboard when entering. Proceeding up the loch keep rather to the E. side, for the W. side shoals as the spit is approached. The spit extends from the W. shore 1 mile below the Cairn Ryan Lighthouse (gp. (2) fl. wht. lt. ev. 10 sec.) to 1½ miles above it and is marked at its S.E. extreme by the spit lt. buoy, blk. con., showing a wht. fl. lt. ev. 6 sec. There is also an unlit buoy (blk. con.) to N.W. of Cairn Pt. to be left to starboard coming in and care is necessary not to confuse this with the lit buoy.

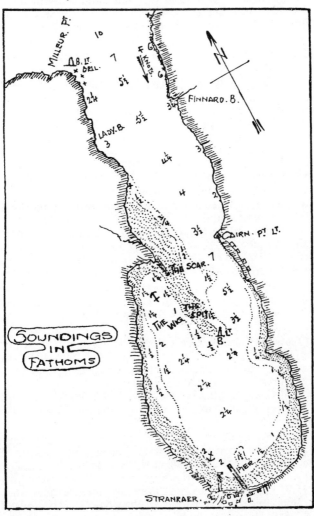

LOCH RYAN

The passage between the spit and the eastern shores in vicinity of Cairn Ryan lt. is only about 3 cables broad (see Plan).

Wharves and jetties line the E. shore from about ½ cable N. of Cairn Ryan lt. to about 2¾ miles S. of it. Most of these are deep water quays.

Inside the spit is good anchorage known as "The Wig", which is sheltered by the spit from wind and sea setting into the loch. The upper part of the loch for about 2 miles to Stranraer is shallow all over, having only about 2 fath. of water, and anchorage may be had anywhere out of the steamer track.

Stranraer Harbour, at the head of the loch, has two long piers. There is a small shipping trade and daily steamers to Larne.

Anchorages

Lady Bay—On W. side of loch about 1 mile from the entrance, is a convenient shelter from S.W. and N.W. winds, and is useful as a jumping-off place if bound on a cruise to Ireland. Anchor anywhere in the bay, in 3 to 5 fath., a suitable distance off-shore avoiding salmon nets at N. end of bay.

Finnart Bay—On the E. shore, opposite is available also in N.E. winds but is not so good an anchorage.

The Wig—In heavy N.W. winds, run up and anchor in "The Wig" not too far up, as the water is shoal there. If coming in on ebb give spit buoy a wide berth and steer for cottage to N. of hangar-like structure and anchor when Ailsa Craig closes with Kirkcolm Pt. In the anchorage (and also on W. side of loch near the head) there are moored a number of 40-gallon oil drums. These are racing marks and care is necessary to avoid them if coming in after dark. This is headquarters of Loch Ryan Sailing Club and visitors are welcome at the clubhouse at the top of the slip.

Stranraer—Anchor near the pier, anywhere out of the steamer track, or off the W. pier. The water is shoal to the westward of the W. pier and between the piers. Water and stores may be taken on at the W. pier but, before berthing, it is advisable to row ashore and contact the Harbour Master at the W. pier.

Stores—Shops. P.O. Tel. Hotels. Train and bus connections. Half-holiday—Wednesday. **Const.** + 0 hr. 44 min. Dover. Sp. 9½ ft., Np. 7½ ft. Calor Gas.

Inside Corsewall Point—In settled weather temporary anchorage in 8 fath., ½ mile E. of Corsewall Light, 1 cable off the shore, which is rocky and steep-to at this point.

South of Corsewall Point. Chart 2198—The shore is bold and rocky. Laggan Bay, 2 miles S.W. of Corsewall Light, is a convenient anchorage in off-shore winds, 2 fath., sandy bottom. Craig Laggan beacon, on an outlying rock, marks the N. end of the bay.

6½ miles S. of Craig Laggan is Black Head of Killintringan Lighthouse, showing a wht. gp. fl. lt. 2 ev. 30 sec. Fog siren, 3–2½ sec. blasts (all of same pitch) ev. 90 sec.

Portpatrick Harbour. Chart 2198—Lies 1½ miles S. of Killintringan and, though now disused, is available for sheltering small yachts. Entering between the ruins of the breakwater at the S. side and the point opposite, and avoiding a rocky patch at the inner end of this point which is submerged at H.W., turn sharp to port into the inner harbour and anchor, using a trip line, and run a stern line to the quay. Depth of water 1 fath. on bar and 2 fath. inside harbour.

The fairway is sometimes indicated at night be a red and green lt. in transit, but reliance should not be placed on the presence of these lights.

Note—It is reported (1968) that there is only 9 ft. in centre of harbour at L.W.O.S.

Stores—Fishmonger and occasional butcher carts. Half-holiday—Thursday. P.O. Tel. Hotel near Coastguard Station. Bus connections. **Water**—At tap on wall of cottages near entrance to inner harbour. Drinking hydrant by lamp at end of channel.

Port Logan—Lies 9 miles S. of Portpatrick. Temporary anchorage in 3 fath. outside breakwater, which dries out inside. Exposed to W. and S. but yachts can lie against the inner breakwater, taking ground about half tide, in complete shelter.

Stores—Shop. **Water**—At village.

South of Portpatrick the coastline, which is bold and rocky, trends about S.S.E. for 15 miles to the Mull of Galloway. At Crammag Head, about 6 miles S. of Portpatrick, there is a beacon showing a fl. wht. lt. ev. 10 sec. and giving a siren fog signal of a 5 sec. blast ev. 30 sec.

The lighthouse on the Mull shows a wht. occ. lt. bright 15 sec., eclipsed 7½ sec. Fog siren 2 quick blasts ev. 60 sec.

Const. + 0 hr. 17 min. Dover. Sp. 15 ft., Np. 12 ft.

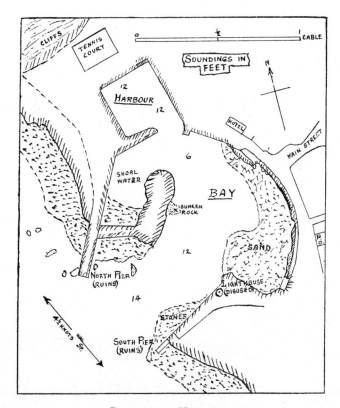

PORTPATRICK HARBOUR

Ailsa Craig. Chart 2199—This remarkable rock which is about 1100 ft. high and ½ mile in diameter, lies 8 miles W.N.W. of Girvan and, being visible for a long distance forms a good leading mark for entering the Firth. The shores are precipitous all round, except on the E. side, where there is a small piece of flat land used for the quarrymen's houses and the lighthouse. Water may be had at the lighthouse, but the soundings off the island are too deep for anchoring. There is a small jetty and landing-place on the N.E. corner (see also under Firth of Clyde, Garroch Head to Mull of Galloway).

Coming up the channel in thick weather in the morning, when the fog is often low on the sea, a rounded hill, Knockdolian, 2 miles N.E. of Ballantrae, has an outline very similar to Ailsa Craig and is sometimes mistaken for it. This should be guarded against by taking careful bearings. Knockdolian is commonly called the "False Craig". Ailsa Craig is known as "Paddy's Milestone".

PART II

MULL OF GALLOWAY

TO

URR ESTUARY

SOLWAY FIRTH

ADMIRALTY CHARTS

GROUP I

1826   Burrow Head to Liverpool

GROUP II

1346   Firth of Solway

GROUP III

1344   Kirkcudbright Bay

C.C.C. SKETCH CHARTS

*41   Firth of Clyde to Belfast and I.O.M.

* Used in previous section

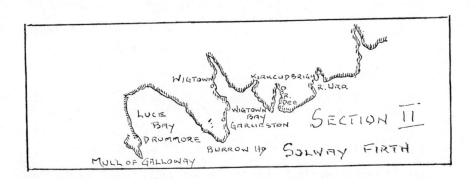

SOLWAY FIRTH
Charts 1346, 1826, and 45

The navigation of the Solway Firth between the Mull of Galloway and the estuary of the Urr presents little difficulty, as there are few out-lying dangers, but eastward of the Urr the Firth is much obstructed by shifting sandbanks and is unsuitable for cruising.

All the harbours on the Scottish shore dry out at low tide and yachts using these waters must be capable of taking the ground and should carry legs. The channels into the estuary change from year to year, but as the banks are all mud it is fairly easy to enter with the flood, which will float you clear if you ground. The appearance of the water shows where the tide is running in the channels.

The tidal stream is moderate except round the headlands and in the estuaries. On the flood it sets into the large bays on the Scottish shore.

The average spring rise is about 20 ft. and the neap rise about 15 ft.

It is usually advisable to give the shore a wide berth as it shoals very far out.

The passage between the Clyde and the Solway requires care. The race at the Mull of Galloway is not so bad as that at the Mull of Cantyre, but it can be bad enough and small boats should wait for settled weather before attempting the passage.

Departure should be arranged so as to reach the Mull at slack tide, and yachts should keep close in-shore to avoid the race (Tidal Constant at Mull + 0 hr. 15 m. Dover). When making the passage westward from the Isle of Whithorn against the flood it is advisable to follow the shore for 4 miles round Burrow Head to take advantage of a flood eddy setting into Luce Bay, and then to hold over to the Mull, passing S. of the Scares.

The Scares are an extensive unlighted group of rocks in the middle of Luce Bay. Big Scare, the southernmost and the highest, is a pyramid about 60 ft. high.

To avoid them, yachts crossing Luce Bay at night should keep the Mull of Galloway light bearing N. of W. until they open the Little Ross light. Can and con. buoys painted yellow with red vertical stripes and showing wht. or red fl. lts. are established in Luce Bay marking an Air Firing Area. These, together with a triangular target float, lie at the head of the bay towards the eastern side.

Mull of Galloway lighthouse stands on the top of the cliffs at the head-land and has a fl. 20 sec. 325 ft. 28 M. The fog siren gives 2 quick blasts of equal pitch each of 3 sec. ev. min.

There is a bad race off Burrow Head which should be avoided by holding well in-shore or well out across the Firth.

From Barsalloch Pt. round Burrow Head eastward almost as far as Garlieston the tide is strong. In-shore the tidal streams turn 2 hr. before H and L.W.

Between Burrow Head and the Urr estuary there are no dangers.

Little Ross lighthouse on the summit of Little Ross Island marks the entrance to Kirkcudbright Bay. It shows 1 quick fl. of 1 sec. ev. 5 sec.

Hestan Lighthouse on Hestan Island marks the entrance to the Urr estuary. It shows 2 quick wht. fl. ev. 10 sec.

Anchorages

East Tarbert Bay—Inside Mull of Galloway, $\frac{1}{4}$ mile to N.W. of light-house. Good anchorage in 2 to 4 fath. about 1 cable out from small jetty. Sand. Shelter from S. and W. winds.

Stores—At Drummore, 3 miles to N.

Drummore—This is the port nearest to the Mull of Galloway and is convenient for yachts awaiting the tide or suitable weather for passage round the Mull.

The harbour is completely sheltered. It dries out but can be entered 2 hr. before H.W. A breakwater extends eastward from the pierhead.

There is a shingle bank in the middle of the harbour and this has silted up to beyond the end of the pier. There are 4 thin iron bn. poles with red and wht. bands. Enter $1\frac{1}{2}$ hours either side of H.W. keeping just N. of a line from the red con. buoy off-shore and the church until you pick up the most N'ly of the beacons. It bears 210° (magnetic) from the church.

Leave it close to port and steer parallel to the shore on an inclined rectangular painted wooden post which is the stern post of a wreck, leaving all the iron poles well to port. Carry on towards a big concrete slip running down from a hangar before turning to port towards the pier off the seaward end of which is a stout timber bn. Tie up anywhere from between 50 yd. in-shore of this mark and a similar distance from the in-shore end of the pier. Inside is sheltered from all directions and the yacht dries out in soft smelly mud.

Temporary anchorage in 2 to 3 fath. in bay outside harbour in line with main street of village and outside the line where the Mull lighthouse bears over a prominent white farm on a ridge $\frac{1}{2}$ mile S. of the village.

Stores—Shops. Tel. P.O. Hotel. **Water**—In village. Half-holiday—Wednesday. Sp. 15 ft., Np. 12 ft. **Const.** + 0 hr. 15 m. Dover. Calor Gas.

Port William—This very small harbour is the only one in Luce Bay between Burrow Head and Drummore. It consists simply of a projecting L-shaped pier. Yachts can tie up against the inner face of this pier, but the only completely sheltered spot is at the shore end where the quay is recessed for the bed of a small stream, making a pocket in which two yachts can tie up. There are no outlying dangers and no marks. The harbour dries out but can be entered soon after half-tide.

Stores—Shops. P.O. Tel. Hotel. **Water**—In tap at village square at head of harbour. Early closing—Thursday. Sp. 18 ft., Np. 14 ft. **Const.** + 0 hr. 9 m. Dover.

Temporary anchorage in 4 fath. in Monreith Bay, 2 miles S. of Port William. Completely exposed from S. to N.W.

Isle of Whithorn—This is the most convenient port for the Isle of Man. The harbour itself dries out to 100 yd. S. of the pier but yachts can enter soon after half-tide.

The entrance would be difficult to distinguish from the seaward but for the low square white tower on a knoll (the isle) on the E. side of the entrance. At the mouth of the bay there is a rock off the E. shore and a reef (the Skerries), marked by a perch (reported 1963 as bent over and difficult to distinguish), running out from the W. shore. The tide sets strongly on to the Skerries. These dangers make it advisable only to enter with a leading wind or under power and to keep to the middle third of the apparent channel. Inside of the mouth there are no outlying dangers, but there are projecting rocky points on both sides.

Yachts should keep well clear of the ruined end of the harbour pier and tie up against the quay on a mud berth.

Larger yachts can anchor in 8 ft. in the middle of the channel between the concrete slip (reported 1963 as dismantled) on the E. shore and the second point from the entrance in the W. shore (i.e., the next point after the Skerries)

Smaller yachts can anchor in 6 ft. in the middle of the channel further in, opposite the prominent concrete slip (reported 1963 as dismantled) on the W. shore.

There is a bank between the two anchorages and a sand bar (with only 2 ft. at L.W. beyond it) lies about mid-way to the end of harbour pier. Exposed to S.

Stores—Shops. P.O. Hotel. **Water**—In village. Early closing—Thursday. Sp. 18 ft., Np. 14 ft. **Const.** + 0 hr. 9 m. Dover.

Garlieston—Garlieston Bay dries out completely, but there is sufficient depth to enter the harbour soon after high tide. The only outlying dangers are a reef running out from Eggerness Pt. on the N.E. and a rocky point opposite on the S.E. side of the entrance. The latter is marked by a perch. The entrance is wide. Yachts can tie up against the pier on a mud berth.

Stores—Shops. P.O. Tel. Hotel. **Water**—At tap on pier near the end of the railway siding. Early closing—Thursday. Sp. 20 ft., Np. 14 ft. **Const.** + 0 hr. 4 m. Dover.

Ross Roads—Behind Ross Island in 2½ to 3 fath. This is the only fairly sheltered anchorage on the Scottish shore of the Firth accessible at all states of the tide. There is a bar on the S. entrance with only a few inches at L.W. In the centre of the Sound there is Richardson's Rock, which shows above H.W. This passage should only be used after half flood.

A dangerous sugar-loaf rock which dries about 1 ft. lies in N. approach channel. It lies about mid-way between the N. point of Ross Island and Manor Pt. to the N.W. of Ross Island. If coming in, hold well down to Ross Island before turning in to anchorage. Anchor about two-thirds of the distance across from the jetty on W. side of Ross Island to the mainland.

In E'ly winds, anchorage can be found off Torr Pt. on the mainland shore to the eastward.

Dee Estuary. Chart 1344—The Dee estuary dries out at L.W. except for the river channel, which is not navigable at L.W. At any state of the tide yachts should enter the channel near the lifeboat station on the E. shore. The approach should be made on a line keeping the lighthouse and leading mark on Ross Island at the river mouth in transit over the taffrail till close to the start of the buoyed channel off the L.B. House. There is a fl. G lt. on the L.B. House. The channel from here to Fish House is marked on the port side by 5 red spherical buoys fl. R Nos. 2, 4, 6, 8, 10. The rock just below Fish House is marked by a red perch No. 21. The S. side is marked by four black spherical buoys fl. Nos. 3, 7, 11, 13 (No. 13 is at the corner at Fish House). There is a black perch, No. 9, fl. just upstream from the rocks at the foot of St. Mary's Isle. There is a fl. G light on the shore at Fish House. The channel on to Sawmill Slip is marked on port side by red perches fl. R, mostly with cans on top Nos. 16, 18, 20 and on the S. side by black perches fl. Nos. 15, 17. Beyond Sawmill Slip the port side is marked by red perches fl. R Nos. 22, 24 and on the S. side by a black perch fl. No. 19 upstream of some nets and at the bend by two black spherical buoys fl. Nos. 21, 23. When going upstream keep close to No. 20, head slightly to port side to miss the nets which are unmarked and then head for No. 22. Just above Nos. 21, 23 is a large mud flat with several shoal draft boats moored. It dries out completely. The tide runs strongly and it is advisable to time arrival and departure to run with it.

Anchorage with 6 ft. at L.W. giving shelter in winds from N.W. through E. to S.E. can be found just S. of the southern buoy off the lifeboat house.

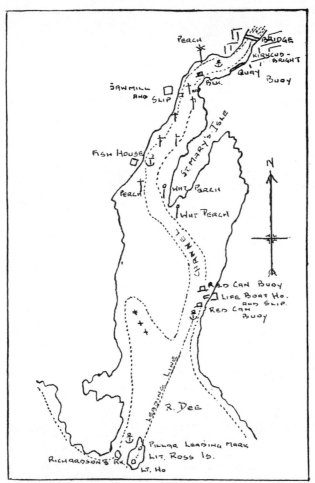

DEE ESTUARY

Note—In above Sketch alter red can buoys off Lifeboat Slip to red barrel buoys.

Kirkcudbright—The anchorage is in the middle of the river 100 yd. below the warehouses opposite the corner of the garden walls. The eastern half of the town quay has been dredged and yachts can now take the ground alongside. Do not attempt to use the western end where there is a steeply shelving bottom. An L-shaped wooden pier has been built just downstream of the old quay for use of yachtsmen, etc. There is a strong ebb stream off the town especially after rain when sluices higher up are opened near L.W. A riding light must be shown at night as vessels come up to the quay.

Stores—Shops. P.O. Tel. Hotels. **Water**—At shops or houses. Half-holiday—Thursday. Flood tide runs for $5\frac{1}{2}$ hr. Sp. 22 ft., Np. 11 ft. Calor Gas. **Const.** + 0 hr. 25 m. Dover.

Urr Estuary—The Urr estuary affords the most E'ly anchorages practicable for yachts. It dries out completely at L.W. except for the bed of the river, which is not navigable at L.W. At high tide the banks are well covered but yachts should keep to the channel.

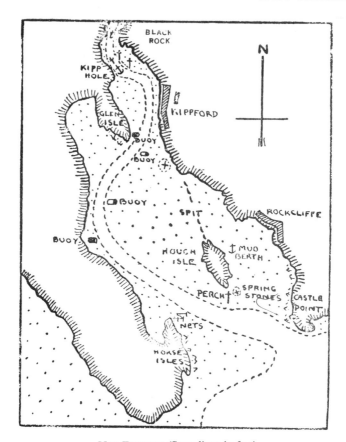

URR ESTUARY (Soundings in feet)

Enter the channel at Castle Pt. on the E. side 1 cable from the shore (see plan) then hold over at once to the stake nets at White Horse Pt. on the W. shore. To clear the Craig Roan Rocks, which run out to the S. from near the point, keep Rough Isle showing clear of Castle Pt. Keep close to the W. shore and then hold over past Glen Isle Pt. to the middle of the river where it narrows between Glen Isle and Kippford. The channel is marked at present with 3 barrel buoys—one to S. on apex of acute bend, two to port further up., but owing to the muddy water the buoys all look the same colour. There are no outlying dangers. The race-start perches have the channel mid-way between them and it is advisable to keep well away from them except at H.W.

Balcary Point and **Hestan Island**—Temporary anchorage when waiting for the tide in the estuary. In W'ly winds anchor in 3 fath. 1 cable out from lifeboat slip, which is on Balcary Pt. S.E. of the square tower on the shore. In E'ly winds anchor in 3 fath. 1 cable from the shore off Hestan Island and directly opposite. Exposed from S. to S.E. Beyond the square tower Auchencairn Bay dries out at L.W.

Rockcliffe—Mud berth behind Rough Island. Dries out after half-tide. A spit between Rough Island and the shore across the W. entrance of Rockcliffe Bay only covers near high tide.

Kipp Hole—On the W. side of a crescent-shaped mud bank, where the river narrows above Kippford. This bank is marked by a perch at each end, 6 ft. at L.W., but depths are liable to change through silting. This is the most convenient anchorage for the village, but there is only room for two yachts (see plan).

Stores—Shops at Kippford and Rockcliffe. P.O. Tel. Hotels. Kippford Slipway have a floating jetty and supply diesel at marine prices. **Water**—At pump on shore at Kippford or at houses. Local yacht club. Sp. 25 ft., Np. 13 ft. Flood tide for 4 hr.

Blackrock—Anchorage can be obtained with 8 ft. at L.W. opposite Black Rock but it is very constricted and there is **no** swinging room. **Const.** + 0 hr. 33 m. Dover.

Tidal Irregularities

The tidal constants given for Kirkcudbright and the Urr estuary are approximate only as the tides vary in relation to Dover. When the tides are neaping they may be as much as 10 minutes later than the constant, and at springs and neaps 10 minutes earlier.

PART III

MULL OF CANTYRE

TO

ARDNAMURCHAN

BY SOUND OF JURA, FIRTH OF
LORNE AND SOUND OF MULL
INCLUDING LOCHS SUNART AND
LINNHE AND ALL ADJACENT
LOCHS AND ISLANDS

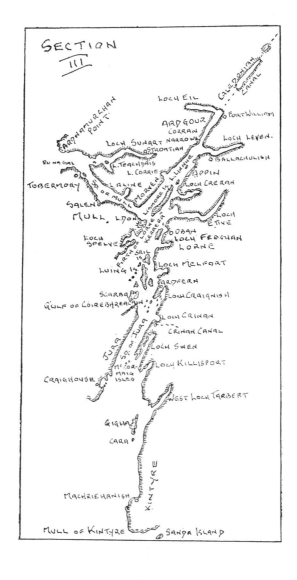

ADMIRALTY CHARTS

GROUP I

NUMBER	TITLE
*2724	Approaches to Firth of Clyde
2722	Islay to Ardnamurchan Pt.

GROUP II

*2144	Kilbrannan Sd. and Approaches

GROUP III

2037	Sd. of Gigha
2477	West Loch Tarbert
2338	Loch Coalisport to Loch Crinan
2326	Loch Crinan to Firth of Lorne
2476	Firth of Lorne
2814A	Loch Linnhe, Southern Part
2814B	Continuation of Lochs Etive and Creran
1426	Loch Linnhe, Northern Part
1791	Caledonian Canal
2813	Lochs Buie and Spelve
3607	Sd. of Mull, Eastern Portion
3718	Sd. of Mull, Western Portion
3185	Loch Sunart
*2472	Loch Crinan
3608	Loch Corrie
3521	Ballachulish Bay

CLYDE CRUISING CLUB SKETCH CHARTS

3	Loch Swen
4	Gigha Sound
5	Crinan to Pladda Island
6	Pladda Island to Puilladobhrain with Cuan Sound
7	Forth of Lorn (N. Section), Kerrera Sound
8	N. Section of Lynn of Lorn and Entrance to Loch Creran
9	Approaches to Corran Narrows and Corpach and W. Section of Loch Leven
10	Sound of Mull, East Section
11	Lochs Spelve and Aline
12	West Section of, and Entrance to, Sound of Mull and Loch Cuan
13	Entrance to Loch Sunart
14	Central Section and Head of Loch Sunart
*41	Firth of Clyde to Belfast and I.O.M.
43	West Loch Tarbert

* Used in Part I

CAMPBELTOWN TO GIGHA SOUND

Charts 2515, 2159, 2144, and 2199

The passage from Campbeltown round the Mull of Kintyre is one which requires great care owing to the tremendous seas which arise in the race off Deas Pt. (Sron Uamha), when wind and tide are opposed. Conditions can deteriorate rapidly and the timing of the passage is most important. A small craft unless provided with a watertight cockpit and means for battening securely all hatches should not attempt this passage except in settled weather.

The flood stream towards the Firth of Clyde flows from the North and West. The main stream, South of Sanda, flows East on the flood (begins + 06 h. 10 m. Dover) and West on the ebb (begins — 00 h. 20 m. Dover).

There is an inner stream along the South coast of Kintyre which changes direction 1¾ hours before the main stream, this conflict causing the race off Deas Pt. which is present during the last quarter of the main ebb.

Going North, Deas Pt. should be passed well before the inner stream turns East at + 04 h. 25 m. Dover. Failing this, it is wise to give the Pt. an offing of at least 3 miles. The ebb can be carried beyond Deas Pt. and round to the West coast of Kintyre where the rate rapidly falls. The aim should then be to pick up the flood setting North towards the Sound of Jura.

Leaving Campbeltown there are no dangers down to the entrance to Sanda Sound, where the Arranman Barrels, a reef marked on its outer end by a red buoy showing a wht. fl. lt. 2 fl. ev. 12 sec., runs out from Dunnighn Pt. About 2 miles further on lie the Macosh Rocks, off Barley Pt., also marked by a red buoy which shows a red fl. lt. ev. 6 sec. The channel between Cantyre and Sanda Islands is 1¼ miles wide. Sanda Island and the small islet, Sheep Isle, off it, should be given a fair berth. A red perch on the N. side of Sanda marks the entrance to Sanda harbour. The lighthouse on the S. side of Sanda shows a wht. fl. lt. bright 8 sec. and dark for 16 sec. It shows red to the eastward over Paterson Rock, which is also marked by a red staff and cage bell buoy. The fog siren on Sanda sounds for 7 sec. ev. min.

The lighthouse at the Mull of Cantyre stands well up on the headland, below the light-keepers' houses, and has a wht. gp. fl. lt. showing 2 quick fl. ev. 30 sec. The fog siren gives 2 blasts of equal pitch in quick succession, each 3½ sec. ev. 90 sec. Wireless fog signal during thick weather. Fog signal transmits morse signal G.G.C. 15 words per min. for 48 sec., 3 min. silence, wavelength 1000 metres.

From here to Gigha Sound there are no dangers that are not easily avoided.

Anchorages

Campbeltown—This anchorage has been described in Part I of the Sailing Directions.

Sanda Harbour—On the N. side of Sanda Island. The best anchorage is behind the sunken rocks, a little eastward of the anchor shown on the plan. Sp. 4 ft.

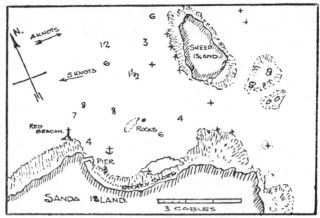

SANDA HARBOUR (Soundings in fathoms).

Machrihanish Bay—Very temporary anchorage in 3 fath. (sand), 1 cable off mouth of burn near S. end of bay. Sheltered from N.N.E. to W.S.W. If unable to round the Mull in S. winds, shelter can be found here, but only as a last resort, as, should the wind veer W'ly, the anchorage would not only be untenable but dangerous as well.

GIGHA SOUND
Chart 2037. C.C.C.S.C. 4

This Sound has a number of very dangerous rocks in it, and only two of them are buoyed, the Gigulum and Badh Rocks. These are sph. red and wht. ringed buoys. A detailed description of the dangers would only tend to confuse, and in using this Sound the detail chart 2037 should be carefully consulted, when, with reasonable care, the navigation should present no great difficulty. The Cora Rocks, the Rhu Mhurachy Rocks, and the Flat Rock have all more than 9 ft. on them, but the others have to be carefully watched.

The tide sets through about 2 to 3 knots Sp., making 1½ hr. before H.W. and L.W. **Const.** + 3 hr. 24 m. Dover.

Anchorages

The anchorages in Gigha are all very foul with rocks and reefs, and great care must be exercised in entering any of them. The detail chart is the best guide. There are good sheltered anchorages in Drum-yoin Bay, Ardminish Bay and Gigulum Sound.

Drum-yoin Bay—Enter either by passing N. and W. of Bhlar Rocks or through the passage between the S. end of the reef and Ardminish Pt. (see plan). The S. channel is narrower than plan would indicate.

Stores—Village. P.O. Tel. and Inn at Ardminish, ¾ mile to the S. Half-holiday—Tuesday. **Water**—Is very scarce in Gigha.

Ardminish Bay—This is the next bay S. of Drum-yoin. An extensive reef runs off each horn of the bay, with a clear passage of 2½ cables between them. Off the jetty there is Kiln Rock, which covers at H.W., and the anchorage is just outside this rock and to S. of it in 2 fath. Exposed to E. Exceptionally good holding ground. In E. winds yachts

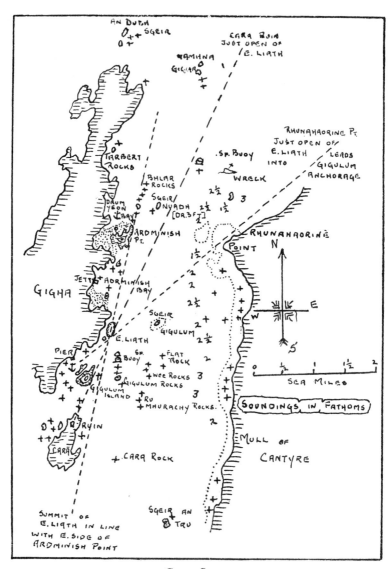

AN DUBH
0 + + SGEIR
0 +

CARA BUIA
JUST OPEN OF
/E. LIATH

TAMHNA
GIGUARO 0
+
+

RHUNAHAORINE Pt
JUST OPEN OF
E. LIATH   / LEADS
INTO   / GIGULUM
/ ANCHORAGE

0 +
TARBERT
ROCKS
BHLAR
+ ROCKS
DAUM
YEON 0
CARA +
ARDMINISH
Pt
SGEIR/
+ ONUADH 2½ ½
[OR.3F²]

.SP. BUOY

WRECK

2½ D 3

RHUNAHAORINE
POINT

N

JETTY + ARDMINISH
+ + / BAY
GIGHA

SGEIR
0
GIGULUM
E. LIATH

½
1½
2
2
2½

+
+

E

W

S

PIER + +
SP.
BUOY
+ FLAT
ROCK
+
+ WEE ROCKS 3
GIGULUM ROCKS
GIGULUM
ISLAND + RU
+ MHURACHY ROCKS.

2

2½

2

3

3

2

+
+
+
+
+
+

0
½
1
1½
2

SEA MILES

SOUNDINGS IN FATHOMS

MULL OF
CANTYRE

0 + 0 RUIN
+ + +
CARA

+ .CARA ROCK

SUMMIT ' OF
E. LIATH IN LINE
WITH E. SIDE OF
ARDMINISH POINT

SGEIR AN
8 TRU

GIGHA SOUND

drawing less than 6 ft. can get shelter under the reefs running N. from S. point of entry. A heavy chain is reported (1963) as sunk approximately on line between Kiln Rock and S. point of entry, possibly with anchor attached.

Stores—Shops. P.O. Tel. Hotel. Half-holiday—Tuesday. **Water**—At head of road, opposite P.O.; well in hedge below Manse garden. Calor Gas.

Gigulum Sound—Between Gigulum Isle and the S. end of Gigha. Going into the Sound from the N. to the anchorages which are off the pier or, in heavy weather from N., between the "Dries 3 ft." and "Dries 2 ft." rocks shown in sketch, N. of pier, there are no dangers if shores are given a fair offing.

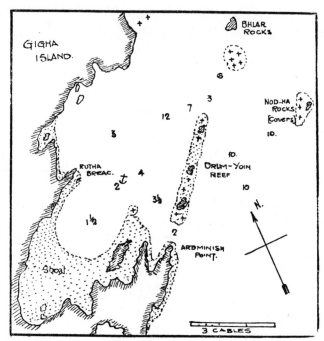

DRUM-YOIN BAY (Soundings in fathoms)

Note—The Drum-yoin reef extends further N. than is indicated and nearly
closes passage S. of Bhlar Rock.

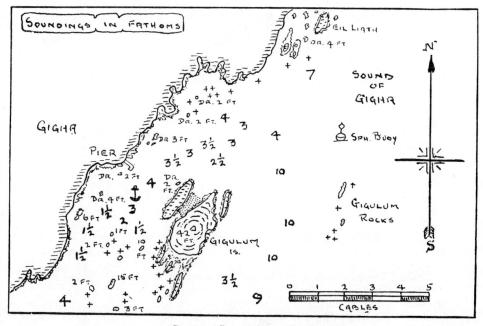

GIGULUM SOUND ANCHORAGE

SOUND OF JURA
Charts* 2724 and 2722. C.C.C.S.C. 3
Gigha to Crinan

From Gigha to Crinan the navigation presents no great difficulty, provided the shores and the islands be given a fair berth. The W. side of Gigha is very foul and should be given a good offing.

Cath Sgeir, a rock off the S.W. of Gigha, is marked by a blk. con. lt. buoy showing a wht. lt. 2 sec. ev. 6 sec.

On the Jura side, $1\frac{1}{2}$ miles off-shore and towards the S. end of the island, lies Cuiltean Rock, marked by a wht. beacon, showing 1 wht. fl. lt. ev. 10 sec., and 5 miles further N. lies Sgeirmaoile, a rock E. of Lowlandman Bay on Jura, about 2 miles off-shore, which is marked by a lighthouse showing a wht. fl. lt. ev. 30 sec. A beacon at S. end of Eiln. nan Gabhar shows a fl. wht. lt. ev. 5 sec. On the mainland side there are some rocks and islands off the mouth of Loch Swen, but they are easily avoided. 3 miles S.W. of Crinan, Ruadh Rock Ledge lies in the fairway. The most southern of this group is marked by a beacon, showing a wht. fl. lt. 2 sec. ev. 6 sec. From here to Crinan the water is free of obstructions on the E. side of the Ledge. If continuing northwards by the W. side of the Ledge towards Scarba Sound on the flood, care must be taken to avoid being caught in the branch of the tide which sets through the Gulf of Coirebhreacain (see under Dorus Mor). In light winds it is advisable to give the Gulf a wide berth, holding over towards Ris-an-tru Island. This is marked on its S. end by a wht. beacon, showing a wht. fl. lt., bright 2 sec., eclipsed 4 sec. Strong tide in Sound which causes bad tide-rips in hard winds.

Anchorages (West Side)

Port Ellen—At the S. end of Islay (see Part V).

Small Isles or **Craighouse (Chart 2037)**—There are several good anchorages behind the Small Isles, which lie off the southern side of Jura. The water is shoal, and it is advisable to have the chart quoted if using this place. The best anchorage is off the distillery, inside Goat Island. Entering from the S. there is a blk. perch 20 yd. inside the outer end of the spit running out from Jura towards Goat Island, and the passage is between this and the island. Anchor well off-shore, in 2 to 3 fath. A beacon at S. end of Goat Island shows a fl. wht. lt. ev. 5 sec.

Holding ground reported poor owing to thick seaweed. It is recommended to tie alongside the new pier in strong winds.

Stores—Shop. Hotel. P.O. Tel. **Water**—Behind cottages to left of stone pier. **Const.** + 6 hr. 8 m. at Dover. Sp. $3\frac{1}{2}$ ft., Np. $2\frac{1}{2}$ ft. Calor Gas. Petrol at pier.

This anchorage is subject to swell but a yacht is out of the worst of it if anchor is let go S. of position shown on plan and about 150 yd. off old stone pier in $1\frac{1}{2}$ fath. The swell passes to the eastward of this position. The S. pier has been extended and if kept open clears Goat Rock to southward.

Lowlandman Bay. Chart 2037—On Jura, N. of Small Isles. Off the entrance to the bay there is a 9 ft. rock marked by a red and wht. ringed buoy, showing 2 wht. fl. ev. 10 sec. The anchorage is in 4 fath. in the centre of the bay, which shoals badly at the head and the E. side, but as the Sp. rise here is only 4 ft., one can anchor fairly well up the bay. It is badly exposed to the S. and in strong N'ly winds the squalls are often very fierce and holding ground is reported to be bad, particularly to the westward of the centre line.

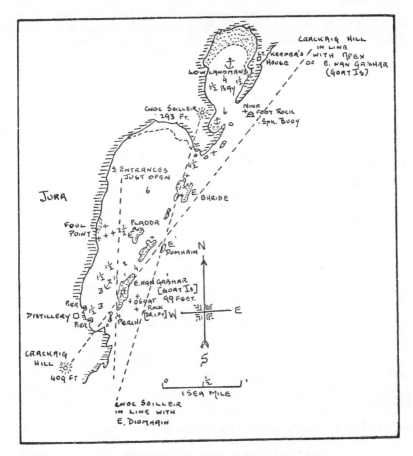

SMALL ISLES AND LOWLANDMAN BAY ANCHORAGES

Just at the W'ly point of the entrance to Lowlandman Bay there is a cove with a white sandy beach. It has 2 fath. at L.W. in the centre, and is quite sheltered from all winds except between E.N.E. and S.E.

Anchor when the little islet off its E. point closes in with the point.

A sheltered anchorage from S.W. winds, in which Lowlandman Bay is bad. It is known locally as Drumnatuadh.

Stores—None. Nearest pillar-box and telephone kiosk at Knookoorna (or Knockrome); letters lifted once a week. **Water**—At a white-painted hydrant on side of road leading up to light-keeper's house.

There are several bays between Lowlandman Bay and the N. end of Jura, which can be used as temporary anchorages, but none of them can be recommended. They are Lagg, Tarbert, S. Ardlussa, Kinuachdrach and Port an Tiobairt Bays. Great care must be exercised entering any of the bays on account of the strong tide sweeping across the entrance. The last two are convenient anchorages if going N. on the flood and awaiting slack water to cross the mouth of the Gulf of Coirebhreacan (see Sound of Jura and Dorus Mor).

Lagg Bay—A small bay on Jura about 4 miles N. of Lowlandman Bay. Sheltered from all winds, except those between N.E. and S.E. and out of the tide but possibly subject to swell in heavy weather. Great care necessary when entering on the ebb. Extreme caution must be taken to avoid fouling the submarine power cable. Terminus for ferry from West Loch Tarbert (Kintyre).

Port an Tiobairt—A small bay, about 1 mile S. of the Gulf. There is a 9 ft. rock lying 1 cable off the E. point, and a small islet about the middle of the bay. The anchorage is in 4 fath., just to the W. of the islet. Exposed to N.E. If the wind is from that quarter, shelter is better in Kinuachdrach Bay. Subject to swell. It is reported that shoal water extends about 45 yd. W. of islet.

Kinuachdrach Bay—Is unnamed on the chart, but lies immediately S. of Kinuachdrach Peninsula. There is a rock with 10 ft. at L.W. about the centre, and a rock awash in the S.W. corner of the bay. Anchorage is in 4 fath., near the centre.

Anchorages (East Side)

Charsaig Bay. Chart 2338. C.C.C.S.C. 3—On Cantyre, 5 miles S. of Crinan. The bay itself is very much exposed, but anchorage can be had in 2 fath., just inside Dubh or Black Isle, the outer of the two islets to the S. of the bay, abreast of a dip in the islet through which two hillocks on Jura can be seen, **care being taken not to go further in than this,** but it is not a good anchorage, and one inside Eilean Traighe (the inner of the two islets) is to be preferred to it. Keep well clear of Eilean Traighe Pt. and anchor in 2 to 3 fath., taking care not to go too far in as it is very shallow in-shore in the middle of the bay.

The best anchorage is in 3 to 4 fath., about 150 yd. inside Charsaig Island, which lies to the N. of the bay. Enter from the S. and anchor close to the island almost abreast of Seal Rock. There are one or two rocks close in-shore at the S. end of the island to be watched, also the Seal Rock about the middle of the bay. This rock covers at H.W.

If coming N. up the Cantyre coast, the bay below Charsaig might be mistaken for Charsaig. Charsaig Island is bluff, and on the Cantyre shore there is a low-lying dip which leads across to Tayvallich on the other side of the peninsula, and houses are visible on shore. The other bay has not these features.

Stores—Shop. P.O. Tel. at Tayvallich, ½ mile across in Loch Swen. **Water**—At house above jetty. Coach from Tayvallich to Ardrishaig. Calor Gas.

Sailean More—Midway between Charsaig and Ardnoe Pt., Crinan. A deep, narrow gut, about 3 cables long and less than 1 cable wide, exposed only to N.E. winds. The head dries out for about one-third of the bay, but the shores are clean, and sheltered anchorage can be had in 2 to 3 fath. The best position being in 2 fath. on the W. side of centre line abreast or a little beyond an old fence that comes down on to beach on E. side. Subject to swell on the ebb tide.

WEST LOCH TARBERT
Chart 2477. C.C.C.S.C. 43

West Loch Tarbert lies on Cantyre, about 5 miles N.E. of Gigha. The tides are irregular, and run about 2 to 3 knots at the narrows. **Const.** + 3 hr. 33 m. Dover.

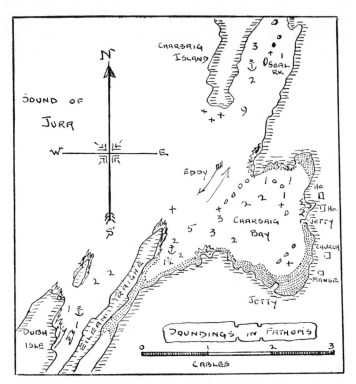

CHARSAIG BAY ANCHORAGES

The entrance is easily distinguishable by the isolated height Dun Skeig, which guards the southern shore. If approaching from the N., keep well off-shore until the loch begins to open to the southward of Eiln. Trein, a small islet just at the entrance. This island shoals considerably, leaving to the N. of the entrance a most treacherous trap for the unwary. The southern shore is fairly clear for small craft within 1 cable, and ought to be held till Ardpatrick House on the N. shore is well in sight. The loch runs E.N.E. from here for 6 miles, and the detail chart, 2477, should be carefully consulted before attempting to navigate the upper reaches.

A perch with red barrel top-mark has been placed on Bo Don Rock in mid-loch about 1 mile N. of Kilmchamiag Ferry and $2\frac{1}{2}$ miles S.W. of steamer pier near head of loch. It exhibits a red fl. lt. ev. 3 sec. and has a radar reflector. Foul ground $1\frac{3}{4}$ cables N.N.E. and 2 and 4 cables S.W. of perch. On Chart 2477 rock is unnamed but is denoted by an "R". About $1\frac{1}{2}$ miles further N. there is a red metal bn. marking the foul ground off Sgeir Liath off W. shore. It shows a gp. (2) fl. red lt. ev. 10 sec. and is fitted with a radar reflector. South of same pier there are 4 blk. spar buoys laid close along the 1 fath. line off E. coast. Each is fitted with a radar reflector and exhibit a fl. wht. lt. ev. 3 sec.

Four bns. off W. shore exhibit from S. to N. quick fl. R., quick fl. R., fl. R. ev. 3 sec. and gp (2) fl. R. ev. 10 sec. The first is S. of Eiln Traighe and others follow at approx. 2 mile intervals. On E. shore there is a bn. showing a quick fl. wht. lt. about half way up loch and near the head on 1 fath. line there are 4 blk. spar buoys each showing a fl. wht. lt. ev. 3 secs. About half way up loch on E. shore there is a car ferry pier.

Anchorages

Above Eiln. Trein—Entering, borrow on the S. shore of the narrows until Ardpatrick House is well open. It is partly hidden by trees, but can be picked out. Then cross to the N. side, anchoring in 4 fath. to the eastward of ferryman's house, where the road terminates.

Good anchorage throughout the loch, and at the head, behind Eiln. Laggan, there is perfect shelter.

Stores—P.O. Tel. at Clachan, about 1 mile S., along the road that skirts the southern entrance. **Water**—At burn. Sp. 4 ft.

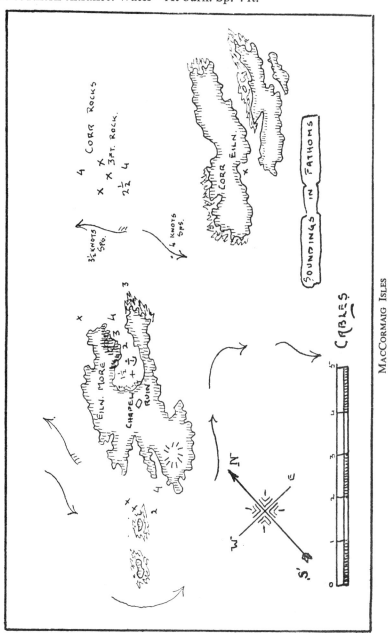

MacCormaig Isles

LOCH KILLISPORT
Chart 2338. C.C.C.S.C. 3

Loch Killisport lies 7 miles N. of West Loch Tarbert. Entering from the S., there are no dangers that are not easily avoided, but if coming in from the N. care must be taken to avoid sunken rocks, Bow of Knap and Brog Rock, which lie about 4 cables off Knap Pt. A concrete pillar with reflector (red over foul ground, wht. otherwise) has been placed on Bow of Knap. (Reflector is 6 ft. above H.W.O.S.T. but is reported missing in 1969.) There is deep water between these rocks and the shore. The navigation of the loch presents no difficulty, the E. shore being the cleaner.

Anchorages

The loch is much exposed to S'ly winds, and should only be used as a temporary anchorage. Suitable depths may be had almost anywhere, but the best shelter is behind Eilean Fad, near the head of the loch.

LOCH SWEN
Chart 2338. C.C.C.S.C. 3

Entering from the S., keep between Eil. nan Leac and Corr Eiln., this channel being free of dangers, and keep to the E. side of the loch to avoid the Lochfoot Rocks, which lie off Dana Island. In approaching from the N., beware of Keills Rock, which has only 4 ft. at L.W. (see note under Loch Keills). The S. end of Dana Island is very foul, so if entering from the N. or W., it should be given a clear berth and the MacCormaig Isles kept well aboard. There are some rocks between these isles, known as Corr Rocks, which lie 3 to 4 cables W. of the N. end of Corr Eiln. (A deep water channel runs between the rocks and the islands.) This passage is preferable if entering the loch on a flood tide with strong W. or N.W. winds, as there is an extremely heavy tide race off the S. end of the Eiln. More at times. The loch is clear of dangers for 3 miles up, when a rock, Sgeir na Amna, locally known as the Coffee Rock, which covers at H.W., lies in the middle of the fairway. The passage to the W. of this rock is clear, but well in-shore on the E. side there are some rocks which dry 1 ft. These rocks are just off a house on shore. From here to the head of the loch the navigation presents no difficulty.

Anchorages

Eiln. More—The largest and most W'ly of the MacCormaig Isles. It has a deep gut on its N.E. side, which affords good sheltered anchorage in moderate depths. There are some rocks off the W. point on entering which must be watched, and also a rock near the head, about the centre, where the pool opens out.

This rock is on the line Keills Pt. (W. side) on with H.W. mark on W. side of entrance to the gut, and the N.E. point of Jura kept in transit with the same H.W. mark clears it to eastward as does a heap of stones on shore below chapel in line with a pillar on summit. It is just N. of a line from a conspicuous patch of quartz on the E. side to a small walled enclosure (fank) on the W. side. There are 3 ft. or 4 ft. over the rock at L.W. Sp. Two red painted stones on the W. shore are in transit with the rock (reported weathered off in 1968). Coming in hold to E. side of mid-channel till past the conspicuous outcrop of quartz on the E. shore, keeping S. of above transit, turn to starboard and anchor off sheep fank. South of outcrop a reef extends westwards to about where the first $1\frac{1}{2}$ fath.

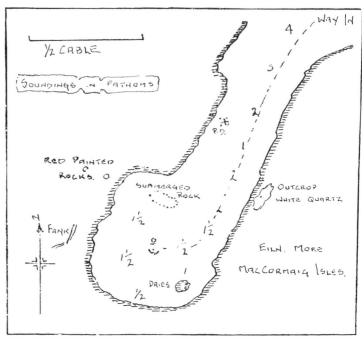

EILN MORE ANCHORAGE

sounding is shown in sketch. Either of above two transits clear it to westward. A rock is also reported (covered 2 ft. 6 in. at L.W.) approximately halfway up channel on W. side.

The water is fairly deep close to the shore at the head, where there is about 1½ fath. There are 4 mooring rings ashore: 2 on S. shore and 1 just N. of outcrop and 1 opposite it on W. shore.

Approaching the anchorage on the ebb, great care must be taken. The island divides the tide into two branches. One branch sets to the eastwards of the anchorage; the other sets on-shore to the W. of the bay.

This second branch runs very strongly and great care must be taken not to get into it. Keep well off the island till the way in is open then come in straight for the entrance. When wind and tide are in opposition a very nasty sea is raised all about these islands.

Water—Well about 50 yd. inland from head of pool.

Anchorage can be had in any of the branches of Loch Swen except Taynish.

Biggar's Gut—A natural harbour lying 2 cables N.E. of Eiln. Laoine. There are rocks close in-shore on both sides of entrance but there are no dangers if mid-channel is kept. Anchor anywhere in mid-channel in 2 fath.

Stores—At Tayvallich.

Tayvallich—On the W. side of the loch near the head. Entering take the left channel between the rock which lies in the entrance and the mainland. This channel is narrow but has 2 fath. in the centre. When through, keep well to the left to clear the rocky patch in the middle of the bay. In the inner harbour there are five ricks which uncover: four in a group

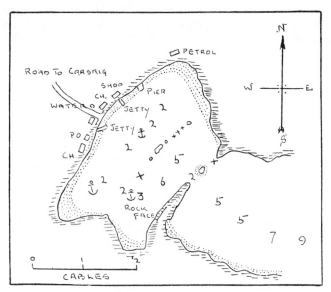

TAYVALLICH ANCHORAGES

in the centre and one off the N.E. shore. In line with them and a considerable distance S.W. of the four, there is a sixth with only 1 ft. on it at
L.W.O.S. (sometimes marked by a locally improvised buoy). Coming in
by the S. passage turn to port as soon as the promontory at the entrance
is passed and proceed S.W. until the S.W. gable of the small tin house
(P.O.), painted yellow with a red roof, only one window on its sea side,
and with a sea wall, is opened before turning to starboard to come up to
the innermost part of pool. On the inside of the promontory there is a
rock face and this should be almost abeam before this first turn to starboard is made. When well past the line of rocks turn to starboard a
second time and come up into the anchorage behind the rocks. Anchor
anywhere off the village in 2 to 4 fath. or, in strong S. or S.W. winds, just
in-shore of the 3 fath. mark in the Sketch Plan. There is also a passage
to the N. of the four centre rocks. Keep close N. of the most northern
of the four as a reef extends S.W. from the single rock to the N.E. for
more than three-quarters of the distance between the two. This passage
is preferable in some winds. Almost landlocked. Bottom slippy mud.

Stores—Shop. P.O. Tel. Butcher's van calls daily. **Water**—Tap on large
tank at foot of road to Charsaig, tap outside P.O. and spring running
into basin on road opposite smithy above wooden pier to left of village.
Bus to Ardrishaig leaves 10.30 and returns 15.00. Calor Gas.

CAOL SCOTNISH
Loch Swen

Owing to the narrowness of the channel and the baffling winds off the
hills, it is useless to try to make the passage under sail. Vessels over 6 ft.
draught should wait for a rising tide (see Plan). Enter between the two
rocks marked with perches. The outer perch is reported to be missing.
The passage is free of dangers till you reach the low rock in mid-channel.
Keep the rock **to starboard and almost aboard** till about 50 yd. past it, for
it is **shallow and foul from the northern shore to mid-channel.** Abreast of

the rock there is just a little over 1 fath. of water at L.W. At the N. end of the channel, keep to the eastern shore till abreast of the covered rock on your port side. All the other dangers are visible except the covered rock close in-shore at Arinafad Pt. Anchor in about 3 fath. in the end basin.

Stores—At Tayvallich. **Water**—At burns.

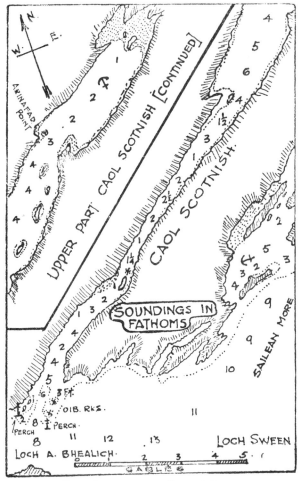

CAOL SCOTNISH AND FAIRY ISLANDS

FAIRY ISLANDS

The anchorage in the Fairy Isles is in 2 or 3 fath. behind Sgeir Bhuide, the first islet on the W. side of Sailean Mor. Entrance is made through a deep passage N.E. of the island. Keep in mid-channel till well into the pool, then turn to port and anchor in 3 fath. A rock is reported approximately in position of the 4 fath. sounding in the Sketch Plan W. of Sgeir Buidhe and a 1 fath. rock just S.W. of the 2 fath. sounding in N.E. corner. Do not anchor to swing S. of a point halfway down Sgeir Buidhe. At H.W. the creeks can be navigated in the dinghy but the area inside Long Island, N.W. of Sgeir Buidhe, has been sealed off by barriers, inside of which a "Fish Farm" has been established.

Kilmorey Bay lies at the mouth of Loch Swen on the neck of land which divides this loch from Loch Killisport.

The bay itself is too exposed for anchorage, but off its northern point lies Eilean na Capull, and on the N. side of this island, between it and the mainland, there is a small bay with good anchorage in 2 fath. in the centre.

Flat Rock, a long reef which covers about half-flood, lies 2 cables N.W. of Capull Isle, but entrance to the bay from the S. is clear, giving the island itself a moderate berth.

Eilean nan Leac, and the other islands off the mouth of Loch Swen, all help to shield the anchorage from the N.W. and it is well sheltered from other quarters.

LOCH KEILLS

This loch lies just on the N. side of Dana Island. Keills Rock, a dangerous obstruction, lies 4 cables W. of Dana Island, at the southern side of the entrance, and, if coming from, or making for, Loch Swen between Dana Island and the MacCormaig Isles, it has to be carefully guarded against, the more so because the strong tide in this area makes compass courses difficult. It has 4 ft. over it at L.W.

The loch is about $1\frac{1}{2}$ miles long, but only about 1 mile of it is navigable, the upper part drying out, but it is free from dangers. Although quite exposed to the S.W., it is reported that the seas do not reach the anchorage at the head, where the shoal water begins. Anchor in N.E. corner off E. shore just S. of jetty and house on foreshore in 2 fath. or in centre of loch in line with jetty. A shallow shelf extends out to near mid-loch from just above jetty.

CRINAN CANAL

The canal is largely a do-it-yourself one except for the bridges and sea-locks which are fully manned.

Hours of working, charges and conditions and instructions regarding working of locks are laid down in a form obtainable from the canal office at Ardrishaig or the lock-keeper at Crinan. Yachtsmen are advised to obtain a copy of this form beforehand.

The anchorage at Ardrishaig is described in Part I.

On entering or leaving the sea-lock of the canal at Ardrishaig, steer parallel to the breakwater, from the centre of the gates, as it is shallow on either hand near the shore. At Ardrishaig, the sea-lock can be entered at any state of the tide at any time. **Const. + 1 hr. 03 m. Dover. Sp. 6 ft., Np. 4 ft.**

The canal is 9 statute miles long and runs from Ardrishaig, Loch Gilp, to Crinan. At Ardrishaig, the sea-lock leads into the basin (water hose in S.W. corner), and then through 3 locks into the canal proper. There is a stretch of 4 miles from here to Cairnbaan, with one swing bridge at Oakfield Wharf, near Lochgilphead.

Here there are other 4 locks, the first of which is closely followed by a bridge and which, as both bridge and lock are worked by one man, must be approached slowly coming from the W. in case both have to be opened. If man is attending bridge he probably will not be available to take ropes and a hand should be ready to jump ashore. Then, at the summit, a stretch of about 1 mile to Dunardry where there are 5 more locks. The W. reach from Dunardry to Crinan is about 3 miles long, with swing bridges at Bellanoch and Crinan Ferry, and at Crinan one lock leads into the basin, and thence out into the sea-lock which can be entered at any time at any state of the tide. **Give warning approaching bridges, particularly in the West Reach.**

It takes about $4\frac{1}{2}$ hr. to go through.

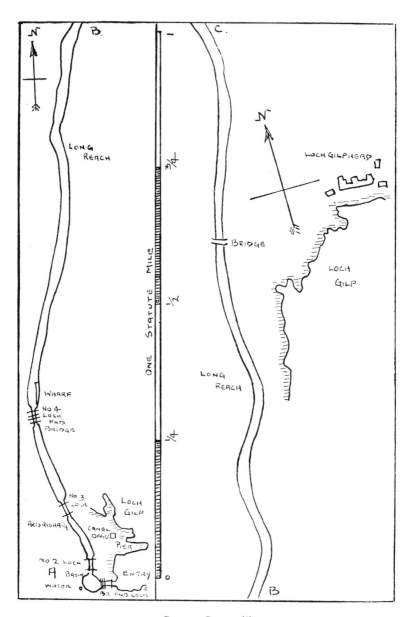

CRINAN CANAL (1)

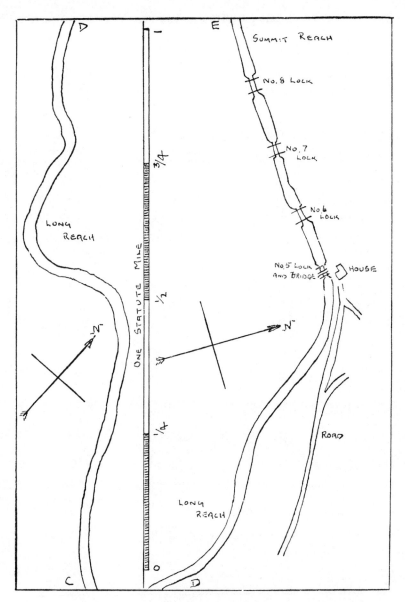

CRINAN CANAL (2)
NOTE.—Bridge at No. 5 Lock is W. of Lock not across it as shown.

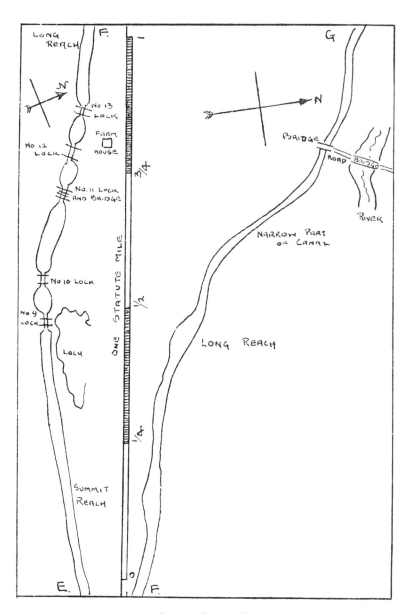

CRINAN CANAL (3)

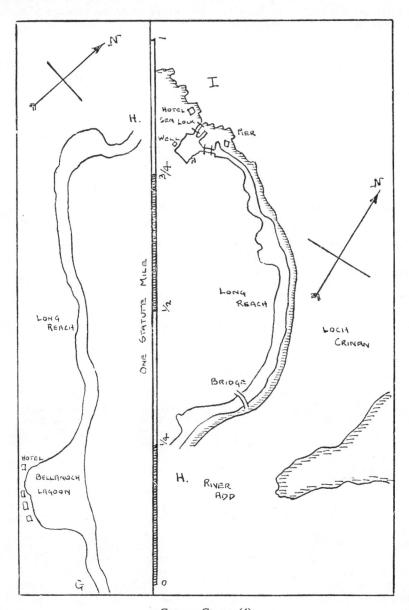

CRINAN CANAL (4)

A pass for the canal must be obtained at the Canal Office at Ardrishaig before W. going passage or on completion of E. going passage. Canal dues are always paid at this end.

Maximum length of yachts going through (overall) .... 88 ft.
Maximum beam of yachts going through .... 20 ft.
Maximum draft of yachts going through .... 9 ft.

Help can be hired at Ardrishaig for the journey to Crinan—cost as mutually arranged. Fenders can be hired at the sea-locks.

Rule of the Road in the Canal

Yachts going E. must cast off their tow rope on meeting yachts going W., the latter having the right of way, tow path being on the northern bank of the canal, i.e., keep to the right on meeting a boat.

Yachts under power keep clear of yachts being tracked.

Hints for going through the Canal

Before going into the sea-lock, have 2 or 3 fenders ready, also 2 check ropes, one forward and one aft and, if the tide is low, 2 heaving lines attached to the check ropes, which should be about 12 fath. in length with a bowline of about 18 in. at the end. For yachts up to about 10 tons, good supple rope of $1\frac{3}{4}$ or 2 in. circumference is best. Yachts make fast to either side, as directed by the lock-keepers, and should enter with sufficient way on to stem the sometimes quite strong out-flowing current caused by overspill from the basin. For the same reason it is advisable to throw the bow line first to avoid being swept back out of the lock. In locks other than sea-locks, less way should be carried when entering, and the stern line should be thrown first. Yachts make fast to the N. side in the locks (starboard side to going W.).

LOCH CRINAN
Chart 2472. C.C.C.S.C. 5

There is a small islet, the Dubh Rock, and some rocks round it, lying about 2 cables straight off the canal entrance. They should be given a wide berth. The point on the Duntrune shore, directly opposite Crinan, has an exposed rock off it and is also very foul and the head of the loch, inside the islands of Ghuir and Glas, dries out at L.W.

Anchorages

Crinan Harbour—A fixed light is exhibited from a wht. tower with a red band on the E. side of the sea-lock entrance. Red from S. 75° E. to S. 15° W. White from S. 15° W. to N. 75° W. (mag. from seaward). On the sea-lock entrance E. wing, there are 2 green fix. lts. vert. (the lower one changed to red when gates are closed), and on the W. wing a green fix. lt. Leading lts. are shown only when vessels are expected to enter lock; front lt. on the lock gate is fix. red and the rear lt. fix. wht. at S. end of basin. The lights in line lead, from seaward, through sea-lock into basin. The best anchorage is to the W. of the canal and the bluff upon which the hotel stands, on the E. side of Eiln. na Vain, keeping well off-shore in 2 fath. This bay is very shoal on the Vain Is. side, so one should keep over to the Crinan side, and not too far up the gut. Well sheltered.

Stores—Vans. Tel. Hotel. Calor Gas. Diesel Oil. Yacht yard. **Water**—Tap at Canal Store. Well on side of Canal Basin. Well opposite quay at No. 14 lock. **Const.** + 5 hr. 52 m. Dover. Sp. 7 ft., Np. $4\frac{3}{4}$ ft. P.O. Shop—confections and limited stores.

Gallanach Bay—On the N. side of the loch, on Craignish shore. Anchor just inside line between 2 outer points of the bay in 2 to 3 fath. Exposed W.S.W. to W.

LOCH CRAIGNISH
Chart 2326. C.C.C.S.C. 5

Entering Loch Craignish between Rabbit Island and the shore, give
Rhuda Minnard Pt. a wide berth as it is foul, and keep mid-channel.
The passage between the islands of Macaskan and Righ and the E. shore
is quite navigable, but there are some rocks to be watched, particularly
on the N. and E. side of Macaskan Island. The chart should be carefully
consulted, and a mid-channel course taken. The N. end of Righ Island
is foul, and at this point the mainland shore must be kept to until abreast
of the N. point of the island which must be given a good berth.

The Black Rock, above water (covers H.W. Extra Sp.), which lies
about ¼ mile S. of Iscan Island, off Ardfern, should be given a wide berth
on its N.E. end, as it shoals out for fully 1½ cables with a rock with 5 ft.
at L.W. on it at the outer end.

The navigation of the loch to the W. of the islands of Macaskan and
Righ presents no difficulty.

Anchorages

East side of Righ Island—There is excellent anchorage on the E. side
of Righ Island, below the farm about halfway down and also at its S.
end, between Righ and Gabhar Islands, but there are some rocks in the
latter which must be watched.

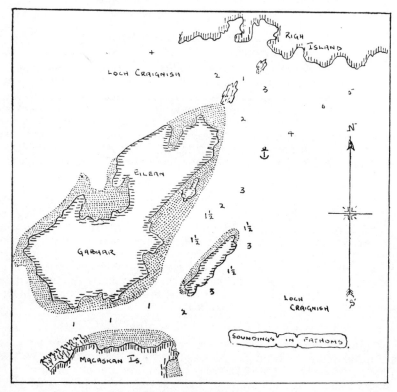

EILEAN GABHAR ANCHORAGE
(Soundings in channel S. of Eiln Gabhar should only be ½ not 1)

In farm anchorage a point of shoal water runs out for 50 yd. in line with the gable end of the two-storey part of the farm house. Boats using power should anchor at the S. end of the bay off the jetty, as the N. end is very foul with seaweed.

Port nan Lion—On the W. side of the loch, ¾ mile N.E. of Craignish Pt. Anchor round the S.W. point, in 3 fath. A sunken rock with 6 ft. on it at L.W., lies in the middle of the bay.

Behind Macnevan Isle—Enter between this isle and More Isle, keeping towards the former, and to the N. of the small islets in the passage. Anchor round the S.W. point of Macnevan Isle or in bay at N.W. end of More Isle, both in 2½ fath. A perfect anchorage under all conditions but landing is difficult owing to the shoal beaches.

Ardfern—On the W. side of the loch near the head. Anchor off house on shore, inside Iscan Island, in 3 fath., midway between the island and the shore, or if the wind suits, nearer up to the small stone pier at Ardfern (not the ruined one further up the loch), where there is plenty of water for a yacht to lie. There is 10 ft. alongside the floating pontoon. Some moorings have been laid for visitors.

Stores—Hotel. Fuel at pontoon. Vans from Kilmartin. Small shop. P.O. Tel. **Water**—At pontoon.

DORUS MOR and GULF OF COIREBHREACAIN
Chart 2326. C.C.C.S.C. 5
Craignish Point to Ardluing Point

The Dorus Mor is the channel between Craignish Pt. and Garraeasar Island. It is a deep channel 3½ cables wide, free from outlying dangers. The tide sets through at 6 to 8 knots Sp., changing 1¼ hr. before H.W. and L.W. **Const.**—6 hr. 8 m. Dover. Working against the tide near slack water, hold in to the Craignish side, taking care to watch the rocks inshore, and round Craignish Pt. close in. An eddy sets along the Craignish shore. Going N. either of two passages may be taken, one between the islands of Ris an tru and Ris an vic faden and the other between the latter island and the Craignish shore. The one between the islands is not recommended in light weather, going N., as a branch of the flood sets straight over to the Gulf of Coirebhreacain. This gulf is considered the worst in the West Highlands, and strangers are warned against it. The tide sets through at 8 knots Sp., and the overfalls caused by the uneven bottom make it extremely dangerous. There is only ¼ hr. of slack water at Sp. and 1 hr. at Np. in the Gulf, when it is possible to pass through, keeping towards the Jura side to avoid the overfall off Scarba as much as possible. **The ebb sets through from W. to E. and the flood from E. to W.** After even moderate W. winds, the Gulf is impassable on the flood, and at any time there is such risk that it is inadvisable to attempt it. On the flood a turbulent race extends about 5 miles to westward.

Note—For anchorages in Coirebhreacain, see Jura West Coast.

Coming S., however, the passage between the islands may be used, care being taken to avoid the McIsaac and Red Rocks on the W. side of Ris an vic faden and the **2 ft. rock**, 2 cables off the S. end of Corr-easar Island in line with Craignish Pt., which should be given a wide berth whichever passage is being taken. If making for Crinan in light weather, take care not to be carried too far to the southward by the ebb.

Ret Corryvreckan: TIDE RUNS WEST STARTING—0100 DOVER S
—0015 DOVEL N

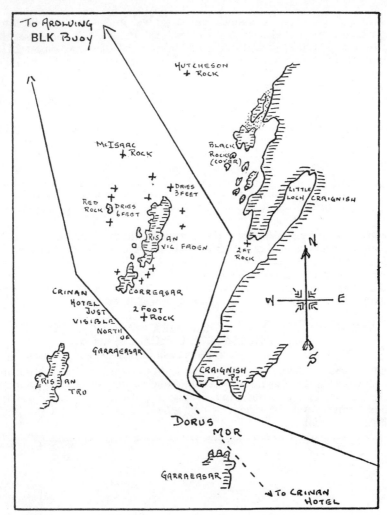

COURSES INTO AND OUT OF DORUS MOR

Taking the passage between Ris an vic faden and Craignish, this 2 ft. rock must also be watched if beating. There is another 2 ft. rock just off the mouth of Little Loch Craignish and a 3 ft. rock, 1 cable off the N.E. end of Ris an vic faden. Going through the N. entrance to this channel, give the N. end of the island a clear berth of 2 cables as it is very foul. The McIsaac Rocks, with 4 ft. on them, lie 4 cables to the N.N.W. of the N. end of the island, and must be watched if beating; but a course to the blk. buoy off Ardluing Pt. clears them if with a leading wind.

The Black Rocks lie to the eastward of the northern entrance, about 2½ cables off the Craignish shore and are mostly above water, but the Hutcheson Rock with 9 ft. on it lies about ½ mile to the northward and is unmarked. From here to Ardluing Pt. the water is clear and free from hidden obstructions. Ardluing Pt. is marked by a blk. buoy and is very foul and rocky.

There are strong eddies round Hutcheson Rock, and a reverse stream close to the coast N.W. of Craignish Pt. on the north-going stream.

TIDE RUNS EASTWARD + 0515 DOVER SPRINGS

— 1. — + 0600 DOVER NEAPS

Although there are so many rocks described in this section, the only one which is at all awkward to avoid is the **2 ft. rock off Corr-easar.** Its position is not easily picked out in old editions of the Chart Sheet 2326, owing to the many other marks and soundings shown in the vicinity. Crinan Hotel, **just visible** N. of Garraeasar clears it to the S. (There is some doubt as to whether this rock really exists as it is not shown in latest edition of Chart 2326, but it is reported in 1969 as having been seen at an exceptionally low Spring tide.)

Note—If proceeding N. from Crinan through the Dorus Mor, the favourable
   flood tide will be carried for maximum time if time of departure from
   Crinan is 1 hr. before the G.M.T. of H.W. at Dover. Therefore,
   when B.S.T. is in force, you should leave Crinan at the same hour
   B.S.T. as the G.M.T. of H.W. at Dover. But during or shortly after
   heavy N'ly weather it is advisable to time departure so that the passage from Pladda to Sheep Isle is done as near slack water as possible.

Anchorages
Little Loch Craignish—Bay on Craignish shore. Can be used as a temporary anchorage. Anchor just inside the point in 2 fath. Beware of a 2 ft. patch W. of N. point of entrance, ½ cable off. Very shoal at the head.
   Stores—Occasional vans. **Water**—Burn.
   Barachan Bay—One mile N. of Black Rocks, on Craignish shore. Anchor in middle of bay in 3 to 5 fath. Exposed to W.

LOCH SHUNA, LOCH MELFORT AND SEIL SOUND
Charts 2326 and 2476. C.C.C.S.C. 5 and 6
LOCH SHUNA—Between Shuna Island and Craignish Shore

On the Shuna Island side the water is quite clear, but, if beating up, the Craignish shore has a few outlying dangers. These can all be avoided by keeping outside of a line from Ashnish Pt. to Craigach Isle. If passing inside Craigach Isle beware of a reef which extends S. from the point halfway to the Isle.

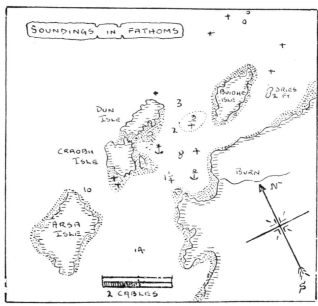

CRAOBH HARBOUR

Anchorages

Behind Craobh Island (pronounced Creuv-e)—A snug anchorage in 2 to 4 fath. It can be entered from the S. through a narrow passage but the rocks off the S. end of Craobh Isle must be watched if coming in by the channel between Craobh and Arsa Isles.

On entering from the N., through the passage between Buidhe Isle and Dun Isle, tend towards the Dun Isle side of mid-channel to avoid a 4 ft. patch in the middle of the channel. The N.W. end of Buidhe Isle is fairly shoal at L.W. A rock awash lies about ½ cable eastward of the eastern end of Dun Isle; and a rock with 3 ft. over it lies about ½ cable northward of the northern end.

Anchor where marked on the plan when Arsa Island closes the passage between Craobh Island and the mainland. This position is out of the swell that sets through in strong southerlies. Alternative anchorage is to the N. of the tidal islet E. of Craobh Island. Sheltered from all winds but subject to swell. It is, however, very confined. Beware of the rocks to the N. of Dun Isle. If entering or leaving under power the southerly passage is to be preferred as the northerly one is very foul with seaweed.

Stores—Good shop and P.O. about 1 mile up road to N. **Water**—Burn in bay on the mainland side.

Anchorage reported off jetty below store in Ashnish Bay.

North End of Shuna Island—Anchor in a small bay just inside the points, in 2 to 3 fath., not further up than stone pier on starboard hand going in; 1 fath. only there. There is a rock off the E. point to be watched. Exposed to N.E.

SHUNA SOUND
Between Shuna Island and Luing Island

All clear water except at Ardluing Pt., which should be given a wide berth. Little tidal stream once N. of S. end of Shuna.

Anchorages

Ard Bay—Just N. of Ardluing. Temporary anchorage well off-shore in 2 to 3 fath., free from obstructions. Exposed S.E. to E.

Kilchattan Bay or **Toberonochy**—On Luing shore, about 1¾ miles N. of Ard Bay. Anchor off farmhouse in 3 to 6 fath., not too close in-shore as the bay shoals rapidly.

Stores—Occasional vans. Tel. at P.O. **Water**—At tap 100 yd. down road to S.

Ardinamir Bay—At the S. end of Torsa Island there is snug anchorage in a small pool with a narrow entrance which is further contracted by a rock in the middle of it. There is a least depth of 1¾ fath. in the pool and 1¼ fath. in the channel. The anchorage should be approached on a course S. of W. to clear reef running N.E. from the point at the S. side of the entrance. Head directly for an isolated patch of gravel (sometimes marked by a wht. painted stone) just W. of this point, then hug shore **very** close and pass between the two rocks that dry 5 ft., one-quarter of the distance between them N. of the southerly one. Anchor as shown in the Plan. Care must be taken not to anchor too far up towards the N.W. corner of the pool, as a swift-running overflow from the Cuan Sound pours down the channel between Luing and Torsa Beg for 2 hr. after H.W.

Stores—At Cullipool (Calor Gas and limited stores) 2 miles over the hill. Half-holiday—Thursdays. **Water**—At farm. Bus connection at cross-roads 1 mile along Cullipool road goes to Cuan Ferry and connects with bus to Oban.

D

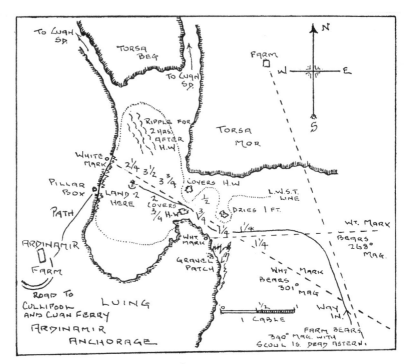

ARDINAMIR

LOCH MELFORT
Chart 2476. C.C.C.S.C. 5

All clear except for the Campbell Rock, with 7 ft. on it which lies in the middle of the loch about ¾ mile above Gamhainn Island. About ¾ mile within the entrance off both the N. and S. shores an unlit mooring buoy has been laid.

Anchorages

Fearnoch Loch—At the end of Loch Melfort. A clear anchorage off the old Powder Works jetty in 5 fath. Berth suitable for beaching at S. side of jetty. A tripod and spar perch has been placed on the "dries 3 ft." rock off the N. shore of the entrance.

Stores—Paraffin can be obtained at store beside Home Farm near river bridge, also shop. P.O., Tel. and Hotel at Kilmelfort, round head of loch and a mile inland. **Water**—At cottages.

Loch na Keil—At the head of Loch Melfort, opposite Fearnoch Loch. There is a reef of rocks on the port hand, just off the church, on entering the inlet, and straight opposite, fairly well in-shore to starboard, a rock with 2 ft. on it at L.W. The anchorage is in the middle of the loch, past the church on the port hand. The head of the loch shoals badly.

A yacht-chartering firm has its headquarters and many moorings are laid down.

Stores—At Kilmelfort, about ¾ mile distant. P.O. Tel. Small shop. Hotel. **Water**—At cottages on shore. Bus to Oban and Ardrishaig.

Kames Bay—About halfway up the loch on the S. side. Anchor in 2 fath. on the W. side holding well to the W. shore coming in as there is a shallow patch with rocks, only some of which show at L.W., stretching from the pier N.W. for about two-thirds of the way across the bay, one of which, off the pier, is marked by a pole beacon with triangular top-mark. Anchor as soon as the steep shore to westwards falls away. The bay to W. of pier dries out for fully half its depth. More sheltered than above anchorages in W'ly winds.

SEIL SOUND—C.C.C.S.C. 6

The sound is navigable for about 2 miles above Torsa Island. The bays in Seil Sound shoal badly and do not offer good anchorage.

Beyond this the channel is narrowed to about ½ cable and is called Clachan Sound. This sound is only navigable towards H.W. by motor boats of small draft. There is a least depth of 4 ft. at H.W. (This figure is reported in 1969 as considerably reduced and is probably not more than 2 ft. at places N. of the bridge.) The ebb sets S. at 1¾ hr. before H.W. by the shore. **Const.**—6 hr. 7 m. Dover. Sp. 8 ft.

Clachan Bridge spans the sound about ¾ mile from the N. entrance. The height of the arch from the bed of the sound is 40½ ft., but the height above H.W. is only about 25 ft. and is less in strong S'ly winds. A telegraph wire, stretched under the bridge, comes a little below the arch and must be noted.

This passage is valuable for motor boats in case of bad weather as it avoids the more open water between Sheep Island and Pladda, but caution must be exercised when using it.

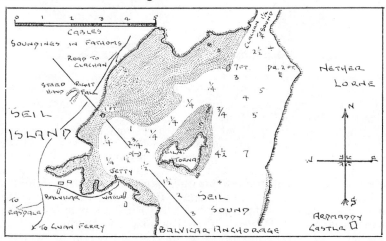

BALVICAR BAY

Anchorages

Balvicar Bay—A perfectly sheltered anchorage in all winds on Seil Island about 1 mile N. of the E. entry to the Cuan Sound. From a point midway between the S. point of entry and the island to N. of it steer for an outcrop of rock on shore below the right-hand fall of ridge on horizon.

Anchor before jetty to port is abeam in 2 to 3 fath.

Stores—P.O. Tel. Frequent buses to Oban on week-days. Petrol at Clachan. Travelling shops—Butcher on Mon., Thur., Fri.; Grocer—Tues., Wed., Fri.; Fishmonger—Wed., Thur. **Water**—At tap 100 yd. inland from jetty.

CUAN SOUND
Charts 2476 (best) and 2326. C.C.C.S.C. 6

Cuan Sound is the narrow channel, about 1 mile long and ¾ cable wide at its narrowest part, lying between Seil Isle on the N., Torsa Island on the S., and Luing Island on the W. It connects the Firth of Lorn with Loch Melfort. The tide sets through at 7 knots Sp., changing 1½ hr. before H.W. or L.W. **Const.**—5 hr. 46 m. Dover.

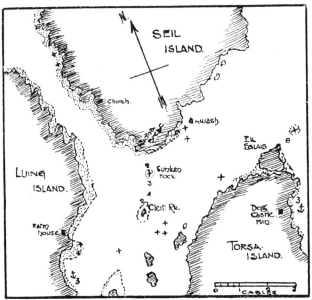

CUAN SOUND AND ANCHORAGE (Soundings in Fathoms)

This sound should never be attempted unless with the tide, on account of the rocks which lie halfway through where it turns at right angles at Rudha Breac Pt. (see Plan). It has a least depth of 3 fath.

Coming in from the Firth of Lorn, if a reasonable berth is given to either shore, it is fairly clear, but at Rudha Breac there is a small islet, the Cleit Rock, 1¾ cables off, and between this and Rudha Breac there is a sunken rock, which shows at L.W. Sp., unmarked, to be avoided. It is almost in the middle of the fairway, rather nearer to the shore than the islet, and is at the turn of the channel which makes it more dangerous. Going round the turn, tend rather towards Cleit Rock than the shore to clear this danger. At H.W. the Cleit Rock has the appearance of two islets. There is a dangerous eddy W. of this rock during the flood stream.

A perch with triangular topmark has been established on the northern underwater spur of the Cleit Rock. Pass about 30 yd. to the N. of this perch. (Reported 1970 as knocked sideways.)

Just W. of Rudha Breac there are 4 telegraph wires and a little further N.W. an electric cable stretching across from Luing Island. They sag in the middle and are over 110 ft. above H.W. though they give the impression of being much lower. The remainder of the Sound is fairly clear if a reasonable berth be given to the shore on either hand. There is a rock, which shows at L.W., ¾ cable off the N. end of Eil. Eaglais, and a 10 ft. rock a little further out to be guarded against before turning into Loch Melfort; by keeping close to the N. end of Eil. Eaglais, these are cleared.

If waiting for the flood tide, anchor off Dog Castle ruin on the N.E. side of Torsa Island, and if for the ebb, anchor at Easdale or Port Mary. A rock is reported off-shore about 30 yd. at N. end of Eiln. Eaglais and to W. of it—near the "S" of "Eaglais" in the plan. In Cuan Sound give the shore of this island a berth of at least ½ cable.

Anchorage

In Cuan Sound—There is a snug anchorage in 2 to 3 fath. on the Luing shore, round the point S. of the farm shown on the plan. The farmhouse is small and inconspicuous, and is further inland than the plan shows. The rocks off the point mentioned must be watched and also a rock about 1½ cables off-shore.

Going in here it is necessary to cut across the tide, which must be carefully done so as to avoid being carried on to any of the rocks.

The Cuan ferry-boat has a mooring laid here.

SCARBA SOUND
Chart 2326. C.C.C.S.C. 5
Ardluing Point to Pladda Light

A strong tide runs through this sound, from 3 knots at Ardluing to 7 knots at Pladda, or Fladda as it is called on some charts. The tide makes 1 hr. before H.W. or L.W. **Const.**—5 hr. 46 m. Dover. With ordinary care, the channel is clear up till abreast of the N. end of Lunga Island on the W., and Blackmill Bay on Luing. With a leading wind, a course from Leaca Pt., the N. point of Blackmill Bay, to Pladda Lt. clears all obstructions, but if beating, the chart must be carefully consulted to avoid the sunken rocks on either side of the channel. General instructions may be given as follows:

Leaving Leaca Pt., tend over toward the N. end of North Fullah Island as the Luing shore is very foul, the only obstruction taking this course being a rock with 13 ft. on it. From here to the passage between Pladda Isle and the Dubh Rock, a 6 ft. rock about halfway between the N. end of North Fullah and Pladda must be avoided. Keep mid-channel. As mentioned the flood and ebb turn 1 hr. before H.W. and L.W. in the middle of the sound, but close to the Lunga side the ebb runs till almost L.W., and this may be taken advantage of if coming S. with the last of the ebb. Pladda Island has a light beacon showing a gp. (3) fl. ev. 18 sec. red and wht. sector. It shows red to the N. over the Bono Rock, which rock is also marked by a red buoy. The Dubh Rock, to the E. of Pladda, is marked by a beacon showing a wht. fl. lt. ev. 6 sec., and should not be approached too closely as it has one or two rocks off it. For boats of 10 ft. draft and upwards, there are a number of other dangers, but from 9 ft. downwards, there are few that cannot easily be avoided with reasonable care.

The lighthouse on Pladda is no longer manned and is reduced to the status of a lit beacon.

The channel between the islands of Scarba and Lunga is known as the Little Coirebhreacain or the Grey Dogs. It is not a recommended passage as the tide runs like a mill race and there is an island in the centre. It should only be attempted at slack water in quiet weather and the channel S. of the islet should be taken. The flood runs W. at up to 8 knots from 1¼ hr. before H.W. to 1¼ hr. before L.W., but this can vary up to ½ hr. according to weather conditions. On the flood a race extends westward for about 2 miles.

P94
GY DOGS. TIDES SAMES AS CORRY.
FLK RUNS W ⊖
BB MORE DANGEROUS THAN FLOOD. PASS THRO' ONLY AT
SLACK OR WITH LAST OF FLOOD.

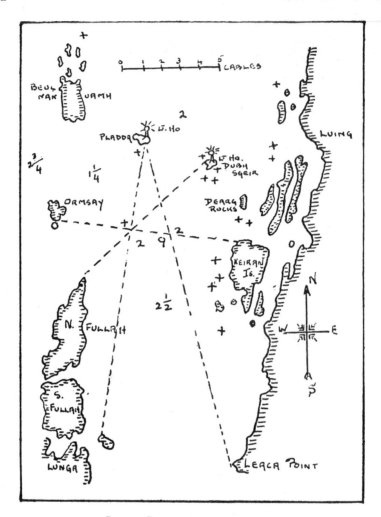

SCARBA SOUND—PLADDA NARROWS

Anchorages (if nipped by the tide)

Blackmill Bay—On Luing, about 2 miles N. of Ardluing Pt. Anchor in 2 to 4 fath. on the N. side of the pier. Out of tide and exposed to W. only. Bay shoals badly.

Stores—None. **Water**—At burns or farm.

Puill a Charrain—Bay on Lunga Island opposite Blackmill Bay. Anchor behind N. islet in S. end of bay in 2 to 4 fath. The E. side of this islet must be given a berth of at least 1 cable as a ridge of rocks (some of which show at L.W.) runs out for about that distance from its N. point into the sound. Quite sheltered all winds.

Pladda Isle—Temporary anchorage can be had on N.E. side of the island off the slip below the light beacon. **Const.**—5 hr. 46 m. Dover. Sp. 11 ft.

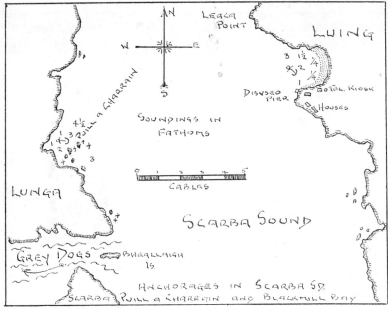

SCARBA SOUND ANCHORAGES

Port Mary—On the W. side of Luing, 3 cables S. of its N. point. A possible anchorage while waiting for the ebb through Cuan Sound. Anchor between the most E'ly of the off-lying islets and Luing in 2 to 4 fath.

FIRTH OF LORN—EAST SIDE
Chart 2476. C.C.C.S.C. 6
Pladda Light to Sheep Island (Insh Island)

Clearing Pladda, keep mid-channel to get the stronger tide running N. The first obstruction is the Bono Rock (Bogha Nuadh) marked by a red buoy.

Note—This must not be mistaken for the other Bogha Nuadh further N. in the Firth (see Firth of Lorn, West Side—Sheep Isle to Lismore).

It can be passed on either hand, giving it a wide berth. Pladda Lt. shows red over this rock, and over a 2 ft. patch which lies $2\frac{1}{2}$ cables to the N.E. of the buoy. From here through Sheep Sound to the N. end of Sheep Island there are no dangers, but at the N. end of this island there are some outlying rocks to be watched. Some of them are above water.

Anchorages

Easdale—Anchorage between Easdale Island and Seil Island, almost landlocked.

The soundings in the Sketch Plan are in feet and are being reduced every year.

All buoys are missing and beacons are being allowed to fall into disrepair and will not be replaced. (In 1968 it was reported that the beacons at N.W. entry to Sound are in good order but those at the pier are falling into disrepair.)

In yachts of 7 ft. draft and over this passage should only be attempted 3 hr. either side of H.W. and even then great care must be exercised as, owing to silting up, the navigable channel and the anchorages are becoming more restricted every year. As an anchorage it is only suitable for shallow draft vessels. Anchor as convenient N. and W. of the pier. Swinging room is restricted.

The S. entrance is midway between Seil and Easdale Islands and at L.W. is less than 60 ft. wide. Keep, if anything, nearer to the Easdale side once the channel begins to narrow in. The line of soundings on the plan shows the passage through at H.W. In working the N. passage hold well to the N. of mid-channel keeping the drying flats on that side well aboard.

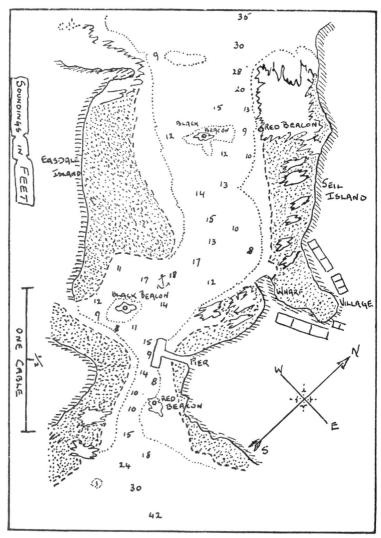

EASDALE HARBOUR

The S. channel is reported in 1961 as having a minimum depth of 12 ft. at L.W. Np.

Stores—Shops on Seil Island. P.O. Tel. Hotel. Water—Tap on shore of Seil Island, beside a small pier. Const.—5 hr. 46 m. Dover. Sp. 11 ft. Bus to Oban.

FIRTH OF LORN—WEST SIDE
Chart 2476. C.C.C.S.C. 6, 7, 10, and 11
Sheep Isle (Insh Island) to Duart Point and Lismore

Leaving Sheep Isle, the Dubh Sgeir Rock, and the other rocks which lie around it, must be guarded against. They lie about ½ mile N.E. of Sheep Isle. About 3 miles N.E. of Dubh Sgeir Rock lie the Dubh Sgeir islets, and 4 cables W. of these is a group of rocks, Bogha Nuadh, marked by a blk. and wht. ringed buoy showing a wht. fl. lt. ev. 6 sec. (There is another Bogha Nuadh in the Firth of Lorn, N. of Pladda Lt., marked by a red buoy—see under Firth of Lorn, East Side—Pladda to Sheep Isle.) From here to Duart Pt., by giving the Mull shore a reasonable berth, there are no dangers. On Musdile Island, which lies just off the S.W. extremity of Lismore Island, there is a lighthouse showing fl. lt. ev. 10 sec. (obscured by land from S. 43° W. to S. 72° W. (mag. from seaward); and the Lady Rock marked by a beacon showing a wht. lt. ev. 6 sec., lies ½ mile S.W. by W. from the lighthouse. Between Lismore Lt. and the Lady Rock, the tide runs at 4 knots Sp., and the race is sometimes very bad. **Const.**—5 hr. 33 m. Dover. On the Mull shore, about ¾ mile S. of Duart Pt., there is a beacon, the William Black Memorial, with a gp. (3) fl. lt. ev. 15 sec. which shows red over the Lady Rock and wht. otherwise. Give the Lady Rock a fair berth.

LOCH SPELVE
Chart 2813. C.C.C.S.C. 11

On Mull. The tide sets through the narrows at the entrance at 3½ knots Sp. **Const.**—5 hr. 35 m. Dover. The entrance is 2 cables wide, but at L.W. the clear channel is only about 50 yd. wide, with 2 fath. On entering, keep fairly close to the N. shore until the loch opens out (see plan) to avoid the rocks and spits off Croggan. The white cairns and marks shown

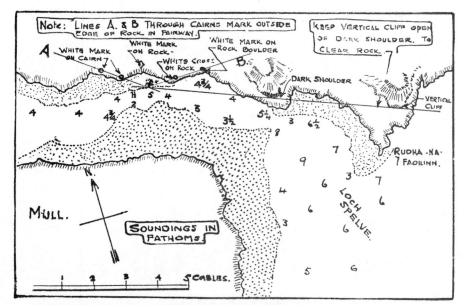

ENTRANCE TO LOCH SPELVE

Note—Marks on Transit "A" above reported (1969) as weathered off.

in Sketch Plan should not be relied upon as they get weathered off. Inside, the shores of the loch are clear on either hand, all dangers being above water except for a foul patch off the W. shore directly opposite the entrance. Anchorage can be had almost anywhere. The N.W. corner to the left of a stone jetty on the shore, and in the bay on the N. shore below farm are both very good. The S.W. corner off two converging narrow jetties is reported as silted up. Above the first anchorage the loch shoals badly at the mouth of Lussa Burn.

Stores—Nearest at Craignure.

LOCH DON—Chart 2476. C.C.C.S.C. 10

The head of the loch dries out, but there is anchorage at the mouth, in the small bay off the ferry-house.

Open out the small bay alongside the ferry pier, but give point and the pier on the port hand going in, a wide berth, as there are some 6 ft. rocks off it. Anchor in 1½ fath., about ½ cable off the pier. Exposed from E.N.E. to S.E. There is a sheltered pool further up, but the shores shoal badly, and it must be used with great caution.

Stores—At Craignure. **Water**—At ferry-house.

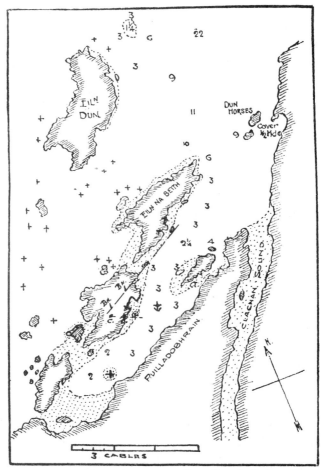

PUILLADOBHRAIN ANCHORAGE (Soundings in Fathoms)

FIRTH OF LORN—EAST SIDE
Chart 2476. C.C.C.S.C. 7
Sheep Island (Insh Island) to Kerrera Sound and Loch Feochan

By keeping a reasonable distance off the Lorn shore, there are no dangers between Sheep Island and Kerrera Sound, which lies about 5 miles E.N.E. from Sheep Island.

Anchorages

Ardencaple Bay—Lies round Ardencaple Pt., about 3 miles N. of Easdale. Entering from the W., from Ardencaple Pt., keep well off-shore until opening Fraoich Eiln., and anchor to the N.W. of this island, in 3 fath. Exposed N.N.E. only, but sheltered places can be got in any wind.

Puilladobhrain (pronounced "Pulldohran")—Just E. of Ardencaple. Enter from N.E. and avoid the N. end of Eiln. Dun, and the Dun Horses off the mainland. A good leading line to clear the Dun Horses is the light beacon on Dubh Sgeir, in Sound of Kerrera, in line with house on Kerrera at ferry. Keep seaward of this line. There is, however, no difficulty in clearing the rocks, if one tends towards Eiln. na Beith on entering.

Take the channel between Eiln. na Beith and the little islet to the S. of it. Anchor anywhere in the lagoon, in about 3 fath. Perfectly sheltered (see plan). The rock and shoal on plan to the W. of the anchorage are dangerous as the shore looks steep-to at ¼ flood. A wht. cross has been painted on the shore, opposite the N. end of the shoal, and 2 cairns each painted with a whit. vert. line have been built on the island. The 2 cairns in line show the S. edge of the shoal.

The rock in the entrance channel on the W. side, about one-third of the length of Eiln. na Beith from its S.W. point, covers at 1 ft. rise and is difficult to locate. Its eastern side has been shown by 2 beacons on the Centre Island (S.W. of Eiln. na Beith) and on rock near figure 3, all with vert. wht. lines. The N.E. and S.W. ends of the rock are indicated by wht. crosses painted on the shore of Eiln. na Beith. A pole beacon has been erected at N. point of Eiln. na Beith.

Note—The above-mentioned painted wht. marks get weathered off and are renewed only occasionally by passing yachtsmen.

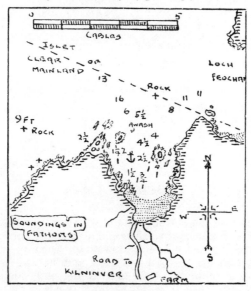

BARNACARYN BAY

Stores—Inn at Clachan Bridge for petrol and milk (row up to shingle beach at head of lagoon before taking path over hill). P.O. and Tel. at Clachan Seil, 1 mile.

Barnacaryn Bay—At the mouth of Loch Feochan. Coming in from the Firth of Lorn, there is a 9 ft. rock lying 2½ cables to the N.W. of the little rocks off the W'ly point of the bay. Give this point a wide berth, as a spit runs out for about 1 cable to the N.E. A rock above water with a rock awash off it, just round the point, and a sunken rock straight off the middle of the bay must be guarded against.

Good sheltered anchorage on the W. side of the bay in 2 fath. Coach to Oban from Kilninver.

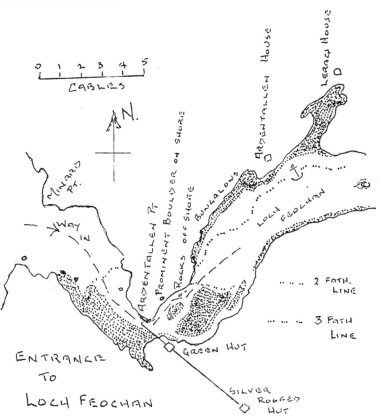

LOCH FEOCHAN ENTRANCE

LOCH FEOCHAN
Chart 2476

The narrows near the entrance to this loch are very shoal and can only be negotiated with a leading wind or under power. Coming into loch hold north of centre line and follow coast round. When approaching Ardentallen Point get on the line of a green hut and, behind it, a silver roofed hut on the south shore and hold this till the east side of Ardentallen Point is well open then turn 90° to port avoiding the shoal water off

Ardentallen Point and keep parallel and close to Ardentallen shore till a conspicuous rock on shore is abeam then alter course 60° to starboard to avoid rocks off shore to port (see sketch). When clear of the rocks turn to port and head up centre of loch to anchor well off shore in 3 to 5 fathoms off Ardentallen House.

The flood runs 4 hours and the ebb 8 hours the flood starting about 2½ hours after H.W. by the shore and runs at about 5 knots in the Narrows. On the way in shown in Sketch there is a least depth of 9 feet for 2 hours either side of H.W.

If waiting for the tide anchor in Barnacaryn Bay or in the bay east of Minard Point.

Const.—5 hr. 30 m. Dover. Sp. 9 ft., Np. 6½ ft.

Once the narrows are negotiated, about mid-channel should be taken till approaching a small islet which lies in the middle of the second narrows, about 1 mile further up. There is a channel by the N. of this islet, keeping about the middle, with a least depth of 6 ft. at L.W. Beyond this the loch is clear till approaching the head, which shoals out for 2½ cables.

SOUND OF KERRERA
Chart 2476. C.C.C.S.C. 7

The sound is well marked by buoys and beacons and presents no difficulty.

Entering from the S. the Cutter Rock, above water, lies to port, and 2 cables further up, on the same side, the Dubh Sgeir Rock, marked by a wht. beacon showing 2 quick fl. ev. 12 sec. Between these two, close in-shore, there are a number of rocks and the point on the opposite shore is foul and should be given a wide berth. Half a mile further on there is a red buoy marking a rock off Little Horseshoe Bay on Kerrera. The Ferry Rocks lie 2 miles further up. The best passage is on the Kerrera side of the first blk. buoy, interrupted rapid fl. 10 sec., but there is water in the Lorn side of the red buoy. Rounding this red buoy, make for the blk. buoy off the Lorn shore and pass it on the Kerrera side. Take the outside of Fraoich, or Heather Island, which lies 1 cable off Kerrera, ¼ mile further up. In the centre of Oban Bay there is a bank lying right in the fairway—the

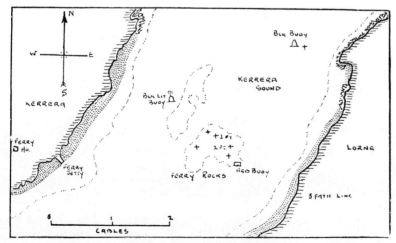

FERRY ROCKS, KERRERA SOUND

Sgeirrat Bank. Its S. end is marked by a blk. and wht. ringed buoy showing a gp. (3) fl. wht. lt. ev. 15 sec., and its N. end by a red and wht. ringed buoy showing a wht. fl. lt. ev. 6 sec. The bank dries 2 ft. at L.W. between these buoys. At the N. entrance to Oban Bay the Coram Ledge runs out from the Lorn shore, and is marked on its outer edge by a red buoy with quick fl. red lt., and there is a blk. beacon on shore ¼ mile N., with a fix. red and wht. lt. on it, showing wht. over the clear passage between the Maiden Isle and Kerrera, and between Coram Ledge and Cow Pt. on Kerrera. The latter point should be given a fair berth, as it is foul. On the N. end of Kerrera there is a red iron beacon showing a fl. G. lt. ev. 3 secs. marking the outer end of Kerrera North Spit. The Maiden Isle lies off the

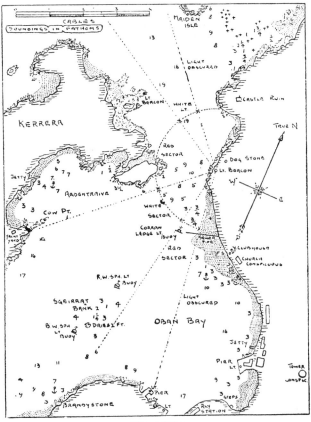

OBAN BAY

N. entrance and should be taken on the outside, noting the rocks just off its S.W. end. If the inside passage is taken, keep close to the island as, there are some sunken rocks lying about midway between the island and the Lorn shore. Tide runs at 1 to 2 knots in the Sound of Kerrera, making about 1½ hr. before H.W. and L.W. The flood runs out of Oban Bay round the N. end of Kerrera. **Const.**—5 hr. 33 m. Dover. The sound is about 4 miles long.

Note—The red buoy on Coram Ledge is an exception to the rule that when going with the flood, blk. marks should be left to starboard and red to port.

Anchorages on Kerrera

Little Horse Shoe Bay—On Kerrera, just inside the S. entrance to the sound. A rock, marked by a red can buoy, lies off the middle of the bay.

Horse Shoe Bay—On Kerrera about ¾ mile N. of Little Horse Shoe Bay. A good anchorage in 3 to 4 fath., but there is an unmarked rock with 6 ft. on it lying to the N. side to be watched. Post and Tel. Office at Ferry House.

Ardentraive Bay—On Kerrera opposite Oban. Anchor as convenient, keeping close in-shore as soundings are deep. Some moorings, at a nominal charge, are available to visiting yachtsmen. A bad spit runs out from S. point of bay at the outer end of which there is a wreck just covered at H.W.O.S.

Stores—At Oban. Yacht yard (wintering facilities and repairs to yachts and engines). **Water** and telephone at yard.

LITTLE HORSE SHOE BAY

Anchorages on Mainland

Port Gallanach—At the S. entrance to the Sound of Kerrera. There is a group of rocks, some of which cover, lying about the centre of the bay, but rather towards the N. side of it, which must be carefully guarded against, and anchorage in 2 to 3 fath. can be had on either side of this patch. As the bay is exposed to S.W'ly winds, it is not recommended.

Brandystone—Just S. of Oban Bay. There is a concrete slip and a boat-house on shore here, beside a large boulder on the beach. This is a favourite anchorage for yachts, but the soundings are deep—about 6 fath., fairly close in-shore.

Stores—At Oban.

Oban Bay—There are a number of anchorages, but in all cases very deep. Ardentraive makes a better anchorage, except for the drawback of being across the bay. The usual place is off Great Western Hotel to the N. of the bay, close in-shore in about 6 or 7 fath., or for small yachts close in-shore between old and new piers at S. side of bay. Let go anchor in 5 fath. when red post on old pier to starboard is in transit with flagpole on high ground behind. To prevent swinging a warp may be taken from the stern to a ringbolt ashore on the ramp at railway pier.

Stores—Shops. P.O. Tel. Hotels. Half-holiday—Thursdays. **Water**—At garage behind hotel. Train, bus, steamer connections. **Const.**—5 hr. 31 m. Dover. Sp. 11½ ft., Np. 8 ft. Calor Gas.

FIRTH OF LORN
Chart 2476
Sound of Kerrera to Loch Nell Bay

By keeping a reasonable distance off-shore, there are no dangers. Off Rudha Garbhard and Rudha Fion, the two points to the W. of Loch Nell Bay, there are dangerous rocks to be guarded against if going into the Lynn of Lorn. The one off the former is 3 cables off the point, and at the latter 1½ cables off.

LOCH ETIVE
Charts 2814a, 2814b,

The entrance to Loch Etive lies about 4 miles N. of Oban. The island of Dunstaffnage and a small islet, Eiln. Beg, N.E. of it, lie at the mouth, and the detail chart, 2814a, should be carefully consulted if going up, to avoid the shoal water off Ledaig Pt. and Ru ard nan leum, the N. and S. points of the actual entrance. About 1 mile further up the channel narrows suddenly at Connel railway bridge, and the navigation becomes very difficult for sailing craft. The height of the arch is 45 ft. above H.W. level. To pass under bridge going E., steer between the bottom points of first and second slanting uprights from the right-hand apex (see sketch). Close above this bridge, which spans the narrows, there is a ledge of rocks forming a submarine causeway. Part of this, in the centre, dries at about

half ebb and is always defined, except at slack water, by a ripple along its S. edge. There is 3 to 5 fath. at L.W. between the centre rock and the S. shore, the clear passage being straight and about ¼ cable wide. Owing to the S. pier of the bridge and several indentations on shore both above and below it, there are many and various eddies along the S. shore, both on flood and ebb tides. There is also on that shore a ledge running out 3 or 4 yd. from the rocks at the E. end of the channel, which only un- covers at L.W., dangerous because the flood tide sets on to it. Towards L.W. there is a heavy overfall over the centre rock, but through the actual channel only a smooth rapid stream, and if the tide is running strongly the eddies are very bad. Yachts without power should not attempt the passage except at or near slack water and with a leading wind. Any wind which is not straight or nearly straight through will not be true under the bridge, thus causing command of the vessel to be lost at the critical time when the eddies, if any tide is running, are apt to take charge. Coasters occasionally negotiate the narrows in a calm, with the aid of sweeps or dinghy to keep them in mid-channel, but only near slack water. The leading mark for the channel is the centre of Dunstaffnage Castle on with Ru ard nan leum, but keeping nothing S. of this line. The castle is now overgrown by the trees and cannot be seen from eastward. (Many of these trees felled in 1965.) Its position is, however, fairly easy to fix. **Const.** for finding time of **High Slack Water at Connell Falls**—2 hr. 50 m. Dover L.W. slack is about—6 hr. later, and yachts should arrange to pass through as near slack water as possible. Times of tides are very irregular, so these figures are only approximate. Three hours after L.W. by the shore has been given as the time to start up the Falls of Lora, as they are known.

There is a margin of 1 hr. either side of both H. and L.W. slack when the passage can be made with safety. If arriving off the Falls too early to go through, anchor off the Dunstaffnage Arms Hotel (W. side) or off the Falls of Lora Hotel (E. side). Off the slipways in both cases as close in as swinging will allow.

A mark which will indicate when clear, E. of the "submarine causeway" referred to, is when the W. garden wall of the second villa E. of the bridge on the S. shore, is in line, end on. This wall is overgrown and not too easy to pick out. It starts from the road and runs up the hillside. When clear, keep to the N. shore until past the second or Kilmaronaig Narrows. It is essential to get over to the N. shore after passing through Connell Narrows, as the strength of the flood will tend to set a vessel on to the rocks on the S. shore, where there are fierce eddies round the point, locally known as Dunfiunary—a high rocky point having a house with a round turret on it. At Kilmaronaig Narrows, the channel is about ½ cable wide with 2 fath. The N. shore is clean, except for one rock which only uncovers at L. W. Sp. It is about 30 yd. off the H.W. mark at W. end of channel. With the wind from W.N.W. to N.N.E., it will be found that the yacht is becalmed when passing through the narrows, owing to the high land and trees in the N. shore. The rocks on the S. side of the channel can always be located by a ripple if there is any tide running. There is always a strong eddy behind them.

To pass through the Kilmaronaig Narrows, keep 50 yd. off the N. shore until well clear of the Narrows and the rock mentioned above. After passing the Narrows (going up the loch) it is best to steer a course to the S. of the middle of the loch so as to avoid Ardchattan Shoal which is nearly in mid-loch off Ardchattan Priory (on N. Shore). This shoal is always covered by at least 4 ft.

Tides are comparatively little felt from here till Bonawe Narrows are reached. There are H.T. electricity cables giving minimum clearance of 40 ft. at H.W. across the Narrows. Better clearance close in-shore on N. side.

The tides are strong, and the wind, unless a leading one, very fluky. Being about a cable wide, this channel is easy to beat through, the position of the shoals on S. side being generally seen. Keep close to the N. shore (Eiln. Duranis) as the shoals on the S. shore off the Ferry slipway and the mouth of the River Awe run out deceptively far. **Const.** —3 hr. 04 m. Dover. Above Bonawe the navigation presents no difficulty, but the wind is very fluky unless setting either up or down the loch. The only real danger is a bad reef the outer rock of which dries 3 ft., lying just N. of Inverliever Bay on the E. side about $3\frac{1}{2}$ miles above Bonawe Narrows. There are some islets with shoal water round them close in-shore on the N. side about 1 mile E. of the Narrows. There are also shoal waters which run out a considerable distance off the mouths of the River Kinglass (about 1 mile N. of Inverliever Reef) and of the River Eas on the N. shore due N. (true) of the mouth of the Kinglass. From what has been written it will be seen that the tides are of first importance; but there is this advantage, they are usually so strong that they can be easily seen, and the ripples they make over rocks or shallow water are also apparent.

Anchorages

Dunstaffnage (Plan in Chart 3739)—At the mouth of Loch Etive. Enter between Dunstaffnage Island and point, and anchor off the pier on the castle side of the bay in 3 to 5 fath., or a little further up and closer in-shore. The bay dries out at L.W. for about half its depth. Perfect shelter and the surrounding trees kill any wind. When approaching from the S. keep to island side and well off castle peninsula's W. shore as shoal water extends fully a cable out from the pebble beaches thereon. The Scottish Marine Biological Association have erected a new laboratory near the castle and are operating research vessels from the bay and a permanent mooring and a wooden raft have been anchored between laboratory and pier. When anchoring yachts should keep clear of these obstructions and the fairway from the entrance to the bay.

Stores–General merchant and ironmonger-electrician beside P.O. on housing estate near Oban-Glasgow road. **Water**—At farm. Bus services to Oban.

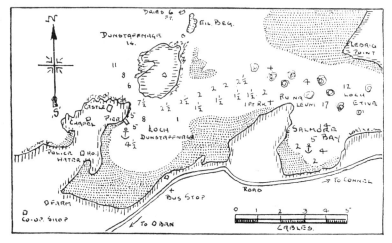

LOCH DUNSTAFFNAGE AND SALMORE BAY

Salmore Bay—On the S. side of the loch, just round Ru ard nan leum. Approaching, keep towards Dunstaffnage Island and do not turn to enter bay until it is fully opened out to avoid the shoal water on the S. shore and the 1 ft. rock which is just at the W. point of the bay.

The bay dries out for a considerable distance at its head and shoals rapidly, so anchor well off-shore in 2 to 4 fath. The bottom is foul with stones and weeds, but it is a convenient anchorage while waiting for the tide up the Falls of Lora. The next bay is also good for this purpose, and is quite clear, but the tide is more troublesome. An experimental raft showing a fix. wht. lt. belonging to Biological Association is moored off Ru ard nan leum.

Stores—P.O. Tel. Hotel at Connel. **Water**—At houses. At Connel, water can be obtained from a pipe on beach, below road on S. shore, about 200 yd. W. of submarine cable mark.

Stonefield Bay (Linnhe na Craige Bay)—On the S. shore, about 2 miles above Connel Bridge. A clear bay, except for two small islets (Abbots Islands) off the E. point. The anchorage is in 2 to 4 fath., well up the bay. There is very snug anchorage in approximately 1½ fath. to the S.E. of the islets. Approach to the N.E. leaving Rudh a Choirn Beg to port and anchor well into the bight between the islets as, at certain states of the tide, there is a tidal eddy between them and the mainland.

Stores—At Taynuilt. **Water**—At houses.

Park Bay—On the S. shore, 2 miles above Stonefield Bay, and just before rounding Airds Pt., there is a small bay with an inner lagoon which affords splendid shelter in 2 to 3 fath. The head of the bay must be avoided, as there are some rocks and shoal water.

Stores—P.O. Tel. Hotel at Taynuilt (2 miles). **Water**—At burn.

Airds Bay—A deep bay on the S. shore just W. of the Bonawe Narrows. An excellent anchorage except in strong E. winds. Best anchorage is immediately to W. or E. of a private slipway built a little to the E. of a large rock on the shore (Clach na Nessum). There is a 6 to 8 fath. shelf then a steep drop to over 10 fath. but a line can be taken from some yacht moorings, usually laid there during summer. Using the lead anchor inside the line of these moorings. Anchorage can also be had off the pier on the E. side of the bay. This position is more convenient for Taynuilt and Bonawe, but care is necessary if using it owing to the strong currents and shoal water off the mouth of the River Naint. An experimental raft showing a fix. wht. lt. belonging to Biological Association is moored in mid-loch E. of Airds Pt.

Achnacreamore Bay—On the N. side of the loch, past Kilmaronaig Narrows. Anchorage can be had in 5 fath., close in-shore off the W. end of three groups of cottages in the N. side of the bay. There is a rock here to be avoided which dries 1 ft. at L.W.O.S. and shows a little kelp at L.W. Neaps. Sp. 6 ft.

Achnacloich Bay—On the S. shore, the next bay E. of Stonefield Bay. A good sheltered anchorage off the pier in 2 to 4 fath. A large motor boat uses this pier, so anchor clear of the fairway leading to it. This motor boat does a daily trip to the head of the loch and back. Convenient for both railway station and main road.

Water—At cottages.

Glenoe Bay—A small bay on the E. shore about 2 miles E. of Bonawe Narrows, where the loch bends more northerly. Sheltered from all but S.W'ly winds. Anchor at head of bay in 2 to 4 fath.

Stores—Farms only. **Water**—Burns.

Creag Bay—On the W. shore directly opposite Glenoe Bay. A fair anchorage in 3 to 5 fath., with shelter from winds from S.W. to N. Anchor off the jetty below cottage.

Inverliever Bay—A deep narrow bay on the E. side just S. of the Inverliever Reef. Well sheltered from all winds but strong W. or S.W. Good holding ground in 2 to 6 fath. at head of bay.

Green Bay—A small bay on the W. shore round Ru Aird (the N. point of Creag Bay). Sheltered from all W'ly winds. Anchor in 2 to 5 fath. as close as possible to the shore. Soundings increase rapidly.

Dail Bay—On the W. shore between the mouths of the rivers Cadderlie and Eas. The loch narrows to about half its previous width immediately N. of this bay. Sheltered from all but S. and S.E. winds. Good holding ground in 3 to 4 fath. immediately W. of remains of old pier (piles projecting out of water).

Note—In the last five anchorages there are no stores and only hill paths leading to main roads. Only occasional farms.

Head of Loch—On the W. shore in 2 to 3 fath. beyond the pier and about halfway between it and an islet that is joined to mainland at L.W. The head of the loch dries out for 2 to 3 cables. P.O. and telephone 1 mile up Glen Etive. Exposed to S'ly winds.

LYNN OF LORN
Chart 2814a. C.C.C.S.C. 8
Loch Nell to Shuna Sound

Entering from the S., there is a group of islets lying off the E. side of Lismore. Either side of this group may be taken, but it is inadvisable to go between Stirk Isle (Eiln. nan Gamhna) and Pladda Isle, as there are a number of rocks there to be avoided. Also keep well off the W'ly point of Loch Nell Bay, as it is foul. Eiln. Dubh, a small islet with foul ground extending about $2\frac{1}{2}$ cables off its western shores, lies 3 miles further up and Branra Rock, marked by a blk. open ironwork beacon, lies $\frac{1}{2}$ mile N.E. of this islet, but there are really no dangers that cannot easily be avoided, up to the mouth of Loch Creran. Just N. of Loch Creran, the Appin Rocks, marked by a blk. buoy showing a wht. fl. lt. ev. 6 sec., and some rocks off Lismore on the other side, narrow the channel to $2\frac{1}{2}$ cables and care must be exercised going through the remainder of the sound. Off the N.E. of Lismore lie Inn Isle and Sheep Isle (Eiln. na Caorach) and they have a number of hidden dangers about them, and the Appin shore opposite shoals badly. There is a clear channel about $2\frac{1}{2}$ cables wide, the middle of which should be taken. Sgeir Buidhe Lt., a beacon on a rock off the Appin shore, shows red over Shuna Island and Sound, and wht. elsewhere (2 fl. ev. 7 sec.).

If going into Loch Linnhe between Shuna Island and Sheep Isle, give the latter a wide berth and keep over towards Shuna Island to clear the rocks N.E. of Grey Isle (Eiln. Glas) which lies 4 cables N. of Sheep Isle and those which dry 2 ft. and 5 ft. between Grey and Sheep Isle. Between Shuna and the shore lies Shuna Sound, the southern entrance to which is very shallow and narrow, and can only be taken near H.W., and with a leading wind. Great care must be taken if using this channel on account of the many rocks and shoals which lie on either hand. Keep Knap Pt.

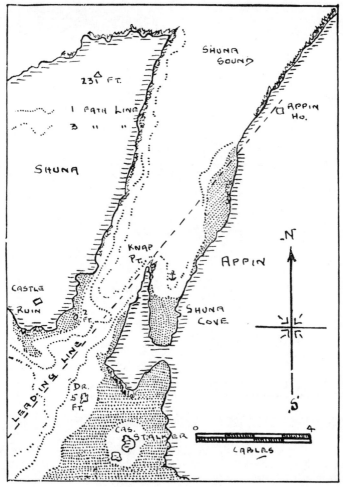

SHUNA SOUND

on left tangent of Appin House, and this line leads clear through with over 6 ft. at half tide. Past Knap Pt. the sound is clear of dangers.

The tide sets through the Lynn of Lorn at 2 to 2½ knots. **Const.** —5 hr. 35 m. Dover. Both ebb and flood tide run southward along the shore of Lismore, below Stirk Isle.

Anchorages

Aird's Bay—Just N. of the mouth of Loch Creran. A temporary anchorage in 2 to 4 fath., in the centre of the bay. The head of the bay dries out for about half its depth. Exposed to S.W. winds.

Stores—At Port Appin. P.O. Tel. **Water**—Burns.

Eiln. nan Caorach (Sheep Isle)—In the bay on E. side of the island. Approaching from the E. there are 2 wht. marks painted on rocks S. of white cottage—keep just N. of a line joining them to clear some bad rocks to the southward and anchor in 2 to 3 fath. The rock marked in chart 2814a as being in bay is shown too far to the N. and the above leading line clears it. Exposed between E. and S.E. but only to a short carry.

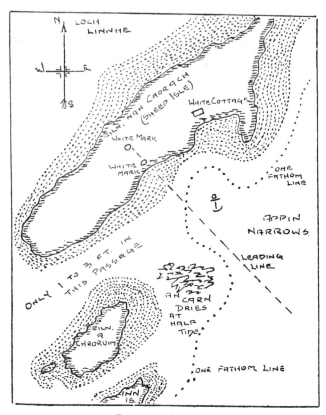

EILN NAN CAORACH

Shuna Cove (Dallens Bay or Knap Bay)—Between Shuna Isle and Appin. It is better to enter from the N. as the S. passage through Shuna Sound is only practicable near H.W. as already stated. The bay dries out for about half its depth.

A very temporary anchorage in good weather may be found in 1 to 2 fath. immediately N. of the ruined Port Appin pier about 80 yd. off-shore.

Stores—At Appin, ½ mile inland. P.O. Tel. Hotels at Port Appin and Appin. **Water**—Farm and at public taps 200 yd. N. of Port Appin pier. Sp. 12 ft., Np. 8½ ft. Half-holiday—Thursdays. Calor Gas.

LOCH CRERAN
Charts 2814a and 2814b. C.C.C.S.C. 8

The entrance is in the Lynn of Lord 1 mile S. of Appin, and lies between Eriska Island and Airds Pt. The narrows are 1½ cables wide but the actual entrance is narrowed to ¾ cable by outlying rocks off Airds Pt. and a group of rocks off the N. side of Eriska.

There is a coloured sectored light fl. WRG 2 sec. on the dries 11-ft. rock S.W. of Airds Pt. The wht. sectors show over Glas Eiln and Airds Pt., the red sector over the approach from the N.W. and the green sectors over the approach from the S.W. and the narrows to the E. A quick fl. lt. on the N.E. pt. of Eriska shows from N.W. through N. to S.E. and is obscured elsewhere. A black conical buoy fl. 3 sec. situated at the N.E. extremity of

Sgeir Caillich marks the end of the narrows. The tide sets through at over 6 knots. Sp. **Const.** —5 hr. 35 m. Dover. With a leading wind Branra Rock beacon in line with N. end of Glas Eiln clears the rocks off Eriska but if beating care must be exercised until inside Airds Pt. From here for 6 miles to Crigan narrows there are no dangers which cannot be avoided with ordinary care. Over Crigan narrows there is a railway bridge with two spans and there is a narrow channel through with 6 ft. at L.W. in it (see plan). Less than this has been reported off the spit further up. The height of the arch is 42 ft. above H.W. level. Going up take the right-hand span and then keep to the left taking care to clear the shoal spit running out from the left bank. From here to the head of the loch the N.E. corner of which dries out at L.W. the water is clear. There is anchorage at the head and in various parts of the loch below the narrows in almost any of the bays.

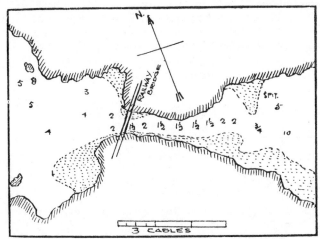

CRIGAN NARROWS (Soundings in Fathoms)

Anchorages

South Shian—Between the E. side of Eriska Island and Sgeir Cailleach, at the entrance to the loch. Anchor straight off the S. ferry-house in 3 to 4 fath.

Head of the Loch—Above Crigan Narrows. Anchor on the S. shore at the head of the loch.

Stores—At Fasnacloich, 1 mile inland. P.O. Tel. **Water**—Well beside fisherman's hut.

LYNN OF MORVEN
Chart 2814a. C.C.C.S.C. 8 and 10
Duart Point to Loch Corrie

Going up the Lynn of Morven from the Sound of Mull, the Morven side is clear of dangers up to Loch Corrie, but off Lismore Island, which lies to the eastward, there are some rocks and islets. The Laith Sgeir, which lies midway between Lismore Lt. and the W'ly point of Bernera Isle, dries 7 ft. at L.W., and should be guarded against. Between the N.E. point of Lismore Island and Shuna Isle there are a number of dangers, but they are clear of the fairway unless going into Shuna Sound, when the chart should be carefully consulted.

Anchorages

Port-na-Morlach—At the N.W. end of Lismore Island. Enter from the S., between Dubh Sgeir and Lismore, giving the former a clear berth, and anchor in the little bay in the S.W. corner, off ruins of lime kiln, below Creagan Breac Hill, in 4 to 6 fath. Well sheltered, even from a S.W. swell. Bay shoals for about half its depth.

Port Ramsay—On the N. end of Lismore Island (see plan). Enter on either side of rock as marked by soundings. The rocks are low lying and are rather difficult to pick out at H.W. Anchor inside Eil. nam Meann and about halfway up it, abreast a dip. From a few feet up the mast the ruin on W. shore should be seen through the dip. Well sheltered. There is a submerged rock about the middle, where marked by a + on the plan. At H.W. when the "Rock" in sketch plan is covered a leading line that leads through the channel between it and the "dries 10 ft." rock to the north of it is: Keep open the face of the S'ly pair of cottages (and theirs only) that lie to the eastward (marked "crofts" in the plan).

If approaching from N. or E. entrance can be made at all states of the tide by passing midway between the "dries 10 ft." rock and the outside rock due E. of it.

Stores—None. **Water**—Well beside pier to left of the crofts.

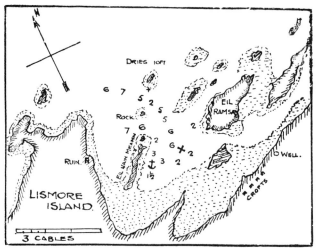

PORT RAMSAY (Soundings in Fathoms)

LOCH CORRIE

Charts 2814a and 3608 (best)

There are a few rocks off the N.E. point going into the loch, but they are close in-shore. The head of the loch dries out for some distance at L.W., and there is an 8 ft. rock there, just off the L.W. mark. There is good anchorage about 100 yd. off the boat slip and a 100 yd. to the E. of it on right-hand side and off gamekeeper's house on the other side. Violent squalls may be expected in strong winds.

Stores—None. **Water**—At gamekeeper's cottage.

LOCH LINNHE Chart 1426. C.C.C.S.C. 8 and 9
(Note—Chart 1426 is not on vertical axis)—**Loch Corrie to Loch Leven**

There is no difficulty in the navigation of Loch Linnhe. On the Morven side, about 4½ miles up from Loch Corrie, there are one or two rocks, but they are close in-shore and some of them are above water. Two miles further up, Sanda Shoal, marked by a red buoy, lies off the Morven shore. Keep outside of a line from this buoy to the red and wht. horizontal striped beacon on Salachan Pt. at the western side of the entrance to Corran Narrows, as there are several bad patches inside this line. A blk. buoy showing a wht. fl. lt. ev. 6 sec. off the end of Culchenna spit, marks the eastern side of the entrance to Corran Narrows, and the northern side of the entrance to Loch Leven.

Anchorages
Cul Bay—On the Appin shore. Anchor round the second point of Rudha Mor, off a fisherman's hut on shore. Both points shoal badly and should be given a clear berth. Exposed W. to S.W.

Stores—At Duror, 1 mile inland. P.O. Tel. Hotel. **Water**—Burns.

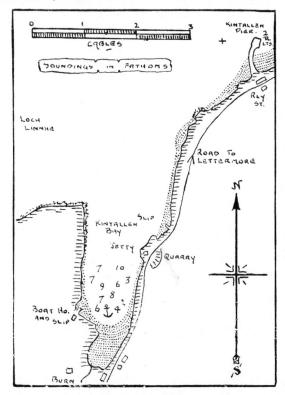

KINTALLEN BAY

Kintallen Bay—Three miles N. of Cul Bay. The pier at Kintallen station, just N. of the bay, shows 2 fix. red lts. The anchorage is deep, as much as 8 fath., within reasonable distance off the shore. Anchor well in-shore on a line joining a ruined boathouse to starboard and a conspicuous railway bridge to port.

Stores—Shop at Lettermore, 1½ miles towards Ballachulish. P.O. Tel. at Kintallen ruined railway pier. **Water**—Burn beside houses on shore.

LOCH LEVEN
Charts 1426 and 3521. C.C.C.S.C. 9

Entering from the loch from the W., leave the blk. buoy on the outer end of Culchenna spit to port. It shows a wht. fl. lt. ev. 6 sec. Off Lettermore, just N. of Kintallen, on the Appin shore, a blk. buoy marks a rock, Sgeir nan roin, which dries 10 ft. at L.W. The water is clear from here to Peter Straits. Both points, on entering the Straits shoal badly, the S. point particularly, so keep mid-channel which is clear of obstructions, 1 cable wide and 1 mile long. Coming out with the ebb, keep towards the S. shore as a branch of the tide sweeps round Port-an-Dun (see plan). The tide runs strongest on the S. shore, 5 to 6 knots Sp., the flood making 1 hr. after L.W. and running 5 hr. and the ebb for 7 hr. **Const.** —5 hr. 35 m. Dover. If making for Port an Dun note that the beacon on the 3 ft. rock no longer exists. The position of this rock is correctly shown on chart 3521 (halfway between △ 40 islet and the point). When through, keep S. of Eil. Choinich Isle, but either side of St. Mungo can be taken. The upper narrows have been dredged out since the aluminium works were started at Kinlochleven, and perches erected to mark the channel. Chart 1426 is advisable.

Two lines of unlit mooring buoys have been laid on both sides of the channel from about abreast Kintallen pier to Peter Straits.

Anchorages

Onich—On the N. shore of the entrance to the loch, 1 mile E. of Culchenna Spit. Anchor in bay on E. side of pier, in 4 fath. It is reported that the pier is surrounded by broken piles and landing should be made on the beach. Exposed S.W.

Stores—Shop at pier. P.O. Tel. **Water**—Burn opposite anchorage. Bus to Fort William. Calor Gas.

North Ballachulish—On N. side of loch, outside Narrows. Anchor in 3 fath., not too close in, opposite private jetty, a little to the E. of the church. Exposed S.W.

Stores—Shop ½ mile E. of church at crossroads. P.O. on shore facing Narrows. **Water**—At burn. **Const.** —5 hr. 31 m. Dover. Sp. 12 ft., Np. 8½ ft.

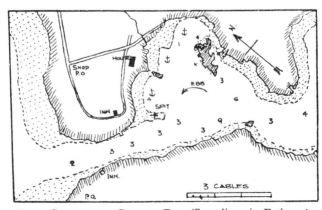

PETER STRAITS AND PORT-AN-DUN (Soundings in Fathoms)

Port-an-Dun (Bishop's Bay)—In basin of Narrows. Anchorage can be had in the outer bay, below the Bishop of Argyll's house, but the inner anchorage is perfectly sheltered. There is a rocky ledge, ending in a rock awash at L.W., off the end of the small islet on the starboard hand, and shoal ground off the rock on the port hand. Entering the inner anchorage, keep to port, but not too close to the rocky promontory on that side as a rock, awash at L.W., lies off it. Anchor where shown on the sketch plan. Moorings laid here restrict room.

Coming out, care must be taken as the ebb tends to drive the yacht on the shoally spit (see plan).

Stores—As for N. Ballachulish. **Water**—From house close in. Ferry across to S. Ballachulish. Bus to Kinlochleven.

Ballachulish (Glencoe)—On the S. shore, inside the Narrows, opposite St. Mungo's Island. Anchor between quarry loading harbour and black slate-stone jetty to the E. of it, off wooden hut, well in-shore in 3 to 4 fath.

Stores—Shops. P.O. Tel. Hotel. Petrol. **Water**—Well on road above black slate jetty to E. of anchorage. Calor Gas.

St. Mungo Islands—This group of islands lies off Ballachulish. There is good anchorage in 3 fath., W. of the second island of the group, coming from the W. (This island has no trees on it.) Enter round the S. of the large St. Mungo Island (with graveyard and ruined chapel). This island may be passed fairly close-to. There is a rock which covers at H.W.O.S. to the E. of the anchorage, and a 4 ft. rock further E. to be watched. Squalls are bad in strong winds.

Stores and **Water**—At Ballachulish.

Kinlochleven—Temporary anchorage can be found at the head of the loch.

Stores—Water and fuel at village.

UPPER LOCH LINNHE Chart 1426 . C.C.C.S.C. 9

(Note—Chart 1426 is not on vertical axis)

Corran Narrows to Fort William

Entering upper Loch Linnhe from the S., on the port hand is Salachan shoal, which runs from Salachan Pt. to Corran Narrows. The outer margin is marked by a red and wht. ringed beacon with ball on top, on Salachan Pt., and two red buoys, the first showing 2 wht. fl. ev. 15 sec., between the point and the Narrows. On the starboard hand is Culchenna spit, marked on its outer end by a blk. buoy, staff and globe and wht. fl. lt. ev. 6 sec. If beating up, be careful to keep outside the line of buoys to port and a line between the blk. buoy and Culchenna Pt. to starboard, as the latter is very shoal near the shore. There is an unwatched lighthouse on Corran Pt. Isophase (1 sec. lt., 1 sec. eclipse) red and wht. sectors (see sketch).

Flood tide makes through the Narrows at 6 knots Sp. and 2 knots Np., about 1 hr. after L.W. and runs 5 hr. **Const.** —5 hr. 15 m. Dover. The Narrows are about 1 cable wide, the Lochaber shore being the deeper. If working through against the ebb near slack water, advantage may be taken of an eddy on the Corran side, working short boards with caution and using the lead. Hold the Corran shore to Camus Asaig Bay. A triangular shoal off the Corran shore is marked at its N.E. point by a red can buoy exhibiting a quick fl. red lt., and about 5 cables N. of ferry pier on Lochaber side a bn. exhibits a fl. wht. lt. ev. 5 sec.

From Corran Narrows to Fort William, a distance of 8 miles, the navigation presents no difficulty. Above the Narrows, the tide runs at about 2 to 2½ knots.

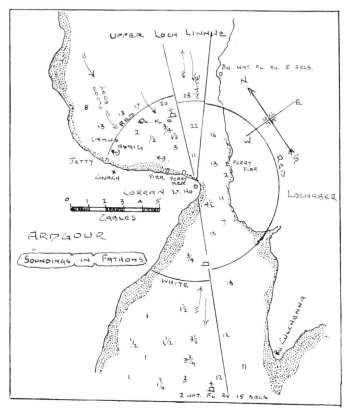

CORRAN NARROWS AND CAMUS ASAIG

Anchorages

Camus Asaig—Just above Corran Narrows (see plan). Anchor anywhere off the shore between the hotel and the jetty W. of the church, but between church and jetty soundings are deep till close in-shore. Exposed N.E. to E.

Stores—P.O. Tel. Inn at Corran Pier. Shop, 1 mile S. of lighthouse on Ardgour side. **Water**—Burns. **Const.** —5 hr. 15 m. Dover. Sp. 13 ft., Np. 9 ft.

Inverscadle Bay—Two miles N. of Corran, on N.W. side of loch. Main bay dries out at L.W. Anchor on S.W. side, just round Ru Dearg, in 2 to 4 fath. Exposed N.E. to E.

Stores—None. Corran nearest. **Water**—Burns.

Fort William—Anchor anywhere S. of piers for ½ mile, in moderate depths. Exposed N.E. through N. to S.W. A fix. wht. lt. is shown on the pier, and a fix. red lt. on viaduct.

Stores—Shops. P.O. Tel. Hotels. Petrol. Half-holiday—Wednesdays. **Water**—At any of the boat slips, or at pierhead. **Const.** —4 hr. 55 m. Dover. Sp. 14 ft., Np. 8 ft. Steamer and train connections. Calor Gas.

Camus-na-Gall—Nearly opposite Fort William. Anchor off the ferry house in 3 to 4 fath. Well sheltered (see plan).

There is another good anchorage just round Ru Dearg in 2 fath., not too close in (see plan).

Stores—At Fort William or Corpach. **Water**—Pipe at ferry house or at burns. Ferry to Fort William which stops at 6 p.m. unless previously bespoken.

LOCH EIL
Chart 1426 and 1791. C.C.C.S.C. 9
(**Note**—Chart 1426 is not on vertical axis)

Above Fort William on the E. shore there is a bad shoal, the Lochy Flats, locally known as the "Long Bank". Its outer edge is marked by five buoys: Lochy Flat S., B. Con. quick fl.; Lochy Flat Middle, B. Con. fl. 6 sec.; Lochy Flat N., B. Con. fl. 3 sec. radar reflector; Corpach Channel No. 1, B Pillar, gr. fl. (3) 6 sec.; Corpach Channel No. 2, B. Con. fl. 2 sec. radar reflector. Off Camus na Gall is a group of rocks and between this and Annat Narrows there are four islands all of which shoal badly. The main channel is to the E. of these obstructions and is marked on its W. side by a red can buoy gp. fl. (2) red 12 sec. off the McLean Rock; a red can buoy, int. quick fl. red 10 sec., 2 cables E. of the shoal water and a red can buoy fl. red 6 sec. $\frac{1}{2}$ cable N. of the shoal. A fixed sectored light on the N. side of the entrance to the sea-lock shows white over the approach channel and red over the islands S. of it and over the Lochy Flats. It is obscured W. of the islands.

The flood sets through Annat Narrows at 5 knots Sp., making about $1\frac{1}{4}$ hr. after L.W. **Const.** —4 hr. 55 m. Dover. In going through, keep to the middle of the channel, which is 1 cable wide and 1 mile long, free from outlying obstructions, but occasionally shoaling on either side. From the Narrows for 6 miles to the head of the loch, part of which dries out at L.W., there are no dangers. Clear of the Narrows the tide runs from 1 to 2 knots.

The new pulp mill has caused a pipe bridge to be built from Annat Pt. to the most W'ly of Corpach Islands with an extension and 2 dolphins running a short way E. of island. There is also laid, about halfway through Narrows, laid on the bottom, a discharge pipe running about seven-eighths of way across Narrows from N. shore. This is buoyed and marked. A septic tank discharge pipe, 2 ft. below L.W.S.T., runs a short way out from N. shore about halfway between the above two constructions.

Anchorage

West of Annat Narrows on the N. side of the loch in 2 fath. Anchor off where the railway has a stone retaining wall with a culvert under it. There is a railway signal (lattice mast) on the wall. A white villa stands slightly E. of the anchorage. Do not go E. of the culvert and come in at right angles to the shore to avoid shoal water on either hand.

Stores—At Kinloch Eil station, Corrybeg, 4 miles above the Narrows on N. side of loch. P.O. Tel. **Water**—Burns. Train connection at Kinloch Eil station. **Const.**: At Corpach —4 hr. 55 m. Dover. Sp. 12 ft., Np. $8\frac{1}{4}$ ft.; At head of Loch Eil —4 hr. 31 m. Dover.

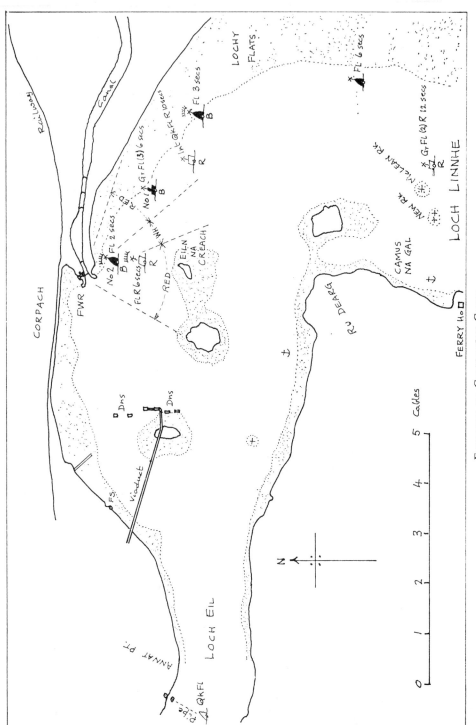

ENTRANCE TO CALEDONIAN CANAL

CALEDONIAN CANAL
Chart 1791

Yachtsmen should obtain before hand the latest information from the Canal office at Corpach or the lock-keeper at Clachnaharry as regards charges and operation of canal as both these are subject to changes and alterations.

The Caledonian Canal cuts across Scotland in a N.E'ly direction, from Corpach, at the head of Upper Loch Linnhe, to Clachnaharry, near Inverness, in the Beauly Firth.

The through passage is about 60 statute miles, $38\frac{1}{2}$ of which are through Lochs Lochy, Oich, and Ness, and the remainder by canal.

There are altogether 29 locks—15 between Corpach and the summit of Laggan, Loch Oich, 100 ft. above sea level, and 14 between this and Clachnaharry, with 10 bridges swinging horizontally.

Road bridges at bottom of Banavie locks, Moy, Gairlochy, Laggan, Aberchalder, Fort Augustus, Tomnahurich and Muirton. Railway bridges at bottom of Banavie locks and at Clachnaharry.

At Corpach the tide runs strongly, and it is best to arrive here at the top of the flood, advising the canal officials before entering, and to leave with the first of the ebb. This also applies to Clachnaharry entrance.

The canal is available for vessels up to 150 ft. long and 13 ft. 6 in. draft or up to 160 ft. with draft limited to 9 ft. maximum beam in either case 35 ft.

Notices are posted along the canal banks giving instructions to vessels. These should be carefully observed.

Caledonian Canal Speeding. The British Waterways Board announce that they are introducing a timing control system on the Caledonian Canal to combat speeding by craft.

The new system comprises a number of electrically operated time clocks which are being installed, initially at Muirtown top lock, Dochgarroch, Gairlochy bottom lock and Banavie top lock. Subject to satisfactory testing, similar equipment will be installed at Fort Augustus top lock, Kytra and Cullochy and also at Banavie bottom lock and Corpach top lock.

Before the departure of craft, the lock-keeper concerned will insert a card into the time clock which will record the earliest time at which the craft can arrive at the far end of the reach whilst observing the speed limit under the Board's bye-laws. The card will be inspected by the receiving lock-keeper on arrival and if the craft has arrived at a time later than that shown on the card, it will be allowed to commence locking immediately.

The Board feel sure that users of the Caledonian Canal will appreciate the need to ensure that craft observe the speed limits in force on this waterway. Speeding causes damage to banks and endangers those in other craft.

All marks to the N.W. are red, and all to S.E. blk. Lights are exhibited at Corpach, Gairlochy, Fort Augustus, Bona Ferry and Clachnaharry. There are no lights on the cairns, beacons and posts nor on any of the buoys.

Before each lock a heavy chain may be suspended, and it is dangerous for a vessel to approach a lock until this has been lowered.

Note—In some cases the painting on above-mentioned posts is faded and identification can be difficult. Between Lochs Lochy and Oich one bridge-keeper is in charge of two bridges, so delay in opening may be expected.

Craft in transit may tie up for limited times at sites at Corpach, Banavie, Gairlochy, Laggan, Fort Augustus, Dochgarroch and Muirton. For craft wishing to make more extended stays there is more room at the top of Banavie Locks, above or below Fort Augustus Locks and above or below Muirton Locks. Craft may also spend the night against the bank in the vicinity of other locks but care should be taken so as to avoid damage to hulls by the stone pitching to the canal banks. There is ample wintering accommodation afloat at Muirton, Inverness. All jetties, piers and landing stages in the lochs are private property and should **not** be used.

At Torvean, near Inverness, an electric cable crosses the canal at 125 ft. above canal level. Masts must not exceed 120 ft. from waterline.

Sea-locks are both tidal. The general rule is that ships are passed from 4 hours before to 4 hours after H.W. The canal is open from sunrise to sunset with a maximum of from 0630 till 1930. Late locking requests will be met subject to the availability of staff and adequate notice. The Board reserve the right to refuse movement.

Single through passage for Yachts (Sail or Motor)

L.O.A. below 7 m (22 ft. 11¾ in.)	£8·00
7 m. but below 12 m. (39 ft. 4½ in.)	£11·00
12 m. and over per complete whole m.	£1·00

Lying-up Dues per Week

L.O.A. below 5 m. (16 ft. 5 in.)	£0·30
5 m. but below 18 m. (59 ft. 0½ in.)	£0·55
18 m. but below 27 m. (88 ft. 7 in.)	£1·25
27 m. but below 36 m. (118 ft. 1½ in.)	£1·90
36 m. and over	£3·20

Late Lockings (L.O.A. below 160 ft.)

Sea-locks	Weekdays	£1·50
	Sundays	£3·00
All other locks and bridges (per gate or per bridge)		
	Weekdays	£0·37
	Sundays	By arrangement

The above charges were extant at time of going to press and *may* be altered.

Reduced charges for partial passages and special terms for long period lying up.

Dues are paid at either end, and a chart and book of regulations can be had at the offices.

Hints for canal work will be found under Crinan Canal.

Corpach—A visitor's mooring has been laid off the Lochaber Y.C.

Loch Lochy—The anchorages are on the N.W. side: in the bay just after leaving the Gairlochy Locks; in the bay N.E. of the glen to Loch Arkaig; at Letter-finlay, half way up the loch on the S.E. side; and in the bay to the N.W. just before leaving the loch. The loch is free from dangers.

Loch Oich—The anchorages are off Port MacDonnell pier; S.W. of Eileann Drynachan and to the W. of the channel. This loch is not so clean as the other two, but it is well buoyed throughout.

Loch Ness—The anchorages are at Invermoriston; in the bay behind Castle Urquhart; and at Templehouse on the opposite side of this bay; all to the N.W. side of the loch. On the S.E. side at Foyers. The loch is free from dangers.

Stores—At Clachnaharry, Inverness, Fort Augustus and Corpach.

Consts.: for Corpach −4 hr. 55 m. Dover; for Clachnaharry +1 hr. 16 m. Dover.

SOUND OF MULL
Charts 2155, 3718, and 3607. C.C.C.S.C. 10, 11, and 12

The sound is about 19 miles long and lies between the island of Mull and the mainland of Morven. It is well buoyed, and if reasonable berth is given to the shore and the marks, the navigation presents no difficulty. The Grey Rocks lie in mid-channel and should be given a wide berth. The largest is marked by a wht. cylinder showing a wht. fl. lt. 2 sec. ev. 6 sec. The passage is clearest on the Morven side; also keep to that side of the red buoy marking the Yule Rocks, a little further on. On the Mull side, Scallasdale Pt. is foul for 4 cables off-shore. Some of the rocks are above water, and the clear channel between the outermost of them and the Grey Rocks is 4 cables wide, but the Yule Rocks with 3 ft. to 6 ft. on them just through must be watched. They are marked, as stated above, by a red can buoy. Two miles further up, the Avon Rock, with 9 ft. on it lies 3 cables off the Mull shore and is marked by a red buoy. Ardtornish Pt. just S. of Loch Aline is marked by a beacon showing a gp. (2) fl. lt. ev. 10 sec. red green and wht. sectors; wht. over the fairways to E. and W. and over the clear water S. of the light green N. of fairway to eastward and over the Avon Rock, red N. of fairway to westward, and over the Yule Rocks, Grey Rocks, and the foul ground off Scallasdale Pt. From here there are no obstructions for 5 miles when there is Bo Rock,

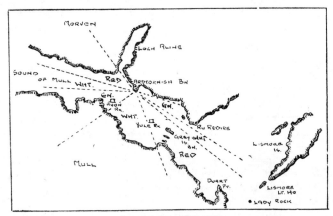

ARDTORNISH BEACON

a foul patch, on the Mull side, off Salen, marked by a blk. buoy, and the Green Isle, marked by a wht. beacon with a wht. fl. lt. eclipsed 4 sec. ev. 6 sec. on its outer end. Between these two marks are patches with 9 ft. on them, and near the buoy one or two rocks. Right opposite, off the Morven shore, lie the Fiunary Rocks, marked by a blk. buoy, which should be given a wide berth. The passage between these and the Green Isle is about 1 mile wide. From here up to Tobermory there are no dangers that are not easily avoided, but both shores, close in, are foul, particularly the Morven shore. Passing Ardnacroish Pt. on Mull about 4 miles up from Green Isle, tend rather towards the Mull side to avoid Sgeir-na-Fennag (Bogha Bhuilg), a rock marked by a small blk. buoy, which lies $\frac{1}{4}$ mile off the Morven shore.

Sgeir Calve, a rock that dries at L.W., lies off the E. shore of Calve Island. It is about $\frac{1}{2}$ cable off-shore and is directly off the point that lies to the southward of the point that has on it a large up-ended rectangular-shaped boulder just above H.W. mark.

E

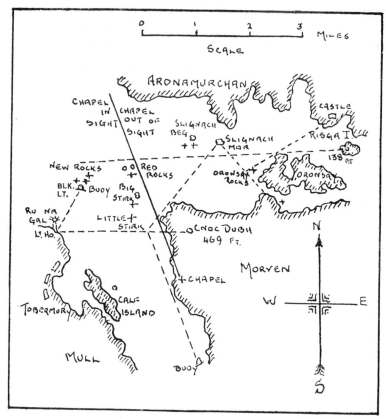

SOUND OF MULL. ROCKS OFF MOUTH OF LOCH SUNART

In light W'ly winds, it is advisable not to go too close in to Duart Pt., at the S. entrance to the sound, nor to Calve Island off Tobermory, as there is frequently a calm patch at these places.

At the western end of the Sound, the Stirk Rocks, Red Rocks, and New Rocks, at the mouth of Loch Sunart, must be watched. The last named are marked by a blk. buoy. This buoy shows a wht. fl. ev. 6 sec. It is said locally that if the seas are breaking on the Stirks there is a heavy sea running at Ardnamurchan. The water from here to Ardnamurchan Pt. is clear. On Mull, about 1 mile W. of Tobermory, there is a lighthouse on Ru na Gal Pt. showing a fl. lt. ev. 2 sec., green, red, and wht. sectors (unwatched). It shows green over the Stirk, New, and Red Rocks; wht. down the Sound of Mull; and red to the N. over the clear water towards Ardnamurchan. At Ardnamurchan Pt. there is a lighthouse showing a gp. (2) fl. lt. ev. 30 sec. Visible from N. 18° E. through E. to S. 53° W. (mag. from seaward). Fog siren, 5 sec. blast ev. min. On Ardmore Pt. on Mull there is a beacon showing a gp. (2) fl. wht. lt. ev. 10 sec.

Anchorages on Morven Shore
Charts 2155 and 3607. C.C.C.S.C. 10, 11, and 12

Camus Redire—A sheltered anchorage behind the islands at Ru Redire, on the N. side of the E. entrance to the Sound of Mull.

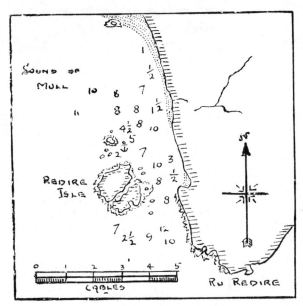

CAMUS REDIRE

It can be entered from either side, keeping the Morven shore aboard. Anchor in 4 fath., close to Redire Isle, behind the three rocks off the N. end of it. These rocks show at H.W. and form good shelter at L.W.

Loch Aline (Chart 3608 and C.C.C.S.C. 11)—The narrows at the entrance are about 150 yd. wide and 3 cables long. A spit runs out from the E. side of Bolorkle Pt., and there is shoal water on the opposite side, between the pier and the village. Bolorkle spit runs a good way out and is dangerous. The tide sets through the narrows at about $2\frac{1}{2}$ knots Sp., and mid-channel should be taken, with the tide or with a fair wind. Two orange leading marks on shore in line give the course through. **Const.** —5 hr. 23 m. Dover. Anchor just round Kyle Pt., the E. point of the inner end of the narrows, in 3 fath., mud bottom, $1\frac{1}{2}$ cables off the H.W. mark. This spot is well sheltered and out of the tide. The loch is fairly clear, but shoals badly here and there. The head dries out for about $\frac{1}{2}$ mile at L.W.

Anchorage out of the tide and more sheltered in N. and W. winds than Kyle Bay can be found in about 4 fath. on the W. side of the loch just S. of the more N'ly of the 2 concrete leading posts.

Stores—Shops. P.O. Tel. **Water**—At store at new jetty. Sp. 14 ft., Np. $10\frac{1}{2}$ ft. Mean depth on bar at L.W.O.S., 6 ft. Steamer connection to Oban daily and ferry to Fishnish Bay and Craignure.

Kinlochaline—The anchorage is in 4 fath., mud, off the boat jetty on the E. side of the head of Loch Aline. A beacon about halfway up marks the end of a spit running out from E. side, and a 1 ft. rock on N.W. side, near the head, is also marked by a beacon, and anchorage can be found close in-shore S.W. of this beacon N. of burn mouth.

Stores—At Loch Aline village. **Water**—Spring at roadside.

Ardtornish Bay—One mile E. of Loch Aline. Good anchorage in 4 fath. off a boathouse on shore, just round Ardtornish Pt., which has an old ruined castle on it. A beacon light is erected on this point (see Sound of Mull). The bay shoals off the house at the head of it. Exposed to S.S.E.

Anchorages on Mull Shore

Charts 2155, 3718 and 3608

Duart Bay—At the E. end of sound, just round Duart Pt. The bay shoals badly. Anchor just round the point below the castle in 3 fath. Exposed N.E. to N.

Stores—None. **Water**—None. **Const.** −5 hr. 27 m. Dover. Sp. 14 ft., Np. 9½ ft.

Craignure Bay—One mile N. of Duart. Anchor in 2 to 3 fath. N.W. of pier, opposite P.O., well off-shore. Bay dries out inside stone part of pier. Exposed N. to N.E. Motor ferry from Oban.

Stores—Shop. P.O. Tel. Inn. **Water**—Well. Steamer connections to Oban and bus to Tobermory. Calor Gas.

Scallasdale Bay—One mile up from Craignure. Scallasdale Pt. is very foul and must be given a wide berth coming in from the S. Anchor anywhere in the bay, in moderate depths. Exposed N.N.W. through N. to E. but only to the carry of seas across the sound, which is 1¾ miles wide at this part.

Fishnish Bay—About 4½ miles up from Scallasdale Pt., opposite Loch Aline. Anchor in 3 to 4 fath. at the head of the bay, not too close in-shore as it shoals badly. Exposed to N'ly winds across the sound. Ferry to Loch Aline.

Salen Bay—Lies 3½ miles up from Fishnish Bay. Salen is a splendid centre for excursions in Mull, but the approach to the anchorage is foul with rocks, and it is uncomfortable in N'ly winds. Approaching up the Sound of Mull, the blk. buoy off Ru More, the E'ly point of the bay, must be left to starboard, and the anchorage is in 2 fath., just S. of a line between the red buoy which lies N.W. of the pier and which marks Antelope Rock, and the pier end.

Coming in from the N., give the shore W. of Antelope Rock a good berth. Some of the rocks are marked but not all. Round the red buoy into the anchorage (see plan).

Stores—Shops. P.O. Tel. Hotel. Petrol. **Water**—At pier.

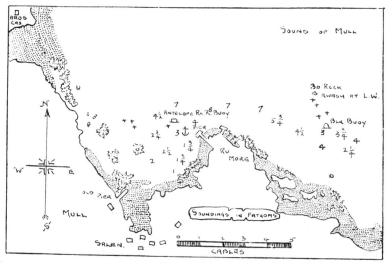

SALEN, MULL

Aros Castle—Alasaid Head is the N. point of Salen Bay, and on its northern side there is a small cove, with good anchorage, well in-shore in the middle of it, off a short stone pier. There is also shelter from N'ly winds on the S. side of the Head, but well off-shore, as this is the beginning of a bad shoal which extends across the mouth of Aros Water.

Stores—Nearest, Salen. **Water**—At house.

Tobermory Bay (Chart 1836 and C.C.C.S.C. 12)—Inside Calve Island. The N. entrance is free from dangers, except for a rock which shows at L.W. lying off the E. side of Calve Island. For its position, see Sound of Mull. The rock, Sgeir Calve, and shoal lie about ½ cable off the shore and extend in a N.W. and S.E. direction about 1 cable. The Doirlinn Narrows at the S. end, between Calve Island and Mull, are only 90 yd. wide at H.W. and dry out at L.W. This passage is only possible for boats of shallow draft, near H.W. The navigable channel even then is very narrow. It used to be marked by a perch on either hand. These are missing but their bases remain and are covered about half tide. A wht. perch has been placed on eastern base (existence unreliable). When that base is awash, there is 4 ft. 6 in. in channel. If leaving Tobermory the depth of water at the steps of the old pier is the same as at the Narrows at that time. There is a depth of fully 6 ft. for 2 hr. each side of H.W. The flood stream enters Tobermory Bay by this channel then flows **out** of bay N. of Calve Island.

A fix. lt. on Tobermory pier shows red to the Doirlinn passage and wht. elsewhere. (Red glass reported in 1970 as broken and lt. showing wht. all round.)

Anchor ¾ cable off the old pier (the one with the clock tower at its head) in 4 fath. After heavy N.W. or N. gales a swell sets into the harbour. There is also good anchorage further up the bay towards the Doirlinn, off demolished Aros House, fairly close in-shore off boathouse and jetty. In E. and N.E winds there is a very good anchorage in the basin at S.E. end of the Doirlinn, in 6 fath. or less.

Stores—Shops. P.O. Tel. Hotels. Petrol. Half-holiday—Wednesdays. **Water**—Hydrants on road between the two piers. **Const.** −5 hr. 19 m. Dover. Sp. 14 ft. ,Np. 11 ft. Steamer connection. Calor Gas.

Kilchoan—About 6 miles E. of Ardnamurchan Lt. There is about 4 fath. in the centre of the bay well off the jetty but both shores are foul. When making this anchorage the large-scale chart is essential.

Stores—Shop. Petrol. Hotel. P.O. Calor Gas.

LOCH SUNART
Charts 2155 and 3185. C.C.C.S.C. 13 and 14

Loch Sunart is 19 miles long, and lies N. of the Sound of Mull.

Entering from the S. round Auliston Pt., there are the Stirk Rocks lying about ½ mile to the westward. One of them is 1 ft. above H.W., but they should be given a wide berth, keeping towards Auliston Pt. To the N.W. of Auliston Pt., beyond the Stirk Rocks, there is a foul patch, the Red Rocks and the New Rocks. The western side is marked by a blk. buoy showing a wht. fl. lt. ev. 6 sec. and the whole patch should be given a wide berth. Runa Gal Lt. on the Mull shore (fl. lt. ev. 2 sec.) shows green over the New, Red and Stirk Rocks, wht. to the eastward of them down the Sound of Mull, and red to the westward towards Ardnamurchan. Keep to the S. of Slignach More Island, as there is a group of rocks, Slignach Beg, lying about 3 cables to the westward to be watched. The

Oronsay Rocks, with 6 ft. on them, lie ¼ mile W. of Oronsay Isle, but they are not in the way unless beating. (See plan of Sound of Mull—rocks off mouth of Loch Sunart.)

The best passage going up is between Resga and Charna Isles, taking care of the Ross Rock with 2 ft. on it off the S.W. end of Resga and the Broad Rock with 4 ft. on it, between Resga and the N. end of Charna, about mid-channel. The other passage between Resga and the shore, can be taken with a leading wind by keeping close to Resga, which is steep-to on its northern side, but a rock which dries 2 ft. lies 2 cables to the W.N.W. of the N.W. end of the island. The N. ends of Charna and Resga in line, clears it.

One and a half miles E. of Salen the loch bends from an E'ly to a S.E'ly direction opposite a fairly wide valley with houses and a bridge, on the N. shore. At the turning point some rocks under water run out from the S. shore terminating in a rock 3 ft. deep about 2½ cables from the shore. A course nothing S. of mid-channel should be held until well into the next reach.

A mile W. of Laudle Narrows the loch is narrowed by islets and rocks to the N. and a shoal running out from the S. and caution is necessary.

The tide runs through Laudle Narrows at about 4 knots and mid-channel should be taken, tending if anything towards Eiln. More islet as the other side shoals. **Const.** —5 hr. 12 m. Dover.

It is clear from here to the head of the loch if the shoal water off Strontian is avoided.

Anchorages

There is good anchorage in almost any of the many bays and bights in the loch, but the following may be noted:

Loch Drumbuy (Dromna na Buidhe)—Between Oronsay Isle and the Morven shore. A perfectly sheltered anchorage. The entrance is about ½ cable wide, steep-to on both sides, but just through, off the S. point of the narrows there is a 3 ft. rock to be watched. Anchor in 3 fath., just round this point, in S.W. corner of loch directly off a big isolated boulder on the beach. Shoal water extends off-shore and the highest point on the Ardnamurchan peninsula should not be any to the left of the S. point at E. end of entrance. If anchoring in the next bay E. of this, keep well off-shore, as it is shoal.

Bay just to W. of Laga Bay—Opposite Charna Island on the N. shore of the loch. There is a house on the shore, back a little from the beach. Anchor in the middle of the bay in 2 fath. The E. point is foul. A beautiful little spot, well sheltered, but holding ground is poor.

North Oronsay—A narrow gut on N. side of Oronsay affords good shelter for **small** yachts. Anchor in 2 fath. immediately inside entrance. Ground N. of E. side of entrance is very foul.

Charna Island—There is excellent anchorage in 2 to 4 fath., mud, on either side of Charna Island, in the channels leading to Loch Teachdais (pronounced "Teachus"). On the E. side, if going in further than the immediate entrance, see under "Loch Teachdais". In the western channel, there is a small islet, leaving a small gut between it and the E. entrance to Loch Drumbuy, where a small yacht can find perfect shelter but reported as subject to swell in N.W. gales. There is a ring on the rock off

W. shore. It must be entered carefully and there is not much room for swinging, the islet side being the clearer. On the other side the anchorage is abreast the middle of the islet.

Stores—None. **Water**—Burns and from a butt at the back of the deserted cottage above the W. shore.

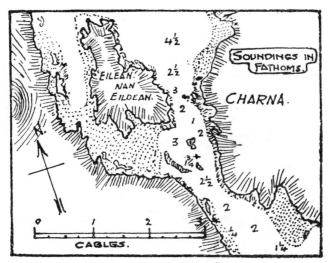

CHARNA ISLAND (WEST SIDE)

Loch Teachdais (Chart 3185)—This loch runs for 2 miles S.E. from the S. end of Charna Island. Both entrances require care and should be attempted only with the aid of the chart mentioned and in the first quarter of the flood, when many of the rocks are visible. The W. channel is difficult and is not recommended but the route lies close by the islet (Eiln. nan Eildean) mentioned in the paragraph headed Charna Island, above, until past the rocks running out from Charna, then (just before reaching the S. end of the islet) very close along the Charna side for 1½ cable, then mid-channel past Eiln. nan Gabhar (the islet S. of Charna) towards the second narrows.

Taking the E. entrance, keep in mid-channel (there is a "dries 1 ft." rock just to the W. of mid-channel) until Drochaid Charna, a ridge of rock extending from the mainland side almost across the channel is reached. Take the middle of the remaining fairway and go on in mid-channel for 3½ cables to the next obstruction off Ceannamuir More, a small headland jutting out from Charna. Just off it is a long rock, covered at H.W., extending up and down the channel and looking like a part of the headland. Abreast of this rock, is a second rock, with less than 6 ft. of water over it, on the mainland side, and close S.E. of the long rock is Sgeir Liath, a large drying rock. Swing round to leave Sgeir Liath to starboard (the line of soundings in Sketch Plan shows way in), then proceed to the second narrows keeping at least a cable from the E. shore. There is an isolated and uncharted rock with 3 ft. on it at L.W. about 50 yd. S.W. of Sgeir a Chuilein about 4 cables S. of Sgeir Liath.

The second narrows are about ½ mile long and should be taken in mid-channel with the aid of chart. The anchorage is towards the head of the loch, which dries out a long way. A good spot is in 1½ fath. on the S.W. side well off-shore, opposite a wall running up the hill.

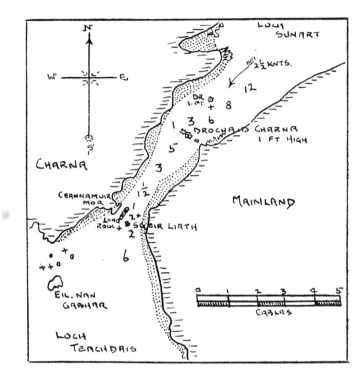

EASTERN ENTRANCE TO LOCH TEACHDAIS

Good anchorage can be found N.E. of Drochaid Charna but there is a bad uncharted rock which must be guarded against when coming in to anchor. It has about 4 ft. on it at L.W. and lies about halfway between the "dries 1 ft." rock and Drochaid Charna. Hold the mainland shore coming in until almost up to Drochaid Charna then head for the more S'ly of the two cottages on Charna keeping its S. gable open. There is a small islet (almost covers) off the mainland shore and this should be almost aboard before turning into the bay. Do not go further into the bay than the N. end of Drochaid Charna as a strong tide sweeps through the channel between it and Charna. In strong N.E'lies complete shelter can be obtained in the lagoon S. of Drochaid Charna making the passage round its N. end any time except during period 1 hr. either side of L.W. At H.W. only 1 ft. of the highest point (about its centre) of Drochaid Charna shows.

Salen—On the N. side of the loch, about 5 miles up from Charna Island. There is a rock off the E. point of the bay and about halfway up the bay there is a drying reef showing 3 heads at L.W. which stretches across the whole middle third of the bay. Pole bns. have been erected at E. and W. ends of reef. On entering keep to the E'ly third of inlet giving the shore a reasonable berth then cross over to the W. side and anchor in 3 to 4 fath. off the stone jetty, giving it a good berth, or off a boathouse at head of bay. The anchorage off the jetty is reported (1962) as fouled by heavy sunk chain or cable.

Stores—Shop. P.O. Tel. Hotel. **Water**—At burn.

Camus na h'Eireachd—A bay on the S. shore sheltered from all but N'ly winds, 3 miles E. of Salen and almost apposite Eiln. Garbh.

Eiln. Garbh—There is good anchorage in the bay between Eiln. Garbh and Ru Daimh, on the N. shore of the loch, 1 mile W. of Laudle Narrows. Entering from the W., there is a rock which dries 10 ft. at L.W., off the W. end of Eil. Garbh to be avoided. The anchorage is in 3 fath., towards the island side of the bay.

Liddesdale—On Morven shore, 1 mile above Laudle Narrows. Good anchorage in 2 to 3 fath. off the houses on shore.

Strontian—Anchor above the shoal caused by Strontian Water in 2 to 3 fath. off ferry pier. There is a granite obelisk which is a good mark for making the anchorage. In E'ly winds this anchorage is subject to fierce squalls from Glen Tarbert.

Stores—Shop. Inn. P.O. Tel. **Water**—Houses. **Const.** −5 hr. 17 m. Dover. Sp. 13½ ft. Calor Gas. Modern model village has been built.

E2

PART IV

ARDNAMURCHAN POINT

TO

PORTREE

WITH ADJACENT LOCHS

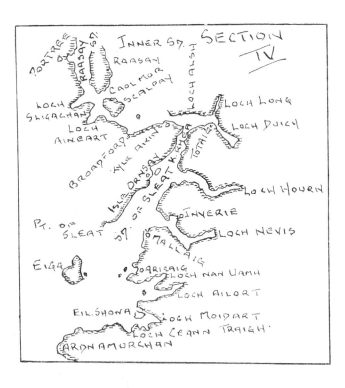

Admiralty Charts

GROUP I	2721	Ardnamurchan Pt. to St. Kilda
GROUP II	2507	Ardnamurchan Pt. to L. Brittle
	2551	Isle of Skye N. of Sd. of Sleat
GROUP III	2496	Sound of Sleat
	2497	L. Hourn
	2676	Lochs Alsh and Duich
	2498	Southern Part of Sd. of Raasay & Inner Sound
	3302	Narrows of Raasay and Caol More
	1839	Portree Harbour
	3292	Loch Alsh and Kyle Rhea

C.C.C. SKETCH CHARTS

15	Lochs Arisaig and Nevis
16	Loch Hourn
17	Kyle Rhea and Kyle Akin
18	Loch Alsh, Loch Duich and Loch Long (Eastern Section)
19	Approaches to Caol Mor, Raasay Narrows, Loch Sligachan
44	Loch Moidart
45	Loch Ailort and Loch Nan Uamh

TOBERMORY TO ISLE ORONSAY (SKYE)
Charts 2507 and 2496. C.C.C.S.C. 15 and 16

Leaving Tobermory, the New Rocks lie ½ mile off Runa Gal lighthouse. Runa Gal lt. (fl. ev. 2 sec.) shows green over these dangers, also over the Red and Stirk Rocks which lie to the eastward, red over the clear water to Ardnamurchan and wht. down the Sound of Mull. A blk. lt. buoy, showing a wht. fl. ev. 6 sec., marks the most S'ly of this group, but they are well clear of the course to Ardnamurchan Pt., distant 10 miles, and there are no dangers that are not easily avoided to the point. It is said locally that if the seas are breaking on the Stirks there is a heavy sea running at Ardnamurchan. On Ardmore Pt. on Mull there is a beacon showing a gp. (2) fl. wht. lt. ev. 10 sec. At the N.W. point of Ardnamurchan Peninsula stands a stone lighthouse showing a gp. (2) wht. fl. ev. 30 sec. Fog siren 5 sec. blast ev. min. There are no outlying dangers at the point, but it is completely exposed to the westward, and a very considerable sea rises in even moderate winds. Thus small craft should exercise caution in attempting to round it, unless in settled weather. In S'ly winds it is advisable to give the point a berth of about 1 mile, as the seas are much wilder within this radius. In bad weather, also avoid Maxwell Bank which lies 2 miles S. of Eigg, as it causes short, broken seas.

Some 6 miles N.E. by E. from the light, and 2½ miles off-shore, lie Bo Faskadale Rocks, one of which is awash at L.W., and marked by a blk. buoy, showing a gp. (3) wht. fl. lt. ev. 18 sec., and 1 mile S. ½ W. of the buoy, the Elizabeth Rock, unmarked, with 4 ft. at L.W., but from here to Isle Ornsay there are no dangers, provided a reasonable berth be given to the shore. Eigg Island lies 10 miles N.E. ½ N. of Ardnamurchan, and there is an anchorage at Eilean Castle at the S. end of the island, but in case of heavy weather, Loch Ailort is preferable. On the E. point of Eiln. Castle a wht. beacon shows a wht. fl. lt. bright 2 sec. ev. 6 sec. The course from Ardnamurchan to the entrance to Sleat Sound is N.E. $\frac{1}{2}$ E. and the distance to Isle Ornsay, 30 miles. On the S.E. point of Isle Ornsay a lighthouse shows a gp. (2) fl. wht. lt. ev. 7 sec., and on its N.E. point a blk. beacon shows a red fl. lt. ev. 6 sec. On Sleat Pt. a white tower, 67 ft. high, shows a wht. fl. lt. ev. 3 sec. vis. 13 miles, unwatched. The total passage from Tobermory to Isle Ornsay is 41 miles.

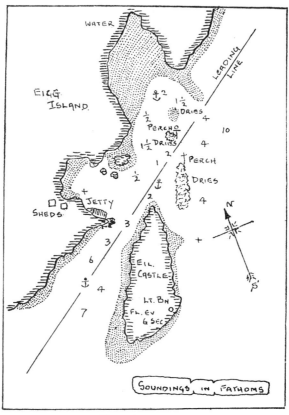

EIGG ANCHORAGES

Anchorages

Eiln. Castle (Eigg Island (Chart 2507))—Good anchorage can be had at Eiln. Castle, off the S. end of Eigg. Eiln. Castle shelters the N. of Flod Sgeir anchorage from S'ly winds, though at times a considerable swell sets in, but it is rather difficult to enter for the first time, owing to the numerous reefs, almost all of which cover at H.W. Only two of these rocks are marked by perches, and the lines of soundings on the plan show the approaches to the anchorages.

Coming in from the N., the starboard hand perch is surmounted by a circle, and the port hand by a cross.

A leading line, which clears the reefs, if entering from the N. between the perches, is Eiln. Castle open of Eigg. The best anchorage which is sheltered from all but N.E. and strong S.W. winds, is just off the jetty, in 3 fath. The narrow channel between the N.E. end of Eiln. Castle and the reef N.E. of it, has 2 fath. at L.W. and is $\frac{1}{2}$ cable wide, and is sometimes used.

A strong ebb tide sets S.W. through anchorage starting 2 hr. before H.W. The flood stream does not run so strongly.

The passage between Eiln. Castle and the shore, through to the S. anchorage, is only ½ cable wide, and there is a bad reef on the Eigg side to be guarded against. The S. anchorage is in the middle of the bay, in 4 fath. Off the S. end of Eiln. Castle the reef extends for 1 cable, and the Eigg shore has a few rocks close in, but otherwise the S. anchorage is clear, though much exposed to S.W. winds.

Silting is taking place in the N. anchorage and anchor should be let go nothing to the W. of the middle section of the leading line. The anchorage shown in the sketch plan in the N. bay is only accessible above half-tide and in 1968 it is reported that shoaling has continued and where anchor is marked in the plan and on the E'ly approach channel there is only a foot or two of water. One fathom reported close W. of the "dries" shoal.

Stores—Limited stores. Calor Gas. P.O. halfway across—2 miles. **Water**—At jetty. **Const.** —4 hr. 39 m. Dover. Sp. 14 ft., Np. 11 ft.

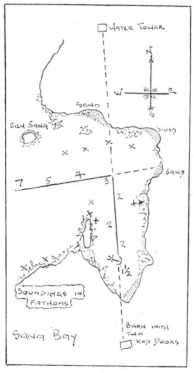

SANA BAY

Sana Bay (Chart 2507)—A small bay about 1¼ miles N. of Ardnamurchan Lt. It is easily distinguished by the white sand on the N. shore. In approaching from the S., care must be taken to avoid Bo Kora Ben, a rock which lies 2 cables off-shore, about halfway between the lighthouse and the S. point of the bay. Eiln. Sana lies off the N. point of the bay, and the shores on both sides are foul with rocks and reefs. Temporary anchorage in off-shore winds can be had in 1½ to 2 fath. in the middle of the bay. There is shelter from all winds behind a rock in the S.W. corner of the bay near the head, but great care must be exercised in making this anchorage for the first time, as a reef runs out to the N.W. from the rock.

Stores—Farm only at Portuairk. Kilchoan, 4 miles S.W. of anchorage. **Water**—At burn.

Anchorages in Sound of Sleat

Camus Darach (Chart 2496)—At Sleat Pt. Temporary anchorage in 3 to 5 fath. in the centre of the bay. There are rocks on either hand going in, which cover about half-tide, to be guarded against, and the W. side of the bay is very foul. Exposed to the S.

Armadale Bay (Chart 2496)—4½ miles N.E. of Camus Darach. Temporary anchorage in 3 fath. off the pier. If coming in from the S. give the shore a good offing as it is very foul.

Stores—Shop, 1 mile inland. **Water**—At farms. Ferry to Mallaig.

Armadale Bay is well sheltered from south east through west to north. In north to north easterly winds a swell sets in and a comfortable anchorage can be obtained three miles north in Knock Bay. Care must be taken at high tide if going close inshore in Knock Bay because of the numerous reefs which cover. In strong easterly winds vessels would be advised to make for Mallaig or Camus Bane on the mainland. All vessels should anchor inside the line of approach to Armadale Pier to avoid obstructing the Car Ferry, as shown on the sketch.

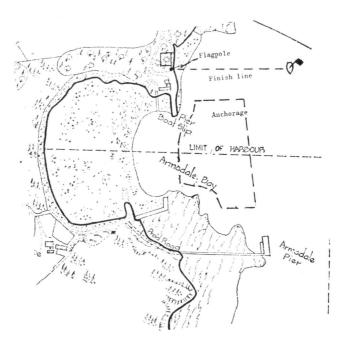

Loch Camus Cross (Chart 2496)—½ mile S. of Isle Ornsay. Temporary anchorage in 3 fath. on the N. side of the entrance, keeping well off-shore as the bay is very shallow and foul near the shore. Exposed to S.W.
    Stores—At Isle Ornsay.

Isle Ornsay (Chart 2496)—Splendid anchorage behind the island. The anchorage is in 2 to 3 fath. in the centre of the bay just inside the N. point of the island. Do not go far beyond the line of the lt. beacon in line with the cliff on Isle Ornsay. The head of the bay shoals badly.

Stores—Hotel. P.O. Tel. on hill, ¾ mile above houses. Petrol 8 miles away at Ardvasar. **Water**—Tap behind hotel, or at well on roadside beyond hotel.

Mallaig Harbour (Chart 1836 and C.C.C.S.C. 15)—At the southern side of the entrance to Loch Nevis. The Red Rocks lie in the entrance and are marked by a beacon which is on the centre rock, showing an occ. ev. 2 sec. wht. lt. The bay can be entered on either side of these rocks, the eastern passage being the clearer.

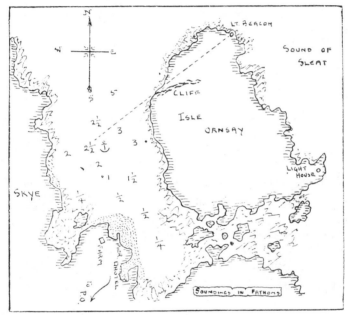

ISLE ORNSAY

A green light with a limited arc of visibility is exhibited from a post on Courteachan Pt. and a red fl. lt. is on Rubha na Acarseid. Entering by either passage keep near mid-channel giving Sgeir Dhearg rocks a good berth. Care should be taken at night when entering from the N. as Sgeir Dhearg light can be obscured by the harbour lights. After clearing the rocks, keep well in the centre of the harbour and anchor in 3 to 4 fath. as shown on the plan. The harbour is under the control of the Harbour-master and is very congested at times with fishing boats. Anchorage should always be sought clear of these. The head of the harbour is foul with moorings.

Leaving Mallaig Harbour, if turning E. to enter Loch Nevis, do not begin to turn until the green corrugated iron hut well up the hill has passed behind the beacons, as the rocks which form the N.E. point of the harbour extend further than appears.

Stores—Chandlers. Shops. P.O. Tel. Hotel. Petrol. **Water**—Hydrant on pier. Railway connections. Half-holiday—Wednesdays. Calor Gas.

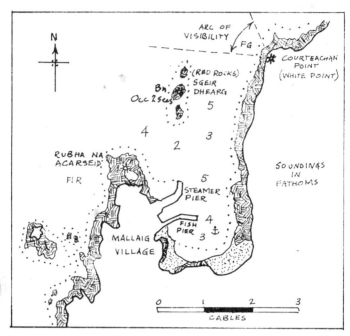

MALLAIG

Dun Bane Bay (Chart 2496)—On the mainland, opposite Armadale Bay, across the mouth of Loch Nevis from Mallaig. A small bay about 2 cables from point to point, and about 2 to head of bay. Much exposed to winds from W. through N. to N.E., with which a heavy, uncomfortable swell sets in. Protected from S.W. through S. to nearly N.E. Anchor in the middle of the bay in 2 to 3 fath. Sand. The shores are rocky to N. and S.

LOCH CEANN TRAIGH
Chart 2507

This loch lies some 10 miles to the eastward of Ardnamurchan Pt. Approaching from the W., the first danger is the Bo Faskadale Rocks, which lie $2\frac{1}{2}$ miles off-shore and are marked by a blk. buoy showing a wht. fl. lt. 3 quick fl. ev. 18 sec.

The Elizabeth Rock, with 4 ft. over it, lies 1 mile S. $\frac{1}{2}$ W. from this buoy and is unmarked. From here to Ru Driminish, the W'ly point of the entrance to Loch Ceann Traigh, the water is clear. About 3 cables E.N.E. of Ru Driminish lies Bo Carach, a rock which dries $8\frac{1}{2}$ ft., and 4 cables S.E. of this and 3 cables off-shore, Bo Ruadh, with 2 ft. on it. Beyond this the loch is clean to $\frac{3}{4}$ mile from the head, when there are some bad rocks lying almost in the middle. The eastern side of the loch is very foul.

Anchorage

The anchorage is near the head of the loch on its western side, in 5 fath., sand. The head of the loch dries out for about 2 cables, so should not be approached too closely. Exposed to N'ly winds.

LOCH MOIDART
Chart 2507. C.C.C.S.C. 44

Loch Moidart lies just to the eastward of Loch Ceann Traigh. Coming in from Ardnamurchan, care must be taken not to mistake Caolas Ardtoe, which runs off Loch Ceann Traigh and which dries out completely, for the entrance to Loch Moidart. The entrance is about 1 mile further N. than this. The navigation is rather intricate, owing to the number of rocks and islets which abound at the entrance. The following directions and the accompanying plans show the dangers to be avoided on entering. The soundings on these plans are in **ft.**

Less depths than shown on the plans have been reported owing to silting up.

Great caution is necessary in navigating this loch. There are two channels, one N. and one S. of Eiln. Raonul.

Bogha Mor, Carn Rock and Bogha Ruach show only towards L.W. and these and the rocks E. and N.E. of Eiln. Raonul are the main dangers. Eiln. Carnagh and Eiln. Corra are bold rocks with grass on their summits. Coming in by the S. channel keep midway between Farquhar Pt. and Eiln. Roanul and proceed E.N.E. (true) keeping about one-third of a cable from the Eiln. then carry on on that course until Eiln. Corra and Eiln. Carnagh are in line (this to avoid the rock ½ cable E. of Eiln. Raonul) then turn 30° to port and steer for a point about ½ cable S. of Sgeir nan Sgarbh. On reaching this point turn E. (true) until Sgeir nan Claidheamh is clearly open of Eiln. Corra. Make then for Sgeir nan Claidheamh and, passing S. of it turn to port and, holding up to the Eiln. Shona shore, steer for Rudha a Bhaile and, rounding this, anchor off jetty.

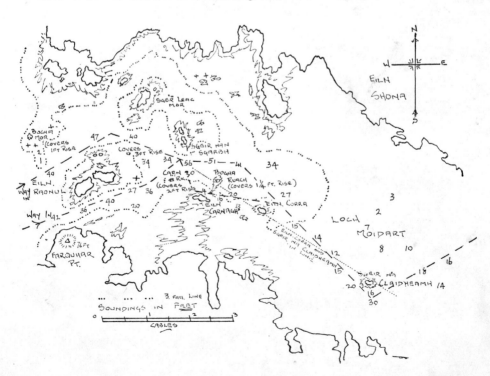

Coming in by N. channel, keep well off entrance to loch until Eiln. Raonul is nearly abeam (to avoid Bogha Mor, covers at 1 ft. rise, and the shoal water S. of it) then come in keeping about 1 cable N.W. of Eiln. Raonul until Sgelr nan Sgarbh is well open to rocks N. of Eiln. Raonul (this to avoid the rock which covers at 3 ft. rise about 1 cable E. of rocks) then turn to make a point ½ cable S. of Sgeir nan Sgarbh then proceed as for S. channel.

Alternative route from the point ½ cable S. of Sgeir nan Sgarbh. Turn S. for Eiln. Carnagh until very close to it (not more than 30 ft.) to avoid a spit running S. from Bogha Ruach. From there turn to port to pass N. of Eiln. Corra then proceed as before to round Sgeir nan Claidheamh.

Coming out the N. channel is preferable except at dead low water when Bogha Ruach and the Carn Rock show but, if using the S. channel, a course from the point S. of Sgeir nan Sgarbh to the summit of Farquhar Pt. clears both Carn Rock and the rock E. of Eiln. Raonul.

The anchorage marked is in 2 fath. but good holding ground is found anywhere in the loch.

The stretch of the loch E. of Eiln. Riasga can be reached by taking the N. side of that island but there is a 5 ft. spit running out from Eiln. Shona to Eiln. Riasga but the upper reaches of the loch abound with shallow parts and require local knowledge.

Anchorage can also be had in the gut between Eiln. Riasga and the castle island, crossing above-mentioned spit above half tide.

A heavy electric supply cable is reported as crossing loch E. of Eiln. Riasga. Its line is **not** indicated by shore marks.

The tide runs strongly, making at H. and L.W. by the shore.

Const. —5 hr. 15 m. Dover. Sp. 13½ ft., Np. 9¼ ft.

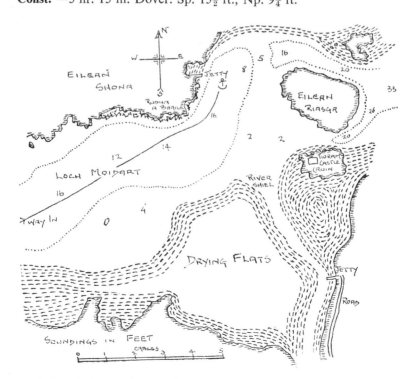

LOCH AILORT
Chart 2496. C.C.C.S.C. 45

Between Loch Moidart and Loch Ailort, which lies 5 miles to the northward, the shore should be given a wide berth. Three islands, Caolas, Gobhar, and Eiln. Glas or Grey Isle, lie in the entrance to Loch Ailort, but the passage to the southward of Eiln. Glas is clean. About 1 mile further up, the loch narrows to 4 cables between the shores, but it becomes very shallow, and the tide runs very strongly, and there are numerous rocks and shoals, which make it difficult to go further up. The Priest Rock, which dries $3\frac{1}{2}$ ft. and is unmarked, lies about 4 cables N.N.W. of Eiln. Glas, and must be carefully avoided if entering from the N.

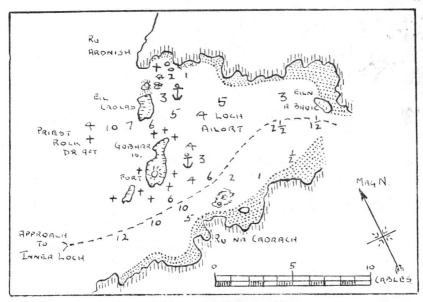

LOCH AILORT (OUTER ANCHORAGES)

Anchorages

Eiln. Gobhar—There is good anchorage behind Eiln. Gobhar and behind Eiln. Caolas, but both islands must be given a good berth on entering (see plan). The latter is reported as less subject to swell. The anchorage behind Gobhar is in 3 fath., just off the low-lying portion in the middle of the island but is very uncomfortable in strong S.W'lies as a considerable swell works in. Train connection at Kinlochailort, at the head of the loch.

Inner Anchorage—Perfect shelter can be obtained further up the loch, but first approach should be made with someone possessing local knowledge, or near L.W. when most dangers show.

From entrance either N. or S. of Eiln. Gobhar hold over to Eiln. a Bhuic, a small, heather-topped, bold, tidal island off the N. shore due E. of Eiln. Caolas (1 mile). Passing S. of this islet, a beacon on Bo Sruth Beg will be seen lying about 2 cables to the eastward. Pass about 50 yd. **north** of this beacon, between it and a rock which dries lying off the N. shore. Follow the shore round till a perch off the W. shore of Eiln. nan

Trom is sighted. Leave this perch about 50 yd. to port. Between Eiln. nan Trom and Eiln. nam Bairneach (to the S. of Eiln. nan Trom) there is a deep water channel used by locals but, if using it, care must be taken to avoid the sickle-shaped reef which curves N.E. from the E. end of Eiln. nam Bairneach. The beacons on Bo Sruth Beg, and W. of Eiln. nan Trom are reported missing. It should be noted that the rock N. of Bo Sruth Beg is bigger than the Bo itself. Beacon on Bo Sruth Beg reported (1962) as replaced but bent over.

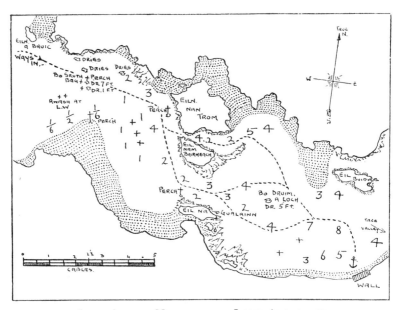

LOCH AILPORT NARROWS AND INNER ANCHORAGE
(Note—Perches are liable to be missing)

After passing the perch off Eiln. nan Trom, keep W. of Eiln. nam Bairneach, and hold down towards a perch lying N.W. of the tidal islet Eiln. na Gualainn. When about 1 cable N. of this perch, turn E. or E.S.E., taking care to avoid the reefs which extend S.E. of Eiln. nam Bairneach.

Beyond the islets the loch opens out, but there is a dangerous rock, Bo Druim a Loch (dries 5 ft.) lying 2 cables due E. of the centre line between the eastern ends of Eilns. nam Bairneach and na Gualainn. It is on a line from the S. end of Eiln. nam Bairneach and a long straight valley with trees on the S. side of the loch.

This rock can be passed either side but, in passing N. of it or if using the channel S. of Eiln. nan Trom mentioned above, care must be taken to avoid a long spit projecting from the N. shore to the W. of Eiln. Buidhe (the next islet to the E. lying off the N. shore). This reef extends further to the S. than the S. end of Eiln. Buidhe. If passing S. of Bo Druim a Loch, hold up to the centre of the loch as soon as you are certain you have passed it, to avoid some rocks with less than 6 ft. on them, which lie S.E. of the rock until 2 cables and about 1½ cables off the S. shore.

Keep in mid-loch until a long, low wall below the road on the S. shore is abeam, then turn to starboard and anchor off it, close in, in about 4 fath.

In the outer loch there is another perch (reported missing) at the outer end of the spit extending from the S. shore about $3\frac{1}{2}$ cables W. of Eiln. nam Bairneach. If the initial approach is made by holding well up to Eiln. a Bhuic, this perch should not confuse. All perches except the bent one on Bo Sruth Beg reported missing in 1966 and a local pilot is recommended for first visit to inner parts of loch.

This anchorage affords perfect shelter in all weathers and no swell works in. But a rock or possibly a reef extending from N. shore to about the centre of bay is reported with 4 ft. at L.W.

Stores—Farms only. **Water**—Burns.

From Eiln. Buidhe the loch runs for another 2 miles in a N.N.E. direction. Eiln. Buidhe itself should be given a good berth as a drying rock lies about $\frac{1}{2}$ cable S. of its S.E. corner. Four cables further on a wide rocky spit runs out $1\frac{1}{2}$ cables from the W. shore, terminating in a large drying boulder, and the remaining channel is obstructed by a cluster of large rocks above and below water in its centre. The boulder is marked by a perch, and if this is in position or the boulder can be seen, vessels may pass close eastward of it, curving round to a N.W. direction to avoid a sunken rock off the central group. The passage E. of the central group is apparently simpler. It is about 150 yd. wide, with a depth of 2 fath., and the E. (mainland) shore is clean.

About 3 cables N. of these narrows lies a small but bold island of dark rock and heather, very close to the E. shore, and in the middle of the fairway opposite this is a very dangerous rock, a second Bo Sruth Beg, which dries about 2 ft. It may be avoided by tending towards either shore. From here the course is up the middle of the loch, past a $\frac{1}{2}$ mile stretch of rocks and islets to starboard, after which the loch opens out into a wide pool, too deep for anchorage except close in-shore in places. A drying shoal extends about $2\frac{1}{2}$ cables from the E. shore.

A good anchorage may be found in 3 fath., S. of and just inside the outer line of the island mentioned above, opposite Bo Sruth Beg.

Camus Gleann Uig—A small bay at the S. side of the entrance to Loch Ailort, just E. of Samalaman Island. The bay dries out for about half its length, and has three rocks in it which show above H.W. Anchor in 2 to 4 fath., just outside these rocks. There is a slip and boathouse here. Exposed N.W. to N.E. winds.

Stores—None. **Water**—At burn beside house E. of slip.

LOCH NA NUADH or NAN UAMH
Chart 2496. C.C.C.S.C. 45

Loch na Nuadh lies to the N. of Loch Ailort. There are no dangers in the navigation of this loch if the southern shore is kept aboard. On the northern side there is a chain of islands, the Borrodale Islands, which must be given a reasonable berth. Two cables S.W. of Grey Isle, the outermost of the group, lies the Astley Rock, with 4 ft. on it, and 8 cables off in the same direction, the Gulnare Rock, with 10 ft. on it, both being unmarked. The loch is much exposed to W'ly winds.

Anchorages

Borrodale Bay—Temporary anchorage may be had in this bay in about 6 fath. Both points on entering are foul, and the head of the bay dries out and must not be approached too closely. Anchorage can also be had behind Eiln. Cabhar (see plan). In entering this anchorage there is a rock in the passage, Rafter's Reef, but it is marked by a red buoy. Keep to the S. of this buoy. (This buoy is reported missing.)

There is also good anchorage at the head of the loch in 2 to 4 fath. behind Eiln. Goblach.

In S. to E. winds anchor close in to Ard nan Buth, the S. shore of the bay, off a sandy bight with a cream-coloured house on the shore in 5 to 6 fath. Small craft can get better shelter by anchoring between the outer points of this bight in 3 fath. but swinging room is restricted. Off-shore squalls in this bay can be fierce.

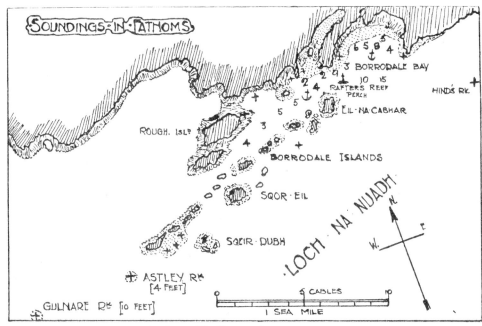

LOCH NA NUADH ANCHORAGES

ARISAIG HARBOUR
Chart 2496. C.C.C.S.C. 15

The entrance to the harbour lies to the N. of Loch na Nuadh, just round Rudha Arisaig. Coming down from the northward it is a little difficult to locate but the S. point of Eigg and the N. point of Muck in line leads almost exactly to entrance.

The channel to the inner harbour is very narrow and winding, and the navigation is hardly practicable unless for auxiliaries or motor boats. A few of the rocks are marked by poles but these are not being maintained and in July, 1968, three only were standing—two starboard hand, surmounted by circles, in the channel and one port hand, surmounted by a cross, just inside the harbour.

Written instructions would only confuse, as the coastline is so broken up, and the rocks and islets are bewildering. Therefore, it would be well to make this harbour for the first time at L.W., or soon after, when the reefs are showing.

It should be noted that the marks are on the highest parts of the rocks, and not on the ends of the shoal water.

If running for shelter, sailing craft should try and make either Mallaig or Loch Ailort, unless they have someone aboard with local knowledge. The anchorage above Cave Rock, about 1 mile within the entrance, is accessible by sailing boats and is well sheltered, but, unless with previous knowledge, it would be unwise to run in during heavy weather.

Stores—P.O. Tel. Hotel at Arisaig village. Half-holiday—Thursdays. **Water**—At hotel or houses. Train connection. **Const.** −5 hr. 05 m. Dover. Sp. 13½ ft., Np. 10 ft.

LOCH NEVIS
Charts 2507 and 2496. C.C.C.S.C. 15

Loch Nevis lies to the eastern side of the Sound of Sleat. Numerous rocks and shoals lie on the N. side of entrance. The southernmost and most dangerous of these rocks is Bo Cas Sruth which dries 4 ft. If entering Loch Nevis from the S., hold a mid-channel course, but if entering from the N. after passing Eiln. Glas (which may be held as close as desired), head for the highest point of the land opposite until Inverie House is open from the peninsula called on the chart Roinn Roanuill. The passage is then clear either up the loch or into Inverie Bay. Similarly, leaving the loch, if making for the N., keep Inverie House in sight behind you until the Mallaig Lt. Ho. is clearly visible; it will then be safe to turn up towards Eiln. Glas.

On the port hand on entering the loch is Bogha Don beacon with a granite cross on top. The rocky ledge on which it stands extends for ½ cable to the S.E. of it. Further in is Sgeir Dearg, a double rock, the S.E. part drying 10 ft. and marked by an iron beacon.

To make the Glaschoille (Shooting Lodge) anchorage at W. end of Inverie Bay it is only necessary to round Bogha Don bn. to port near the bottom of spring tides when the rock upon which the bn. stands will be visible, awash or nearly so. At other states of the tide it is safe to pass midway between the Bogha Don bn. and the 10 ft. rock shown in the sketch or, if this rock is not showing then, about ½ cable from the bn. There is deep water between Sgeir Dearg and the islands in front of the Shooting Lodge, but do not approach within a good cable of the N.W. of the bn.

From Bogha Don bn. for 4 miles up the loch is clear of dangers to Beithe Island, beyond which extensive shallow water is encountered off the N. shore.

Narrows of Loch Nevis (Inset plan on chart 2496)—To negotiate the narrows above Torr an Albannaich, first keep towards this headland until about 2 cables off it. Turn in towards the narrows, heading first for the ruined cottages at the near end of the low ground on the Morar shore and continuing to turn slowly gradually closing the southern shore until you are close in under the southern shore just before you reach the white cottage. At that point, cross the narrows and hold the northern shore some 30 or 40 yd. off until past Ru Torr na Cartach. On leaving the narrows, the rock Bogha an Tachard must be avoided. In the upper part of the loch the dangers are fairly close in-shore.

The tide makes through the narrows at about 5 knots. **Const.** −5 hr. 09 m. Dover. In common with most lochs N. of Ardnamurchan, Loch Nevis is noted for fierce squalls. The high lands on S. side of entrance cause baffling winds which make it difficult for sailing craft to navigate.

Anchorages

Inverie Bay (Chart 2496 and C.C.C.S.C. 15)—A large open bight on the N. shore just inside the entrance to Loch Nevis. The anchorage is in 5 fath., to the W. of the concrete jetty and post office. Keep well off-shore as it gets shallower towards the W. If approaching the anchorage at night, a large mooring buoy off the jetty must be watched. East of a line from the church to Rudha na Cruaidh, the bay dries out at L.W. More sheltered anchorage may be had in 4 to 5 fath. behind Sgeir Dearg, off the shooting lodge, just E. of the jetty and abreast the highest of the islets.

Stores—At Knoydart. P.O. Tel. At Home Farm, Inverie House. **Water**—At well behind P.O. Sp. 14½ ft., Np. 10 ft.

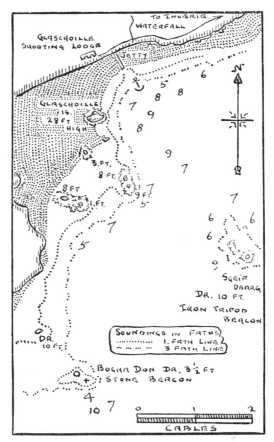

INVERIE BAY—SHOOTING LODGE ANCHORAGE

Glaschoille Shooting Lodge—A good sheltered anchorage particularly in N'ly winds (when Mallaig is uncomfortable). Anchor in 4 to 5 fath. near the jetty as close in-shore as swinging will allow.

Tarbet Bay—On the S. shore, just outside the narrows. Anchorage may be had in this inlet in 4 to 5 fath., off the two rocks below the farm. The bay dries out beyond these rocks. Easy of access and good holding ground, but exposed to a 3-mile drift in N'ly winds. A heavy chain or other obstruction is reported in centre of bay in 8 fath. when church and farm bear approximately 2 points on port and starboard bows respectively.

Stores—Farm only. **Water**—Burn.

Loch Nevis Head—Anchor in 2 fath., close in on S. side of the loch and above Eiln. Maol. A good temporary anchorage. Exposed to W.

LOCH HOURN
Charts 2507 and 2497 (best). C.C.C.S.C. 16

Loch Hourn lies some 7 miles to the N.E. of Loch Nevis. Nearly in mid-channel in the entrance, but a little to the N., lie some dangerous rocks. Sgeir Ulibhe, which dries at L.W., is marked by an iron beacon surmounted by a ball. About 1 cable N.W. of this beacon is a rock awash, and 1 cable S.E. another with 9 ft. The Clansman Rock, with 8 ft. on it, lies in the middle of the N. passage between Sgeir Ulibhe and the shore, but the S. passage is clear of dangers. There is no difficulty in the navigation until 5 miles further up, when Elice Shoal, with 6 ft. at L.W., lies in the fairway. This shoal lies about 4 cables W.N.W. of Coir Island. The passage to the S. of Coir Island should be taken as there are some rocks between it and the N. shore; but immediately on passing the island, the N. shore should be kept well aboard till clear of Barrisdale Bay, which shoals out badly from its eastern point. A mile further up, at Cnoc of Kyle, the northern shore shoals badly, narrowing the channel to about 1 cable, and the southern shore must be kept well aboard till clear. About 1 mile further up, Eiln. Mousker lies in the fairway, leaving a passage between it and the southern shore of less than 1 cable. An 8 ft. rock lies ¼ cable S. of Eiln. Mousker. A mid-channel course should be steered and care taken to avoid the spit running out from the mainland. The passage to the N. of the island should not be undertaken below half tides, as the water is shallower than the chart indicates.

The tides at the narrows run at about 3 knots, making at H. and L.W. by the shore. **Const.** —5 hr. 12 m. Dover. Above Coir Island, the large scale chart 2497 is necessary. The narrows at the head of the loch are very tricky, as there is a winding gut with only ½ fath. at L.W. in the channel. Power is almost a necessity here. The squalls in this loch are erratic and fierce, which make the navigation difficult for sailing craft and, in bad weather, dangerous.

Anchorages

Eilean Rarsaidh, an island off the N. shore 2 miles E. of Sgeir Ulibhe Excellent anchorage N. to E. of this island according to the wind in 3 to 4 fath. The channel N. of the island is about 150 yd. wide and quite clean. On the E. side the L.W. mark runs out a little and S.E. of the island is a large rock, nearly 1 cable off, which seldom if ever covers. East of this rock a 3 ft. shoal extends a further 150 yd. A cable off the mainland shore are two drying rocks (not one only as shown on Chart 2497) roughly 1 and 2 cables E. of the N.E. corner of Eiln. Rarsaidh, and drying about 8 ft. and 5 ft. respectively. If taking the E. entrance, pass 100 yd. W. of Eiln. a Chuilinn, a smaller island S.E. of Eiln. Rarsaidh, heading 100 yd. E. of the latter until level with it, then anchor in about 3 fath.

Camus Bane—A bay on the N. shore, just E. of Tioram Island. The anchorage is off Arnisdale village, but the shore must not be approached too closely, as it dries out for a short distance at L.W. In S'ly winds this anchorage is uncomfortable.

Stores—Restricted at P.O. **Water**—Burn. Sp. 14 ft., Np. 10 ft.

Camus Doin—A bay on the S. shore, W. of Eilean Mhuinteil. Good anchorage on the W. side of the bay, in 4 to 5 fath., fairly well in-shore. The soundings on the E. side are deep. The squalls here are extremely fierce.

Stores—None. **Water**—At burn.

Loch Hourn Head—A land-locked anchorage in the natural basin at the head of the loch. It dries out for about half its length. Anchor in $3\frac{1}{2}$ fath., off the N. boat jetty. Well sheltered from all winds.

ISLE ORNSAY TO KYLE AKIN
Charts 2496, 2676 and 3292. C.C.C.S.C. 17 and 18

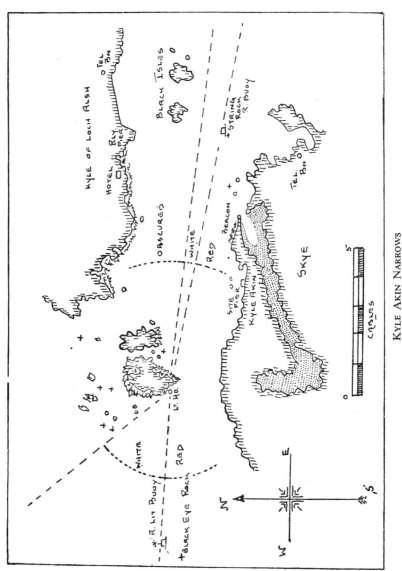

Through the channel, between Skye and the mainland, the tide runs very strongly, and at the narrows at Kyle Rhea, the ebb attains a speed of 8 knots (Sp.) and the flood 6 knots, turning at H.W. and L.W. by the shore. **Const.** —5 hr. 06 m. Dover. In strong S'ly winds the flood makes between 15 and 30 min. before L.W. It is advisable for sailing craft to go through near slack water. A mid-channel course should be taken, and the dangers are well marked by beacons. Coming in from Isle Ornsay, the first mark is a beacon on Sandaig Island on the opposite shore, just N. of Loch Hourn. It shows a wht. fl. lt. 2 sec. ev. 6 sec. About 4 miles further on, the channel suddenly narrows to about 2 cables, and the tide becomes very strong. In S'ly winds there is a **very heavy overfall** off Glenelg on the ebb. A mid-channel course must still be kept until clear of the narrows, as there are eddies on either hand. Halfway through, off the Skye shore, a wht. beacon stands, showing a fl. lt. ev. 3 sec. It shows a narrow sector of red over the fairways of both N. and S. entrances, with wht. to the westward and green to the eastward of these. At the entrance, off Ru na Cailleach on the Skye shore, there is a beacon showing a red fl. ev. sec. marking the Cailleach Stone, with some rocks inside. The water from here to the narrows of Kyle Akin is fairly clear, and the tide slacker. At the eastern end of Kyle Akin Narrows, lie the Black Isles, which can be passed on either hand, giving them a reasonable offing. On the S.E. isle a "Reflector Cluster" has been established. The northern passage is fairly clear, but between the island and Skye lies the String Rock, marked by a red can buoy. The passage between the Black Isles and this buoy is only 1 cable wide. From here to the lighthouse on Ban Island, mid-channel should be kept, giving the island a fair berth, as it has an extensive L.W. mark. Kyle Akin Lt., on this island, is an occ. lt., showing wht. between the Black Isles and the String Rock. North of this sector the light is obscured and S. of it the lt. shows red. By keeping in the wht. sector till off Kyle Akin these dangers are cleared.

Anchorages

Sandaig Bay—On the N. side of the entrance to Loch Hourn. On Sandaig Island, which lies off the N. point of the bay, there is a beacon showing a wht. fl. lt. 2 sec. ev. 6 sec. There is a rock above water

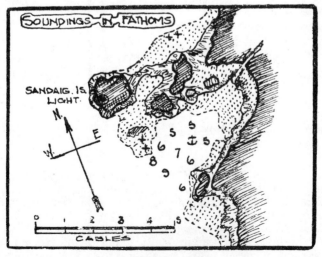

SANDAIG BAY

lying to the S. of the island which must be left well to port going in, as there are some submerged rocks off it, and the shore to starboard must also be given a fair berth. The anchorage is in the middle of the bay in 5 fath. Very exposed to the S. (see plan). This anchorage must not be confused with the Sandaig Bay at the N. side of the entrance to Loch Nevis.

Glenelg Bay—On the mainland, at the S. entrance to Kyle Rhea. A convenient anchorage while waiting the tide through the Kyle. The anchorage is fairly close in-shore, to the S. of the pier at Ru Mhic Cuinn. There is a large rock, Bo Beg, with 6 ft. over it at L.W., lying off this point, to be avoided. The main bay N. of this dries out for a considerable distance. Exposed to S'ly swell, and the shore on Skye, directly opposite, makes a more comfortable anchorage.

Stores—Shop at the point, also at Glenelg village, where there is a P.O. and Tel. **Water**—At well on hillside, behind the houses. **Const.** —5 hr. 06 m. Dover. Sp. 15 ft., Np. 10½ ft. Calor Gas.

Cailleach Anchorage (Chart 2676. C.C.C.S.C. 17)—On the Skye shore, just N. of Sgeir na Cailleach beacon, which shows a red fl. ev. sec. at the N. entrance to Kyle Rhea. A convenient anchorage while waiting for the tide. The best anchorage is off a shepherd's hut, keeping well off-shore, in 2 to 3 fath., good holding ground. Beacon, bearing S. by E., round as far as S.E. by S., 1 to 3 cables.

Both cottages shown on the chart are now in ruins. The shepherd's hut referred to above is the "White Cot" shown on chart—the more westerly of the two.

Balmacara Bay (Chart 2676)—On the mainland, opposite Cailleach anchorage. The bay shoals badly to the eastward of the pier. The anchorage is to the W. of the bay off a boat slip, in 4 to 5 fath. The bottom shelves up very quickly, so care must be exercised if anchoring here in on-shore winds. Very uncomfortable in S'ly winds.

Stores—None. **Water**—Burn beside slip.

Loch na Beist (Chart 2676 and C.C.C.S.C. 17)—On Skye shore, about ¾ mile E. of Kyle Akin. The shores are steep-to, but good anchorage can be had at the head of the loch, on the S. side well in-shore, off the burn. Well sheltered and preferable to Kyle Akin in N.W'ly winds. Holding ground good, but soundings are deep.

Stores—At Kyle Akin, 2 miles over the hill. P.O. Tel. Hotel. **Water**—At spring near beach on port hand entering.

Ob na Partan—A small bay to the W. of Rudha ard Treshnish, and to the E. of Castle Maol. Anchorage is in 3 fath., not too close in and there are several tel. cables and a power cable crossing from Skye to the mainland to be avoided. Entering from the W., keep the red buoy marking the String Rock to starboard. Well sheltered, but the cables above mentioned spoil it as an anchorage.

Stores—At Kyle Akin.

Kyle Akin (Chart 2676 and C.C.C.S.C. 17)—The usual anchorage is W. of the site of the demolished pier, well in-shore, in 4 fath. If making in here after dark a large mooring buoy has to be guarded against. East of the pier, the bottom is cleaner. The shore on both sides shelve rapidly. A bad swell sets in if the wind is from the N.W. To the E. side of the pier there is a small natural harbour. The entrance to this has been dredged and there is a least depth of 6 ft. over the bar at L.W. In a pool on the port hand, on entering, there is a depth of 2 fath., but a kedge should be laid out, as there is not much room for swinging. (Silting to less than **1 fath. is reported** in 1957, at the entrance opposite the ferry jetty.) There is a fishing boat pier opposite the ferry jetty where yachts can berth alongside.

Note—The ferry boats are moored fore and aft at night in the middle of the pool. A secure anchorage in all winds and a convenient place to leave a yacht over for a few days but local fishing boats may be occupying most of available space.

At the head of the pool, on the S. side near the first house by the water's edge, there is a submerged wreck with only a few feet on it at L.W. Two fix. wht. vert. lts. are shown on the ferry jetty while ferry is running. They are extinguished after the last ferry run.

Stores—Shops. P.O. Tel. Hotel. Petrol. **Water**—Hydrant at pier. Train connection at Kyle of Lochalsh opposite and ferry across. Calor Gas. **Const.** —4 hr. 40 m. Dover. Sp. 15½ ft., Np. 11 ft.

Kyle of Lochalsh—The anchorage at Lochalsh, opposite Kyle Akin, is in 6 fath., off the Station Hotel. The pier shows a fix. lt. from each corner, red from W. and green from E.

Stores—In village. **Water**—At hotel. Calor Gas.

Caution—Large mooring buoys were laid in most of above anchorages during the 1939-45 war and bottoms are foul with abandoned chains, etc. These have, however, probably sunk to a safe depth by this time.

LOCH ALSH AND LOCH DUICH
Chart 2676. C.C.C.S.C. 18

Entering from Loch Alsh, Glas Eilean, a low-lying island with extensive L.W. mark, lies in the fairway. The passage to the N. of this island is the clearer, though there are some rocks ½ cable S.E. of Scart Pt. to be guarded against, and also the Racoon Rock with 6 ft. over it at L.W., which lies about midway between Scart Pt. and Glas Eilean. It is marked by a blk. buoy. To make the S. passage, tend towards Ardintoul Pt., but do not approach within 1½ cables of the shore, then keep to the southern shore but not too close. There is a ½ fath. patch in the middle of the fairway at the eastern end of the channel which may be passed either to the S. or W. It lies about 1 cable N.N.W. of Ru Aird a Mhadaich, the first point on the S. shore E. of Glas Eilean. If beating, a shoal, Larach Tigh Mhic Donnuil, which dries 5 ft., has to be guarded against when taking either N. or S. passage. This shoal lies about 3 cables due E. of the centre of Glas Eilan, and shoal water extends fully 1 cable westward from the part that dries. From here the navigation presents no difficulty till the narrows at the mouth of Loch Duich are reached (see plan), when the S. shore should be kept aboard, care being taken to avoid Aile Mor Bank with 6 ft. at L.W., which lies 1 cable off Ru na Totaig. The remainder of the loch is clear, provided a reasonable berth is given to the shores, but at the head it shoals badly. Loch Beg has now been cut off completely by a causeway. **Const.** —4 hr. 57 m. Dover.

Anchorages

Ardintoul Bay (Chart 2676 and C.C.C.S.C. 18)—On the S. shore of Loch Alsh, opposite the Racoon Rock. Anchor in 3 fath. opposite the wood on the western shore, about ½ cable off. The bay shelves quickly on W. side, but less so on the S. side. Both points of the bay shoal badly. **Stores**—Farms only. **Water**—Burns.

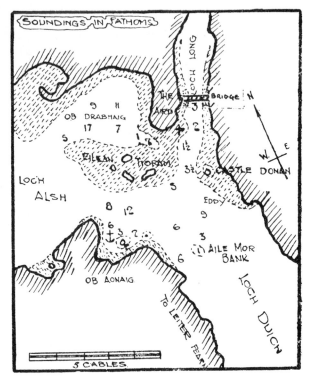

NARROWS LOCH DUICH

Ob Aonig, or Totaig (Chart 2676 and C.C.C.S.C. 18)—A small bay at the entrance to Loch Duich, opposite the mouth of Loch Long and Castle Donan (see plan). There is a rocky patch which shows above H.W. in the centre of the bay, and the anchorage is to the W. of this patch, in 2 fath. (a cairn and rock, painted with a wht. vert. stripe, in line indicate the centre line of the anchorage), or behind islet, fairly close in-shore, small rock off pier only danger. Perfectly sheltered from all winds but fierce squalls can be expected in strong S.W'lies. The point that makes the W. horn of the bay should be given a fair berth as a shelf projects a considerable distance. It is deceptive at H.W. as the point appears to be steep-to. Sp. 15½ ft., Np. 11 ft.

Stores—P.O. at Letter Fearn, a mile up the loch. Ferry to Dornie village for stores. Ferryman's house at first farm on Letter Fearn road past a big house. Bar at ferry slip but though licence maintained, bar does not open. **Water**—Pipe at head of W. bay. Calor Gas.

Ratigan Bay (Chart 2676 and C.C.C.S.C. 18.)—At the S.W. corner of the loch. The bay is on the S. side. There is a wooded point, and beyond it a reddish stony beach, forming a wide bay. Anchor off a small wooden hut on the foreshore, in 4 fath. The southern side dries out for a considerable distance.

Stores—P.O. Tel. at Glenshiel, about 1 mile round the head of the loch. **Water**—At burn beside small hut on foreshore.

LOCH LONG

Chart 2676. C.C.C.S.C. 18

Loch Long branches off from Loch Alsh to the N.E., at the entrance to Loch Duich, but it is spanned by a bridge, with opening span in its centre, at the entrance. (To have it opened requires 24 hr. notice.) The navigable channel is very narrow and is impracticable for sailing boats without a leading wind. With the detailed chart, 2676, it can easily be navigated by auxiliaries and motor boats.

KYLE AKIN TO PORTREE

Charts 2551, 2498 and 3302. C.C.C.S.C. 17 and 19

Leaving Kyle Akin, the first danger is the Black Eye Rock. It lies 7 cables W. of the lighthouse, and must be left to port. A red buoy, showing 2 quick fl. ev. 10 sec., is moored about 1 cable N.E. of the rock, and further out, Bow Rock, which dries 4 ft., is marked by a red buoy (see plan of Kyle Akin Narrows).

Kyle Akin occ. lt. shows wht. over the clear channel, the red sector just clear to the N. of Bow Rock, and covering the water to the S. of it. It also shows red to the N. of the channel, over the rocks off Plock of Kyle.

Between here and Caol Mor, the channel between Raasay and Scalpay Islands, lie Longa Isle and Sgeir Dearg, both of which must be given a good offing. Gulnare Rock, awash at L.W., lies 2 cables S.W. of Sgeir Dearg, and is marked by a blk. buoy, and Sgeir Tarsen, which dries 12 ft., lies 5 cables N.W. of the same islet, and is marked by a red iron beacon. There is deep water round these rocks, but they should not be approached nearer than 1 cable.

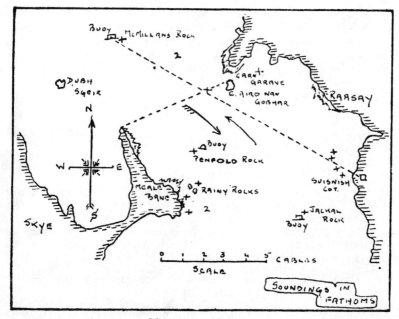

NARROWS OF RAASAY

At Point of Ayre, the S. point of Raasay Island, a wht. beacon shows a fl. lt. ev. 4 sec., red over these dangers, and wht. otherwise. Raasay Narrows lie between Raasay Island and Skye (chart 2498). If dark, after passing Ayre Pt., beware of the pier on Raasay, which is built well out into the fairway. At the narrows the direction of the tidal streams changes, the flood setting **southward** and the ebb **northward,** at 2 to 3 knots, the ebb starting ¾ hr. before H.W. by the shore and running for 7 hr., and the flood starting ¼ hr. after L.W. and running 5 hr. **Const.** —4 hr. 33 m. Dover.

At the S. end of the narrows, a red buoy marks the Jackal Rock, with 2¼ fath. over it at L.W., and well inside this, on the Raasay side, there are a number of dangers. Off Meale Bane on the Skye shore opposite, the Rainy Rocks run out for a considerable distance, and this point should be given a wide berth of about 2½ cables. Lying off Meale Bane, about 2¾ cables N.E., lies Penfold Rock with 1¾ fath. over it, and in the fairway marked by a blk. con. buoy which should be left on the port hand. Carngarave, the northern point of Churchton Bay on Raasay, must also be given a wide berth. The narrows are 4 cables wide at their narrowest part. McMillan Rock, with 2 ft. at L.W., lies at the N. entrance to the narrows. On W. side of this there is a red can buoy showing a gp. (2) wht. fl. lt. ev. 12 sec. It should be passed on W. side, but must be given a wide berth. From here to Portree the navigation presents no difficulty.

Anchorages

Broadford Bay. Chart 2551—About 5 miles W. of Kyle Akin. Coming in from Kyle Akin, the Skye shore must be given an offing of fully 3 cables, as there are dangerous rocks and reefs lying well off-shore, between Bow Rock buoy and Broadford. Seven cables off the S.W. end of Paba Island lies Sgeir Golach, a rock which dries 6 ft. It is marked by a red iron beacon, which must be left to starboard. Entering by the W. side of Paba Island, there are no dangers, if the island and Sgeir Golach are given a wide berth. The S. side of the bay is very foul. The anchorage is in 4 fath. S. of the pier and close to it. Broadford pier shows a fix. red lt. and 2 additional fix. wht. lts. when steamers are expected but these, marble carrying boats, only arrive infrequently and irregularly. Exposed to N. but, for boats drawing 4 ft. or less, shelter can be found on S. side close in under lee of wooden portion of pier.

Stores—Shop. P.O. Tel. Hotel. **Water**—At hotel. Motor connection to Kyle Akin.

Scalpay Sound (Chart 2551)—There is good anchorage in Caolas Scalpay, the channel between Scalpay Island and Skye.

The narrows, halfway through, are only navigable by motor boats or auxiliaries of small draft, as the channel has **only 1 ft.** in it at L.W. and 16 ft. at H.W., and is very narrow. A small staff and globe marks the end of a reef off Scalpay, but a rocky spit running out towards it from Skye, narrows the passage very considerably. There are no dangers in the approach from either end of the sound, and splendid shelter can be had on each side, near the narrows, in 2 fath., but in N'ly winds fierce squalls can be expected coming from over and round Scalpay Island.

East Loch Ainneart (Chart 2551)—This loch runs into Skye from the N. part of Caolas Scalpay, for about 2 miles.

There are no dangers to navigation, and anchorages can be had in convenient depths on the S. side of the loch, keeping well off the head.

Perhaps the best spot is in $3\frac{1}{2}$ fath., just before coming to the first cottage on shore. A bad mud bank runs out into the middle of the bay from the W. and it dries at L.W.

The squalls from the hills in this loch are notable for their fierceness, and it is not recommended except in quiet weather.

Loch Sligachan (Chart 2498 and C.C.C.S.C. 19)—About 3 miles N. of Loch Ainneart. The entrance to this loch is contracted to $\frac{3}{4}$ cable by shoals and is rather difficult to navigate. The detail chart is the best guide and, the leading mark given, Sconser Lodge in line with the peak of Glamaig is easily picked out. Anchorage can be had in convenient depths on the S. side of the loch, but the squalls are exceptionally fierce at times. There is a case on record of a wooden house near the S. ferry pier being blown down during a severe squall. The head of the loch dries out for a considerable distance at L.W.

Stores—Small shop at the S. ferry. Hotel at the head of the loch. Calor Gas. **Water**—Burns.

Camus na Geadaig—A small bay on N.W. end of Scalpay Island, opposite Point of Ayre, sheltered from all but N.E. to N.W. winds. Good holding ground in 3 fath., well off-shore in middle of bay.

Churchton Bay—On Raasay, just N. of Loch Sligachan. There are several rocks in the bay, some marked by perches and one by a blk. buoy. A long pier runs out from the shore, and there is fair anchorage on either side of it. The S. side of the bay is foul and rather shoal.

Portree Harbour. Charts 2498 and 1839 (best)—Approaching from the S. round Am Tom Pt., give the S. shore a fair berth as there are a number of rocks in-shore. The harbour is wide and easy of access, and the anchorage is in $2\frac{1}{2}$ fath. to the N.E. of the pier. The N. side of the bay, at the mouth of the burn, dries out for some distance. Be careful not to anchor directly off the burn, as the holding ground is bad there. A red fix. lt. is shown on the pier. Leave island at entrance to starboard going into the bay. The vicinity of Am Tom Pt. is subject to fierce squalls from all and every direction.

In strong S.W'lies the anchorage off the pier can be very uncomfortable but then good shelter can be found in the bay off a sandy beach, to the E. of Vriskaig Pt. in 2 to 3 fath. Vriskaig Pt. is the bluff at the southern side of entrance to inner harbour.

Stores—Shops. P.O. Tel. Hotels. Petrol. Calor Gas. Half-holiday—Wednesdays. **Water**—At tap on pier (charge $12\frac{1}{2}$p) or in dairy or inn on quay. Diesel fuel at depot at pier. **Const.** —4 hr. 33 m. Dover. Sp. 15 ft., Np. $10\frac{3}{4}$ ft.

PART V

INNER HEBRIDES

WESTERN SIDES OF SKYE, MULL,

JURA AND ISLAY; AND INNER ISLES

PART V

Admiralty Charts

GROUP I	2722*	Islay to Ardnamurchan Pt.
	2721*	Ardnamurchan Pt. to St. Kilda
GROUP II	2507*	Ardnamurchan Pt. to L. Brittle
	2551*	Isle of Skye N. of Sd. of Sleat
	3674	Southern Approaches to the Minch
GROUP III	3116	Island of Islay
	2481	Sound of Islay
	2418	Colonsay and Oronsay
	2326*	L. Crinan to Firth of Lorn
	2813*	Lochs Buie and Spelve
	2617	Sound of Iona
	3015	L. Scridain
	2155*	Sound and NW Coast of Mull
	2652	Loch Tuath and The Isles
	2832	Treshnish Pt. to entrance to Sd. of Mull
	3608	Lochs Corrie and Aline; Gunna Sd.
	3601	Loch Dunvegan and Loch Bay
	1202	Lochs Diubaig, Greshornish and Snizort Beg
	3669	Uig Bay
	3015	Loch Na Keal
	2037	Port Ellen

* Used in previous section

CLYDE CRUISING CLUB SKETCH CHARTS

*12	Western Section of, and entrance to, Sound of Mull and Loch Cuan
20	Island of Rona, North End of Raasay, Rona Sound
21	West Coast of Skye
22	Loch Tuadh, Ulva Sound, Southern Approaches to Loch na Keal
23	Lochs Lathaich and Scridain
24	Iona Sound and Southern Approaches to it
25	Southern Section of Sound of Islay
26	Northern Section of Sound of Islay and West Loch Tarbert, Jura

* Used in former sections

ISLAND OF MULL
West Side

The navigation of the West Coast of Mull requires considerable care. The whole coast is completely exposed to the S.W. and though there are many clean bays which might be used as temporary anchorages, most of the sheltered harbours are rather difficult of access, owing to submerged rocks. Off Caliach Pt., the extreme N.W. point of Mull, there is a tide rip extending out for about 2 miles, which is bad in strong winds, and off the Ross of Mull lie the Torranan Rocks, a foul patch of about $4\frac{1}{2}$ miles by $2\frac{1}{2}$ miles in extent, many of which are only a few feet below water (see under Sound of Iona). About 5 miles W. of the island of Iona, the bottom is very uneven, and this causes dangerous overfalls in heavy weather.

Anchorages

Ardmore Bay. Charts 2155 and 2832 (best). C.C.C.S.C. 12—At the N. end of Mull. A clean bay, but much exposed to the northward. Temporary anchorage in off-shore winds in 2 to 4 fath. A light showing a gp. (2) fl. wht. lt. ev. 10 sec. is exhibited on Ardmore Pt.

Loch Mingary (Chart 2832 and C.C.C.S.C. 12)—About $2\frac{1}{2}$ miles W. of Ardmore Bay. This loch should not be attempted without the chart quoted. It is very foul, and a number of the rocks cover at H.W. It is about $1\frac{1}{2}$ miles in length, and about half of it dries out at L.W. The entrance is between Cuan More Rocks on the N.E. and Eiln. Tarst on the S.W., but the clear channel is contracted to less than 1 cable wide by a sunken rock off the latter. The anchorage is about 3 cables within the entrance, in 3 fath. Small yachts might find fair shelter further in on the E. side in $1\frac{1}{2}$ fath., beyond a reef which juts out from the inner part of Laorin Pt., but great care must be exercised going in. Exposed to N'ly winds.

LOCH CUAN
Charts 2155 and 2832 (best). C.C.C.S.C. 12

About 1 mile S.W. of Loch Mingary. There is a large-scale inset plan of the loch on Chart 2832, without which it is not advisable to attempt this anchorage. There are a number of reefs which cover at 7 ft. flood, and near H.W. great care must be exercised. At half-tide most of the dangers show. Sgeir More, a reef which covers 4 ft. at H.W., lies in the entrance, about midway between Quinish Pt. and Airds Pt., the two horns of the loch, and a little to the S. of this, some rocks 3 ft. below L.W.O.S. This patch may be passed on either side, the western passage being about 4 cables wide and rather clearer than the other. Both shores of the loch are very foul, and the chart must be carefully consulted in using this anchorage. Sgeir Beg, a foul patch which covers about 4 ft. at H.W., extends for 4 cables off the W. shore, but as most of these rocks show soon after H.W., they are easily avoided. There is a small islet, Goat Isle, off Port-Croag in the S.W. corner of the loch, and fair anchorage can be had in 2 to 4 fath. to the E. of this. The islet is easily distinguished by an obelisk on its highest point. There is a narrow gut on the W. side of the islet, where a small yacht can find good shelter in $1\frac{1}{2}$ fath., but there is not much room for swinging. The islet also has an extensive L.W. mark to be guarded against, and one must not go further in than just past its N. end. Exposed to N'ly winds.

Stores—Van calls forenoon Wednesdays and Saturdays at Penmore Mill, $1\frac{1}{2}$ miles S. **Water**—At Croag House.

Langamul Bay. Charts 2155 and 2832 (best)—Just W. of Loch Cuan. An open bight, clean on its W. side if the shore is given an offing of ¾ cable. There is one rock which covers at H.W. lying about the centre of the bay. Temporary anchorage in off-shore winds in 2 to 4 fath.

Calgary Bay. Charts 2155 and 2832 (best)—Three miles S. of Caliach Pt. A large, open bay, but completely exposed to the W. and S.W. Entering from the N., give Arein Pt. a berth of fully ¼ mile as it is very foul. The S. side and the head of the bay are also foul. Temporary anchorage in off-shore winds in 2 to 3 fath., well off the head of the bay, off cottage on S. side, or off stone jetty on N. side.

Stores—None. **Water**—At cottage.

LOCH TUADH
Charts 2155 and 2652 (best). C.C.C.S.C. 22

Loch Tuadh is contained between Ulva and Gometra Islands on the S. and the coast of Mull on the N. It is 6 miles in length, and is clean, except for a 12 ft. rock, Bogha More—which lies 2½ cables off Tiompain Pt. on the N. shore—and at the head, at Ulva Sound.

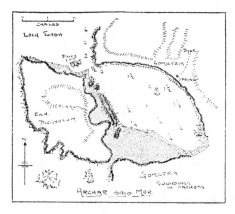

Anchorages

Archar said Mhor (Chart 2652)—There is an almost land-locked pool at the N. end of Gometra Island, but swinging room is very restricted. Eiln. Dioghulum, a small island, lies off the extreme N. of Gometra, and at L.W. is connected with it at its S. end, forming a small bottle-necked loch between the two islands.

There is a narrow entrance at N. side, less than 1 cable, and it is contracted to about 40 yd. by rocks off the W. side. Going in, the port hand must be kept close all the way in, and the anchorage is off the steep-to E. shore in 2 fath. The S. and W. shores of the bay are very shoal and both dry out a good distance and the holding ground, silver sand and thick seaweed, is reported as not too good. Perfectly sheltered in all winds but might be difficult to enter in strong N.W'lies. It is reported (1968) that this anchorage is silting up and 6 ft. at L.W. is maximum anywhere.

Stores—None. **Water**—Spring at end of dry stone dyke.

Soribay Bay. Charts 2155 and 2652 (best). C.C.C.S.C. 22—On Ulva, near the head of the loch. There are some rocks and reefs close in-shore, but this bay is fairly clear and well sheltered. Good anchorage can be had almost anywhere, in 4 fath.

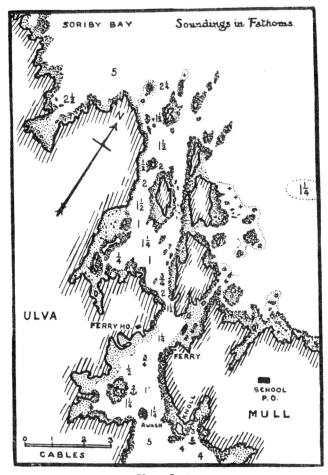

ULVA SOUND

Ulva Sound. Charts 2652 and 3015 (best). C.C.C.S.C. 22 (see plan)—
The channel lying between Ulva and Mull. Entering from the S. there are
no off-shore dangers for the first 4 cables, after which there is to port
Sgeir Beul a Chaolais (dries 11 ft.) which is dangerous when covered but
may be avoided by keeping rather to the Mull side of the visible channel,
but not too far, as a reef runs out S.E. from that side. Mid-channel should
be held until just N. of the ferry, where there is good anchorage in normal
weather in 3 fath. But there is a bar with less than 1 fath. right across
sound and a rock with only 3 ft. on it. This rock is about 60 ft. long and
is right in mid-channel. It lies halfway between the Ulva ferry pier and
the rock awash off Ulva. A line from Ulva ferry pier to the top of Eiln.
Casach, or the "V" in the Mull hills behind clears it. The passage between
Sgeir Beul a Chaloais and the ferry should only be attempted above half-
tide. In exceptionally bad S.E. gales a more sheltered spot for small yachts
with better holding ground and no current, is between the Sgeir and the
rock, 2 ft. high, just W. of it, or a little S. of this, but this anchorage is
awkward for getting ashore.

North of the ferry the channel narrows in places to 50 yd., with many rocks not accurately charted, and if attempting the passage it is advisable to proceed slowly under power or with a leading wind at half flood using the lead constantly. A simple way through at L.W. does exist but the leading mark is hard to identify. After passing through the W. narrows just N. of the ferry, bear to port until on a line between the bend of the E. ferry pier and the end of an overgrown stone dyke, 4 cables ahead, running down Ulva and terminating at a tiny cliff. Hold this direction and, on reaching the dyke, turn sharply to starboard to a steep rocky islet (16 ft. high); pass **East** of this and make for the western H.W. mark of a much larger island (24 ft. high) lying 2 cables to the N. Pass close **West** of this island at first, then bear to port into the open loch as a drying reef runs a long way (fully 1½ cables) N.W. of this island. A reef (dries 7 ft.) lies ½ mile N.W. of the 24 ft. island but there are no other outlying dangers to the westward.

An obstruction, like the shank of a large anchor, awash at L.W., was reported in 1946 in the narrows N. of ferry but has not been reported since. The passage of the sound should only be attempted **above halftide**.

Stores—Farms only. Occasional vans. P.O. Tel. at ferry house. **Water**— At houses. **Const.** —5 hr. 31 m. Dover. Sp. 13 ft., Np. 8½ ft.

Port Ranneach—About 4 miles up the loch, on the N. side. A good anchorage for small yachts, sheltered from all winds, but a 30 ft. boat would have little enough room to swing.

It is rather difficult for a stranger to find this anchorage on coming in from sea, as it is hidden by a low reef named Carraigean. A good leading mark is Torloisk House, a large house among the trees, and when one gets nearer, a wht. perch shows above the reef on its inner end. There is also a small cage or basket for a light at the outer end of the reef. The rock, Sgeir Leathann, off the entrance must be avoided, and the anchor dropped in about 3 fath., sandy bottom.

Stores—None. **Water**—From burn.

LOCH NA KEAL
Charts 2155, 2652 and 3015 (best). C.C.C.S.C. 22

Entering this loch from the W., the shores of Gometra and Ulva must be given a wide berth. Little Colonsay lies off the western end of Ulva, and can be passed on either side, the inside passage being about 4 cables wide between Colonsay and Eiln. Dubh. A rock above water, and also a 10 ft. and a 12 ft. rock, lie in this passage. Inch Kenneth and Gaisgil Islands lie in the entrance to the loch proper, and the former has a bad spit running out to the N.E., the greater part of which covers at H.W. One must be careful not to approach nearer than ½ mile to the N. end of Inch Kenneth. There is a clear passage about 3½ cables wide, on either side of the Gaisgil Isles, all of which are above water, and offer good marks. About 1 mile due E. of the largest of these islands, and ½ mile off, Airde na Cailleach, the eastern point of Ulva, lies Macquarrie Rock which dries 1½ ft. at L.W.O.S. This dangerous rock is slightly to the N. of a line between Gaisgil Isle and the N. end of Eorsa Island, which lies 2½ miles further up the loch. Beyond Eorsa Island, and to the S. side of the loch, there are a number of dangers, but there is little inducement to go so far up, as there is not much shelter.

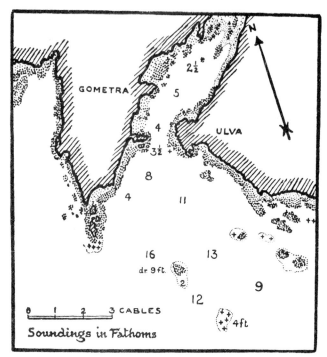

GOMETRA HARBOUR

Anchorages

Gometra Harbour (Chart 2652 and C.C.C.S.C. 22) (see plan)—Known also as Bailachloidh Harbour. This harbour lies between Gometra and Ulva, and affords perfect shelter in 2 to 4 fath. On the E. side, abreast of 5 fath. sounding on plan is best, opposite the cottages on Gometra, as there are some bad submerged reefs off the W. shore. A depth of 4 fath. and good holding has been reported off the E. shore abreast the 2½ fath. sounding or N. of this point close inshore S.S.E. of a cleared boat slip and a 20 ft. high cliff island; 10 ft. at L.W. There are several large boulders on the bottom, so, if possible, drop anchor on sand to avoid a foul anchor. Approaching from the W., Moisgeir Island, which lies S.W. of Gometra, must be left well to port, as a rocky spur runs out from it to the southward for almost ¼ mile. There are several sunken rocks in the approach, and the plan best shows these. It is obvious that great care must be exercised going in, especially in heavy weather. The channel between Ulva and Gometra is only navigable by rowing boats towards H.W.

Stores—Farms. **Water**—Well beside cottage on W. shore. Sp. 12 ft., Np. 9 ft.

Cragaig Bay—A very well sheltered and secure anchorage between Eiln. Reilan and a small peninsula to the E. of it on the S. coast of Ulva, N.E. of Little Colonsay (see plan).

Approach in 3 to 4 fath., leaving Eiln. na H'umha to port and heading straight for a prominent white cottage on shore. When Eiln. Reilan comes abeam to port alter course slightly to port and anchor in gut in 2 fath. sandy mud.

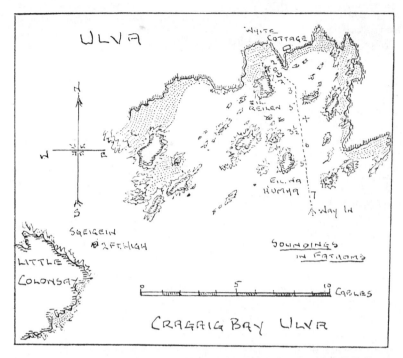

ULVA

SGEIGEIN
2 FT HIGH

LITTLE
COLONSAY

SOUNDINGS
IN FATHOMS

0   5   10 CABLES

CRAGAIG BAY ULVA

The Knoll, Ulva Sound. Charts 2652 and 3015 (best). C.C.C.S.C. 22—
There is good sheltered anchorage in 3 fath. in the small bay beside the
Knoll, a small castle-like rock at the S. entrance to Ulva Sound (see plan
of Ulva Sound). Entering this anchorage care must be taken to keep clear
of the spit which runs to the southward of Eilean a Chasaich, an islet on

Soundings in Fathoms.

INCH
KENNETH

SAMALAN
ISLD

MULL

CABLES

INCH KENNETH

the E. side, and also of the ledge which runs out from the Knoll in the same direction. Both these spits are very deceptive at H.W.

Eorsa. Charts 2155 and 3015 (best). C.C.C.S.C. 22—There is good sheltered anchorage behind Eorsa Island, on its E. side, in 3 to 4 fath. Give the S.E. point of the island a berth of fully 1 cable to clear Sgeir Bhuidhe, a rock which covers at half flood.

Inch Kenneth. Chart 3015 (see plan). C.C.C.S.C. 22—There is perfect shelter in the anchorage behind Inch Kenneth. The entrance is between Samalan on the E. and Inch Kenneth and the plan shows the dangers. Keep towards the Gaisgil group side of channel until the prominent house on Ulva (Ulva House) bears 355° (mag.) before turning into the anchorage on course 175°. Keep Ulva House directly astern on bearing 355° until conspicuous house on Inch Kenneth bears 250° then alter course to 230° and anchor in 3 to 5 fath. in centre of bay. **This anchorage should not be attempted in darkness.**

The best anchorage is about the $2\frac{1}{4}$ fath. sounding on the plan. Another good anchorage is reported in "White Stone Bay" (isolated barnacled boulder) to E. of house and below old schooner boom stuck in the hillside. In hard winds, the squalls from Mull are fierce, and boats sometimes cannot land here in bad weather. Holding ground reported not too good.

Stores—Vans pass from Salen. P.O. Tel. on Mull. **Water**—At houses. Sp. 12 ft., Np. 9 ft.

TRESHNISH ISLES
Chart 2652

Two groups of peculiar-shaped islands, lying about 3 miles to the westward of Gometra. The northern group consists of Fladda and Lunga, and a number of small islets and rocks, many of which cover at H.W.,

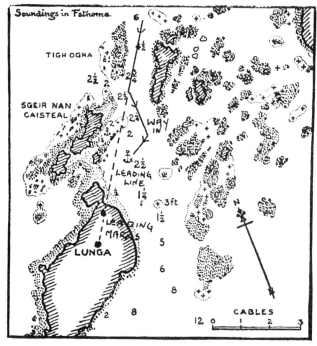

TRESHNISH ISLES

and the southern group of Back Beg and Back Mor or the Dutchman's Cap. These islands are all very interesting, but the approaches require the greatest caution. There is one sheltered anchorage on Lunga, but there are numerous sunken rocks in the approach. Coming in from the N. or W., take either side of Tigh Ogha, but if using the passage between the rock and Sgeir nan Caisteal, great care must be taken to avoid the spits running out on both sides and contracting the channel to about ½ cable. Two beacons on Lunga, one near the ½ fath. sounding shown in the Sketch Plan, and one on the summit of the hill, give a leading line till S. of Tigh Ogha. Once S. of Tigh Ogha, course **must** be altered to the eastward to open the leading marks as the leading line leads over the rocks E. of Sgeir nan Caisteal. The lower beacon is difficult to distinguish but white guano on cliff behind it can be used instead of it.

STAFFA
Chart 2652

This island lies 2½ miles W. of Little Colonsay. There are a number of outlying rocks extending for about 1½ cables from its E. side and also from its S. end, off Fingal's Cave. About 1 cable E. of the cave there is a landing place, distinguishable by an iron railing close down on the shore, and the water is clear just off this, with depths of from 3 to 6 fath., where it is possible to anchor temporarily while exploring this wonderful place. To make the anchorage by a clear channel come in from the S.E. on a line joining Erisgear over the stern to the landing place (distinguishable by the light coloured steps in the shape of an inverted "V" above it) over the bow. There are dangerous rocks that show at L.W. both N. and S. of the anchoring position. Temporary anchorage can also be had off the Clamshell Cave. It is often impossible to effect a landing on account of the swell which sets in during S'ly or W'ly winds.

LOCH SCRIDAIN
Chart 2771. C.C.C.S.C. 23

Loch Scridain lies to the N. of the Ross of Mull. It is about 7 miles in length, and is free from dangers on its northern side, though, if coming S. from Loch na Keal, there are a number of dangerous rocks off Mull. The S. shore is foul with outlying rocks and must be given a wide berth.

Anchorages

Loch Beg (Chart 2771. C.C.C.S.C. 23)—A small harbour right at the head of the loch. The entrance is little more than 1 cable wide, and opens out into a sheltered harbour, where anchorage can be found in 2 fath. up to 1 cable beyond the entrance. The loch shoals badly within 3 cables of its outer points, and the greater part of it beyond this dries out at L.W.

Sgeir Altach (Chart 2771)—About 2½ miles from the head of the loch, and on the S. side, there is a reef of rocks running out, behind which good shelter can be had in 2 to 4 fath. Most of this reef dries 8 or 9 ft. at L.W. but one rock on the E. side of it, Sgeir Chailleach, dries only 2 ft., and there are also numerous other rocks to be avoided. The chart quoted is necessary if using this anchorage.

Bun an Leoib—A perfectly sheltered anchorage under the islets near the entrance to the loch on the S. shore. Reported to be subject to swell in N. and N.W. winds but yachts drawing up to 10 ft. can get out of this by going well into the W. side of the pool under the protecting islets. Coming in, hold towards the islets or the E. shore to avoid a drying rock (Bogha Mor) in the centre of the entry to the bay.

Loch Lathaich. Charts 2771 and 2617 (best). C.C.C.S.C. 23—A splendidly sheltered loch, lying 3 miles E. of the Sound of Iona, on the Ross of Mull. It is about 1½ miles in length, and is easy of access. Eilean Lathanach, a group of islets, lies off the entrance, and is marked on its E. end by a wht. beacon showing a fl. lt. ev. 6 sec. This group can be passed on either hand, giving it a wide berth. The light shows red from bearing S. 77° E. to S. 57° E. (magnetic from seaward) over the western channel but white otherwise. The E. side of the loch is very foul, but by keeping to the W. and giving the shore a fair berth, it presents no difficulty. Goat Island and White Island lie towards the head of the loch, and behind the latter, off its S. end, there is good sheltered anchorage in 2½ fath., entering by the western side of the island. Loch Caol runs off to the westward, but it almost dries out at L.W. Good shelter can be had at the mouth of this loch, in 2 fath., but the centre is fouled by two wrecks.

Stores—Shop. P.O. Tel. Inn at Bunessan. Petrol at garage, 3 miles along Fionnphort road. Bus to Craignure and Fionnphort. **Water**—Pipe about 100 yd. up road from pier. **Const.**—5 hr. 30 m. Dover. Sp. 14 ft., Np. 11 ft.

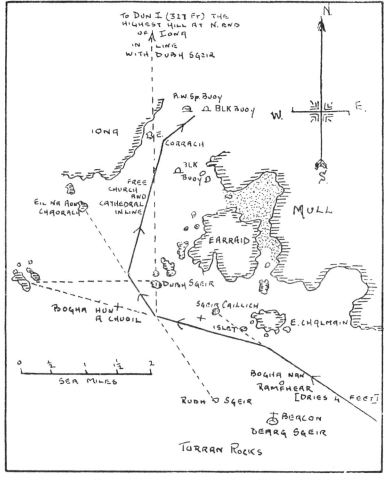

SOUTHERN APPROACHES TO IONA SOUND
(Note—Reverse Rudh Sgeir and Dearg Sgeir)

SOUND OF IONA
Chart 2617. C.C.C.S.C. 24

The Sound of Iona is about 4 miles in length, and requires careful navigation for yachts of more than 6 ft. draft. The maximum depth for the greater part is 5 fath. but at some places there are not as much as 2 fath. at L.W. The chart quoted is the best guide, but general directions may be given. The Mull shore is very foul throughout, and the rocks on the Iona side are all well in-shore. The tide runs strongly through the sound, N. on the flood and S. on the ebb changing at H.W. and L.W. on the shore. Entering from the N., a mid-channel course should be steered until almost abreast of the Cathedral, from which a fixed lt. shows to seaward. Between the Cathedral and the Free Church, which stands conspicuously on a point ½ mile further S., there is a bad bank lying in the fairway with 3 ft. on its shoalest part. It is marked on its S. end by a red and wht. horizontal striped buoy. Yachts drawing up to 9 ft. can pass this bank on the Iona side by keeping parallel to the shore, about 1½ cables off, till past the Free Church; but boats of deeper draft must consult the chart carefully, and pass the bank on its eastern side. Beyond this bank two conical blk. buoys mark rocks, and, coming S., by leaving them to port all dangers are cleared till abreast of the S. end of Earraid Island on the Ross of Mull, and Soay Island, which lies 1½ miles S.W. of Iona. Just beyond this line lies Bogha hun a Chuoil, an unmarked rock which is really the first of the Torranan Rocks. This is a cluster of rocks about 4½ miles by 2½ miles in extent. One of them, Rudh Sgeir, the most eastern of the group, is marked by a stone beacon surmounted by a cross. Many of the others are only a few feet below water, and there is usually a swell setting in which breaks badly over them. The inside passage is usually taken, and is about 1 mile wide between Rudh Sgeir and Eiln. Chalman, which lies ¾ mile S. of Earraid Island, and there are three rocks to be guarded against. With the large-scale chart, this passage should present no great difficulty. Bogha hun a Choil has 6 ft. over it at L.W., and lies 7 cables W. by S. from Dubh Sgeir, a small islet off the Ross, and can be easily cleared by keeping towards Dubh Sgeir. The next danger is a 12 ft. rock lying 2½ cables W. of Sgeir Calliach, an isolated rock above water between Dubh Sgeir and Eiln. Chalman. After this danger is passed, by keeping towards Eiln. Chalman, but not too closely, Bogha nan Ramfhear, a rock which dries 4 ft., and on which the swell generally breaks is cleared. This rock lies 7 cables to the southward of Eiln. Chalman, and is the only real danger in the inside passage. Owing to the swell, always evident here, there is frequently less depth of water over these rocks than noted. Dubh Artach, a large rock, lies 13 miles S.W. of Iona, and is marked by a grey stone lighthouse, with a broad red band painted round it. It shows a gr. fl. (2) 30 sec., 145 ft. 29 M (U). Fog horn one blast of 2 sec. ev. 45 sec., nominal range ½ M. From here to the Firth of Lorn there are no dangers.

Anchorages

There are no good sheltered anchorages for large yachts in the Sound of Iona, and the strong tide running through it makes it uncomfortable. **Const.** —5 hr. 34 m. Dover. Sp. 14½ ft., Np. 10¾ ft.

Bull Hole (Chart 2617. C.C.C.S.C. 24) (see plan)—A sheltered anchorage between Eiln. nam Ban and the Ross of Mull. The entrance is from the S. and is only ½ cable wide. There is a narrow channel entering from the N., but it is studded with rocks, and should only be used towards H.W. The channel is between Eiln. Dubh and Eiln. nam Ban and a leading line

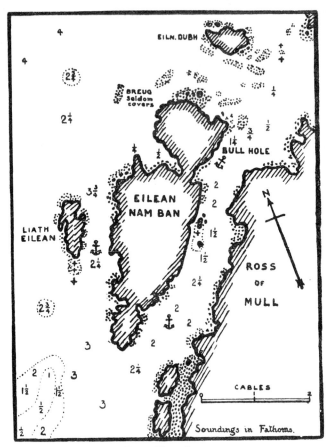

BULL HOLE IONA

is a big boulder on the shore on the point of the Ross of Mull (the most
N'ly one shown in the sketch plan) in line with the gable end of a house
a little way up the hill. Coming in from the S., the Mull shore is clean
and should be kept well aboard. About halfway up there is a bad rock
lying in the fairway, and about 30 ft. off the S.E. end of it there is another,
which is awash only at L.W.O.S. About 15 or 20 ft. off the point, S. of
the second "L" in "Bull Hole" in the Sketch Plan, there is a pinnacle rock
(known locally as "The Limpet") that just shows at L.W. It is dangerous
if making in for the anchorage described above. At the top of the Bull
Hole there is a ring on the island to which a warp can be made fast. This
anchorage is often uncomfortable on account of the swell and the tide.
On the Mull side, about the letter "E" in "Bull Hole" on plan, is the best
spot. Macbrayne's ferry boats moor here about where "Bull Hole" is
marked on plan. Also in channel leading to it.

There is another fair anchorage between Eiln. nam Ban and a small
islet, Eilean Liath, on the W. side, in 2½ fath., which is suitable in some
winds.

Stores—Shop. P.O. Tel. at Fionnphort on Mull, a little to the S. of the
anchorage. Calor Gas. Petrol 1½ miles along Bunessan road.

Martyr's Bay (Chart 2617. C.C.C.S.C. 24)—On Iona. The anchorage is in 1½ fath., fairly well in-shore, midway between the landing slip and the former Free Church, which is situated 4 cables S.S.W. of Cathedral. In this depth a small yacht can get clear of the tide, which runs strongly through the Sound and makes it an uncomfortable anchorage for larger craft.

Stores—Shop. P.O. Tel. Temperance hotels. **Water**—Hydrant on shore at landing slip. Steamer connection to Oban. Calor Gas. Ferry to Fionnphort.

Port na Fraing—On Iona N. of Cathedral. Good holding ground.

Fionnphort—In E. winds when Martyr's Bay is uncomfortable good shelter can be found in the bay off the ferry jetty at Fionnphort. Anchor in 1½ fath. to 2 fath. just S. of the islet off the N. point of the bay. The S. half of the bay is fouled by the tel. cable.

Stores—Calor Gas. Petrol 1½ miles along road to Bunessan.

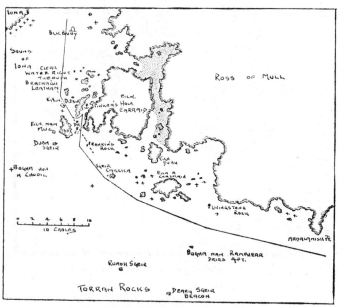

APPROACHES TO TINKER'S HOLE IONA
(Note—Reverse Rudh Sgeir and Dearg Sgeir)

Earraid (Chart 2617. C.C.C.S.C. 24) (see plan)—At the western end of the Ross of Mull. This anchorage is sheltered, but most difficult of access, and only suitable for small yachts handy in stays. The plan shows the dangers in the approach. The shores on either hand leading from the entrance to the pool can be approached closely, and any dangers are easily seen on the white sandy bottom. The pool is about 1 cable across and is known locally as the "Tinker's Hole". In the entrance channel the tidal stream runs N. from 3 hr. after H.W. till the following H.W.

Note—The Iona steamer goes through channel between Eilean nam Muc and the "Dries 8 ft." rock (see plan). Times of arrival and departure should be timed so as not to coincide with her passage.

If using this passage, keep on a steady course that shows clear water ahead and astern between all visible islands and rocks (see plan "Approaches to Tinker's Hole").

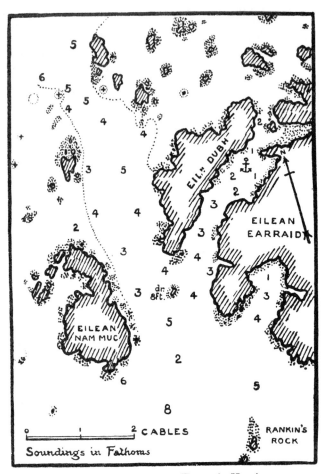

EARRAID ANCHORAGE (TINKER'S HOLE)

Rudha Ardalanish—Good anchorage (though possibly subject to scend in heavy S'ly weather) is reported in the bay **west** of Rusha Ardalanish (not in Ardalanish Bay which lies to the E. of that point) which is the most S'ly point of the Ross of Mull (about 2½ miles E. of Bogha nan Ramfhear).

The approach to the anchorage should be made from the S., giving Eiln. More (6 cables west of the point) and Rudha Ardalanish both a good berth and steering for just W. of the summit of the 411 ft. hill lying to the N. of the anchorage. Do not go E. of the W. extremity of a spur jutting westward from Rudha Ardalanish on its W. side about two-thirds of the way up it. The anchorage is in 4 fath. to 5 fath. behind this spur, between it and the eastern of the two islands beyond it, holding to the spur side of mid-channel.

Carsaig Bay (Chart 2813)—This and the one W. of Rudha Ardalanish (see above) are the only anchorages between the Ross of Mull and the Firth of Lorn. The bay lies 13 miles E. of the Ross, and is clean in its outer part. A group of islets, the Gamnach Islands, lies at the eastern part of the bay, near the head, and the anchorage is behind them. Entering

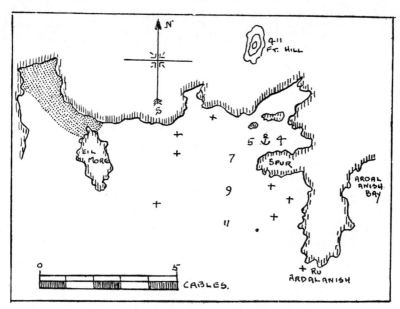

RU ARDALANISH ANCHORAGE

CARSAIG BAY

from the W., care must be taken to give the islands a wide berth, as the rocks extend 1½ cables from them in this direction, the outer one drying 3 ft. If coming in from the E., a good berth must also be given, as a ledge extends in that direction for 1 cable. Off Mull, inside the islands, the shore is very foul with rocks, the two outer of which are shown on the chart as being marked by poles but these are missing (1957). There is a perch on one of the inner rocks. The anchorage is in 4 fath. behind either of the two largest islands, and there are rings (reported as badly rusted) on them to which additional warps may be made fast. There is another rock with 11 ft. at L.W., lying 4 cables N.W. of the islands.

Stores—P.O. Tel. box by the big house, 1 mile from the pier. Water— At houses. Const. —5 hr. 27 m. Dover. Sp. 13½ ft., Np. 10¾ ft. Bus to Tobermory.

ISLANDS OF COLL AND TIREE
Charts 3674 and 3608

These islands lie to the W. of the island of Mull, and are separated from it by the Passage of Tiree, which is about 5 miles wide at its narrowest part. The two islands are separated by Gunna Sound (which see). The Cairns of Coll extend for 1½ miles off the N. end of that island, and dry 11 ft. Suill Gorm, one of these rocks, is marked by a wht. beacon, showing a wht. fl. lt. ev. 12 sec., but the outer rock is unmarked and is very danger- ous when covered, near H.W. The S.E. coast of Coll is clear from here for 5 miles, to Loch nan Eathar, but westward of this the shores must be given a good offing, as there are a large number of outlying dangers. Nine miles S.W. of Tiree lies Skerryvore, a cluster of rocks, on one of which stands a stone lighthouse showing a wht. fl. lt. ev. 10 sec. Com- pressed air fog horn 1 blast of 1.5 sec. ev. min.

In line between Skerryvore and the S. end of Tiree, and about midway between the two, there is a dangerous unmarked rock, which is just below the surface at L.W. There is no shelter to be had on the western sides of Coll or Tiree, and the whole of this coast is entirely exposed to the N. and W. It is also much broken up and studded with dangers, both rocks and overfalls, and should be avoided. There are one or two fairly good anchorages on the inner sides of the islands, but all must be cautiously approached.

Arinagour (Chart 3674) (see plan)—There is sheltered anchorage to be got in Loch nan Eathar, off the village of Arinagour. This loch lies 5 miles from the N.E. end of Coll, and the eastern shore is clear down to this point. The plan shows the entrance and dangers to be guarded against going into the E. anchorage, where good shelter can be got from all winds except S.E. in 1½ to 3 fath. This anchorage is, however, fouled by a mooring and an anchor tripping line should be used. Coming in from the E., there is a rock off the outside point of the Moil to be watched. This is not shown on the plan. A dangerous rock lies in mid-channel and is about 10 yd. N. of a line between the point which juts out on the largest island and a prominent dip in the rock formation of the Moil. A line from the end of the Moil through the N. tip of the first islet to the church with conspicuous steeple only just clears rock. There is another larger rock which dries 10 ft. nearer the Moil abreast the prominent dip. The point on the island opposite these rocks is foul. There is also a shallow shelf near the centre of the channel about two-thirds of the way up the first islet and rather nearer to the Moil side. **A course from a position midway between the S. points of the Moil and the outer island to the white building (hotel) below and on the left of the conspicuous church clears ALL dangers.**

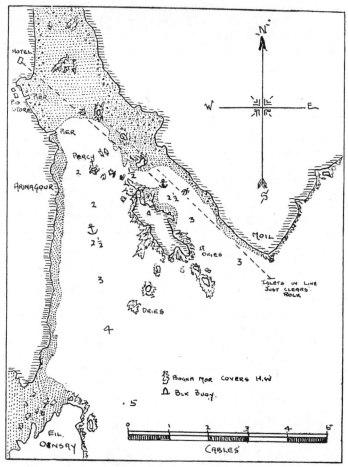

ARINAGOUR

The best position to anchor is off the N. end of the largest island with the most S'ly of the islets to the N. of it shutting out the hotel. There is a ring on this most S'ly islet.

There is also good anchorage between the perch (stone beacon) and E. pier, care being taken to avoid a rock below water about $\frac{1}{2}$ cable N.E. of perch. Approach to this should be made by W. channel or by E. channel above half flood avoiding rock above mentioned by keeping reasonably close to perch.

Off the S. point of the loch lies Eiln. Ornsay, an island which is connected with the shore at L.W., and the entrance to the S. anchorage is between this island and the blk. con. buoy which lies off it. This buoy which shows fl. 6 sec. should be given a very wide berth on E. side as its position has been doubted. The S. anchorage, which is in 2 fath. where shown on the plan, is much exposed to S'ly winds, and a considerable swell sets in when the wind is in that quarter. A pier is built about in-shore from the 4 fath. sounding in sketch and a road leads to it from the village, and another bn. has been built on drying reef 1 cable N.E. of same sounding.

Stores—Two good shops. P.O. Tel. Hotel. **Water**—Pump at cross-roads. **Const.** —5 hr. 12 m. Dover. Sp. 12½ ft., Np. 9½ ft. Steamer connection. Calor Gas. Petrol at garage ¼ mile inland from hotel.

Foill Bay—On S.W. of Coll about 2½ miles up from Gunna Sound. Good anchorage in E'ly weather. Anchor in 2 fath. close in-shore off sandy shore.

Gunna Sound (Chart 3608)—Gunna Sound lies between the islands of Coll and Tiree. The channel is very foul with sunken rocks, and is about ¾ mile wide at its narrowest part. The flood stream runs N.W. and the ebb S.E. at about 2½ to 3 knots and a strong wind with an adverse tide sets up a very nasty sea. **Const.** —5 hr. 12 m. Dover. Sp. 12 ft., Np. 9 ft. Off the centre of the sound, on the E. side, there is a red and wht. ringed sph. buoy, with a gp. (3) fl. lt. wht. ev. 12 sec., which marks Bogha Roan, a rock awash at L.W. and which lies slightly to the N.E. of the buoy. Between this buoy and Tiree lies Eiln. Creach, an islet which can be passed on either side, giving it a wide berth, particularly at its S. end. A little to the N. of this islet there is an 8 ft. patch. Coming in from the S., through the inside passage, the Tiree shore must be given a berth of about 1 cable, as there are a number of bad rocks lying off it. The anchorage is on Tiree, just round the first point past Eiln. Creach, in 3 fath., clay bottom. A P.O. cable has been laid from this bay—see warning in Introduction.

To make the passage of the sound from the S., proceed as follows: Take departure from the Bogha Roan red and wht. buoy and steer N.W. ¼ W. for the centre of the sound and keep in the centre line until on a

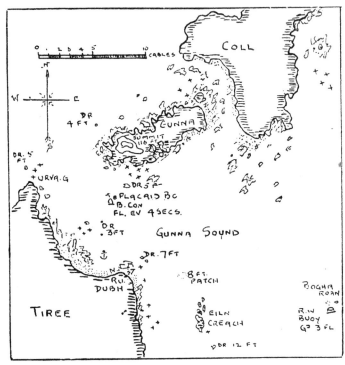

GUNNA SOUND

line joining the house nearest Urvaig (the extreme N.W. point of Tiree) and a peak on Gunna. The house is a good-sized one and is near the shore above a sandy beach and the peak on Gunna is the one that is **not** surmounted by a cairn. When on this line, alter course to N. till well clear of sound.

Entering from the N., approach on a S'ly course, making to enter the sound about one-third of the distance between Tiree and Gunna from Tiree. When on the above mentioned line, alter course to S.E. ¼ E. till in sight of the red and wht. buoy which must be left to port.

A course of N.W. from the red and wht. buoy will lead through the sound, but it passes very close to the middle rock which lies S.S.E. of the E'ly point of Gunna. There is another dangerous shoal to the S. of the course given; it lies about midway between Urvaig and Rudha Dubh (the N.E'ly point of Tiree) and just N. of a line joining their extremities.

A blk. con. buoy exhibits a wht. fl. lt. ev. 4 sec. lies about ½ cable S. of the above mentioned middle rock (Placaid Bo). A course close S. of this buoy to close S. of the R. and W. buoy clears all dangers but if one buoy cannot be seen from the other a course should be set tending to N. of the centre line of channel until second buoy is seen.

Gott Bay (Chart 3674)—In the S.E. end of Tiree. The entrance is between Soa Island and Ru Mealloaidh, and is about 1 mile wide; but the rocks off both sides contract it to 3 cables. On the port hand on entering, there is a jetty, and further in, a pier. Give the shore on this side a good offing. Anchor between the shore side of the pier and the concrete dolphin to W. of it in 2 to 3 fath. The bottom is foul between the shore side of the pier and the breakwater from which pier extends. Keep as close in-shore as possible after passing the pier, so as to get out of the uncomfortable swell which sets into the bay in S'ly winds. The bay dries out some distance at the head, and yachts should not go much past the end of the pier. At the S. side of the entrance to Scarnish Harbour, ¾ mile to W., there is a beacon showing a wht. fl. lt. ev. 3 sec. This harbour dries right out. Exposed to E'ly winds, then shelter can be had behind Soa Island, but great care must be exercised, as there are a number of dangers on that side of the bay.

Stores—Shop. P.O. Tel. at Scarnish (half-holiday—Thursdays). Calor Gas. **Water**—At pierhead. **Const.** −5 hr. 03 m. Dover. Sp. 12 ft., Np. 9 ft. Steamer connection.

Crossapol Bay—This bay lying N. and E. of Gunna Sound affords sheltered anchorage in winds from S.W. through N. to E., but in S.W. winds is uncomfortable owing to swell. Chart 3608 is essential as approach is foul with rocks that cover. Anchor midway between Sgeir Dubh and Sgeir nan Cuiseag in N.W. corner of bay. The farm houses on the shore are deserted and there are no stores of any kind.

ISLES OF THE SEA
(Garvelloch Isles)
Chart 2326

A chain of four islands lying about 3 miles N. of Scarba. There is a temporary anchorage on the S.E. side of Eileach an Naoimh, the most W'ly of these islands. On the S.W. end of this island a wht. beacon shows a wht. fl. lt. 2 sec. ev. 6 sec. There are a number of islets and rocks in the approach, but with the chart noted, they are easily avoided. The anchorage is in 4 fath., between the island and the small islets lying to the eastward, off the chapel ruin. The entrance is from the S.

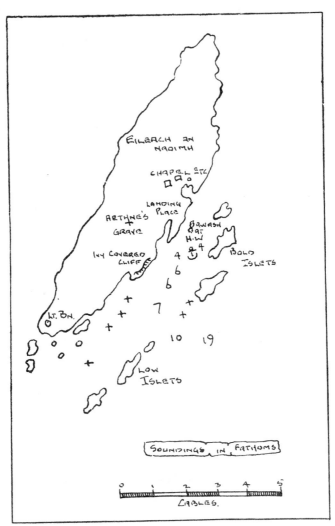

EILEACH AN NAOIMH

There are two chains of islets off the chapel the N.E. one being directly off it, the other more to the S.W. On approaching from the S. hold well in to the most N'ly of the S.W. group to avoid a reef running S.W. from the outermost islet of the N.E. group (the reef extends fully half the distance between the two islets), then stand N.E. towards the main island until it is well aboard then turn towards the channel between the main island and the innermost islet of the N.E. group and anchor in 4 to 6 fath. between some ivy-covered cliffs on the island and the S.W. end of the islet. Small vessels can anchor further up the channel between the island and islet but there is a dangerous rock, that covers lying off the mainland shore to be avoided. It shows white under the water. Exposed to swell in N.E. and S'ly winds but is well sheltered. Spring near shore below chapel.

JURA—West Side

There are two or three clean bays on the W. side of Jura, but they are exposed to the N. and W., and can only be used very temporarily in off-shore winds.

Bagh nam Muc—A convenient anchorage at the extreme N. end of Jura on the S. shore of the Coirebhreacain if coming into Crinan from the W. **in quiet weather.** The tide runs like a mill race across the entrance, and it would be unwise for a vessel without an engine to attempt it. In light weather the wind is blanketed when vessels are still in the tideway, and in heavy weather no vessel should attempt to make this anchorage. Anchor in S. or S.E. corner in 2 to 3 fath.

Perfectly sheltered, but a swell may work in in rough weather.

If making the anchorage on the flood tide, hold over towards the islet on the E. side of the entrance to avoid being swept down on the rocks (some of which cover) which lie just westward of the entrance between Jura and the island Eilean More. There is an islet close N. of the island, and a dangerous rock lying about 1 cable N.W. of it.

This anchorage should only be attempted in settled weather at slack water.

LOCH TARBERT, JURA
Chart 2481. C.C.C.S.C. 26

On the W. side of Jura, just N. of the Sound of Islay, It is about 4 miles in length, but only about 2 miles of the outer portion is navigable, the inner part being foul with rocks and shoals. Four cables S.W. of Rudha ant Sailean, the N.E. point of the entrance, lies Bo Mor, an isolated 7 ft. rock which is unmarked, and off the S.W. shore, about 1 mile within the entrance there is Sgeir Agleann, a rocky spit running out for about $\frac{1}{2}$ mile. Six cables beyond this spit a bad patch of rocks, Bogha-chan Baite, lies in the middle off Rudha Liath. A little further up on the S. side are Sgeiran Bhudregain, islets and rocks extending eastwards. From here the channel into the inner anchorages becomes extremely narrow. Off Rudha Gille nam Orlag, the N. point of the narrows, is a conspicuous islet, approx. 20 ft. high and at the inner end is a 13 ft. islet (dome-shaped). Beyond this islet the loch opens out. The soundings in this bight are very uneven and soon become shoal, and there is a "dries 1 ft." rock towards the E.

Outer Anchorages

Bagh Gleann Righ Mor—An open bay on the N. shore to the E. of Eiln. Gleann Righ. Anchor in 4 to 5 fath. in the middle, a little further in than the anchor shown on Chart 2481. Exposed to S.W. winds and squalls off the hills are fierce.

Gleann Righ Beg (Chart 2481. C.C.C.S.C. 26)—A clean open bay on the N.E. shore about 1½ miles within the entrance. The anchorage is in 3˙ to 5 fath. on the N.W. side of the bay. Exposed to W'ly winds. The squalls off the hills here are very fierce.

West of Gunhann Mor (Chart 2481. C.C.C.S.C. 26)—A bay on the N. side within the narrows, midway between the 20 ft. and the 13 ft. islet. Anchor between the narrow island on the W. side and the point of Gun-hann Mor. A little further in than the 6 sounding on the chart sheet 2481 is a good spot. Beware of an uncharted reef which covers at H.W. a little to the E. of the 4_2 sounding (see sketch plan). Well sheltered and good holding ground in firm mud.

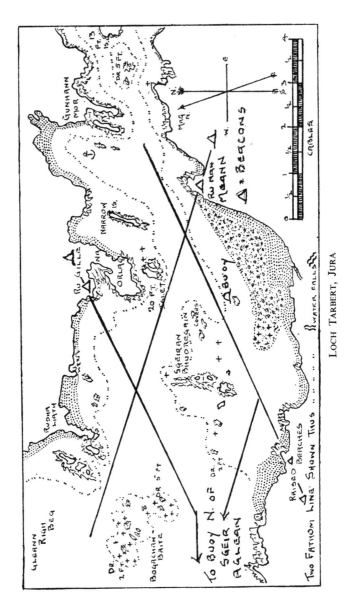

Glenbatrick—On S. shore in 2 to 4 fath. in bay W. of Glenbatrick House. To come in leave a buoy to W. of Sgeir Aglean to port and line up on two leading marks on S. shore to the S. of Sgeir Aglean then, as Rudh Eoghain is closed, turn 20° to port into bay.

Innermost Anchorages

Beyond the Narrows (Chart 2481. C.C.C.S.C. 26)—In the open bight of the loch past the 13 ft. islet, which must be passed on its S. side. Consult chart carefully and keep the lead going to find a reasonable depth in which to anchor.

Approaches to Anchorages

For the outer anchorages there is no difficulty provided Bo Mor is avoided and Eiln. Gleann Righ are given a good offing. The islands are very foul on their W. side.

Approaches to the inner and innermost anchorages require caution. There are alternative courses as follows:

North Channel—After passing Eiln. Gleann Righ, steer for Aird Reamhar (the W. point of Gleann Righ Beg), and pass it close aboard. Get on the stern line Aird Reamhar on end of Rudha ant Sailean. Do no pass S. of this line until past Rudha Liath (the E. point of Gleann Righ Beg), and then make for the 20 ft. islet, and pass close round to the S. of it.

South Channel—After passing Eiln. Gleann Righ, turn S.E. between Sgeir Agleann spit and Boghachan Baite, being careful to give the spit a good offing, and to pass clear to the S. of Boghachan Baite. Then line up with the two leading marks on the shore to the N.E., near Ru Gille na Orlag, and stay on this line until two leading marks on Rudha nam Meann to S.E. are in line—this line leads past the 20 ft. islet and N. of Sgeir Bhudregain.

When past the 20 ft. islet, if making for the inner anchorage, turn N.E. past the narrow island (leaving it to port) into the bay. If making for the innermost anchorage, carry on to the 13 ft. islet and pass to the S. of it.

The local landowner has laid buoys and established leading line marks (conspicuous) for pilotage of loch. A small white buoy lies just N. of Sgeir Agleann and another just W. of it (see Glenbatrick anchorage above). A third buoy lies just E. of Sgeir Bhudregain and leading marks have been established ashore as follows: (A) on S. shore S. of Sgeir Agleann; (B) on N. shore N. of Ru Gille na Orlag; (C) on S. shore S.S.W. of Sgeir Bhudregain; (D) on S. shore on Ru nan Meann.

The sketch shows the various lines of approach to Gunhann Mor anchorage and the inner loch once the buoy N. of Sgeir Agleann or Eiln. Gleann Righ have been passed clearer than any written description.

Note—The marks and buoys are for use of the Estate motor boats which are of shallow draft and the buoys may be removed in winter.

ISLAY

West Side (Chart 3116)

The W. side of Islay is very exposed to all winds from N. through W. to S., and there are numerous overfalls which render the navigation open to considerable risk. The anchorages are mostly exposed, and cannot be recommended. Off the S.W. end of the Rhynns of Islay a lighthouse stands on Oversay Island. It shows a wht. fl. lt. ev. 5 sec. Fog siren, 3 blasts of $2\frac{1}{2}$ sec. each, in quick succession ev. 90 sec.

Anchorages

Naomh Island (Chart 3116)—There is good anchorage behind Naomh Isle, which lies off the entrance to Loch Ghruinnard, at the N. end of Islay. The Balach Rocks, which cover at Sp., lie 1 mile N.E. of Naomh Island and must be avoided. The anchorage is in 3 fath., well off-shore, on the S.E. side of the island. Exposed to N.W'ly winds. A wht. lt. is shown from a pole on shore during the fishing season.

Loch Indail—A deep indentation to the E. of the Rhynns of Islay. On the E. side lies Laggan Head, which has a bad reef running out from it for about 5 cables, but otherwise there are no dangers. The anchorage is in $2\frac{1}{2}$ fath., past the pier at Bowmore, which lies on the E. side of the inner part of the loch. On Dun Pt., which is on the W. side of the entrance, there is a gp. (2) ev. 7 sec. lt., red and wht. sector. The red sector shows to the eastward, between the end of the spit off Laggan Head and the village of Bowmore. The wht. shows to the S.W. over the clear water until past Laggan spit, and over the clear water in the anchorage. The holding ground is good, but in S.W'ly winds there is a heavy scend into the loch.

Stores—P.O. Tel. at Bowmore. Calor Gas. **Water**—At houses. **Const.** —5 hr. 54 m. Dover.

Port Ellen (Charts 3116, 2037)—At the S. end of Islay. The anchorage is much exposed to S'ly winds, and the entrances and approaches are very foul, and should not be attempted without the inset plan on Chart 2037. The coast E. of Port Ellen to the Sound of Islay is very dirty, and must not be approached closer than 2 miles. Coming S. from the Sound of Islay, Chuirn Isle lies S.W. of Ardmore Pt. and has a beacon showing a gp. (3) fl. wht. lt. ev. 18 sec. To avoid the dangers off the shores of Islay steer for the bell and lt. red can buoy, gp. (2) fl. wht. lt. ev. 13 sec. marking the Otter Rock (a 2 fath. rock that breaks heavily at times). The buoy lies about 5 cables 197° from the rock. About $4\frac{3}{4}$ miles S.S.E. of the rock, a red and yellow horizontal striped pillar buoy has been established. Hold on till Tat Sgeir, the outermost rock off Texa Island, bears W., but nothing S. of that, and then approach the bay cautiously, using the plan already referred to. The anchorage is in 2 fath. midway between the pier in the N.E. corner of the bay, and the point opposite, care being taken not to go further in, as it shoals badly beyond this line. In strong S'ly winds a heavy swell sets into the bay, and slight shelter might be found in 3 fath. in the bay behind Carraig Fada lighthouse. This is a square tower on the W. side, showing fl. red and wht. sectors, 1 fl. of $\frac{1}{2}$ sec. ev. 3 sec. It shows wht. down the fairway and red on each side but this is confusing. If coming up in the dark, one does not know which of the red sectors one is in.

Stores—Shops. P.O. Tel. Hotels. **Water**—Tap on wall on left hand at pierhead. **Const.** —5 hr. 54 m. Dover. Sp. 5 ft., Np. 4 ft. Steamer connection.

SOUND OF ISLAY
Chart 2481. C.C.C.S.C. 25 and 26

The Sound of Islay is 11 miles long, and lies between Islay and Jura. The tide sets through at 3 knots, increasing to 5 knots flood and 6 knots ebb (Sp.) and $3\frac{3}{4}$ knots flood and $4\frac{1}{4}$ ebb (Np.) at the narrows at Port Askaig about halfway through. **Const.** —5 hr. 34 m. Dover. Sp. $6\frac{1}{2}$ ft., Np. $4\frac{1}{2}$, stream turning 1 hr. before H. and L.W. by the shore. The navigation presents no difficulty if the Islay side is kept, all dangers on that side being fairly well in-shore. The Jura side has a few dangers. Entering from the S., Brosdile Island lies 1 cable off the S. end of Jura, and 2 cables S.W. of it, an unmarked rock. A little over $1\frac{1}{2}$ miles further on lies Fraoich Island, which must not be approached too closely; and just beyond this the Black Rocks, a foul patch, marked on its outer end by a blk. con. buoy showing a wht. fl. lt. ev. 6 sec., which must be left to starboard going N. The lighthouse on McArthur Head on the S.E. point of Islay shows a fix. lt., red over all these dangers and wht. otherwise. Beyond this there are no dangers that cannot be easily avoided with ordinary care. On Carraig Mhor, a point ½ mile below the narrows at Port Askaig, a beacon shows a gp. (2) fl. lt. ev. 6 sec., wht. over the clear water, and red over the shoal water. A beacon on Carragh an T'sruith on Jura at N. end of Whitefarland Bay shows a 1 sec. fl. lt. ev. 3 sec. green across sound, wht. up and down sound. On Rudha Mhail, on the Islay side of the N. entrance to the sound, there is a lighthouse with gp. fl. lt. with red and wht. sectors. Keeping in the wht. sector leads clear into the N. entrance to the Sound of Islay, and the red shows to the westward and over the land. Gp. fl., 3 fl. of 3 sec., eclipse 2 sec. between groups 7 sec.

Anchorages

Port Askaig (Chart 2481)—On Islay, about halfway up the sound. The tide affects this anchorage making it often very uncomfortable, and the holding ground is not good. A fix. wht. lt. is shown on the quay, and the anchorage is close in-shore in 2 fath.

A new small harbour and a substantial ramp for the vehicular ferry has been built to southward of pier. There is enough water for a small yacht to lie afloat against the N. wall just inside the entrance to the harbour. When ferry boat is in the entrance is blocked.

Better holding ground opposite Caol Isla Distillery, ¾ mile further N.

Stores—Shop. P.O. Tel. Hotel. **Water**—At quay. Steamer connection. Sp. 6½ ft., Np. 4¼ ft. Ferry to Cantyre.

Bun na h abhain Bay (pronounced "Bunnahaven") **(Chart 2481)**— 2½ miles N. of Port Askaig. Anchorage while awaiting the tide, in 2 fath., ½ cable N. of the pier, well in-shore. Out of the main stream of the tide.

Stores—Shop. P.O. **Water**—At shop.

Whitefarland Bay (Chart 2481. C.C.C.S.C. 25)—On Jura, just N. of Port Askaig. A clean open bay. Anchorage can be had almost anywhere in 2 to 4 fath. On the S. side of the bay, near a boulder with an anchor painted on it on the beach, there is a ring to which an additional warp may be made fast. Off above boulder and in bay N. of it the tide does not run uncomfortably strongly.

There are many places along both sides where one could anchor while awaiting the tide, but all are uncomfortable and not well sheltered from all winds, nor is the holding ground good. A chart is a sufficient guide.

COLONSAY AND ORONSAY ISLANDS
Chart 2418

The islands of Colonsay and Oronsay lie 8 miles to the westward of Jura. Between Loch Tarbert (Jura) and these islands, in the Passage of Oronsay, lies the Tarbert Bank, with 6 to 9 fath. on it, and it is marked "not examined" on the charts. The two islands are joined together by a shoal, which dries at L.W., so that they practically form one island. The shores are very foul with outlying rocks, and must be given a wide berth, particularly off the S.W. end. There is no good shelter to be had on the W. side, but there are three fair harbours on the E. side, though all of them are exposed to E'ly winds.

Anchorages

Oronsay (Chart 2418) (see plan)—There are two good anchorages on the E. side of Oronsay, one between Eiln. Gartmeal and the boathouse

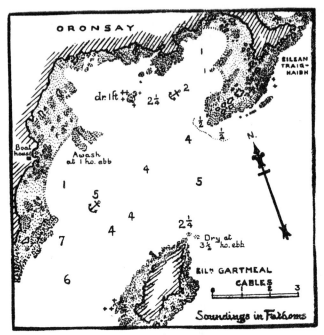

ORONSAY ANCHORAGE

on shore, in 3 fath., and the other behind Eiln. Traighaidh, in 2 to 3 fath. The plan shows the dangers to be avoided. Exposed to E'ly winds. Shelter (but subject to swell) can be had in E. or S.E. winds behind Eiln. nan Ean (to the S. of Eiln. Gartmeal). Water is shallow, bottom is sandy, and there are some rocks in-shore.

Stores—At Scalasaig. Calor Gas. **Water**—At farm.

Loch Stursneg (Chart 2418)—On the E. side of Colonsay about the middle of the island. There are no outlying dangers to be avoided, and anchorage can be had in 2 to 4 fath. almost anywhere in the bay, but the N. shore should not be approached closer than 1 cable as, off it, there are some isolated submerged rocks. Exposed to E'ly winds.

Stores—At Scalasaig. Calor Gas.

Scalasaig (Chart 2418)—Just N. of Loch Stursneg. There is a fix. lt. red and wht. sector on the point between Loch Stursneg and Scalasaig Bay. The lt. shows a narrow red sector along the shore to the N.E. and wht. otherwise.

The northern and southern points of the bay are steep-to and, with the exception of a small group of rocks marked by a beacon, well in-shore to the N. of the pier; there are no dangers.

As there is invariably a swell working round from the S. and N. ends of the island to obtain any degree of comfort in anything except a large vessel it is necessary to go well in-shore. This makes for restricted swinging room if there is a change of wind. A rope made fast to the ring shown on the sketch and one or even two anchors to allow the vessel to lie close to the S. shore of the bay fully halfway between the tip of the pier and the mouth of the harbour (which dries out) is to be recommended. Yachts must keep clear of steamer coming to or leaving pier. (The steamer always comes in to the windward side of the pier.)

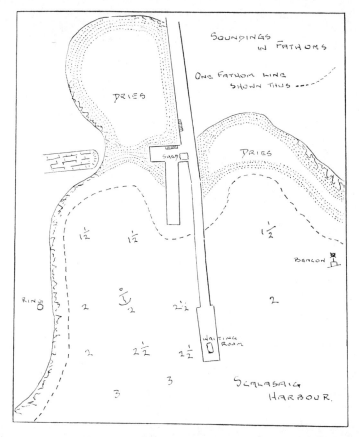

Water on the pier is not recommended but there is a convenient spring a little way up the road to the hotel. Excellent frozen food supplies are available at the P.O. also petrol and diesel.

In the event of excessively severe weather perfect refuge is available in the inner harbour if one is prepared to dry out. Entry to harbour should not be made without consultation with the piermaster.

Stores—Shop. P.O. Tel. Hotel. Calor Gas. **Const.** −5 hr. 36 m. Dover. Sp. 11 ft., Np. 4 ft. Steamer connection on Mondays, Thursdays and Saturdays.

Port Mhor—A bay on the W. side of Colonsay about 5 miles from its N. end. It is a first-class anchorage in E'ly winds. It is easy of access in daylight. Stand 1 mile to the W. of the N. end of the island then turn southwards and a straight line from that point to the rocks guarding Port Mhor (Eiln. nam Bean) clears all in-shore dangers. Do not approach the island nearer than 4 cables so as to avoid the off-lying rocks and reefs until the road passing the cemetery is completely open then come in on the line of this road (see sketch). Bogha na Tuadh (dries 6 ft.) to N. of anchorage makes the above 4 cables distance off essential.

It must be realised, if using this anchorage, that a S.W'ly blow brings in a very heavy swell but adequate shelter is afforded in winds from N.W. through E. to S.

Navigation of the W. side of Colonsay S. of Port Mhor should not be attempted without local knowledge.

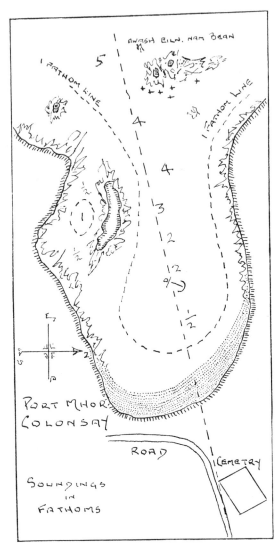

PORT MHOR COLONSAY

THE SMALL ISLES
Chart 2507

The Small Isles consist of four islands—Rum, Eigg, Muck, and Canna —which lie between Ardnamurchan and the coast of Skye. Two miles S.W. of Canna lies Humla Rock, which is marked by a blk. lt. buoy, showing a wht. interrupted rapid fl. ev. 10 sec., and between this and Canna, the Jemima and Belle Rocks, unmarked with 5 and 10 ft. over them respectively, with between them, other rocks with less than 6 ft. on them. Three miles further on in the same direction from Humla Rock, lie the Oig Sgeir, or Hysgeir Rocks, marked by a beacon showing 3 quick fl. ev. 30 sec., Tyfon fog signal 2 sec. ev. 30 sec. and about 2 miles further on still, the Mills Rocks, which are unmarked, with 6 ft. on them at L.W.

Between Muck and Eigg, about 1 mile off the former, lie the Godyke Rocks, some of which cover at H.W. Otherwise the dangers are fairly close in to the islands. The tides run from 2 to 4 knots about the Small Isles, their direction being deflected by the islands, and there are several banks which in heavy weather cause the seas to break badly.

ISLAND OF RUM
Chart 2507

Rum is the largest of the four islands and lies 7 miles W. of Sleat Pt., Skye. The coast is fairly clear if it is not approached nearer than 2 cables, most of the dangers being close in-shore.

Anchorage

Loch Scresort (Chart 2507)—This is the only sheltered anchorage in Rum. The loch is on the E. side of the island, and is about $1\frac{1}{4}$ miles long, the head of it drying out for about 2 cables at L.W. There is a bad reef running out for 2 cables from the southern point of the entrance. Anchor in 2 to 3 fath., well off-shore before reaching the jetty on the S. shore. Exposed to E'ly winds.

Stores—Provisions (except bread and paraffin). Tel. available at Kinloch P.O. at the head of the loch. **Water**—At burn. **Const.** —4 hr. 39 m. Dover. Sp. 14 ft., Np. 11 ft. Steamer connection.

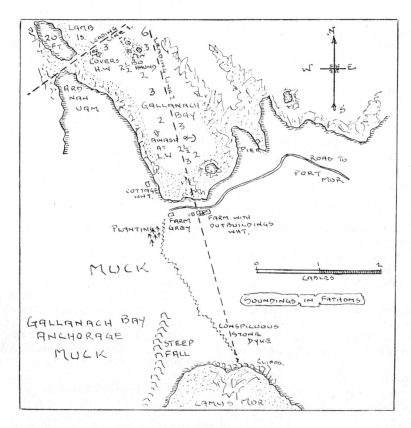

ISLAND OF EIGG
Chart 2507

If the shores are given a reasonable berth, there are no dangers, but between Eigg and Muck the navigation requires care, and at times the seas break badly on the banks off the S. end of Eigg. The anchorages at Eiln. Castle at the S. end of the island are described in Part IV of the Sailing Directions.

ISLAND OF MUCK

Muck is the smallest of the four islands and lies 2½ miles S.W. of Eigg. The shores all round must be given a wide berth as there are a number of outlying dangers. The anchorages are difficult of access, and are only temporary and not recommended for strangers. Abnormal magnetic variation reported E. of Muck. In spring tides there is a very strong set off the N.W. end.

Anchorages

Gallanach Bay (Chart 2507)—At the N. end of the island. In N'ly winds this anchorage is very dangerous to approach, as the swell sets in badly. To the N.W. of the bay lies Horse Isle, which is joined to the W. point of the entrance by an islet and a low water spit, and in the entrance, a little to the E. side, lies Bohaund, which dries 3 ft. at L.W.O.S. There is a narrow 3 fath. passage to the W. of this rock, and a 5 fath. passage to the E. On the latter side, however, there is a long spit running out in a N'ly direction from the island to be avoided. At L.W. the rock shows two heads, and the spit is also uncovered, and forms the E. side of the bay. The anchorage is in 2½ fath. in the centre of the bay and about halfway up it. There is another rock, awash at L.W., on the W. side. Perfectly sheltered, but an uncomfortable swell sets in during N'ly winds. Western passage should not be used by strangers.

Directions for entering from eastward: pass S. of Godag Rocks giving them a moderate berth and steer for N. end of Lamb Is. until Lamb Is. closes Ard nan uam. Alter course slightly S. and keep on leading line 1 (see sketch) until on leading line 2 (see sketch)—the end of stone dyke, conspicuous on skyline with W. end of farmhouse.

All reefs and rocks extend to N.N.W. and S.S.E. but can be approached fairly close on their N.N.E. and W.S.W. sides. Note the 3 fath. sounding close E. of Bo Haund.

Coming from W.: give N. shore of Horse Is. a berth of at least 1 cable then steer E. till on leading line 2 (see sketch).

A mooring buoy with span running E.N.E. and W.S.W. is laid near head of bay.

Port Mor (Chart 2507)—A small bay on the S. end of the island. On the port hand, on entering, there is a rock, Du Sgeir, which shows well above H.W., and on the starboard hand, Bo Rua, a rock which covers. Do not approach Bo Rua nearer than ¾ cable. The entry is the narrow channel between these two rocks. There are 5 fath. in channel between these rocks and entry should be made on leading line—higher edge of plantation above road in line with wht. gable end of cottage at pier (see sketch) but note that, when coming from N.E., rising ground obstructs view of cottage till nearly on the leading line. Be careful of the set of the tide when entering.

Anchor near the motor boat mooring near the head of the bay. Exposed to S. Good holding ground.

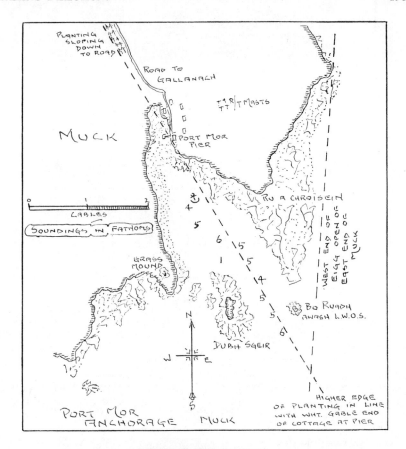

ISLAND OF CANNA
Chart 2507

The most northern of the Small Isles. Coming from the N. it has the appearance of being two distinct islands. The shores must be given a wide berth, and off the S.W. end there are the Jemima and Belle Rocks, Steigh Isle, and other rocks near to the shore. The cliffs are said to be highly magnetic, particularly at the extreme eastern end of the island, but, as one is unlikely to be steering by compass when so close to the shore as to feel any possible effect, this does not constitute a danger. If making for Canna from S.E. the shores of Rum should be given a berth of at least 2 miles until Canna Sound opens as the back scend from the Rum shore can be very bad.

Anchorage

Canna Harbour (Chart 2507)—Sanday Island lies off the S.E. end of Canna, forming a snug harbour between the two islands, sheltered from all but E'ly winds, but even in these, except at dead H.W., shelter can be found behind the drying rock. On the E. end of Sanday Island a beacon shows a wht. fl. lt. 2 sec. ev. 6 sec. (obscured over Humla Rock). The church on the hill on Sanday Island is a prominent mark. The shore of Sanday Island must be given a wide berth, as it is very foul, but one can stand right in to Ru Cirenish, a promontory which runs out in a S'ly

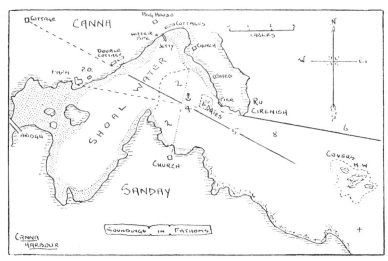

CANNA HARBOUR

direction from Canna, and forms the N.E. point of the harbour. Within the harbour, 1 cable from Ru Cirenish, a large rock which partly dries at L.W., lies about 60 yd. off the N. shore, and is the only danger to be guarded against. It lies just past the pier, and well outside the line of the end of it. A line of farm shut in behind Ru Cirenish clears rock off Sanday, and a line of small cottage on hill open to W. of double cottage near shore clears pier rock. The anchorage is in 2 fath., just beyond this rock, taking care not to go much further up, as the inner part of the harbour dries out at L.W. On a line between the church on Sanday and that on Canna is a good spot.

Stores—Farm, limited stores. Bread on Thursdays. Tel. box beside P.O. near farm. **Water**—At farm. Standpipe in field behind two derelict cottages near church on Sanday. **Const.** —4 hr. 34 m. Dover. Sp. 14¾ ft., Np. 10¼ fet. Steamer to mainland three to four times a week.

COAST OF SKYE
Sound of Raasay
Chart 2551. C.C.C.S.C. 20

Raasay Sound lies between Skye and the islands of Raasay and South Rona. It is 16 miles in length from Raasay Narrows to the N. end of South Rona, and varies in width from 1 to 5 miles. The main flood stream runs southward, starting about ¼ hr. after L.W., and the ebb northwards, about ⅓ hr. before H.W., at a rate of from 1½ to 3 knots Sp. **Const.** —4 hr. 36 m. Dover.

If the shores are given a fair berth, there are no dangers in the Skye side, but the western sides of Raasay and Rona must not be approached too closely. If turning to the eastward, round the N. end of Rona, the island must be given an offing of fully 1¼ miles to clear Guanachan Rock, which is awash at L.W. One can pass S. of Guanachan Rock as follows: N. of Rona are Cow Rock 29 ft. high and showing double peaks at H.W and another rock just E. of it 12 ft. high and shaped like a limpet shell. The solitary rock 2 cables N. of these has been built up with concrete to

form a flat topped polygon about 3 ft. above H.W. The passage between
Cow and the limpet-shaped rocks, and the polygon-shaped rock is wide
and clean and easily picked out. On the N. end of South Rona there stands
a lighthouse showing a wht. fl. lt. ev. 12 sec.

Note—It is reported, 1969, that polygon on rock covers at H.W.

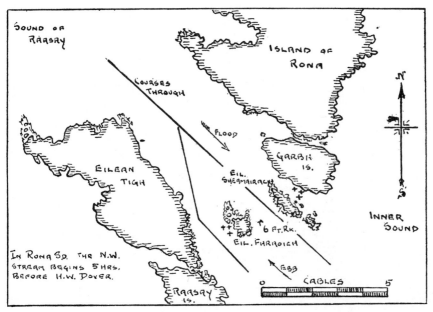

RONA SOUND

RONA SOUND
Chart 2551. C.C.C.S.C. 20

This channel lies between South Rona and Raasay. Eiln. Tigh, an
island which is practically joined to the N. end of Raasay forms with that
island the western side of the channel, and if this is kept aboard, the
passage is clean. The narrowest part is 1 cable wide, between the S.E. end
of Eiln. Tigh and Eiln. Fraoich, which must not be approached nearer
than ½ cable, as rocks extend from its western side for that distance.
Two iron poles with triangular topmarks have been established in the
passage. Going N. the first should be left to port, the second to starboard.
(The latter reported in 1969 as lying flat.) There is also a passage between
Eiln. Fraoich and Eiln. Sheamairach holding over towards the latter to
avoid a 6 ft. rock lying E. of the former. Flood runs S.E. at moderate
speed, setting through 1¼ hr. before L.W. **Const.** —4 hr. 35 m. Dover.

Fladday Harbour (Chart 2551. C.C.C.S.C. 20)—There is a snug
harbour behind Fladday Island, which lies near the N. end of Raasay.
The entrance is from the southward, keeping Ru na Torrin, the N.E.
point of Loch Arnish, well aboard, and passing between it and Fraoich
Island, a small islet lying ½ cable off the point. From here the water is
clear up to the anchorage, which is in 3 fath., between the S. end of
Fladday and Raasay. (**Note**—The houses shown on sketch plan are not
visible when approaching anchorage.)

There is also anchorage in 3 to 4 fath. to the northward, between these two islands, the approach being round the N. end of Fladday keeping fairly close to it as Bo na Faochag, a rock with 6 ft. on it, lies 2 cables N. of the island (see plan).

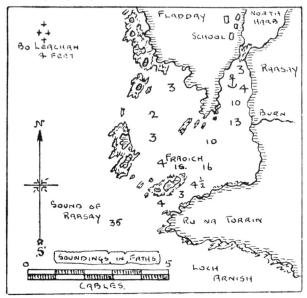

FLADDAY HARBOUR (SOUTH)

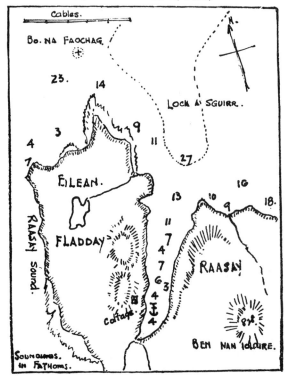

FLADDAY HARBOUR (NORTH)

Acarsaid Mor or Big Harbour (Chart 2551. C.C.C.S.C. 20)—A perfectly sheltered harbour on the S.W. side of South Rona, though a little difficult to locate. A large wht. arrow has been painted on rock face of island to indicate entrance—but this may well be subject to weathering off. It lies just N. of Rona Sound, and when the entrance is open, the house on the hillside can be seen. The entrance is by the S. side of Rough Island, and the plan shows the dangers better than any written description. The first rock, between the two 2 fath, soundings on plan, must be left to port. There is another rock further in between the 5 fath. sounding and the shore, sometimes marked by a wooden post erected by locals. Thereafter, steer for the winding road down the gully at the head of the bay until the islet at the top is reached and this leads clear through. There is a rock with less than 6 ft. on it at L.W. about halfway between the N.W. point of the islet and the rocks to W. of jetty. To avoid hold islet side of mid-channel. The "winding road" above mentioned is not now so easily picked out as it is badly overgrown. The spring at the cottage is reported as polluted.

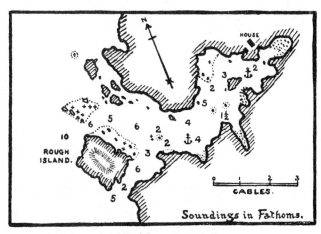

ACARSAID MOR—SOUTH RONA

The rocks on the N. side all cover at H.W.O.S. and the two beside the $1\frac{1}{2}$ soundings are covered at L.W. Anchor in 2 to 3 fath. behind the islet. There is a mooring buoy close E. of islet.

If entering by passage N. of Rough Island there is a dangerous rock, dries 4 ft., 20 yd. off the islet shown just W. of the 4 fath. sounding shown on the plan. The cottage kept in sight clears it.

Stores—None. **Water**—Spring beside path to cottage. Sp. $14\frac{1}{2}$ ft., Np. $10\frac{1}{2}$ ft.

RAASAY SOUND TO LOCH SNIZORT
Chart 2551

If the Skye shore is given a reasonable offing, there are no dangers. Trodday Island lies 1 mile off the N. end of Skye, and the tide sets through the passage at $3\frac{1}{2}$ knots Sp., the ebb setting to the westward $2\frac{3}{4}$ hr. after H.W. and the flood to the eastward. **Const.** —4 hr. 36 m. Dover. On the summit of Trodday Island there is a gp. fl. lt. showing 2 fl. ev. 10 sec. The light shows red over the bad patch of islands and rocks which lie to the N.W. of Trodday; white to the eastward over the clear water between these rocks and a line from Trodday to the outer side of the islands off Loch Staffin; green over Skye between this line and a line from Trodday to Ru Hunish; and white again to the westward over the clear water between this line and the S. margin of the red sector. Yesker Island lies about 3 miles W. of Ru Hunish, and is cleared to the northward by keeping in the wht. sector of the light. From this point to Loch Snizort, the coast is much exposed to the westward, and bad seas may be expected in heavy winds.

Anchorages

Staffin Bay (Chart 2551)—At the N.E. end of Skye, Stenchol Island lies off the S. point of the bay and the anchorage is in 3 fath., 1 cable off the centre of the island, between it and the shore. Much exposed to N'ly winds.

Stores—Shop at Youth Hostel. P.O. Tel. Hotel. Calor Gas. **Water**—At burn.

Kilmaluag Bay (Chart 2551)—Four miles N. of Loch Staffin. A clean bay with good anchorage in 3 fath. near the head of it, keeping the northern shore aboard going in. Much exposed to E'ly winds. Nearest P.O., Tel. at Duntulm, 1 mile inland to W.

Water—Spring on beach at head of loch.

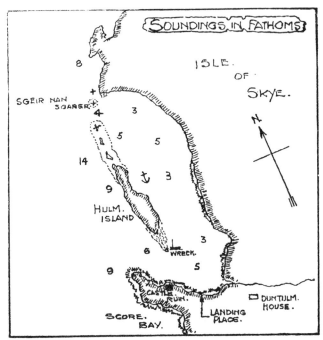

PORT ERISCO ANCHORAGE

Port Erisco (Chart 2551) (see plan)—A sheltered harbour at the N. end of Skye, 1 mile S. of Ru Hunish. Hulm Island shelters the bay from W'ly winds. The harbour can be entered by a passage round the S. end of Hulm Island, keeping towards the point on the Skye shore on which stands the ruins of Duntulm Castle. There is the wreck of a drifter which shows only at L.W. Sp. tides, lying off the spit at the S. end of Hulm Island, which must be carefully avoided. The entrance by the N. end of the island is very narrow, but with about 4 fath. Off the N. end of the island there is a reef of rocks awash at L.W.O.S. and a little further out lies Sgeir na Skarav which just covers at H.W. Sp., and the passage is between this rock and the rocks off the island. The anchorage is in 2 to 3 fath. close in to the island and towards its N. end, with an anchor or additional warp to the shore. The flood stream runs northwards up the W. coast of Skye, and this must be watched if making the anchorage in light winds. Exposed to the northward, and is very uncomfortable if there is any swell running.

Stores—Small shop. P.O. Tel. **Water**—At farms.

LOCH SNIZORT
Charts 2551, 3669 and 1202. C.C.C.S.C. 21

Loch Snizort lies some 5 miles W. of Trotternish Pt. The entrance is between Dun Lea on the E. and Vaternish Pt. on the W., and is about 6½ miles across, and the distance to the head of the loch is about 12 miles. Vaternish Pt. has a lighthouse, showing 1 wht. fl. ev. 20 sec. The Ascrib Isles lie in the western side of the entrance towards the Vaternish side. This group consists of four islands and a number of rocks, most of which are above water. Two cables off the western side of the South Island lies Skate Rock, a submerged rock with 4 ft. on it at L.W., and this constitutes the only real danger round these islands in daylight. If the shores of the loch are given a reasonable berth, there are no dangers till at the head, where it splits into two branches, Loch Snizort Beg to the E. and Loch Greshornish to the W. At the entrance to the latter there are some islets and rocks to be guarded against.

There is very little tide in the loch and the rise at Sp. is 14½ ft. and at Np. 10 ft.

Anchorages
Uig Bay (Chart 2551 and 3669 (best). C.C.C.S.C. 21)—A deep bay on the E. side of the loch, about 4 miles from Dun Lea. Coming in from the N., round Ru Idrigil, there is a spit running out for over 1 cable off Rudha Dubh, a point ½ mile within the bay. The anchorage is in 2 fath., just beyond the pier, which shows a red fix. lt. at its head. The head of the bay dries out for about 2 cables at L.W.

Stores—Shop. P.O. Tel Hotel Calor Gas. **Water**—At pier. Steamer connection daily to Outer Isles and bus service to Portree.

Port na Ella (Chart 2551 and 3669 (best). C.C.C.S.C. 21)—A small bay, 1¼ miles S. of Ru Chorachan, the southern point of Uig Bay. Coming S., the shore must be given a wide berth to clear Christie Rock, which lies ¼ mile N. of the bay and 1½ cables off-shore. This rock dries 6 ft. The northern point of the bay is foul, and must be given a berth of about 1 cable. On the southern side there is a small islet with a castle ruin on it, and the bay behind this dries out at L.W. The anchorage is in 2 to 3 fath., abreast of this islet, and is well sheltered, unless in W'ly winds.

LOCH SNIZORT BEG
Charts 2551 and 1202 (best). C.C.C.S.C. 21

South of Port na Ella the loch narrows to 4½ cables and runs inland for about 5 miles, forming Loch Snizort Beg. On the E. shore, a little over 2 miles S. from Port na Ella and 1 cable off-shore, lies Beatson Rock, with 4 ft. over it at L.W., and this constitutes the only hidden danger in the loch. This rock lies a little to the N. of some boathouses on shore, below Kingsburgh House. At the head, the loch divides into three branches, the most E'ly of which, Loch Eyre, completely dries out; but the other two offer splendid shelter.

Anchorages

Little Loch Snizort—The middle loch of the three at the head. This branch dries out for half its length, and there is splendid anchorage in 2 fath., mud, just within the outer points, at the mouth of Loch Eyre. The eastern shore at the entrance is very shoal, and must be given a fair berth. Sp. 14 ft., Np. 10 ft.

Stores—Shop. P.O. Tel. ¾ mile at Bernisdale village. Tel. at Skeabost Bridge at head of loch. **Water**—At burn.

Loch Treaslane—The most W'ly of the three branches at the head. There are some rocks off the eastern point of this loch on entering, and it dries out at L.W. for about half its length. The anchorage is just within the outer points, in the middle of the bay, in 2 fath.

Clachamish Bay—A small bay lying 1 mile N. of Loch Treaslane, with a rock off its E. point. There is good anchorage in the middle of the bay in 4 fath., but the head dries out for fully 1½ cables.

LOCH GRESHORNISH

Charts 2551 and 1202 (best). C.C.C.S.C. 21

This loch lies to the W. of Loch Snizort Beg, and has its entrance between Lynedale Pt. on the E. and Greshornish Pt. on the W. Off Lynedale Pt. lie Eiln. Beg and Eiln. More, and 1 cable off the S.W. end of the latter, Bo Eilean, a rock which dries 3 ft. Scart Rock lies off the N.W. end of the same island, and is 8 ft. above H.W. One cable off Greshornish Pt. lie Clinligin Rocks, which dry 5 ft. and 1 ft. The shores of the loch are fairly clean. About halfway up it narrows to about 2 cables, and 3 cables beyond this Crachan Rock, with 5 ft. over it at L.W., lies 150 yd. off the eastern shore with 100 yd. S.E. of it Graham Rock which dries 2 ft. The anchorage is in 2 to 3 fath. off this shore just before the loch narrows in from the W. Beyond this point the loch dries out to the head at L.W. On the western side here, there is also an extensive L.W. flat. Sp. 14 ft., Np. 10 ft.

Stores—On E. side at head of loch. Inn. P.O. Tel. and Hospital. **Water**—Springs. Buses to Portree.

Loch Diubaig (Charts 2551 and 1202 (best). C.C.C.S.C. 21)—An open bay to the W. of Loch Greshornish. A temporary anchorage in off-shore winds in 4 fath. in the centre of the bay. The head dries out for a considerable distance at L.W. Exposed to N'ly winds.

Aros Bay (Chart 2551. C.C.C.S.C. 21)—A clean open bay, lying 4 miles N. of Loch Diubaig. Temporary anchorage in off-shore winds in 3 to 4 fath., off clear part of beach.

Stores—Small shop among cottages on hill. P.O. Inn and tel. at Stein, 2 miles towards Dunvegan. **Water**—At small burn to E. of bay.

LOCH BAY AND LOCH DUNVEGAN
Charts 2551 and 3601 (best). C.C.C.S.C. 21

Lochs Bay and Dunvegan lie to the W. of Loch Snizort, and are separated from it by Vaternish peninsula, on the outer end of which is a lighthouse, showing a wht. fl. lt. ev. 20 sec. Vaternish Pt. must be given a good berth, and from here the coast is clear for about 4 miles to Ard More, at the N. side of Loch Bay, provided the shore is given a reasonable offing.

LOCH BAY
Charts 2551 and 3601 (best). C.C.C.S.C. 21

Loch Bay is the eastern arm of Loch Dunvegan and its entrance is $2\frac{1}{2}$ miles wide. Ard More is the N. point, and is easily distinguished by a fine natural double arch on its outer side. Between this point and Groban na Sgeir, the S. point of the loch, lie three islands, Issay, Mingay, and Clett, which shelter the loch from W'ly winds. The whole N.W. shore and the head of the loch are clean, but between Issay Island and Groban na Sgeir there are some dangerous rocks. Sheep Rock, which dries 5 ft., lies in the middle of the channel, and between it and the island there are some other rocks; but there is a passage, 2 cables wide, between Sheep Rock and Groban na Sgeir, the only obstruction being a patch with 9 ft. at L.W. Biast Rock, a large rock which covers at Sp., lies in line between Ru Maol, the western point of the upper part of Loch Bay, and the centre of Mingay Island, and 6 cables off the former.

Stores—At Stein. P.O. Tel. Inn.

Anchorages

Ard More (Charts 2551 and 3601 (best). C.C.C.S.C. 21)—There is good shelter to be had in N.W. winds behind Ard More, off the outer part of the point. The best place is between Ardmore Pt. and Ardmore House, rather towards the latter, keeping fairly well in-shore in 3 to 5 fath., but the holding ground is not very good. The bay behind the point is very shoal, and dries out for some distance at L.W.

Stores—Nearest at Stein, 4 miles up the loch. **Water**—At house.

Issay Island (Charts 2551 and 3601 (best). C.C.C.S.C. 21)—There is splendid sheltered anchorage behind Issay Island, between it and Mingay Island, anchoring in 3 fath. off the ruins on the former. Coming in from the S., the rocks off that end of Issay must be carefully noted.

Anchorage can also be had in 5 fath., off the village of Stein on the N. side of the loch, 1 mile from the head; and at the head of the loch in 3 fath., off the houses.

Stores—P.O. Tel. Shop at Stein. **Water**—At houses. Steamer connection at Stein thrice weekly.

LOCH DUNVEGAN
Charts 2551 and 3601 (best). C.C.C.S.C. 21

The entrance to Loch Dunvegan is between Dunvegan Head on the W. and Groban na Sgeir on the E. It is about $2\frac{1}{2}$ miles in width at the entrance, and for $3\frac{1}{2}$ miles up, the navigation presents no difficulty. Lampay Island lies 3 cables off Groban na Sgeir, and must be given a wide berth, as it is very foul; but if the shores are given a reasonable offing there are no dangers till near the head, when there are a large number of rocks and islets lying in the channel. A description of these would only confuse, and the sketch plan best shows the dangers. On Uiginish Pt. there is a lighthouse showing a lt. red and wht. sectors, fl. ev. 5 sec., red over the dangers to the westward and wht. over the channel to Dunvegan, and a blk. buoy further in marks Bo na Famachd, a rock lying in the fairway.

Anchorages

Totaig or Leinish Bay (Charts 2551 and 3601. C.C.C.S.C. 21)—On the western shore of the loch, about 3½ miles up from Dunvegan Head. The anchorage is near the head of the bay, on its western side, in 4 fath. Part of the head dries out at L.W. There are rocks to the S. of the bay to be guarded against. Much exposed to N'ly winds. Red Rock, which dries 13 ft., lies to the N. of the bay, and the shores all round shelve rapidly.

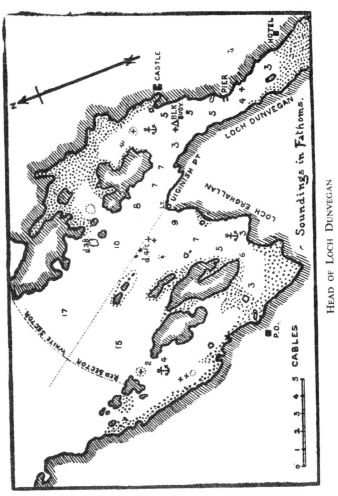

Lochs Dunvegan and Erghallen—The sketch plan shows the various anchorages at the head of Loch Dunvegan, and also the dangers to be guarded against. The blk. buoy in the upper loch should be left to starboard if making for the pier, and the anchorage there is just a little past the pier, and not too close in-shore. The pier has a fix. lt. showing red to seaward. There are also good anchorages, below the castle; in Loch Erghallen; and at Colbost where the other anchor is shown on the plan.

Stores—P.O. Tel. Hotel. Petrol and shops at Dunvegan village, ½ mile from the pier. Calor Gas. **Water**—The water at the pier is not good, but there is a pipe at tin-roofed shed, to right of road, a little inland towards the village. **Const.** —4 hr. 45 m. Dover. Sp. 15 ft., Np. 11 ft. Steamer connection.

LOCH DUNVEGAN TO LOCH BRACADALE
Chart 2551. C.C.C.S.C. 21

Leaving Dunvegan Head, the first mark is Meal a Veg Head, which lies 4 miles to the S.W. and forms the western point of Loch Pooltiel. Just off this point there stands a detached basaltic column, 60 ft. high, called the "Merchant". It is not very conspicuous. Two miles S. of this is Neist Pt., on which stands a lighthouse showing a wht. double fl. during 5 sec., ev. 30 sec. Fog siren, 2 quick low blasts ev. 90 sec. Between here and Ru Idrigill the coast is completely exposed to the S. and S.W., but if the shores are given a berth of 2 cables there are no hidden dangers until 3½ miles from Ru Idrigill. Here a bad reef, the Mibow Rocks, extends from shore for 1½ miles. The outermost rock is Dubh Sgeir, which is 16 ft. above H.W., and from its N.E. side the reef extends 4 cables towards the shore. There is a 3 fath. channel between these rocks and Big Mibow Rock, which dries 9 ft., and which lies 3 cables nearer the shore, and 4 cables further in still, and 1½ cables off-shore, lie the Little Mibow Rocks, which dry 3 ft. The surf generally breaks on Big Mibow. The channels on either side of Big Mibow Rock are navigable, but the inner one is preferable. Half a mile W. of Ru Idrigill stands the McLeod's Maidens, three remarkable isolated basaltic columns. The inner one is 200 ft. in height, and the two outer ones about 100 ft. Coming southwards, if the largest of McLeod's Maidens is kept bearing ahead, S.E. ¼E., this course leads clear between the Outer and Inner Mibow Rocks.

Anchorages

Loch Pooltiel (Chart 2551. C.C.C.S.C. 21)—Loch Pooltiel lies 3 miles S.W. from Dunvegan Head. It is about 1½ miles in length, and the eastern side is steep-to. Off the western side there are some rocks to be guarded against. The anchorage is at the head of the loch, in 2 to 3 fath., mud, but as it is completely exposed to the N. and N.W., it should only be used temporarily in off-shore winds.

Camus Bane (Chart 2551. C.C.C.S.C. 21)—A clean open bay lying behind Neist Pt. Temporary anchorage in 3 fath. near the head of the bay. This anchorage is much exposed to S'ly winds, and should not be used unless in settled weather. Neist Pt. lt. is shut out by a hill, when at the head of the bay.

LOCH BRACADALE
Chart 2551. C.C.C.S.C. 21

The entrance to Loch Bracadale is 3 miles wide and lies between Ru Idrigill on the N.W. and Ru na Clach on the S.E. Wiay Island lies in the centre of the loch, and its shores are clean to within 1½ cables. The loch is divided into three branches, Loch Vatin and Loch Caroy to the N., and Loch Harport to the S. Lochs Vatin and Caroy are separated by a point, Ru Harlosh, off which lies Harlosh Island.

LOCH VATIN
Chart 2551. C.C.C.S.C. 21

Loch Vatin lies on the N.W. side of Loch Bracadale. The loch is much exposed to the swell from the S.W., and is not recommended as an anchorage. There is a small bay in the N.W. corner, where fair shelter can be had close in-shore in 2 fath.

LOCH CAROY
Chart 2551. C.C.C.S.C. 21

Loch Caroy lies to the eastward of Loch Vatin. Tarner Island lies in the entrance, and $1\frac{1}{2}$ cables to the N.E. there is a rock above water, leaving a channel with 3 fath. between it and the island. Between this rock and the Skye shore there are a number of rocks which cover at H.W. About 1 mile N. of Tarner Island and in the centre of the loch lies the Ocean Rock, which is 6 ft. above H.W., and should not be approached nearer than 1 cable. The loch is much exposed to the S'ly swell, making it untenable as an anchorage; but fair shelter can be had behind Tarner Isle on its N.E. side, close to the island, in 5 fath., entering preferably from the S.

LOCH HARPORT
Chart 2551. C.C.C.S.C. 21

Loch Harport branches off to the southward from Loch Bracadale. The entrance is between Oronsay Island on the W. and Ru aird Tearc on the E., where a lt. is exhibited from a small wht. tower, high up. If the S.W. and E. ends of Oronsay are given a wide berth, there are no dangers to the head of the loch, a distance of about 5 miles, but it dries out at the head for about 1 mile.

Anchorages

Oronsay Island (Chart 2551. C.C.C.S.C. 21)—This island is practically joined to the mainland at L.W., and there is good anchorage on the N. side of the isthmus for small yachts in 2 fath.

Fiskavaig Bay (Chart 2551. C.C.C.S.C. 21)—This bay lies to the westward of Ru aird Tearc, and temporary anchorage can be had close in-shore, in 4 fath., not further up than the burn, which runs in on its western side.

Loch Beg—This loch branches off to the N.E. near the entrance to Loch Harport, but it dries out for about half its length, and it is too much exposed to the W. to offer good shelter. The anchorage is not further up the loch than a line between a wall running down the hillside to the shore on the S. side, and the small slip below the house on the N. shore. The tide at the anchorage is objectionable.

Gesto Bay, the bay next to Loch Beg, is also too exposed to be recommended.

Stores—Small shop. P.O. Tel. at Struan, $\frac{1}{4}$ mile inland. **Water**—At house.

Port na Long (Chart 2551. C.C.C.S.C. 21)—Within Loch Harport, just to the eastward of Ru aird Tearc. Sheltered anchorage, except for a short carry from the E., in 4 fath., close in-shore. This bay is free of dangers and affords splendid anchorage to W. of ruined slip, the holding ground being very good.

Stores—Small store. P.O. $\frac{3}{4}$ mile up road. Tel. **Water**—At first house on road.

Carabost (Chart 2551. C.C.C.S.C. 21)—On the western shore of the loch, 1½ miles from the head. The anchorage is off a corrugated iron shed on shore, between the distillery and the pier, in 5 fath. Bad shoal off distillery burn.

Stores—Shop. P.O. Tel. Temperance hotel. **Water**—At Talisker Distillery. Half-holiday—Wednesdays. Steamer connection at Struan, Loch Beg. Sp. 14 ft., Np. 10 ft.

LOCH BRACADALE TO SLEAT POINT
Charts 2551 and 2507

There are no dangers between Loch Bracadale and Sleat Pt. that cannot be avoided with ordinary care. Sleat Pt. is marked by a wht. tower 67 ft. high, showing a wht. fl. lt. ev. 3 sec. Visible 13 miles (unwatched). Most of the rocks are within 1½ cables of the shore, and almost all of them show above H.W. The whole coast is, of course, completely exposed to the S.W. and, this being the prevalent wind, a heavy swell is usually experienced, which makes many of the anchorages untenable.

One and a half miles S.W. of Ru na Clach, the S.E. point of Loch Bracadale, lies Talisker Bay, which can only be used temporarily, as the holding ground is bad and the bay much exposed. Four miles further S. lies West Loch Ainneart, which is clean on both its shores, but which dries out at the head for 8 cables. Sgurr Beg, the N. point of the entrance, must be given a wide berth, as rocks awash at ½ ebb lie off it and off the opposite shore lies Dubh Sgeir, an islet with a clear channel on either side.

The holding ground here is good, but the loch is subject to fierce squalls, and is much exposed to the W. Three and a half miles further S. lies Loch Bhreatal (Brittle) which is clean, but is also too much exposed to be used as an anchorage. Between Ru an Dunain, the southern point of Loch Bhreatal and Straithaird Pt., which lies 8 miles to the S.E., is the entrance to Loch Scathvaig. Between these two points lies Soay Island, which must be given a wide berth to avoid the rocks which lie off its western side. Straithaird Pt. must also be given a wide berth to clear Eiln. na Haird, an island with an extensive L.W. mark, lying about 3 cables off Ru na Heasgahn, the southern extremity of the point. Loch Slapin and Loch Eishart branch off between Straithaird Pt. and the Point of Sleat, the distance between the two points being 7½ miles.

LOCH SCATHVAIG
Chart 2507 (see plan)

The approach to Loch Scathvaig is between Ru an Dunain on the W. and Straithaird Pt. on the E. Heasghan, the E. point of Straithaird, has a long dangerous spur running out from it. Soay Island lies in the entrance and can be passed on either side, giving the S.W. end a wide berth to clear Gamhna and Coileach Rocks, which extend off-shore for ½ mile. Caol Soay, the western passage which is ¾ mile wide at its narrowest part, is clean and presents no difficulty and in the eastern passage between Soay and Straithaird Pt. the only obstruction is Bogha Carrach, a rock with 12 ft. over it at L.W., which lies about the middle of the fairway.

Loch Scathvaig lies in the N.W. corner at the head of the bight. There are a number of rocks which are awash at L.W., and the plan shows these better than any written description. The western side should be taken, as Eiln. Reamhar and Sgeir Doghigh are both above water. The anchorage is in 2 fath., at the head of the loch, behind Eiln. Glas. Going in, the rock off the western end of this islet is dangerous and must be carefully guarded against. It is awash at ½ ebb and it is **not** shown on chart sheet 2507. The exact position of this rock is as follows: the rock is 40 yd. long from E. to W. and its E. edge is 60 yd. from the nearest point of Glas Island. Its W. edge is 100 yd. from the W. shore of the loch.

To make the anchorage behind Glas Island, pass between the rock and the island, in the centre of the 60 yd. channel.

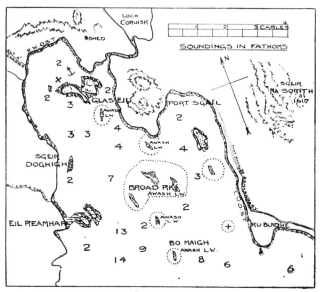

SCATHVAIG

The centre of this channel shows whitish from the sand below, and the shoal water on either side shows black from kelp on the rock and the island When the rock is showing it is easy to pick out the passage, but when covered it is rather deceptive. There is a detached rock with 2 ft. at L.W.O.S., lying 25 yd. off the N. side of the eastern end of Eiln. Glas, and silting is reported E. of a line joining the N.W. point of this island and the landing steps. Care must be taken if using the moorings on the island (see chart).

There are rings on the island and on shore to which additional warps can be made fast. The principal danger in Loch Scathvaig is the terrific squalls for which this place is noted, and in strong winds from any quarter caution is necessary. It is advisable always to have shore warps, as the anchor might readily start in the vicious gusts which come down from the hills from all quarters. It is pronounced "Skavaig". A fall of rock at the back of the loch shows up white from a long way off.

Stores—None. **Water**—At burn. Steamer calls once a week in summer. Motor boat from Mallaig calls at 1300 on Tuesdays and Thursdays and steamer on Thursdays during the summer months.

Soay Harbour (North)—On the N. side of Soay Island. There are reefs which cover on both sides of the entrance and approach must be made on a S.S.E'ly course from well off-shore, making for the centre of the entrance. About ¾ cable in from the entrance the loch narrows and across the narrows runs a bar about 20 ft. wide. On both sides boulder spits run out toward the centre with, between their extremities, a shingle bottomed

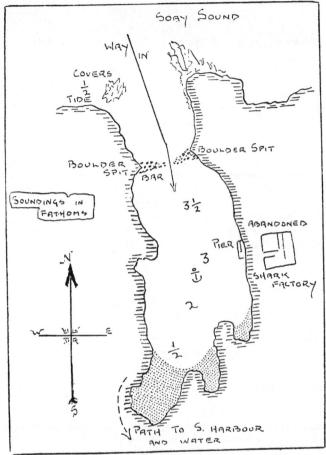

SOAY HARBOUR

channel about 50 ft. wide. This channel is actually a little to the eastward of the centre of the narrows but appears to the eye to be about the centre. There is about 1 ft. in it at L.W.O.S. and about 9 ft. at H.W. Np. Under some conditions the bar dries right off and retains water inside some 18 in. higher than outside, with a consequent fierce stream on last of ebb or early flood.

Entry should only be attempted, if without local knowledge, on a rising tide and towards H.W. Two sticks have been placed above shore on S. side about 1½ cables inside entrance. These in transit lead over the deepest part of bar. They should not be relied on owing to shifting of bar.

Once over the bar anchorage can be had anywhere in 2 to 3½ fath. down the centre line as far as about 1 cable S. of the pier beside the abandoned shark factory. This is a well sheltered natural harbour with good holding ground and not subject to swell (though at H.W. in strong N.W'lies a little lop finds its way in and in strong S'lies swell, reflected from Skye, comes in towards H.W.). The shore is generally steep except at extreme S. end where a mud bank dries out for about ¾ cable.

Stores—Nil. Calor Gas. Communications, Radio tel. **Water**—Nearest at burn flowing into S. harbour across island. The burn at N. harbour dries in spells of dry weather and is reported as not clean.

LOCH SLAPIN
Chart 2507

Loch Slapin branches off inland to the N.E. just round Straithaird Pt. After rounding Ru Heasgahn, which must be given a wide berth, the coast is clean for $2\frac{1}{2}$ miles, when Bogha Ailean, a rock with 7 ft. at L.W., lies 2 cables off the western shore. Between this rock and Ru Suisnish, the point on the E. side, is the entrance to Loch Slapin proper. The loch runs inland for 4 miles. On the W. side, a little beyond Bogha Ailean, there is a bay, Cille Marie, which dries out, and 1 mile beyond this there are some rocks lying 2 cables off a point on the same side. Either side of the loch may be safely kept aboard to this point, but on clearing these rocks, the W. side should be taken, as there are a number of dangers on the other side, just before the loch narrows, as it does $\frac{1}{2}$ mile further up.

Anchorage

The anchorage is just beyond the narrows, in 2 to 3 fath., on the western side, taking care not to go too far up, as the head dries out for $\frac{1}{2}$ mile at L.W. This anchorage is well sheltered, but if there is a swell from the southward, the scend comes right up to the head of the loch. On E. side the anchorage is in $2\frac{1}{2}$ fath., off schoolhouse, a house walled round and the furthest up on that side.

Stores—P.O. Tel. at Torrin, $\frac{1}{2}$ mile towards entrance on E. side. Mobile shop makes a short call at 2000. **Water**—At schoolhouse. Burn water is dirty.

LOCH EISHART
Chart 2507

Loch Eishart lies to the E. of Loch Slapin. It is about 5 miles in length, but about 2 miles within the entrance it narrows to $2\frac{1}{2}$ cables, and the passage is studded with rocks, many of which are below water. There is a passage through, about $\frac{1}{2}$ cable wide, almost in the centre of the narrows, but unless with local knowledge it is inadvisable to attempt it, particularly as there is no large-scale chart of this part. After passing the narrows, if the S. shore is kept aboard, there are no dangers to the head of the loch, a good portion of which dries out at L.W. Off the northern shore there are a number of outlying rocks off Heaste Island, which lies on the N. side, about 1 mile past the narrows.

Anchorages

Heaste Island (Chart 2507)—There is perfect shelter behind Heaste Island in 4 fath. Entering, one must keep the S. shore of the loch well aboard till the bay to the E. of the island is well open, and then round up into the anchorage.

Tocabhaig Bay (Chart 2507)—A small bay on the Sleat peninsula, 3 miles W. of the narrows of Loch Eishart. Eiln. Ruairidh, a small islet with an extensive L.W. mark, lies off the E. point of the bay, and there is a rock also off this point. The anchorage is in the middle of the bay in 5 fath. Exposed to N.W'ly winds.

PART VI

MAINLAND COAST

KYLE AKIN TO CAPE WRATH AND

LOCH ERIBOLL; WITH ADJACENT LOCHS

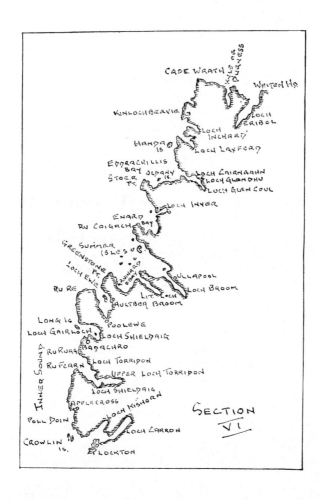

PART VI

Admiralty Charts

GROUP I   2721*   Ardnamurchan Pt. to St. Kilda
                  2720   St. Kilda to Cape Wrath
                  1954   Butt of Lewis to Noup Head

GROUP II   2551*   Isle of Skye, Northward of Sound of Sleat
                  1794   Rubha Hunish to Pt. of Stoer

GROUP III   2639   Lochs Carron and Kishorn
                  3564   Loch Kishorn and Approach to Loch Carron
                  2498*   Southern Parts of Sound of Raasay and Inner Sd.
                  2638   Lochs Torridon and Shieldaig
                  3441   Loch Gairloch
                  3146   Loch Ewe
                  2509   Red Pt. to Priest Island
                  2500   Approaches to L. Broom and Little L. Broom
                  3192   Loch Broom—Upper Portion
                  2501   Priest Island to L. Inver
                  1953   Loch Inver, incl. Lochs Roe and Kirkaig
                  2502   Eddrachilles Bay, including the Glens
                  2503   Lochs Laxford and Inchard and approaches
                  2076   Loch Eriboll
                           * Used in previous sections

CLYDE CRUISING CLUB SKETCH CHARTS

27   Outer Loch Carron, Strome Narrows
28   Loch Kishorn and Head of Inner Loch Carron
29   Outer Loch Torridon
30   Loch Shieldaig, Upper Loch Torridon
31   Head of Loch Gairloch
32   Summer Isles
46   Loch Ewe
47   Loch Broom
48   Loch Cairnbahn
49   Lochs Laxford and Inchard

KYLE AKIN TO LOCH EWE
Chart 2551

The passage from Kyle Akin to Loch Ewe is made by the Inner Sound.
The Inner Sound lies between the islands of Raasay and South Rona,
and the mainland of Scotland. It is about 5 or 6 miles wide and about
16 miles long. The flood tide sets S. down the sound and the ebb N.,
but at no great strength. A torpedo testing range is being established in
Inner Sound. **Const.** —4 hr. 36 m. Dover.

Rounding Kyle Akin Light and proceeding northwards by the Inner
Sound, a number of dangerous rocks lie to starboard, off Bleat Island, at
the southern side of the approach to Loch Carron. This island and the
shore should be given a wide berth. Kyle Akin Lt. shows red over these
dangers, and also over Black Eye and Bow Rocks, which lie to the southward of the channel leading from the Kyle. The lt. shows wht. over the
clear water.

Off the northern side of the entrance to Loch Carron, about 4 miles
N. of Kyle Akin, lie the three Crowlin Islands, which are close together
and practically form one island. On the N. end of this group there is a
wht. beacon showing a wht. fl. lt., bright 2 sec. ev. 6 sec., and a bad spit
which covers shortly after L.W. runs out here to the N.N.E. for over 3
cables.

The channel between the Crowlins and the mainland is about 1 mile
wide, and is clean towards the island side.

Crowlin Islands—There is good anchorage between Eiln. More and
Eiln. Meadhonach, the two southern islands. Coming from the N. or W.,
give a very wide berth to the spit running N. from Eiln. Beg until the
long straight channel W. of it is open. Steer for this channel, holding the
Eiln. More side until past H.W. mark on the other side and, in fine
weather, anchor in 2 or 3 fath. before the first narrows. Enter by N. end
of channel only.

In N'ly weather a vessel can move a further $2\frac{1}{2}$ cables into the channel
obtaining perfect shelter in a pool of 2 fath., just N. of a reef running out
from Eiln. Meadhonach. At half flood there is a least depth of 8 ft. in
the centre of the channel in the narrows. The bottom is sand and very
clear and the centre of the channel is clean as far as the pool. A fairly
strong current sets through channel and this can swing boat across the
wind.

Stores—None. **Water**—Restricted supplies only.

Cow Island lies off the mainland, a little further N., and it should be
given a fair berth all round. It can be passed on its inner side by keeping
the mainland aboard, but when abreast of the N. end, the mainland must
be given a wide berth to clear a bad spit running out.

The remainder of the Inner Sound is clear, none of the outlying rocks
being more than 3 cables off-shore.

On the N.E. end of South Rona there is a lighthouse showing a wht. fl.
lt. ev. 12 sec. Guanachan Rock lies almost 1 mile N.N.E. of the island and
is awash only at L.W. For the passage between Guanachan Rock and
South Rona, see Sound of Raasay.

Loch Torridon lies directly E. of South Rona, and from here for 17
miles to Ru Re, the W. point of the entrance to Loch Ewe, there are no
dangers to navigation.

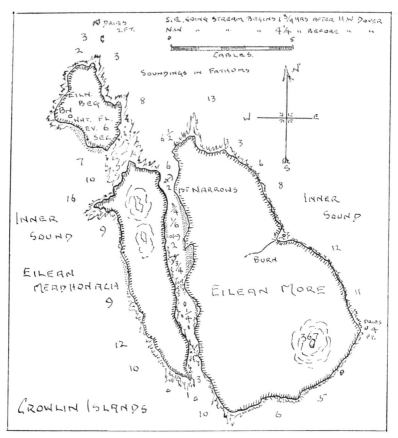

The whole coast N. of this is wild, and quite exposed to N'ly and W'ly winds, and should the weather be bad, the seas may be very heavy for a small yacht.

A lighthouse on Ru Re shows a wht. gp. fl. lt. 6 fl. of $\frac{3}{4}$ sec. each during 13 sec., eclipse 17 sec. during 30 sec., and the fog siren gives 4 blasts ev. $1\frac{1}{2}$ min.

The point of Ru Re is foul, and the tide runs about 3 knots Sp. off the headland. Heavy seas may be expected in strong adverse winds. The flood sets about N.E. and the ebb about W., starting 3 hr. after L.W. and H.W. by the shore.

LOCHS CARRON AND KISHORN
Charts 2639 and 3564. C.C.C.S.C. 27 and 28

Loch Carron lies immediately N. of Kyle Akin. Off Plock of Kyle, the southern shore of the entrance, it is very foul with rocks, round Bleat Island, and the whole shore on this side should be given a wide berth for 5 miles up, where the loch divides into Loch Kishorn to the N., and Inner Loch Carron to the S.

The navigation of Loch Kishorn presents no difficulty. The N. shore is clean, and on the S. after passing Kishorn Island which lies off the southern point of the entrance, the water is clear up to $\frac{1}{2}$ mile off the eastern end. Inside this distance, there are a number of rocks and shoal water.

In the N.E. corner of the loch there is a gut running inland for $1\frac{1}{4}$ miles. This gut completely dries out. Fool's Pt. is the E. point of the entrance to this inlet, and off it there runs a spit to the S.W. with a rock, showing 2 ft. above H.W., towards its outer end.

Some industrial expansion connected with North Sea oil is under consideration in area.

The entrance to Loch Carron proper is very foul with rocks and reefs. Off the Airde, which is the promontory which divides Loch Kishorn from Loch Carron, lie the Garra Isles, and around them a large number of reefs and islets. The outermost to the S. are Sgeir a Chinn and Sgeir Buidhe, both of which are above water, the former being 5 ft. high.

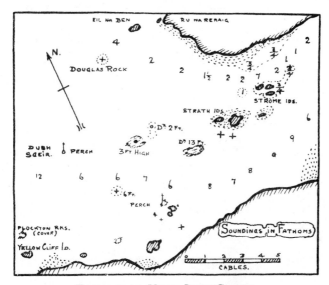

ENTRANCE TO UPPER LOCH CARRON

There is a clear channel of over 3 cables between these islets and Sgeir Golach, a bad patch of reefs which cover, and which lie $3\frac{1}{4}$ cables S. of Sgeir a Chinn. Between Sgeir Golach and the southern shore is Hawk Rock, also the Cat Islands, on one of which is a stone tower 35 ft. high, and other islets and rocks. One may enter either by the passage N. or the passage S. of Sgeir Golach. See sketch plan of Plockton.

If taking the northern passage, when Sgeir a Chinn and Sgeir Buidhe are picked up, keep towards them and pass S. of them, and when clear, steer for the Strome and Strath Islands, which lie at the entrance to Strome Narrows, leading into Upper Carron. The only danger taking this course is Douglas Rock with 6 ft. over it at L.W. It lies 2 cables W. of Eiln. na Ben, a small islet off Ru na Reraig on the N. side of the narrows, before coming to the Strath Isles.

Provided Hawk Rock is carefully guarded against, there are advantages in taking the southern passage. Keep midway between the Sgeir Golach beacon (which stands on the S.W. extremity of the patch) and the tower on Cat Island. The red buoy marking Hawk Rock is missing. The High Stone (nearly covers at H.W.) at S.E. end of Sgeir Golach patch in line with Sgeir Buidhe leads eastward of Hawk Rock.

PLOCKTON, LOCH CARRON
(Soundings in Fathoms)

On approaching the Strath Isles, the chart must be carefully consulted and the passage made 2 hr. after L.W. When there is sufficient water for a yacht of 9 ft. draft (see plan). The tide runs through the narrows at 2 knots Sp. **Const.** —4 hr. 27 m. Dover.

In the S. passage there is a deep water channel, available at all states of the tide, and leading to the S. of Strome and Strath Isles. This channel is wider and deeper than the northern one, and though encumbered with rocks, there are none which cannot be avoided given reasonable care and the help of detail chart 3564. From Cat Island steer for Dubh Sgeir beacon, then keep on the stone cairn (marked "perch" on plan) on Ullava. Pass within reasonable distance N. of Ullava, and keep slightly on the S. side of the channel to avoid several rocks, such as Sgeir na Clach (dries 13 ft.) which lie S. of Strath Islands (see plan).

The perches shown on the plan are liable to be washed away.

About ¾ mile above Strome Isles, the Strome Narrows begin, and for another ¾ mile the channel is not much over 2 cables wide. The narrows are fairly clean, if somewhere about mid-channel is taken.

Through the narrows, the shores of Upper Loch Carron are clean till near the head, when Slumbay peninsula runs out from the N. shore, and 4 cables E. of it. Broad Island lies in the middle of the loch. Long Island, which shoals out from both E. and W. ends, lies still further up, and the head of the loch shoals and dries out from a little beyond it.

Anchorages

Kishorn Island—There is splendid anchorage in 3 fath. behind Kishorn Island. Entering from the N. there are no dangers, if the island is given a moderate berth, and depths of from 2 to 5 fath. can be found anywhere between it and the shore.

Fools Point—In the bay to the E. of the reef off Fools Pt. in the N.E. corner of Loch Kishorn, good anchorage can be had in 3 fath., 1 cable off-shore.

Stores—Shop. P.O. Tel. **Water**—Burn.

There is also good anchorage in 3 to 4 fath. outside the shoal water in the S.E. corner of Loch Kishorn.

Plockton (see plan)—Plockton Harbour lies on the S. shore of Outer Loch Carron. To make the anchorage, take the passage N. or S. of Sgeir Golach, until the castle on the S. shore of the harbour, S. of Yellow Cliff Island which lies at the entrance to the harbour, shows midway between Cat Island tower and perch on Dubh Sgeir (see sketch). Hawk Rock, with 3 or 4 ft. over it at L.W. Sp., lies between Sgeir Golach and the shore. To the W. are Cat Isles, on one of which is a conspicuous stone tower. To clear Hawk Rock keep either E. or W. of a line joining the centre of Yellow Cliff Island and a waterfall on the shore behind (and above) it.

The lines of soundings on the plan show the course in. The rock shown off Ard Vourar is uncharted, and the perch on Plockton Rocks is carried away.

The anchorage is in line between Yellow Cliff Island and Eiln. nan Gamhainn, which lies up the harbour, but keep well over towards Yellow Cliff, as it is very shoal on the other side, and also inside of this line. Sp. $16\frac{3}{4}$ ft., Np. $11\frac{3}{4}$ ft.

Stores—Shops. P.O. Tel. Hotels. Petrol. Calor Gas. **Water**—Numerous public taps. Train connections to Kyle and Inverness. Air landing strip.

Slumbay Harbour and Jeantown—There is excellent anchorage in 2 fath. behind Slumbay peninsula, but the point must be given a berth of 1 cable as a spit runs out from it. One and a half cables from Broad Island, towards this point, is Red Rock, awash, which must be also cleared, and the anchorage is well off the pier. Great care must be taken not to go too far in as the shore is very shoal for fully 1 cable out, and an extensive flat dries off the N.E. side. The channel between Slumbay peninsula and Sgeir Chreagach (Broad Island) is reported to have shoaled considerably (see Chart 2639).

Jeantown lies further up on the N. side, inside of Long Island, and, if anchoring off the village here, the chart is the only guide to avoid the shoals off-shore and around the island.

Stores—Shops. P.O. Tel. Hotel. Calor Gas. **Water**—At pier.

Anchorages in Inner Sound
Chart 2498

Loch Toscaig—Just N. of Crowlin Islands. This loch is too deep for convenient anchorage, and it is exposed to southward.

There is a bad rock, Bo Du, which dries 3 ft. at L.W., lying $2\frac{1}{2}$ cables S.W. of the W'ly point of the loch.

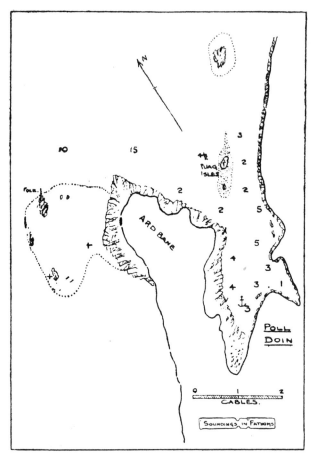

POLL DOIN

Poll Doin (see plan)—About 1 mile N. of Cow Island. The entrance is N. of Ard Bane on which is a conspicuous patch of white sand S. of some cottages. Coming from the N. or S., give the mainland a berth of ½ mile till roughly N.W. of the entrance, then steer for Ruag Isles, a long drying reef with two heads above H.W., lying close to the mainland and forming the E. side of the entrance, i.e., keep 1 cable off Ard Bane until the position is clear, then steer S. into the anchorage. Do not anchor too near the head as there is a steep-to reef. Drying rocks (the pole shown in sketch plan is missing) extend over 2 cables W. of Ard Bane, and to the N., Eiln. nan Naomh is very foul. The channel E. of Ruag Isles is not recommended as a rock (dries 9 ft.) lies E. of them nearly in the fairway.

An excellent anchorage even in N'ly winds. Sp. 15 ft., Np. 11 ft.

Poll Creadha—One mile N. of Poll Doin and at the S. side of Applecross Bay. The entrance is very foul with rocks. The nine poles shown on the chart cannot be relied upon, but two B. and W. poles near the shore at the southern end, kept in line, lead straight in clear of all dangers. Good local knowledge is required for this anchorage.

Applecross Bay—Five miles N. of Crowlin Islands. A wide open bight, much exposed and very shoal at the head. Only temporary anchorage.

Ob Chuaig (Chart 2638. C.C.C.S.C. 29)—A bay just S. of the entrance to Loch Torridon. A small islet lies in the centre of the entrance, and a rock which dries 4 ft. at L.W. lies N.E. of this. The islet is steep-to on its S. end. The head of the bay shoals, and there are two rocks, one of which dries at L.W. at the head of the bay, and one 2 ft. below L.W. off the S. point of the bay. Ob na Uag lies just N. of Ob Chuaig, but there are two rocks in it; and Murdoch Breac, a dangerous rock, lies off the approach (see under Loch Torridon). Both of these bays are much exposed to the N. and are only very temporary anchorages.

LOCH TORRIDON
Charts 2551 and 2638. C.C.C.S.C. 29 and 30

The entrance to Loch Torridon is about 3 miles wide, and lies between Ru Ruag on the N. and Ru Fearn on the S.

Murdoch Breac, a rock which dries 3 ft. at L.W., lies 3 cables off-shore to the W. of Ru na Uag and is the only danger in entering from the S. It must be carefully guarded against as it lies further out than one would think. Sgeir na Trian, a small islet 7 ft. above H.W., lies $1\frac{1}{2}$ miles S. of Ru Ruag and should not be approached too closely.

Loch Torridon is very clean and chart 2551 is all that is necessary.

At Diabaig Pt., about 5 miles further up, on the N. shore, the loch narrows to $\frac{1}{2}$ mile, and $1\frac{1}{2}$ miles further on are the narrows of the entrance to Upper Loch Torridon (which see).

Past Diabaig Pt., Loch Shieldaig branches off to the S. for about 3 miles. **Const.** —4 hr. 26 m. Dover.

Anchorages

Loch Creagach, or Craig—On the S. shore, 3 miles from the entrance to Loch Torridon.

By keeping a reasonable distance off-shore, there are no dangers till close to the bay. A submerged rock about 1 cable off an island $\frac{1}{4}$ mile W. of the bay, and some outlying rocks off the western point on entering, are the only dangers, and they are easily avoided. Keep well off this point, and turn into the bay and anchor fairly well in-shore in the N.W. corner, in 5 to 6 fath., off the four or five houses of Kenmore village.

Ru Ruag, the N. point of entrance to Loch Torridon just open to eastward of Sgeir na Train astern leads directly to this anchorage.

There is a small waterfall running into the bay at its head. A splendidly sheltered anchorage and good holding ground.

Stores—Telephone at cottages. **Water**—At burn. Sp. 17 ft., Np. 12 ft.

Loch Beg—To W. of isthmus leading to Ardheslaig. The entrance is 3 cables wide but narrows to 1 cable. Hold down to S. shore in outer portion to avoid a rock (dries 3 ft.) which lies a cable N. (mag.) of the eastern point of the entrance to narrower portion. At the head there is a rocky beach, with rocks on the W. side. Anchor well up in $1\frac{1}{2}$ to 2 fath. Rather exposed to N. otherwise well sheltered, but bottom is reported as being very thick seaweed.

Stores—None.

Loch Shieldaig—Entering the loch, keep well clear of Ru Ardheslaig, the W. point of the entrance, as there are some submerged rocks lying well off-shore to the W. of it. Also keep off the W. side of the loch after entering.

Shieldaig Island lies near the head, and should be given a wide berth on its N. end. Between this point of the island and Shieldaig village there is a gut with good anchorage in 2 fath., towards the island side, but do not go too far in, as it shoals badly.

Off the village, at the S. end of the island, the water is deep until close in-shore, but fair anchorage in 5 fath. can be got here.

The best anchorage for yachts of up to moderate size is in a small bay on the W. side of the loch about opposite Shieldaig Island. It is just to the W. of the bay that forms the head of the loch. In making the approach, the E. point of the bay must be given a good berth as a shoal runs N. and W. from its extremity. Hold over to the W. shore and anchor in 2 fath., just to the southward of the cottage that stands above the shore. The head of the loch dries out for about 2 cables. To port, below a cliff cut to make a road, there is a rock which dries 8 ft.

Stores—Shops. P.O. Tel. **Water**—Hydrant near head of stone jetty. Sp. 17 ft., Np. 12 ft.

Upper Loch Torridon—The narrows at the entrance are under 2 cables wide, and the tide sets through at 3 knots Sp. **Const.** —4 hr. 26 m. Dover.

The loch is clean, except for the shoal water at the head, which extends out for about $\frac{1}{2}$ mile, and some outlying rocks on the S. side just within the entrance. The anchorage is in 2 to 3 fath., mud, near the head of the loch off a boathouse and slip W. of hotel. The small shallow bay containing slipway is reported fouled by metal posts (covered) making approach dangerous for dinghies.

Diabaig Bay—Behind Diabaig Pt. on the N. side of the loch. A fairly clean bay, but not recommended, as the water is deep, and it is exposed to the W.

Ru Ruag—There is a bay behind Ru Ruag, shoal at its head, which affords good temporary anchorage in N'ly winds, but is quite impossible in S'ly winds. There is an islet, Sgeir Ghlas, with reefs off its W. side, which must be given a wide berth, and the anchorage is in 2 to 3 fath. between this and Ru Ruag.

LOCH GAIRLOCH (Ross-shire)
Charts 2551, 2509 and 3441. C.C.C.S.C. 31

Gairloch lies 5 miles N. of Loch Torridon. Long Island lies off the N. point of the entrance, leaving a channel between it and the N. shore of $\frac{1}{2}$ mile, but this is contracted to under 3 cables by shoal water on both sides. Mid-channel should be taken if using this passage.

The entrance is about 3 miles wide, and the loch runs inland for $3\frac{1}{2}$ miles. At its head it divides into three branches, Flowerdale Bay, Loch Kerry, and Loch Shieldaig. Loch Kerry, the middle branch, is a poor anchorage. The holding ground is good, but a bad scend sets into the loch during and after W'ly winds, and there is a submerged rock in the centre of the entrance.

The shores of Gairloch are fairly clean, except in Loch Shieldaig. Glas Eilean, a small island clean all round, lies about the centre of the fairway when the loch begins to narrow. A beacon on it shows a red fl. ev. 6 sec. **Const.** —4 hr. 26 m. Dover.

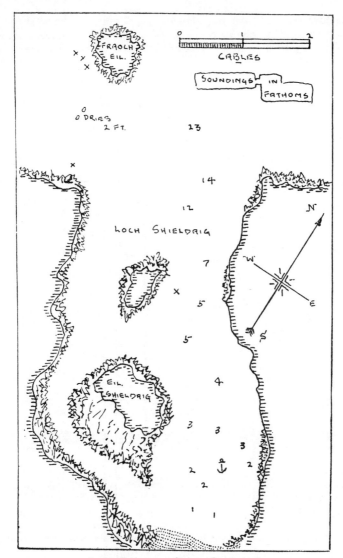

LOCH SHIELDAIG (LOCH GAIRLOCH)

Anchorages

Flowerdale Bay—The northern branch at the head of the loch. The bay is clean, and the anchorage is in 3 fath., mud, in the centre of the bay, not further up than the outer end of the pier. The bay shoals badly further in, off the burn at the head.

Stores—P.O. Tel. Garage at bridge. Butcher and good general store at crossroads 1 mile past hotel. Hotel, ¾ mile W. of bay. **Water**—Tap on shed, inner end of pier. Sp. 14 ft., Np. 10 ft.

Loch Shieldaig (see plan)—The southern branch at the head of the loch. A splendid anchorage in 3 to 4 fath., behind the islets in this loch. The plan shows all the dangers better than any description. **Water**—At hotel.

Some fishing boats' moorings have been laid in this anchorage with heavy chains running to Eiln. Shieldaig.

Badachro (see plan)—Behind Horrisdale Island, on the S. shore of the Gairloch. Access by channels either W. or S. of Horrisdale Island, but the latter only with local knowledge. Perfectly sheltered from all winds, but the entrance is less than 1 cable wide at L.W. Passing in, keep towards the pier on the island, to clear the rock off-shore on the opposite side, and anchor beside the fishing boats in 3 fath. Anchorage in $1\frac{1}{2}$ fath. can also be had inside the perch about where the "P" of PERCH is in the plan, or at swinging room off the largest island due W. of the "P". The bay shoals out further than shown in the plan and the whole bay between jetty and S. end of biggest island is shoal.

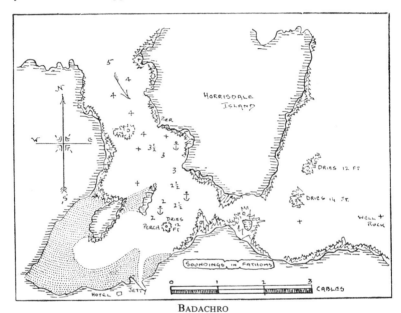

BADACHRO

There are two moorings laid in the bay and a heavy chain is reported to stretch from the more E'ly of them to the more E'ly of the two islands in the bay. A rock with $5\frac{1}{2}$ ft. on it at L.W. is reported in a position about 60 ft. E.S.E. from the N. point of that same island. Fishing boats are liable to come in to take up above mentioned moorings during the night.

Stores—Shops. P.O. Tel., $\frac{1}{4}$ mile up hill. Inn. Petrol at Port Henderson, 1 mile. **Water**—At inn.

LOCH EWE
Charts 2509 and 3146. C.C.C.S.C. 46

From the lighthouse at Ru Re (see Kyle Akin to Loch Ewe) 8 miles above Loch Gairloch, the coast trends eastward for 4 miles to the entrance to Loch Ewe, and by keeping a reasonable distance off-shore, there are no dangers. The entrance to Loch Ewe is about 1 mile wide, and the loch runs to the S. for about 7 miles. The shores are free from outlying dangers. Ewe Island, and the two small islets, Sgeir an Araig, $\frac{1}{2}$ mile N.W. of it, lie in the centre of the loch, 2 miles up, and can be passed on either side, keeping near mid-channel if using the eastern passage.

There are several unlit mooring buoys established in this loch.

A mile and a half past the S. end of the Ewe Island, the loch divides into two branches, Loch Thurnaig to the E. and Poolewe Bay to the W. **Const.** —4 hr. 25 m. Dover.

The Boom Defence pier near the entrance to the loch (E. side), with convenient anchorage off it in 3 fath., offers good facilities for watering. The Admiralty have built a new pier in the vicinity with, off it, four mooring dolphins. A channel marked by lit buoys leads E. of Ewe Island.

Anchorages

Poolewe Bay—Entering Poolewe Bay, there is only one danger, Boor Rock, which lies off the W. shore, about halfway up. It is 9 ft. above H.W. but has sunken rocks running out for 1 cable off both its N. and S. ends. The anchorage is in 2 to 3 fath., mud, not more than ½ mile past this rock. Be very careful not to go further up than this, as the head of the bay shoals out for a considerable distance, and the rise and fall at Sp. is 15 ft. Anchor off the first white house on starboard hand going up.

Stores—Shops. P.O. Hotel. Petrol. **Water**—Burn. Sp. 15 ft., Np. 11 ft.

Loch Thurnaig—This is a fairly clean loch, about ½ mile long, with a small cove in the S.W. corner, where there is perfect shelter, with limited swinging room, and a depth of 2½ fath., but there is good enough anchorage, though fairly deep, elsewhere in the loch. Coming in hold to the S. shore of cove as there are three reefs (all of which cover) which extend from the N. shore and reach more than halfway across loch.

Gavenn Point—There is a good anchorage in W. winds to the N. of this point, which is easily recognised as it rises in two steep summits.

Aultbea—On the E. side of the loch, behind Ewe Island. This bay is very shoal, and the anchorage is in the middle of the bay in 5 fath., in line between the pier and the hotel. Do not go in further than this. Outside this line, and to the S. of the hotel, there is also good anchorage in 3 fath.

Stores—Shop. P.O. Tel. Hotel. Petrol. Butcher twice a week. **Water**—At hotel.

Camus Angus—In S.W. winds, Aultbea anchorage is very exposed and splendid shelter and holding ground can be had in the bay nearest to N.E. point of Ewe Island, on the E. side of this island. There is a rock off the S. point of this bay, and the anchorage is in 3½ fath., within 1 cable of the shore.

LOCH EWE TO RU COIGACH
Charts 2509, 2500 and 2501

Between Greenstone Pt., which is the eastern headland of the entrance to Loch Ewe, and Ru Coigach, a headland 12 miles to the N.E., there is a deep indentation containing Gruinard Bay, Little Loch Broom and Loch Broom, and towards the N. side, a group of some thirty islands and islets known as the Summer Isles.

Priest Island, the S.W. island of this group, is 250 ft. high and clean all round.

Taking the southern shore of this indentation, and coming in from the W., round Greenstone Pt., the first inlet is Gruinard Bay. **Const.** —4 hr. 21 m. Dover.

GRUINARD BAY
Charts 2509 and 2500

The entrance is 4 miles across, and the bay runs in for 3 miles. Towards the eastern side lies Gruinard Island, **landing upon which is prohibited as it is dangerously contaminated.**

Rudha Beg is the W'ly horn of the bay, and the second bay past this point must be given a good offing, as Carr Rocks, which dry 11 ft., lie 2 cables off-shore. Two miles further in is Laid Bay, which gives temporary shelter in winds from W. to S.E., in 3 fath., rocky bottom, well off-shore. A rock, which is awash at L.W.O.S., lies off the E. point of this bay.

Stores—Small shop. P.O. Tel. at crossroads, $\frac{3}{4}$ mile inland. **Water**—Burn.

Rounding Gruinard Island, there are some rocks off its E. side which require to be watched, and also Stirk Rocks, over 1 cable off the N. end which are awash only at L.W.

The bottom all round the island is rocky, and not very suitable for anchorage. The shore on the E. side of the bay should be given a fair berth up to Stattic Pt., the E. horn of the bay and the S. side of the entrance to Little Loch Broom.

LITTLE LOCH BROOM
Chart 2500

The entrance is between Stattic Pt. on the S.W. and Cailleach Head on the N.E. about $1\frac{1}{2}$ miles across. On Cailleach Head an unwatched beacon with lt. showing a gp. (2) fl. wht. lt. ev. 12 sec. has been established.

Ardross Rock, which only shows at exceptionally low tides, lies in the entrance, 4 cables E. of Stattic Pt. and it can be passed on either side. The loch runs inland to the S.E. for $7\frac{1}{2}$ miles, and has no outlying dangers, but is noted for its fierce squalls, and is locally known as "The Loch of a Hundred Winds". The head of the loch dries out for 7 cables.

Anchorage

Camus na Gal—This bay lies on the S. shore, round the last point before reaching the head of the loch. There are four houses on this point, and further up, a war memorial. Anchor in 4 fath., fairly well in-shore. Sp. $14\frac{1}{2}$ ft., Np. $10\frac{1}{2}$ ft.

Stores—Shop. P.O. Tel. 2 miles and hotel at Dundonnell, $1\frac{3}{4}$ miles up the loch. Petrol. Calor Gas. **Water**—At burn.

LOCH BROOM
Charts 2500 and 3192. C.C.C.S.C. 47

Approaching from Cailleach Head, the N.E. point of the entrance to Little Loch Broom, the first headland is Carn Dearg, which lies $1\frac{1}{2}$ miles to the E. One cable off this point lies Iolla Dearg, a rock which shows 2 ft. above H.W.O.S. It should be given a fair berth. Between this and the entrance to Loch Broom, there is a wide open bight, Annat Bay. The shores of this bight are clear and there is one bay, Camus Fheoir, on the W. side, which affords temporary anchorage in 4 fath., 1 cable off-shore.

The entrance to Loch Broom is about 4 miles further E. and is 7 cables wide. The loch runs in a S.E. direction for 8 miles inland. The W. side of it is perfectly clean, but on the E. side, $2\frac{1}{2}$ miles from the entrance, Ullapool Pt. juts out, and off Ullapool River on the N. side of this point there is an extensive flat which dries out for over 2 cables at L.W. A red, wht. and green unwatched, sectored light beacon 29 ft. high, showing a 1 sec. fl. ev. 6 sec., has been established on Rudha Cadail at E. side of entrance to loch. Coming from W. it shows white over the fairways N. and S. of the Carn Skerries lying N. of Carn Dearg, and over Isle Martin in Loch Kanaird. It shows green over Carn Skerries and red over Horse Island and the reefs off it, over Horse Sound, and the waters between Horse Sound and Martin Island, over Iolla Dearg and Annat Bay, and over the W. half of Loch Broom as far down as Ullapool. White down the centre of the loch as far as Ullapool and green over the eastern side of the loch and over the flats above mentioned. It cannot be seen from anywhere E. of Isle Martin. There is a fixed green lt. on Ullapool Pt. and, about 4 cables W.N.W. of it, a red can buoy showing a quick fl. red. lt.

One and a half miles past Ullapool, the loch narrows to 2 cables, but both shores are clean, and there are no dangers till the head, which dries out for about 1 mile. The tide runs about 2 knots Sp. in the narrows. **Const.** —4 hr. 21 m. Dover.

Anchorages

Ullapool—Behind Ullapool Pt. there is a wide bay, affording good shelter in 3 to 4 fath., off the pier and a little beyond it. The pier is being extended and two dolphins built all to S. of it.

Stores—Shops. P.O. Tel. Hotel. Petrol. Calor Gas. Half-holiday—Tuesdays. **Water**—Hydrant at pier. Sp. $14\frac{1}{2}$ ft., Np. $10\frac{1}{2}$ ft.

Port Young—There is splendid anchorage in 3 fath., in a little bay on the W. shore, just through the narrows. There is a ruined house above this bay, on a bright grassy point.

LOCH KANAIRD
Chart 2500

Just N.E. of the entrance to Loch Broom lies Isle Martin and, between it and the E. shore, lies Loch Kanaird. The southern entrance is contracted $4\frac{1}{2}$ cables to 1 cable by a spit which runs out $2\frac{1}{2}$ cables from the shore, and another which runs out 1 cable from the S. point of the island. The entrance by the N. of the island is quite clean. There is splendid shelter in this loch, the bay on the E. side of Isle Martin being clean outside of 1 cable off-shore. On the shore-side, the bay is clean on its N. side, but the E. side is very shoal and there are reefs off the S. side There is an inset plan of this loch on chart sheet 2500.

THE SUMMER ISLES
Chart 2501. C.C.C.S.C. 32

A description of all the Summer Isles would only confuse, but with the chart quoted the navigation of the channels between the islands should present no difficulty.

There are several anchorages, but in most cases the approaches are intricate and it will be sufficient to describe the three best ones and the approaches to them.

Tanera More (see plan)—This anchorage is on the E. side of Tanera More, the largest of the Summer Isles, and is the best in the whole group.

Risdale (or Ristol) Island and Eilean Mullagrach lie to the W. of the
northern horn of the bight which contains the Summer Isles, and form
with the mainland the northern side of the approach from the N.W. The
southern shores of these islands and of the mainland are clean and can be
kept well aboard.

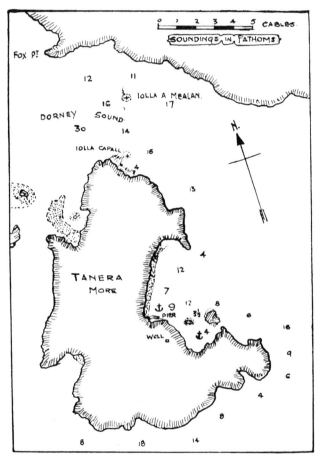

TANERA MORE ANCHORAGE

The Tanera group, which consists of about a dozen islands and islets,
lies to the S. Glasleac More is the NW. island and Tanera More the
most E'ly of the group, and the N. ends of these two islands in line form
the southern limit of a clear channel of about ½ mile wide.

Keeping in this channel, there are no dangers till coming to Dorny
Sound which is between Tanera More and the northern mainland. Iolla a
Mealan, a dangerous rock which is awash at L.W., lies in the sound,
2½ cables off the mainland and 3½ cables off the N. end of Tanera More.
The mainland can be kept close aboard if passing to the N. of this rock,
but if passing to the S. give the N. end of Tanera More a berth of 1½
cables, as Iolla Capall, a rock which dries 6 ft., lies off this point (see
plan). From here round to the bay on the E. side of the island the shores
are clean.

Coming to the anchorage from the W. and passing to the S. of Tanera More, the shores of this island and also of Tanera Beg, which lies to the W., are clean, and all dangers round to the anchorage are above water.

Approaching the anchorage from the S., round Greenstone Pt., make for the channel just mentioned, by passing between Priest Island and Glasleac Beg, which lies about 1 mile N.N.E. of it.

The shores of both these islands are free from outlying dangers, but keep well clear of Angus Stack, an islet which lies 1½ miles E. of Glasleac Beg and 8 cables S.W. of Tanera Beg, as it has rocks 4 ft. below L.W., lying 3 cables off its western side.

It is advisable to have chart 2501 if using the other channels.

The main anchorage in the bay, which is clean, is in 5 fath. off the old fish-curing house and its ruined stone pier.

There is a perfectly sheltered nook, locally known as "The Cabbage Garden", in the S. corner of the bay, in 4 fath., behind two islets there. The passage is in mid-channel between these two islets.

It is reported that in strong N.N.E. winds this anchorage can be un-comfortable and perfect shelter can then be found in N.E. corner of main bay.

Stores—None. **Water**—At well. Sp. 14 ft., Np. 10½ ft.

Tanera Beg—Approaching from the N. by the channel described under Tanera More (para. 4) identify Skeir na Feusgan, a rocky islet 250 yd. long lying 5 cables W. of the N. end of Tanera More. The islet is con-tinued S. by Skeir Glas and drying reefs to Eiln. Fada More, a big island 115 ft. high; and between the line of islands and rocks thus formed and Tanera More runs a channel widening to open water to southward whereas the channel W. of the line is blocked by Tanera Beg, 262 ft. high. Turn S. out of the approach channel and proceed down W. side of Skeir na Feusgan, and succeeding islands. A drying rock lies 100 yd. W. of the highest point, a cliff, on Eiln. Fada More and the island shore should be held until past the rocky islets lying off it. South of islets and between Eiln. Fada More and Tanera Beg is a clean pool, 6 fath. deep and nearly 2 cables across, which is suitable anchorage for large yachts, but small vessels should keep on S. then E. round Eiln. Fada More anchoring almost immediately after the turn to E. in 2½ fath.

Coming from S.W., follow directions as for Tanera More until past Angus Stack, a remarkable long jagged rock, 80 ft. high, then head into gap between Tanera More and Beg, holding the latter well aboard right up to the anchorage described above. The entrance lies between Tanera Beg and Eiln. Fada More, but a sandbank, least depth 3 ft., extends across mouth, and there are two rocks, both covering at half flood; one is close to Eiln. Fada More, nearly 1 cable N. from entrance, but the other lies slightly W. of mid-channel at the very entrance. The ideal time to enter is about 2 hr. flood when both rocks still show. Soon after the entrance the shore of Tanera Beg trends to the W. and, following it, the anchorage described above is reached.

Stores—None.

Risdale (or Ristol) Island—Splendid shelter can be found in the lagoon between Risdale Island and the mainland. Entrance must be made from the S. as N. entrance dries out. The S. entrance is narrowed by a spur projecting from the mainland shore and a point on the island. Anchor in the centre of lagoon in 3 fath. The bay on Risdale immediately through the narrows dries out as do the N. entrance and the bay on the mainland N. of lagoon. Land at jetty at entrance to this last named bay.

RU COIGACH TO RU STOER
Charts 2501 and 1794

Leaving the Summer Isles and passing northwards, the coast should be given a fair berth up to Ru Coigach, which lies about 4 miles further on. This is the S. point of another indentation which contains Enard Bay and Loch Inver. It also contains several other small lochs and bays, but a swell usually sets in from the W., making many of them uncomfortable. The best shelter is in Loch Inver.

The northern headland of this bight, about 8 miles across, is Ru Stoer. Close in-shore, off the N. end of this headland, there stands a remarkable isolated pillar of rock. On South Ear, the southern point of the headland, there is a lighthouse which shows a wht. occ. lt. bright 30 sec., eclipsed 15 sec. Storm signals.

In strong winds, when the tide is contrary, the seas off Ru Stoer are very heavy. **Const.** —4 hr. 18 m. Dover. The stream turns 3 hr. before and after H.W. and L.W. by the shore, flood setting N.E. and ebb S.

Lochan Salainn—Good shelter free from swell can be found in Lochan Salainn on the E. shore of Enard Bay. The approach should be made from the N. keeping midway between the mainland and the chain of islets (Grey Is.) lying to W. Anchor in 3 fath. in centre of pool. There is a rock to be watched off the E. shore of the lochan a little N. of centre.

LOCH INVER
Chart 1953 (see sketch plan)

Rounding Ru Coigach, the position of Loch Inver is easily picked out by the mountain Suilven, which is S. of it. This mountain has an unmistakable "sugar loaf" shape. On approaching Loch Inver, Clette Island lies about $1\frac{1}{2}$ miles off-shore, and should be given a fair berth, particularly on its E. side, where rocks extend for about 1 cable. About 1 mile N.E. of Clette Island lies Soya Island, with some rocks off its E. end, and between it and the northern shore, a red perch marks foul ground.

The entrance to Loch Inver is between Soya Island and Kirkaig Pt., which is on the mainland, $\frac{1}{2}$ mile to the S.E. The southern shore of Soya is fairly clean, but there is a rock about 50 yd. off Kirkaig Pt., drying 4 ft. at L.W.

Leave Soya Island and the red perch to port, going up, and also a small islet off the northern shore, 1 mile further up, as sunken rocks extend $\frac{3}{4}$ cable off its N. point.

On this islet a concrete pillar carries a W., R. and G. sectored lt., 1 fl. ev. 3 sec. W. from 103° to 111°; R. from 111° to 243°; W. from 243° to 251°; R. from 251° to 071°; W. from 071° to 080°; G. from 080° to 103° Bearings true from seaward. White over fairways.

At the head of the loch, a point juts out from the S. shore, forming a bay behind it, at the head of which is a small stone pier. On this point there is a blk. perch, marking a rock, which must be left to starboard, and the anchorage is in 3 fath. in the middle of the bay off the pier. The N.E. side of the bay is shoal. Perfectly sheltered from all winds.

Stores—Shops. P.O. Tel. on N.E. side of bay. Hotel at pier. Calor Gas.
Water—Tap beside hotel. Key at hotel. Sp. 15 ft., Np. $10\frac{3}{4}$ ft.

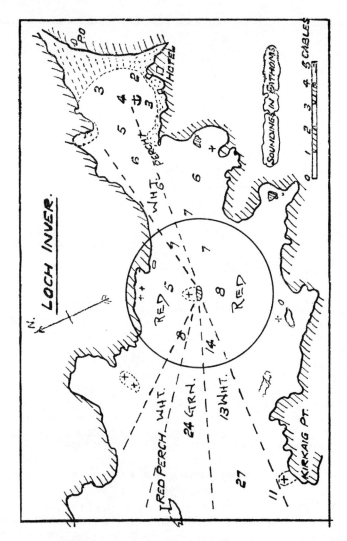

Good anchorage, though possible subject to swell in strong N.W'lies, can be found behind Eiln. Bad nam Ban, the islet in the E. end of the bay E. of Kirkaig promontory. Entry can be made by passing either N. or S. of Bo an Tairbh (the skerries off the W. end of the same bay) keeping mid-channel in the latter case, and by either E. or W. of Bad nam Ban, keeping mid-channel in both cases. There is a minimum depth of 8 ft. at L.W. in the E. channel, the more shallow one, the one between Bad nam Ban and Sgeir Buidhe to the E. of it.

LOCH ROE
Chart 1953

Loch Roe is a small loch, about 2 miles N.W. of beacon at entrance to Loch Inver.

The approach by the S. shore is fairly clear up to the entrance which is contracted to $\frac{1}{2}$ cable by a point jutting out from the S. shore. This

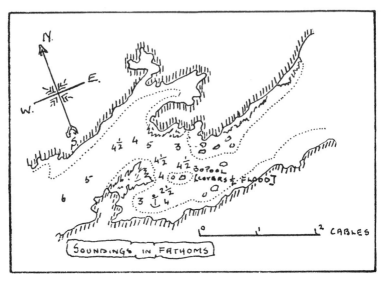

POOL BAY ANCHORAGE, LOCH ROE

point continues in a N.E'ly direction as two islets (tidal) with reefs running eastwards from them for 20 or 30 yd. About 45 yd. E. of the S.E. end of these reefs is an isolated reef about 50 yd. in length. The western end of this reef is awash at L.W.O.S. and the eastern end (Bo Pool) dries 5 ft. About 80 yd. E.N.E. of this reef is a rock close to the N. shore which dries 4½ ft. and has foul ground between it and the shore. The channels each side of the central reef have depths of 3 to 4 fath.

The anchorage is in the small sheltered bay S. of the two tidal islets, in depths of 2 to 4 fath. The mainland side is deep right up to the cliffs, and the stony beach shown on Chart 1953 does not exist.

EDDRACHILLES BAY
Chart 2502

Rounding Ru Stoer, the land falls away to the eastward, forming a large indentation called Eddrachilles Bay. At the northern end of it is Handa Island, which lies 8½ miles N.E. by E. from Ru Stoer. From the centre of this bight, Loch Cairnbahn runs inland for some 6 miles.

Close to the S. shore of this bight, 4½ miles E.S.E. of Ru Stoer, lies Oldany Island, and about 4 miles further on, in the same direction is the entrance to Loch Cairnbahn.

Two miles N.E. by E. of Oldany lie two islands, Meall Mor and Meall Beg, and inside of a line between the W. side of Handa Island, there are a number of dangerous rocks and islets known as the Badcall Islands. Keep outside of this line, and on approaching Handa Island, care must be taken to clear Bo More, two rocks which cover and which lie 2 cables S.W. of Handa. **Const.** —4 hr. 18 m. Dover.

There are many snug anchorages, though some are subject to swell in heavy weather, N. of the entrance to Loch Cairnbahn and also along the southern shore E. of Oldany Island. These can be made with little difficulty with the aid of Chart 2502. The best approach to the Badcall Bay anchorage is by the south channel.

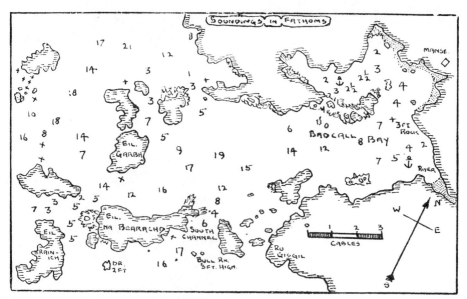

BADCALL BAY ANCHORAGE

Van calls at anchorage on Fridays and at Scourie (2 miles to N.) there is a P.O., hotel, shops (half-holiday—Wednesdays) and bus to Lairg.

In the sketch plan of Badcall Bay anchorage, the reef between the 3 and 4 fath. soundings in the top right-hand corner is an island about 30 ft. high.

Culkein Drumbeg (Chart 2502)—A sheltered anchorage lying about 1 mile S.E. of Oldany Island.

Care is needed making approach as entrance is hidden at L.W. by rocky outcrops. To assist identification a white mark has been painted on the seaward side of island lying immediately to W. of entrance (see plan).

Great care should be taken to avoid the two rocks which lie to seaward. These rocks are only visible at L.W. Sp. but breaking waves **may** indicate their position.

It is recommended that first visit be made at L.W. when dangers from rocks in entry can be clearly seen.

Entry should not be attempted if a N'ly swell is running.

On passing Oldany Island coming from W., steer for the white mark mentioned above (160 mag.) then alter course to port and steer 130° (mag.) for the S. tip of N.E'ly island. Once clear of the seaward rocks alter course to starboard to make for the white transit marks which lead through entrance channel. On passing the rock outcrops to port, a sharp turn must be made to port to line up on the second set of white transit marks which lie at far end of bay. Anchor in open section of bay (sand and kelp) but care is needed to avoid rock (visible at L.W.) in centre of bay.

Note—It is reported that very thick seaweed in entrance channel may cause a false reading on echo sounder and the white marks on the island and the mainland at the W. end of the anchorage are barely discernible.

Stores—At Drumbeg, 2 miles.

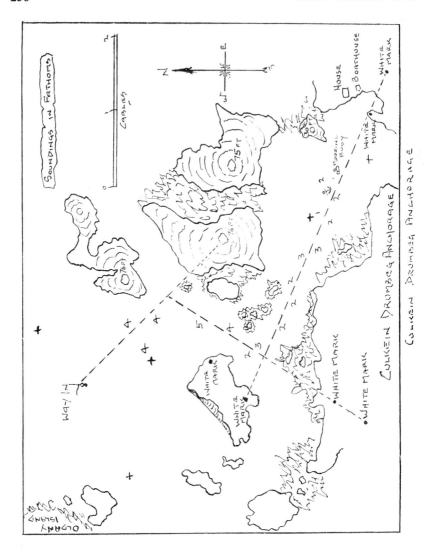

Loch Drumbeg—A very good anchorage and handy for stores etc., lying about 1½ miles from the N. tip of Oldany Island. Coming from the W. care is needed to identify the entrance, but just 1½ miles E. of the tip of Oldany (¾ mile E. of island lying off Oldany's N.E. corner) is a prominent yellow-green rocky islet (67 ft.) S. of which on the mainland is a grassy headland (191 ft.) higher than any island. Turn S.E. round N. end of islet and make for a bold black rock about 30 ft. high lying just E. of the headland. On approach this rock will prove to be two rocks close together. Pass close E. of them and keep to mainland (W.) side of channel till past the next (50 ft.) to port, then steer straight on S.S.E. to the end of the visible channel, anchoring in 2 to 3 fath. This spot is a little exposed to the N.W., but shelter can be obtained by small yachts in a 7 ft. at L.W. channel running E. along the mainland shore in 7 to 10 ft. Approaching from the E. the most E'ly islet off the loch is Sgeir Liath (75 ft.). Pass E. and S. of this islet keeping well off mainland shore then head S.W. for the 7 ft. channel mentioned above between a bold island and the mainland keeping to the island side of mid-channel. There are dangerous rocks lying W. (2 cables), S.W. (1½ cables), and N. (1 cable) of Sgeir Liath.

Stores—Shop. P.O. Tel. Hotel. Half-holiday—Wednesdays. **Water**—At taps.

Loch Nedd (see plan)—This loch lies 1½ miles S.W. of Ru Fiasin outside of Loch Cairnbahn and on the S. shore. Keep well off the S. shore coming in from the W., and stand towards Ru Male, the E'ly point of the entrance, until the loch opens out.

From seaward, houses will be seen on the side of the hill above the entrance to the anchorage, which helps as a landmark. Keep well to the E. side of the loch on entering, as there are a number of rocks off the western point.

In the centre of the lagoon at the head of the loch opposite a small islet there is a wreck that shows at L.W. Sp. The loch narrows to little more than 1 cable N. of this lagoon, and the anchor should be let go in the narrows or immediately the lagoon opens up.

Stores—At Drumbeg village, 1½ miles to W.; also P.O., Tel. **Water**—Small burn opposite island on W. side.

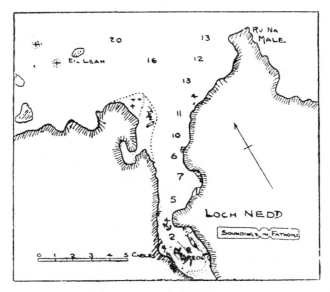

LOCH NEDD

Loch Ardvar—An inlet about 1½ miles E. of Loch Nedd, which affords perfect shelter in all weathers and which is easy of access. There are rocks which dry 8 and 14 ft. at the entrance, but these are easily avoided by holding over to the eastern shore. Anchor in 2 fath. in the S.W. corner of the outer loch. Without local knowledge the passage into the inner loch should **not** be attempted, as the narrows are very foul and fast running tides are encountered. The holding ground is good and this is probably the best anchorage in the district.

Stores—None. **Water**—Springs only.

Calva Bay—Between Calva More and the mainland N. of entrance to
Loch Cairnbahn. A good anchorage and easy of access. Approaching
from the W., close Sgeir a Chlaidheimh (35 ft.) lying ¾ mile S.E. of Meall
Beg (see Eddrachilles Bay). Pass either side of the Sgeir (giving it a berth
of at least 1 cable if passing S. of it) and proceed E. for 1 mile to give the
N. end of Calva Beg a berth of at least 2 cables then a further 6 cables E.
to round the N. end of Calva More. Turn S. into the anchorage, keeping
to the E. (or mainland) side of the channel until past a rock, 6 ft. high,
on the Calva More side. Off this rock about ¾ cable to the E. of it is a
dries 9 ft. rock. Anchor well into the narrows at S. end in 2 to 4 fath.

Stores—None.

LOCH CAIRNBAHN
Chart 2502. C.C.C.S.C. 48

The approach to Loch Cairnbahn is between the Meall Islands and
Oldany Island, and is clean up to the entrance, by keeping 2¼ cables off
the southern shore. The entrance to the loch is ¾ mile wide, between the
two Calva islands which lie off the N. side and Ru Fiasin, which is the
S. point.

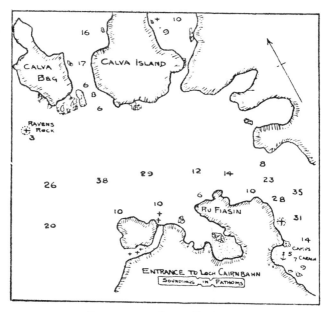

ENTRANCE TO LOCH CAIRNBAHN

Raven Rock lies 2 cables W. by S. of Calva Beg, the outer of the two
islands, and it dries 4 ft. at L.W. This rock is dangerous, and the S. shore
should be kept aboard until the entrance is reached.

The loch narrows here to 2½ cables, and the N. side should be held, to
clear a rock which covers at half-tide, ½ cable off the southern shore, just
within the narrows.

There are no other outlying dangers in the loch. Eiln. na Ghamhna
lies off the southern shore, 2 miles up, and 1 mile further on, Garbh
Island off the N. shore, narrows the channel to ½ cable and just E. of
narrows a ferry plies across the loch.

In the centre of these narrows there is a patch with 9 ft. at L.W. over it. After passing through, the S. shore should be kept aboard, as there are a few rocks to the N.

The loch splits here into two branches, each about 2 miles long, Loch Glen Dhu to the E. and Loch Glen Coul to the S.S.E.

The former is clean to the head, where it shoals for a short distance, but the latter has some dangers on its W. side, and at the head there is shoal water with a narrow channel leading into Loch Beg, a continuation of the loch of ¾ mile.

Chart 2502 is necessary here, as the entrance is rather foul.

Anchorages

Camus Carach (see plan of Loch Cairnbahn)—A small bay just within the entrance, on the S. shore.

There is a lobster fisher's hut on the shore, at the head of the bay, and the anchorage is in 5 fath., off this white hut.

Approaching from the W., keep well off-shore until the bay is open, for the N. point of it is foul. The S. side is steep-to with rocky cliffs. The bottom on the W. side is gravel covered with thick seaweed, and shelves rapidly.

Stores—None. **Water**—At hut. Sp. 14½ ft., Np. 11 ft.

Behind Eiln. na Ghamhna—There is good anchorage in 3 to 6 fath. in the bay inside of Eiln. na Ghamhna. The head of the bay shoals out for ½ cable, and there is a rocky shoal just off the S. point of the island with 11 ft. on it at L.W.

South Ferry Bay—The bay on S. shore immediately E. of ferry jetty. Anchor in 3 to 4 fath. well into bay keeping clear of ferry-boats' moorings. Hotel. Vans only.

North Ferry Bay—Behind Eilean na Rainich on N. shore. Through narrows hold the S. shore till Eilean na Rainich (the most E'ly of the islets) is abaft the beam to avoid the rocks lying off it, then turn to the N. and, giving the islet a fair berth, anchor in 3 to 4 fath. well up the bay, holding to islet side to avoid rocks off the N. shore. Hotel across no-charge ferry.

LOCH LAXFORD
Chart 2503. C.C.C.S.C. 49

The entrance to Loch Laxford lies about 2½ miles E.N.E. of Handa Island. The W. point of the entrance is Rudha Ruadh, which is steep-to and of unmistakable red-coloured rock. The E. point is Ardmore Pt. or Dougal Head, and the distance across 6 cables.

The loch runs inland to the S.E. for about 3½ miles. Along the S.W. shore there is a chain of islands, all of which are clean on their northern sides, and there are several bays on this side which afford good anchorage.

There are no dangers more than ½ cable off this side of the loch until the head, off the River Laxford, where it shoals out gradually. The same holds good of the northern shore until near the head when a berth of 1½ cables clears all dangers. **Const.** —4 hr. 09 m. Dover. Sp. 13 ft., Np. 9 ft.

Anchorages

Loch a Chadh Fi—On the northern side, 1 mile S.E. of Ardmore Pt., a large island—Paddy Island—lies close to the shore. To the E. of it is a clear channel, 1 cable wide leading into this loch.

Anchorage can be had in 4 fath., off the N.E. side of the island, within the entrance.

Six cables up from the entrance, Eiln. Chadh Fi lies in the fairway, and mid-channel through the passage to the W. of it leads into the inner loch, where perfect shelter can be had on the W. side, just N. of the narrows, in 2 to 4 fath. or off the E. side of this island in 3 fath. The channel is $1\frac{1}{2}$ cables wide, but a rock above water off each side contracts it to $\frac{3}{4}$ cable. A rock, dries 7 ft., lies about 100 yd. off the E. shore of the outer loch about 3 cables up from the entrance, and there are shoal patches S. of Eiln. a Chadh Fi, off the N. shore of the inner loch, 3 cables E. of the island, and at the head of the loch.

Fanagmore Bay—Eilean Ard, or Crow Island, the highest island on the S.W. shore of Loch Laxford, 1 mile within the entrance, lies off a bay on the mainland. Entering this bay round the E. side of Eiln. Ard, there are no dangers, and splendid anchorage in 5 fath. can be had well up the bay, off the schoolhouse. There are no dangers except a rock which dries, very close in-shore, at the head of the bay.

Stores—Can be had from Lairg, if the car is met at Laxford Bridge, at the head of the loch. Order by telephone from schoolhouse at head of bay. Telegrams can also be phoned. **Water**—Burn, or at schoolhouse.

Weaver Bay—On the S.W. shore, $1\frac{1}{2}$ miles up from Eiln. Ard. The N. point on entering must be given a fair berth, and the anchorage is in 3 fath., in the middle of the bay, abreast of Eiln. Port a Choit, which lies off the E. point.

Stores—Good shop, butcher, baker, P.O., tel., and inn at Scourie Bay. The road is $\frac{1}{4}$ mile up the burn at head of bay, and Scourie 6 miles W. **Water**—Burn. Calor Gas.

Handa Island—The island is under the care of the Royal Society for the Protection of Birds. They have equipped a bothy and a shelter hut for use by ornithologists. Maps and information on the island are available at the shelter. The flagpole is used to call out the ferrymen and warden from the mainland should their presence be required.

Anchorage

There are two anchorages, the first, Port an Eilein, is on the south-east corner and shelter may be had in $1\frac{1}{2}$ fath. off a cave located on the east side of the bay from all winds that may be expected during the summer. The second anchorage is in the sound of Handa off a ruined chapel in 2 fath. The bottom in both cases is sandy with patches of kelp.

The approach to both anchorages should be from the S. end of the sound and care should be taken to allow for a 3 knot tide in the sound during springs. The Bo More rocks which cover lie 2 cables S.W. of the island.

Water—A tap is available near the shelter supplying water from the loch further up the hill. Stores are not available on the island but a First Aid kit is located in the shelter.

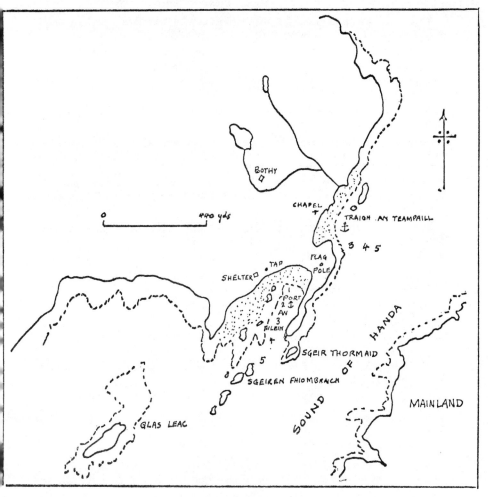

HANDA ANCHORAGE

LOCH INCHARD—Chart 2503

Loch Inchard lies 3 miles N.E. of Loch Laxford. The Dubh Sgeiran Isles lie about 1 mile off the mainland, above Loch Laxford, and $1\frac{1}{2}$ cables off the S. end of Whale Island, the south-western islet of the group. There is a bad rock which dries 10 ft. and on which the sea usually breaks.

There is a channel about 4 cables wide between this group and another chain of islets and rocks which lie nearer shore, but the chart quoted is necessary if using this passage.

The entrance to Loch Inchard is difficult to make out from seaward. Glas Leac Isles lie off the S.W. point and are fairly clean, and Rudha na Leacaig is the N.E. point, $3\frac{1}{2}$ cables across. It is marked by a small inconspicuous concrete tower showing a gp. (2) fl. wht. lt. ev. 10 sec.

Ceann na Saile or Kinsale Rock, with 7 ft. over it at L.W., lies about the middle of the fairway, 4 cables within the entrance, and can be passed by keeping the northern shore aboard. There are no further dangers to the head, which shoals out gradually for 4 cables. Sp. $14\frac{1}{2}$ ft., Np. $11\frac{1}{2}$ ft.

Anchorages

There are three anchorages in the loch, which can be used in most weathers, but the whole loch is open to the N.W.

Camus Blair—At the mouth of the loch, on the S. shore, 1 mile up from Glas Leac Isles, there is a little bay, where anchorage can be had in 3 to 4 fath. It is exposed to any swell setting in, but one has to go fairly well inshore to get 4 fath., and only scend comes in there.

Stores can be got at Kinloch Bervie. Hotel. P.O. Tel. Petrol and paraffin at hotel. Half-holiday—Wednesdays.

Loch Bervie lies on the N. shore right opposite Camus Blair and is well sheltered in any wind. The entrance is narrow but has a depth of 8 ft. at L.W. Sp. Two iron-work beacons exhibiting a green lt. from a red lamp at head of loch if kept in line lead up centre of narrow channel. Anchor in 2 or 3 fath. below or above pier. Several fishing boats have permanent moorings here.

Stores—Van at pier every evening, 7 to 8 p.m. Chandler at Loch Clash. Shop at Badcall, 1 mile. Petrol at garage. Calor Gas. **Water**—At pier.

Achriesgill Bay—This bay is on the N. side of the loch, near the head. It is a wide open bay, rather deep, but temporary anchorage can be had in 7 fath., well off the head.

Stores—Small shop. **Water**—At burn.

Rhiconich—At the head of the loch. The anchorage is in 2 to 3 fath. on the N. side of the loch, well off the head, and well off the southern shore which is very shoal.

The best place is just where the road leaves the side of the loch and runs a little inland up to the hotel.

Stores—Limited at P.O. Tel. Petrol at good hotel, ¼ mile. **Water**—At burn or hotel.

LOCH CLAISE OR CLASH
Chart 2503

A small loch lying just northward of Loch Inchard, round Rudha na Leacaig. It is only a summer anchorage, for although an island more or less guards the mouth, the swell sets in badly if the wind is W'ly. The anchorage is off the pier, in about 2 fath.

Stores—Van at pier every evening, 7 to 8 p.m. Chandler on quay. Shop. P.O. Tel. at Badcall (1 mile). Half-holiday—Wednesdays. **Water**—At pier.

LOCH INCHARD TO LOCH ERIBOLL
Charts 1954 and 2720

It is hardly necessary to state that even in a moderate-sized yacht the greatest care must be taken to pick the weather for navigating this exposed coast.

From Loch Inchard to Cape Wrath, a distance of about 12 miles, the coast is fully exposed to N. and N.W.

Roan Island lies off the northern point of the bight, which contains Lochs Laxford and Inchard, and should be given a wide berth on its S.W. end, as Bo Roan, a rock which is awash at L.W., lies 1 cable off it.

The mainland N. of this should be given a fair offing, to Bulgie Island, which lies 4 miles further on.

This island lies off the Herd Pt., leaving a clear channel between of 8 cables, mid-channel of which should be taken if passing through as rocks lie off both sides for about 2 cables.

From here it is 6 miles to Cape Wrath, the north-western headland of Scotland.

The lighthouse stands on the northern side of the cliff at the headland and shows a fl. lt., alt. wht. and red, of $1\frac{1}{2}$ sec. each, eclipse between fl., $28\frac{1}{2}$ sec. ev. 60 sec. The fog siren gives a blast of 6 sec. ev. $1\frac{1}{2}$ min.

The flood tide sets to the E. and the ebb to the W. round the headland at about 3 knots Sp., commencing $1\frac{1}{2}$ hr. after L.W. and H.W.

Const. —3 hr. 39 m. Dover.

Close in-shore the stream sets to the westward.

Unless in calm weather, the headland should be given a wide berth when wind and tide are opposed, as the seas are then exceptionally heavy.

The Stag Rock, which covers at half flood, lies $\frac{3}{4}$ mile N.E. by E. from the lighthouse. This rock is very dangerous, but usually shows in the hollows of the swell which is always here.

It can be cleared by keeping towards the headland, and the marks for clearing it on the outside are:

Bulgie Island open of Cape Wrath, until the high part of Fairaird Head is open to the northward of Garve Island.

Garve Island lies 4 miles E. of the light and $\frac{1}{4}$ mile off-shore, and Fairaird or Far Out Head, 3 miles further on, forming the E. side of Kyle of Durness, which dries out completely.

The shore is fairly clear as far as Fairaird Head, when Loch Eriboll begins to come in view.

Hoan Island is seen lying off the W. shore, $3\frac{1}{2}$ miles S.E. by S. of Fairaird Head, and off its E. end is Dubh Sgeir, 35 ft. high. Stand towards this rock, keeping well off the W. shore, to make the entrance to the loch.

LOCH ERIBOLL
Chart 2076 (see plan)

Whiten Head is the eastern headland of the entrance, and can be identified by two prominent white stacks or pillars of rock, called "The Sisters" (or "The Maidens"), which show up against the cliffs.

After rounding Dubh Sgeir, make for the eastern side of Klourig Island, which lies 1 mile to the S. and 4 cables off the western shore. On clearing this island, the loch trends to the S.W. and narrows at White Head, on the eastern side.

A fl. ev. 3 sec. lt., red and wht. sector, on White Head, shows white over the clear water between Klourig Island and the eastern shore, and red to the W., between the western shore and the island.

The cliff below the light can be picked out in poor visibility in daylight by white splashes of carbide (discharge from former gas plant).

Two and a half miles further up, Chorrie Island lies in the fairway and can be passed on either side, keeping to mid-channel if using the western passage, and the water is clear from there at a reasonable distance off-shore to the head, which shoals out for about 2 cables. Because of the funnelling effect S.W. winds are fierce throughout the loch. **Const.** —3 hr. 17 m. Dover. Sp. $14\frac{1}{2}$ ft., Np. $10\frac{1}{2}$ ft.

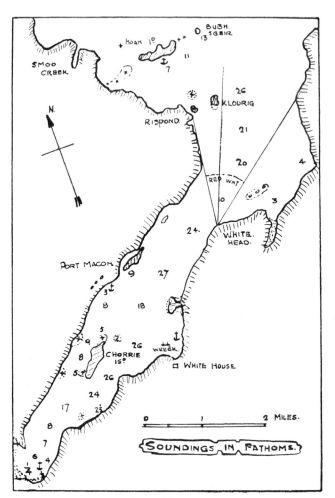

LOCH ERIBOLL

Anchorages

Hoan Island—There is anchorage behind Hoan Island in the W. end of the bay, in 3 fath., but a swell comes in during N'ly winds.

Rispond Bay—A tiny hidden harbour but reported uncomfortable in a N'ly wind and unsafe in a N.E'ly. Small pier.

Port Macon (or Portnancon)—The best anchorage is at the head of the loch on the E. side, in 3 to 4 fath., but the most convenient is at Port Macon village, on the W. side of the loch, about halfway up.

The anchorage is in 3 fath. N.E. of the pier.

Stores—Van daily about 2 p.m. Tel. at Laid. **Water**—Burn.

PART VII

THE

OUTER HEBRIDES

FROM THE BUTT OF LEWIS TO
BARRA HEAD; WITH ST. KILDA

PART VII

Admiralty Charts

GROUP I	2721*	Ardnamurchan Pt. to St. Kilda
	2720*	St. Kilda to Cape Wrath
GROUP II	1796	Barra Hd to Skye
	1795	The Little Minch
	1794*	Rubha Hunish to Pt. of Stoer
	3674*	S. Approaches to Minch and Monach Isles
GROUP III	1144	Village Bay, Castle Bay, Sd of Bernerav
	2770	Sound of Barra
	618	Loch Boisdale
	2750	Loch Skiport
	3168	Eigneig More to Black Leversay; L. Carnan
	2825	Loch Maddy
	2642	Sound of Harris
	2905	E. Loch Tarbert
	1154	Loch Erisort, Leurbost Grimshader
	512	Approaches to Stornoway
	3422	E. Loch Roag
	3381	W. Loch Roag
	3331	Flannan Islands
	2841	Sound of Harris to Aird Brenish
	1919	Stornoway Harbour

CLYDE CRUISING CLUB SKETCH CHARTS

33	Loch Grimshader and Entrances to Lochs Luirbost and Erisort
34	Loch Maddy
35	Lochs Skiport and Eynort
36	Scalpay Island and Entrance to East Loch Tarbert in Harris
37	Head of East Loch Tarbert in Harris
38	Loch Boisdale and Eport
39	South-East Section of Sound of Barra
40	Sound of Barra—Passage through
50	Stornoway Harbour

THE OUTER HEBRIDES—Eastern Side
Charts 2720, 3674, 1795, 1796 and 1794
C.C.C.S.C. 33 to 40 and 50

The Outer Hebrides form a continuous chain of islands running almost parallel to the coast of Scotland, from 30 to 40 miles distant to the westward.

The northern island is Lewis and Harris, the N. end of which is 40 miles W. by N. of Cape Wrath, and the southern islands are Mingulay and Bernera, which lie 45 miles N.W. by W. of the Sound of Mull.

The chain is about 100 miles long, and consists of a large number of islands and islets. The principal ones are Lewis and Harris in the N. then North Uist, Benbecula, South Uist, and Barra at the S.

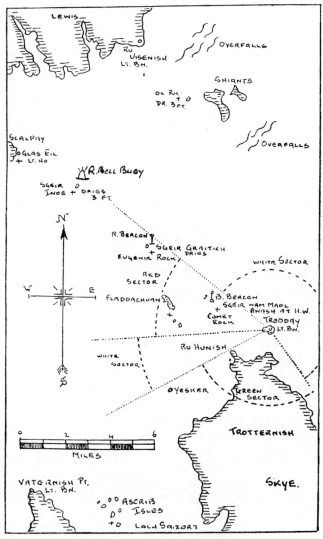

PASSAGE BETWEEN SKYE AND LEWIS

Between Lewis and the mainland, the channel down to the N. of Skye is called the North Minch. In the northern part of this channel, the flood tide sets S'ly, and in the southern part it sets N'ly.

The North Minch is free from outlying dangers, but about 11 miles N. of Skye and $3\frac{1}{2}$ miles off Lewis lie the Shiant Islands, and around them the tides run from 2 to even 4 knots. **Const.** —4 hr. 21 m. Dover.

They vary in time and direction, and when the wind is opposed the irregular bottom causes heavy overfalls. Through Shiant Sound the ebb runs S.W. till 3 hr. after L.W. and the flood N.E. till 2 hr. after H.W.

In bad weather or when a heavy swell is running, this part of the Minch should be avoided altogether, as it is considered the most dangerous part between the Butt of Lewis and Barra.

Off the N.W. point of the largest of the Shiant Islands, rocks extend W. by N. for $1\frac{1}{2}$ miles. They are all above water except Ox Rock, the outermost, which dries 3 ft. It bears N.W. by W., 4 cables from Galta More, the outermost but one, and also the largest and highest of these rocks.

After passing the Shiants there are some rocks between Harris and the N. end of Skye. The first of these is 3 miles off Harris, and they are described under Lewis and Harris, East Side. They lie across the northern entrance to the Little Minch, which is the channel between Skye and the Outer Hebrides.

All around the vicinity of these rocks the tides are deflected, and when running strongly there are eddies and overfalls which make this a place to be avoided. The flood runs till 2 hr. after H.W. at Sp. and $4\frac{1}{2}$ hr. after H.W. at Np. at this point, about N.E.

The rest of the Little Minch is clear of dangers, but the shores of the islands should be given a berth of $1\frac{1}{2}$ miles.

It is advisable to pick the weather for crossing the Minch at any part, as in bad weather the seas can be **very** bad.

The distances across from the usual points of departure are:

	Miles
Staffin Bay (Skye) to Stornoway (Lewis)	32
Ru Re (Loch Ewe) to Stornoway (Lewis)	26
Ru Re (Loch Ewe) to Loch Shell (Lewis)	23
Ru Hunish (Skye) to E. Loch Tarbert (Harris)	15
Dunvegan Head (Skye) to Loch Maddy (N. Uist)	14
Canna Island to Loch Boisdale (S. Uist)	25
Canna Island to Castle Bay (Barra)	35
Ardnamurchan Point to Castle Bay (Barra)	45

The whole eastern side of the group is broken up with lochs and islets and plentifully strewn with rocks, and requires very careful navigation. The anchorages are numerous and splendidly sheltered, but in many cases the rocks in the approaches are unmarked and are so numerous as to be bewildering.

The largest scale charts are necessary for anyone navigating close inshore about the Outer Hebrides, particularly S. of Lewis and Harris.

LEWIS AND HARRIS—Eastern Side
Charts 2720, 512 and 1794
C.C.C.S.C. 33, 36, 37 and 50

Lewis and Harris is the largest and most N'ly of the Outer Hebrides. The island is 53 miles long from the Butt of Lewis on the N. end, to Ru Renish, the southern point of Harris.

There are few outlying dangers along this coast and none outside ½ mile off-shore.

A lighthouse on the Butt of Lewis shows a wht. fl. lt. ev. 20 sec. Fog siren, 2 blasts of 4 sec. in quick succession ev. 90 sec.

About 20 miles down the coast, Eye Peninsula stands out like a large island off the coast, forming a bay on each side of the isthmus. It is not very prominent at a distance. The northern point of the promontory is Tiumpan Head, which shows a wht. gp. fl. lt., 2 fl. during 5 sec., ev. 30 sec. Fog signal of 3 blasts of 2½ sec. in quick succession ev. 90 sec.

The bay on the N. side is Broad Bay, clean except for McIver Rock which dries at L.W.O.S., lying right in the centre of the bay. By the S. side of the peninsula is the approach to Stornoway.

About 10 miles further down the coast is Milaid Pt., on which is shown a wht. fl. lt. ev. 15 sec.

Six miles further down, the Shiant Islands lie 3½ miles off-shore, and the caution already given about them above should be noted.

Other 6 miles down, Scalpay Island lies close in-shore, and on Glas Island, its outer end, is shown a gp. (3) fl. wht. lt. ev. 20 sec. Fog siren, 1 blast of 7 sec. ev. 90 sec. Three miles S.E. of it a blk. con. buoy is moored 5 cables 010° from Sgeir Inoe, a rock which dries 3 ft. It shows a fl. wht. lt. ev. 6 sec. and has a bell sounded by the motion of the buoy. Sgeir Graitich lies 7 miles S.E. by S. of Glas Island Lt. and is marked by a red iron beacon. The whole vicinity of this patch, particularly on the flood, is to be avoided, as it is subject to dangerous whirlpools and overfalls. Eugenie Rock, with 3 ft. over it at L.W., lies 4 cables S. by E. of Sgeir Graitich, and between these rocks and Trotternish Pt., Skye, there are other bad patches (see sketch plan).

The Little Minch is now entered and from here to Ru Renish there are no further lights or marks, but the coast is clean outside of ½ mile off-shore.

Anchorages

Port of Ness—A couple of miles S. of Butt of Lewis. A shallow indentation with sandy bottom and good holding ground but only suitable in off-shore winds. Subject to swell. The harbour is silted up but boats drawing up to 5 ft. can enter at H.W. and dry out, but even the harbour is subject to swell.

Stores—Shop. P.O. Boatbuilder.

Stornoway (Charts 512 and 1919. C.C.C.S.C. 50)—Stornoway harbour lies in the N.W. corner of the bight, to the S. of Eye Peninsula. In the approach to the anchorage all dangers are either above water or marked by perches, and if these are given a reasonable berth, there is no difficulty.

The entrance to the main harbour is 4 cables wide and is between Arnish Pt., on the W., and Holm Pt. on the E. Off Holm Pt. there is a **red** beacon, marking the Beist of Holm, a rocky patch.

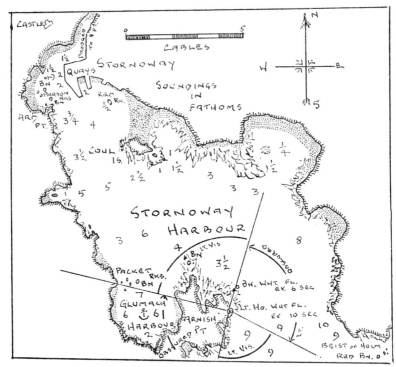

STORNOWAY HARBOUR

On Arnish Pt., a lighthouse shows a wht. fl. lt. ev. 10 sec., and on the outer end of the reef a little N. of it, a wht. beacon shows a wht. fl. lt., 2 sec. ev. 6 sec. The latter has been demolished by heavy seas and a red can buoy has been laid temporarily in a position 047° 500 ft. from bn. It shows a gp.(2) fl. wht. lt. ev. 6 secs.

Behind Arnish Pt. lies Glumach harbour, the best and most sheltered anchorage. The dangers in this bay are:—Another spit off Arnish Pt., marked by a **black** beacon, and inside, off the W. side Packet Rocks, also marked by a perch. The anchorage is in 3 to 4 fath., at the head of the bay, clear of the hulks which lie here.

Further up the main harbour, Coul Island (Eilean na Gothail on the large-scale charts) lies off the N.E. shore and must be left well to starboard, going in. A causeway joins this island to the mainland. Ard Pt., the western point of the inner harbour, should be given a fair berth as it shoals out, and further in, off the same side lie Parson Rocks, marked by two iron perches. The piers at Stornoway lie on the other side, and the anchorage is just beyond the Parson Rocks, off the walled erection on shore below the castle. A fix. wht. and red sector lt. is at S.W. corner of pier and a fix. wht. lt. at N.E. corner.

The anchorage is sometimes rather crowded, and is restricted, for, if anchoring further out, one is in the way of the fishing vessels, of which there is a large fleet. Any swell from the southward rolls into the anchorage and makes it uncomfortable.

Stores—Shops. P.O. Tel. Hotels. Boat slip. Petrol pump on W. pier. **Water**—Fountain by steamer pier. **Const.** —4 hr. 28 m. Dover. Sp. 13¾ ft., Np. 10 ft Daily steamer to Kyle of Lochalsh.

LOCH GRIMSHADER
Charts 1154 and 512. C.C.C.S.C. 33

This loch lies 3 miles below Stornoway. The approach is clear of dangers if the N. point of the entrance is given a berth of ½ cable off a small islet there.

Sgeir a Caolas, which covers at ¾-flood, lies about the centre of the loch, ½ mile up from the entrance. It is rather nearer the S. shore, and is between a fence and dyke running down to the beach on that side and a bay on the opposite shore. It has a 2 fath. channel on either side. Taking N. channel the rock is easily avoided by curving slightly into the bay, which incidentally is reported as quite a good anchorage.

The loch runs inland for another ½ mile through a clean channel about 150 yd. wide, and then opens out into a basin, shoal at the head, where perfect shelter can be got anywhere, in 3 to 4 fath., but the bottom, both in loch and lagoon, is soft mud and very poor holding ground. In the event of strong winds, a line ashore is advisable. A narrow canal leads from the N.E. side of this basin into another lagoon, Loch Beag, which is perhaps the most perfect anchorage on the W. coast. About ordinary L.W. there is a clean channel through with 1 to 2 fath. and, inside, an area

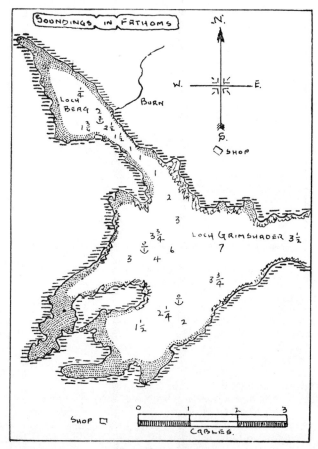

LOCH GRIMSHADER

off the burn with 2 fath. in it for anchoring (see sketch plan) but an over-head power cable crosses approach channel giving a clearance of about 50 ft. above H.W.

It is reported that Loch Beag is silting up badly, and the soundings, both in Loch Beag and in the channel leading to it, may already be reduced. The silting is, however, **very** soft mud.

Stores—Small store towards Rhanish village, on S. shore, $\frac{1}{2}$ mile inland.
Water—Burn. P.O. and tel. at Crossbost, $\frac{1}{2}$ mile S.E.

LOCH ERISORT
Chart 1154 (see plan). C.C.C.S.C. 33

Aird Ranish, or Ru Ranish, is the promontory between Loch Grim-shader and Loch Erisort, and forms the northern side of the entrance to the latter. The southern side is formed by the peninsula of Cromore, and a number of islands off its E. side.

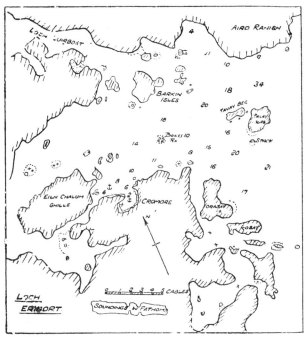

LOCH ERISORT

The entrance is a little over 1 mile wide, and the loch runs inland to the W. for 9 miles, about 7 of which are navigable.

Tavay Beg and Tavay More, and a small islet 50 ft. high, off the S. side of the latter, lie in a cluster in the centre of the entrance, and can be passed on either side.

The Barkin Islands lie to the N. side off the entrance to Loch Luirbost, which branches off to the N.W. for $2\frac{1}{2}$ miles.

Both these lochs abound with perfectly sheltered anchorages, but there are so many rocks and islets that any description of them would be useless for navigation. With Chart 1154 they are quite accessible, but without it, it would be inadvisable to attempt any save Cromore Bay. Bones Rock, off the N. side of Cromore Peninsula, has 15 ft. over it at L.W.

Anchorages

Cromore Bay (Chart 1154. C.C.C.S.C. 33)—On the S. shore of the loch, W. of Cromore Peninsula, Eilean Chalum Ghille, an island joined to the mainland at L.W. and with four or five islets off its N.E. point, forms the W. side of a bay between it and Cromore.

Entering the loch by the S. side of the Tavay Islands, a small islet lies off the N.E. point of Cromore. Keeping 1 cable off the southern shore, there are islets off the next two points of Cromore, and round the second islet, which is 11 ft. high, is the E. point of the entrance to the bay. Anchorage can be had in the centre of the bay in 4 to 6 fath.

In the S. corner there is a pool with 2 fath., the entrance to which is 1 cable wide. The centre of this passage should be taken and the anchor dropped immediately the pool opens out. Sp. 15 ft., Np. 11 ft.

Loch Mariveg—At the S.E. entrance to Loch Erisort, is an excellent anchorage and well sheltered (see plan). Enter S. of Eilean Thorraidh, but this passage has only $1\frac{1}{4}$ fath., with an outlying rock at N. end $\frac{1}{2}$ cable off

LOCH MARIVEG ENTRANCE

the island. The best entrance is S. of Rosay Island, with better depths, but pass N. and W. of 1 fath. patch shown in plan, not S. and E. as indicated by dotted line.

There is a rock with 6 ft. on it at L.W. fairly close in off S.E. point of Rosay Island which is dangerous if a swell is running. This rock is **not** shown on large-scale Admiralty chart.

The anchorage in S.W. corner is reported as being fouled by a heavy mooring chain (1967).

P.O. and tel. on S. side.

LOCH ODAIRN OR OUIRN
Charts 2720 and 1794

This loch lies 4 miles below Loch Erisort. Coming S., there are no hidden dangers, Owen's Rock, just outside Loch Erisort, having 4 fath. on it. Loch Odairn runs inland to the W. for 2 miles and is quite free of dangers. It is exposed to the E. but no swell reaches the head. The anchorage is in 4 fath. off a boat slip on the N. side near the head, below the village.

Stores—Shop near slip. P.O. Tel. at Grabhir, 1 mile. **Water**—Well at cottage near slip.

LOCH SHELL
Charts 2720 and 1794

Loch Shell lies 3 miles below Loch Odairn. The coastline between the two is clean. Halfway down is Milaid Pt. on which is shown a wht. fl. lt. ev. 15 sec.

There is no large-scale chart of this loch.

The entrance to the loch lies between Ru Ailltenish (S.) and Streanach Head (N.). The latter is steep-to and can be approached closely. Iuvard Island, with Sgeir nan Caorach close off its western extreme, lies in the centre of the fairway. The N. channel leads only to Little Loch Shell (see below). If proceeding up Loch Shell proper, the island should be kept to starboard with a berth of ½ cable, and the centre of the loch held until past Orosay. The S. shore of the loch is clean, but the high cliffs at the entrance may blanket a sailing yacht.

Anchorages

Tob Eishken—An islet, 2½ cables wide at its entrance, which lies about 4½ miles within the entrance on the N. side of the loch. A sunken rock lies about ½ cable from the W. shore about 2 cables from the head. The anchorage is at the head of the inlet, but it is reported to be foul with lost moorings.

South Shore—A bight S.E. of Tob Eishken is used by fishermen, and is sheltered from the prevailing winds. The beach dries off a good distance.

Head of Loch—Sheltered except from the E. The very head dries out for some distance.

Little Loch Shell—Known locally as Tob Iimervay (or Lemreway). The anchorage is entered by the passage N. of Iuvard Island. The shores of this passage are clean for about 1 mile except for a dangerous rock, Sgier Phlathuig, which dries 3 ft. It is about 1 cable off the N. shore, about 9 cables from the entrance, off a ravine with large boulders at its mouth where the shore changes from cliffs to steep hills. West of the direct passage to Limervay the strait N. of Iuvard Island is very foul.

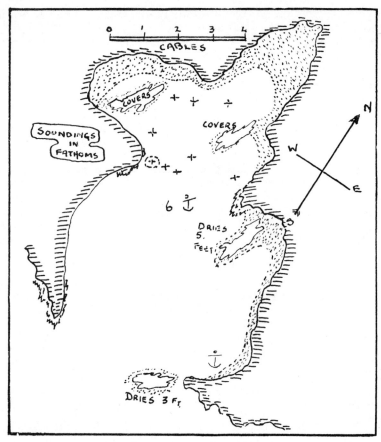

LITTLE LOCH SHELL—TOB LIMERVAY

On entering Tob Limervay itself, keep well in the centre, as there is a bad reef off the point on the E. shore. Proceed up the inlet towards the school, and anchor in 4 to 6 fath. (hard mud and rock) before reaching the school or the rocky bluffs that narrow in the loch, and just short of the fishing boats. Beyond this the head is foul with rocks.

Sheltered in winds from W. through N. to E. In S'lies it is subject to swell and fully exposed to a drift of over a mile.

Anchorage is also reported to be found in S.E. corner of the loch, where shown on the sketch.

Stores—Shop in Limervay. P.O. Tel. **Water**—Burns only.

SHIANT ISLANDS
Chart 1795

The Shiant Islands is a group of two islands and several islets and rocks lying 6 miles S. of the mouth of Loch Shell and 3½ miles off-shore. The western island is 1½ miles long and consists of Garav Eiln. to the N. and Eiln. Tighe to the S., connected together by a low neck of gravel. Eilean Mhuire lies to the E. of Eiln. Garav, and near the middle of its W. side a spit runs out and narrows the navigable passage between the islands to less than 1 cable.

If entering from the N., keep towards Eiln. Garav. The E. side of Eiln. Tighe is steep-to if entering from the S.

Ox Rock and the others to the N.W. of Eiln. Garav are described under Outer Hebrides, East Side, and also remarks about the tides, which should be carefully considered.

The anchorage is on the E. side of the neck of gravel between the high parts of Eiln. Garav and Eiln. Tighe.

It is exposed to winds from N.E. and S.E. and a heavy swell sets in during S. W. winds, but it is sheltered from winds from N. through W. to S. The water is deep, there being as much as 8 ft. about 10 yd. from the shore.

Abreast of the Shiants is Rudh' Uisenish (not to be confused with Ushinish), a smooth sloping headland. On it stands a wht. tower exhibiting a wht. fl. of 1 sec. ev. 3 sec.

With a weather going tide there is a confused sea off this point, and yachts wishing to wait for the tide or take shelter might enter Loch Bhrollum.

LOCH BHROLLUM

This loch lies 2 miles W.S.W. of Rudh' Uisenish and runs N. for about 2 miles. The entrance is about 5 cables wide between bold headlands, and is clean. The anchorage is on the E. shore, 6 cables from the entrance, N. of Aird Dubh, a peninsula of black rock and grass, 50 ft. high; about 3 cables further N. is a bold headland 220 ft. high, which seems almost to close the passage N. To enter keep 30 yd. from Aird Dubh to avoid two rocks, one a cable N.W. of it (dries 1 ft.) and the other $\frac{1}{2}$ cable N.N.W. (1 ft. deep). The anchorage is N.E. and E. of Aird Dubh, with depths of 2 to $3\frac{1}{2}$ fath., good holding ground. It is well sheltered, but with S'ly winds some swell enters, but this may be avoided or mitigated by mooring in the small pool in the S.E. corner.

There is also an anchorage for small yachts by an island at the head of the loch, which is about 220 yd. wide for the last $\frac{3}{4}$ mile. The depths on the E. side of the island decrease gradually to about 6 ft., and there is only about 4 ft. just N. of the island. The bottom is however of soft mud and yachts sink in without listing. There appear to be no dangers in the upper loch, which provides good shelter, especially behind the island, and is used by fishermen in bad weather.

LOCH CLAY

Loch Clay lies about 2 miles W. of Loch Bhrollum. The shores between are rocky and indented and should be given a wide berth. The loch runs in a N.N.W. direction for about 3 miles, and is about $\frac{1}{2}$ mile wide for most of that distance. Drying rocks extend $\frac{1}{2}$ cable from the E. side of the entrance, and rocks above and below water extend 4 cables S.E. from the W. point. Vessels entering should get the loch well open before turning N., tending towards the E. shore.

About 1 mile up the loch, on the E. side, is Eilean Hingerstay, a green islet about 80 ft. high, and the anchorage is on the N.E. side of this, entering from the N. It is about 150 yd. wide with depths of 3 to 4 fath., and has no rocks except close in-shore. Some swell probably enters with S'ly winds, but could be avoided by going well up the inlet. Apart from the dangers at the mouth of the loch, this anchorage is easier to identify and enter in bad weather than that at Loch Bhrollum.

LOCH SEAFORTH
Chart 1795

Aird Pt. runs out, forming the W. side of Loch Clay, and the E. side of Loch Seaforth, and the western side of the latter is formed by Rudha Crago, $2\frac{1}{2}$ miles to the S.W. About 2 miles N. of Rudha Crago, the loch narrows to about $\frac{1}{2}$ mile when the loch proper begins. Loch Seaforth is the longest loch in the Outer Hebrides. It runs N. for 6 miles, when Eiln. Seaforth lies in the centre, leaving a clear passage on either side. Beyond the island it runs inland to the eastward for other 6 miles. It narrows very much 3 miles above the island, and the tide runs up to 7 knots Sp. here. South of the eastern point of the entrance proper lies Sgeir Shail, and this rock, which is 6 ft. high, should be given a wide berth, as there is foul ground round it especially to the S. for 2 cables. It may be passed on either side, but about 4 cables W. of it, and $2\frac{1}{2}$ cables southward of western entrance point lies Iolla More, awash at L.W. To avoid all these rocks:—On the port tack keep the N. end of the Shiants open of Eiln. More; on the starboard tack keep Great Sea Head open of the W. side of the loch. When these lines meet, make very short tacks on the latter line until just within the entrance, when all danger will be past.

Inside, the loch is steep-to on both sides except for a small rock 80 yd. from the western shore 3 cables northward of a small green island about $1\frac{1}{2}$ miles within the loch. The rock dries 7 ft.

The best anchorage is in Loch Mharuig on the western side of Loch Seaforth, $2\frac{1}{2}$ miles from the entrance proper.

In Loch Mharuig a spit of rocky land runs out from the N. side called Goat Pt. There is a rock about 50 yd. off its western end.

The anchorage is to the westward of Goat Pt., but not too far, as the loch shoals at the head. Anchor well off the cottages on the N. shore in about 4 fath.

Stores—Van from Stornoway on Tuesdays. **Water**—From burns. Buses to Tarbert and Stornoway.

EAST LOCH TARBERT, HARRIS
Chart 2905. C.C.S.C. 36 and 37

The next inlet is East Loch Tarbert, the entrance to which lies between Crago Pt. on the N.E. and Ru Bocaig on the S.W., the distance across being 4 miles, and the loch runs inland for about 5 miles.

Towards the N. side of the entrance lies Scalpay, a large island, and on Glas Island, the S. point of it, is shown a wht. gp. (3) fl. lt. ev. 20 sec. (see Lewis and Harris, East Side).

In entering the loch by the S. of Scalpay, there are several dangerous rocks, and the chart quoted is necessary, as it also is for making the anchorages on the S.W. of Scalpay and those on the S.W. shore of the loch. On Dunn Corr, one of the Glorigs, there is a quick fl. wht. lt.

Coming from Loch Seaforth, the only danger up to Crago Pt. is Ox Rock, which lies about $\frac{1}{2}$ mile off-shore and bears N.E. of Crago Pt. This rock is 14 ft. above H.W. and must be given a wide berth.

Caolas Scalpay is the channel between Scalpay and the northern shore. This channel varies in width from 4 cables at its eastern end to 1 cable at its western end, and the ebb tide sets inward at $1\frac{1}{2}$ to 2 knots Sp., starting 3 hr. after H.W. The flood stream sets outward. **Const.** —4 hr. 48 m. Dover.

Entering round Crago Point there are no real dangers until the head of the loch is reached, provided the northern shore is kept to. The shore at Crago Pt. is steep-to and clean, and Elliot Rock, with 7 ft. over it at L.W., lies 2½ cables S.W. of it.

Off the point of the first bay on the N. shore, about ¾ mile within the channel, rocks run out for ½ cable, but the island side is steep-to and clean here.

About 2 miles further along the N. shore, Urgha Rock, 3 ft. above H.W., lies ¾ cable off-shore and should be given a wide berth. The N.E. point of the bay, in the extreme N. of the loch at its head, about 1 mile further on, is Black Pt., and N. of a line between Urgha Rock and this point lie Oban Rocks, which dry 4 ft. at L.W.

Anchorages

Tarbert—This bay is an inlet ½ mile long and about 1½ cables wide, in the extreme N. corner of East Loch Tarbert. It is free of hidden dangers and the anchorage is in 2 fath., off the pier just past the church on the N. side. Perfectly sheltered except in E. wind. A heavy wire cable is

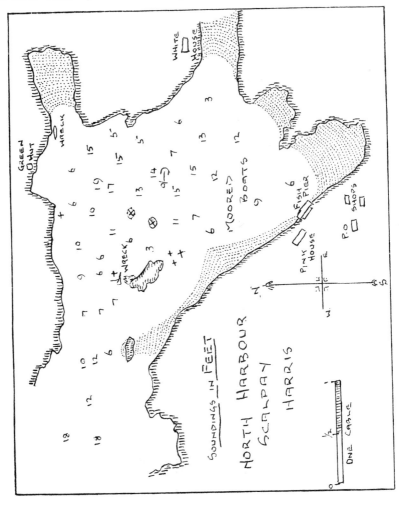

reported running from the W. side of pier across loch. Anchor either well beyond the pier or to the E. of it. On the pier there is a red and wht. sectored lt. occ. (4 sec. lt. 2 sec. eclipse). Wht. 298° to 306°, red elsewhere.

Stores—Shop. P.O. Tel. Hotel. Petrol. Calor Gas. **Water**—Tap at pier. Sp. 13½ ft., Np. 10 ft. Daily ferry to Uig in Skye.

North Harbour, Scalpay—North Harbour is easy of access. The approach is through Caolas Scalpay, avoiding Elliot Rock which lies just S. of mid-channel at the E. end of it, and the harbour lies behind Ard na Aiseig, or Ferry Pt., the N. point of Scalpay Island. There is one rock off this point, and if coming in from Scalpay Sound, give this point a wide berth before turning into the harbour. If approaching from the S., the point to the southward of the entrance must be given a wide berth of more than 3 cables to avoid McQueen's Rock.

There is perfect anchorage in 2 to 2½ fath. for yachts of moderate draft in the pool beyond the islets in the narrows (see sketch).

Access is obtained by passing N. of the islets holding one-third of channel's width from the N. shore to avoid a spit, upon which is the remains of a wreck, which runs out in a N'ly direction. Bottom is grey mud. Rocks with less than 6 ft. on them are reported as being in positions marked in sketch east of islets.

The best shelter and most convenient anchoring positions are immediately N. of the fish pier but the area is occupied by local craft and the bottom is reported fouled by permanent moorings.

Stores—At village on S. side of bay. P.O. Tel. **Water**—At schoolhouse. Calor Gas.

South Harbour, Scalpay (Chart 2905)—Enter between Hamarsay and Rossay Islands and keep mid-channel until the Inner Harbour is clearly visible. Then turn towards the Inner Harbour and keeping a third of the way out from the western shore anchor about 1½ cables S. of the harbour, as shown on the chart. If entering the Inner Harbour, hold close to the W. side and anchor in the centre of the pool clear of the local boats which restrict the swinging room. In the entrance there are extensive drying rocks on the E. side. Depths are about 7 fath. outside the harbour and about 2 fath. inside. Bottom is medium black mud.

Stores—as for North Harbour.

Eileanan Diraclett—Behind the islets at S. entry of Tarbert Bay (see above). Many reefs cumber the approach, but all save one, Mid-Sound Rock with 8 ft. over it, show at L.W. Mid-Sound Rock lies about 4 cables due W. of centre of Scotasay, the first big island W. of Caolas Scalpay. Pass fairly close N. of Scotasay and head to pass close S. of the point at the N. side of entry to Loch Ceann Dibig (the wide bay due W. of Scotasay). Paterson Rock (dries 1 ft.) lies immediately N. of this line, and Little Duncan Rock (dries 1 ft.) lies immediately S. of it and about 1 cable N.N.E. of Duncan Rock, which lies in centre of entrance to Loch Ceann Dibig. Immediately the lagoon W. of Diraclett Isles opens up, turn N. and anchor in E. centre of lagoon. Do not go further up than the S. end of third island. The lagoon narrows after that and there are some bad rocks in the fairway.

Obe Meavag, Bagh Buidhe, Plocrapool Bay—Bays on the S. shore all difficult of approach owing to the reefs and rocks, and to make them, the large-scale chart 2905 is essential.

LOCHS BETWEEN EAST LOCH TARBERT AND
SOUND OF HARRIS
Charts 1795 and 2642

Between East Loch Tarbert and Ru Renish, the southern point of Harris, a distance of 10 miles, the coast is clear if given a moderate offing. There are several small lochs along this coast which afford good anchorage, but the approaches are intricate.

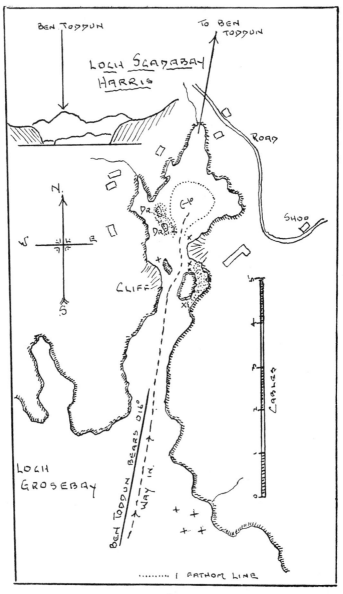

LOCH SCADABAY

Loch Grosebay—The first loch S.W. of East Loch Tarbert is Loch Grosebay, which is fairly clean and offers moderately good shelter at the head. Coming from the N., give a wide berth to Ru Reibinish, the headland dividing the two lochs, and go up the middle of the loch between the islets to the S.W. and the N. shore. About two-thirds of the way up is John Rock, which lies ½ cable off the N.E. shore and 4 cables N. of Glas Sgeir, the last islet on the port hand. This rock dries 10 ft. and can generally be seen. Beyond it, about 100 yd. from the N.E. shore, is Sgeir a Chais, a group of rocky islets with a cairn. One hundred yards S.W. of this group are two rocks, which dry 5 ft., and there is a channel 1 cable wide between these, and the S.W. shore.

Steer close W. of Sgeir a Chais, and anchor in the pool N. of the group. This anchorage is rather exposed to S'ly winds and swell, and is not recommended by local fishermen who prefer Loch Scadabay (see below).

Stores—None. **Water**—At houses.

Loch nan h'Uamha—The first bay on the N.E. side on entering Loch Grosebay is unsafe and is not advised.

Loch Scadabay—About 4 cables further up the N.E. side of Loch Grosebay than Loch nan h'Uamha. A canal-like channel running N. between low cliffs, which after 2½ cables is almost blocked by cliffs and a rocky tidal islet extending from the eastern side. (Ben Toddun bearing 016° clears these rocks. See sketch.) To the W. of this islet is a short channel about 30 yd. wide with steep sides and a minimum depth of 7 ft. over a sandy bottom. On passing through the channel, bear to starboard to avoid the drying rocks off the scree at the foot of the port hand cliff, then follow round the rocky point to starboard keeping same distance off until the pool opens up (as shown in sketch) and anchor in centre of pool, which is about 1½ cables in length. This course avoids the shallow spit with two drying patches lying across entrance to the pool which covers at 2 hr. flood, but weed shows for a further 2 hr. The depth in the pool is only about 6 ft. at L.W.O.S., but the bottom is soft mud, and a vessel of greater draft would sink in without listing. This anchorage affords perfect shelter and is used by fishing boats during winter gales, and the entrance is not difficult.

Stores—Small shop. **Water**—At houses.

Loch Stockinish—From the S.W. corner of Loch Grosebay the coast trends S.S.W. for about 1 mile to Rudha Cluer, a headland 156 ft. in height, bounded by steep cliffs. It is marked by a small cairn, and some houses show through a cleft in the rock wall. The southern face is about 2½ cables in length, and the coast then turns N. into Loch Cluer, a deep bay running about 8 cables inland and useless as an anchorage. The S.W. corner of Loch Cluer is formed by Stockinish Island and outlying islets, whose S.E. end is about 5½ cables W. by S. from Rudha Cluer. In case of doubt it should be noted that the island has islets off its southern face, which is fairly green, and it should not be approached within 3 cables. Rudha Cluer is steep-to, and dark in colouring and from just S. of it Eiln. Glas Lighthouse and Reibinish are still in view.

Between the W. side of Stockinish Island and Ard Mor, a headland 7 cables to the W., is the entrance to Loch Stockinish, which runs N. for about 2 miles. This channel, known as Caolas More, contains many drying rocks and requires the greatest care in navigation, but after about 1 mile the loch bends to the N.N.W. and narrows to about 2 cables, almost free from rocks and forming a good sheltered anchorage.

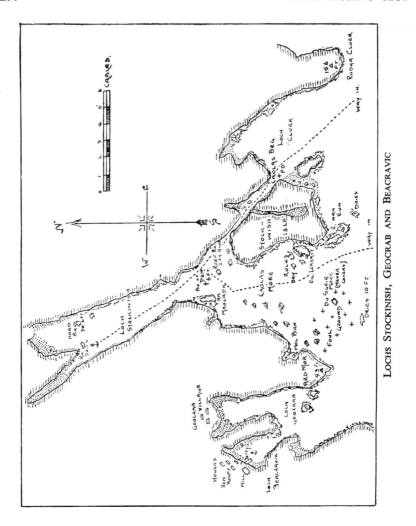

LOCHS STOCKINISH, GEOCRAB AND BEACRAVIC

The better entrance to the loch is by Caolas Beg, a narrow channel leading from the western side of Loch Cluer up past the N.E. shore of Stockinish Island. It runs very straight to the N.N.W. and, although only 90 ft. wide at the northern end, has a least depth of 2 fath. Yachts taking this route should at first tend rather to the N.E. side until clear of a rock reported to lie off the S.E. point of the island, but should then keep rather to the S.W. side of the channel to avoid a shoal patch just round the E. point of entrance. There is no room to tack, and vessels without engines should make sure of a leading wind and a favourable tide (during part of the flood the stream runs outwards and inwards during part of the ebb). On emerging from the narrows, the channel should be kept open for 4 cables to clear a 6 ft. rock, Bo of the Den, lying about ½ cable east-ward of Am Maoladh, a prominent tidal island near the bend in the western shore of the loch, described above. The anchorage is in about 5 fath., sand, off the entrance to a long narrow arm at the N.W. corner of the loch abreast a little rocky gully. There is, however, a rock, drying

1 ft. about 1 cable S.E. by S. from the point on the E. side of this N.W. arm. Also, as shown in sketch plan in Caolas Beg, well sheltered and good holding ground.

In Caolas More, drying rocks extend for 5 cables E. and S.E. of Ard Mor, and in this foul ground is one rock, Du Sgeir More, which never covers. It is nearly 4 cables E. of Ard Mor, and so about halfway between that headland and the islets S.W. of Stockinish Island. The W. shore of Stockinish Island, like the S. is foul, and islets and rocks extend 2½ cables S.S.E. from its S.W. corner. Vessels attempting entrance by Caolas More should approach these islets from between S. and S.W. and keep about 150 yd. from them, curving out to about 250 yd. to clear some drying rocks just N. of them. They should then steer halfway between Am Maoladh and Reef Rock, which is 2 ft. high and lies N. of Stockinish

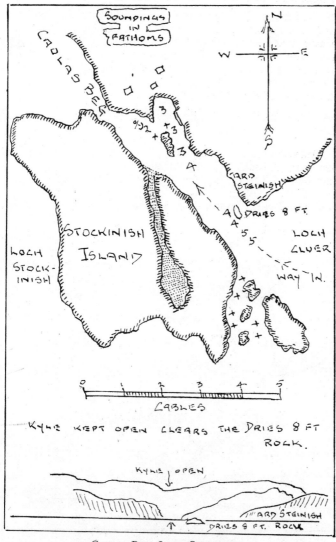

CAOLAS BEG, LOCH STOCKINISH

I

Island, holding this course until Caolas Beg begins to open up, then steer up the loch to the anchorage described above.

Stores—Shops and P.O. on E. side of loch.

Loch Geocrab with Loch Beacravik—Loch Geocrab lies W. of Ard Mor and E. of Ard Manish, a low-lying headland. The entrances to this loch, Loch Stockinish and Loch Cluer, form one wide bay when viewed from seaward, and the foul ground extending S.E. from Ard Mor must be avoided if entering from E. or S.; but there are no other dangers in the outer approaches, except a foul patch near Manish Island, extending about 2 cables eastward from the Harris shore. The outer rock, Earr Manish, 2 cables eastward from the Harris shore. The outer rock Earr Man dries 6 ft. The large woollen mill in Loch Beacravik, partly painted red, kept in sight leads in well clear of this danger.

Inside the loch is Glas Sgeir, a group of islets which should be left to starboard, and northward of them the loch divides into two arms. The eastern arm is not recommended, but the western one, Loch Beacravik, has a good sheltered basin with a depth of 5 fath. At the entrance a reef runs out from the E. side, covering at H.W. and blocking half or more of the passage, but the rest of the passage is of good width and depth, and the western shore is clean and steep-to.

Stores—Very small shop. **Water**—Tap behind factory. Occasional buses to Tarbert.

Loch Flodabay—This loch lies W. of Ard Manish. It is an open bay with many sunken rocks and quite unsuitable as an anchorage. Its western shore continues S.S.E. for another mile to Rudha Quidnish, 126 ft. high, and from off this headland Eilean Glas Lighthouse again becomes visible 9 miles to the E.N.E., just open of Rudha Cluer.

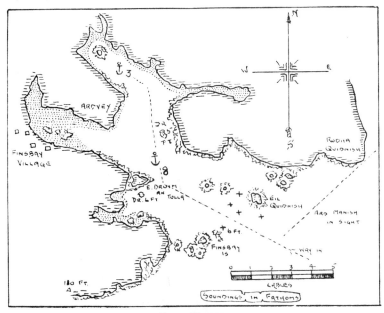

LOCH FINSBAY

Loch Finsbay—About ½ mile W. of Rudha Quidnish, Loch Finsbay runs N.W. for about 1 mile, forming a good sheltered anchorage fairly easy of access. The entrance is narrowed by Finsbay Island and some islets on the S.W. side, and Eiln. Quidnish and rocks on the N.E. side, to an apparent width of about 3 cables, but as foul ground extends outwards from each, the actual channel is only about 1 cable wide. The S.W. side of the loch is divided into three minor sheets of water by two headlands, the first running almost to a point at Eiln. Druim an Tolla, a tidal islet, and the second having a much broader front. The northernmost arm is the only one suitable for anchorage and it provides good sheltered holding ground in 3 fath., mud.

Yachts entering should give the islands a good berth until the loch is well open and steer straight up for Eiln. Druim an Tolla, about N.W. by W., keeping rather to the Eiln. Quidnish side. When nearing Eiln. Druim an Tolla, they should alter course to starboard and keep up the northern arm of the loch holding to the westward of the centre line of channel, then turn to port following the loch round, up the arm mentioned above, anchoring about halfway up in 3 fath., mud. To clear to the westward of the "dries 5 ft." rock and a reef extending from it for 50 yd. in a N'ly direction of E. of Ardvey, keep the lower left-hand peak of Eiln. Quidnish open of cliff N.W. of it.

In sketch plan the "dries 5 ft." rock should be shown more to the westward, one-third of the way across channel, so the course showing way in N. of Eiln. Druim an Tolla should bend more towards Ardvey Pt.

Stores—Small shops. P.O. Tel.

From Finsbay Island the coast runs S.W. for 3 miles in a series of rocky, headlands and bays to Loch Rodel, which is described with the Sound of Harris (see below).

Lingara Bay—About 1 mile W.S.W. of Loch Finsbay and 1¾ miles N.E. of Loch Rodel is Lingara Bay, behind Lingarabay Island, 108 ft. high, and some smaller islands of comparable height: above it a light-coloured patch caused by an old quarry shows up for many miles (see under Rodel Bay). The eastern entrance is wide and clean and vessels can anchor in about 3 fath. just past Eiln. Collam, which lies on the N. side. The western entrance and end are foul. Excellent shelter in winds from S. round by W. to N. but untenable in E'ly weather. Fishermen report that all dangers show at L.W.

Stores—None.

SOUND OF HARRIS
Chart 2642

The Sound of Harris is the channel between Harris and the island of North Uist. The N.E. point of the entrance is Ru Renish on Harris, and the S.W. point is Leac Lee, the N.E. point of North Uist. The distance across is 6 miles.

The sound is a perfect labyrinth of islands, islets, and rocks, many of the last covering. No one would be justified in attempting to negotiate the sound without the chart quoted, and in reasonably clear weather.

The tides through the sound are peculiar. According to the Admiralty Directions, in summer, during Neap tides the stream sets through from the Atlantic during the whole of the day, and in the reverse direction during the night. At Spring tides, it sets through from the Atlantic during

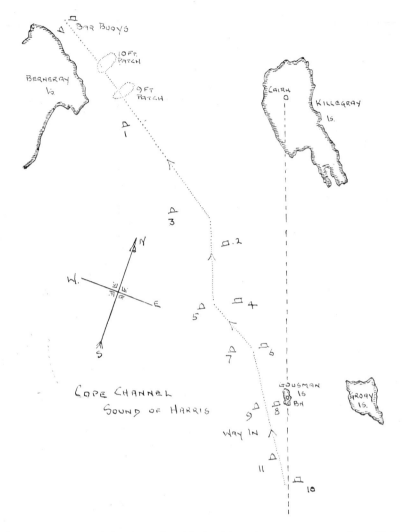

the greater part of the time the tide is rising, but never more than $5\frac{1}{4}$ hr., and in the reverse direction for the remainder of the tidal period. The speed varies, according as the channel is obstructed with islets and rocks, from 2 to 6 knots. During the winter there is a variation both in time and direction.

A buoyed channel through (Cope Channel—see sketch) has been established. Approach from southward on the line a beacon on Gousman Island and a cairn on Killegray Island. The bearing of this leading line is 338° and its outer end is marked by a R and W can buoy fl. R 5 sec. N.E. of Hermetray. The most E'ly pair, Nos. 10 and 11, lie S.S.E.of Gousman Island and S.S.W. of Groay Island. There are no hazards in this passage provided the track is **strictly** adhered to but there are two shallow patches (9 ft. and 10 ft.) to S.E. of the Bar Buoys.

High water is approximately 40 min. before H.W. at Stornoway and there is a 14 ft. rise at Sp. and 10 ft. at Np. West of No. 3 buoy the bottom of sand and weed shows up clearly.

Passing between the Bar Buoys alter course to N.N.W. to a blk. con. buoy showing a wht. fl. lt. ev. sec. lying about 8 cables W. of Pabbay.

It is said that if there is a deep swell at the Bar Buoys conditions are not suitable for a visit to St. Kilda.

The other channel through is on the Harris side of the sound (see plan). Entering round Ru Renish, give this point a wide berth, as it is foul, and steer for Cook Rock. If Cook Rock is not visible, keep Jane Tower between the two highest point of Ben Chaipabhall, i.e., above Cape Difficulty, and this position will bring your port bow on the blk. buoy.

This rock is awash at L.W. and is marked by a blk. buoy. Leave this mark to port and steer for the centre of the passage between the wht. beacon on Black Rock and Jane Tower. **The beacon on Black Rock is of conventional shape and resembles a disused lighthouse while Jane Tower is a cement cairn, shaped like a hay-rick and painted white on its S.E. side. Black Rock beacon having open water background is the most conspicuous mark.**

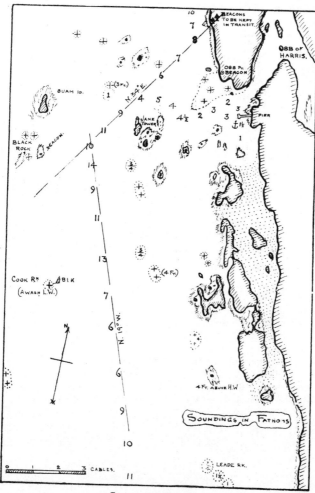

SOUND OF HARRIS

Keep on through these narrows until the two beacons on shore N. of Obb Pt. are in line (light steel structures on concrete bases painted white, with beyond them, also on the line, a white painted rock), then turn to starboard and keep them in transit until closing the land.

If making for the Obb of Harris (or Leverburgh) hold on this line till 1 cable past Jane Tower, then steer E. for a point just S. of the pier and keep the lead going and watch particularly the long spit off Obb Pt. The beacon on Obb Pt. is of white stone, with what appears to be a disused lantern on its top.

If making through the sound, carry on until close to the land, still keeping the beacons in transit. From Obb Pt. to Ru Carnan, which lies about 1 mile further on, the shore should be kept aboard. A red beacon off Ru Carnan marks Sgeir Voulinish, a rock which dries 3 ft. and, leaving this to port, steer to the westward of a blk. beacon which lies about $\frac{3}{4}$ mile to the northward, on Red Rock. This beacon is about $1\frac{1}{4}$ cables W. of Strome Island, off the Harris shore, 6 cables N. of Ru Carnan. Leave this beacon to starboard, and steer to the westward of Coppay Island, which lies off Toe Head, at the N.E. end of the sound. Keep on this course for $\frac{3}{4}$ mile, and then the water is clear to Shillay Island, the outer island at the N.W. end of the sound. St. Kilda Islands lie 42 miles W.N.W. from Shillay.

Approaching from the westward, the landmarks are Pabbay Island and the high hill at Cape Difficulty. The leading lines into the sound are: the two beacons on Red Rock and Sgeir Voulinish in line (to the eastward), and the beacons on Sgeir Voulinish and Obb Pt. (to the westward). If beating into the sound, consult the chart carefully on going outside these lines. If, due to bad visibility, the beacons cannot be picked up, the greatest care must be exercised after passing Cape Difficulty to avoid Colla Sgeir and the rocks off the Harris shore. Leave the blk. beacon to port and the red to starboard. For remainder of the passage, see directions above.

This is the only passage through to the W. side of the Outer Hebrides for over 90 miles. There is only one light, and the passage must be made in daylight.

Anchorages

Rodel Bay—This bay lies on the E. side of Ru Renish. The square tower of St. Clement church on the E. side of the bay, forms a good landmark, and a scar on the hillside a mile or so beyond the head of the bay shows up well even in hazy weather. Ru Renish must be given a good berth, and Duncan Rock, with $4\frac{3}{4}$ ft. over it at L.W., lies on the W. side of the bay, just within the entrance.

Otherwise it is clean to near the head. The anchorage is in 4 fath., opposite the shingle beach on the E. side. Do not pass beyond a line joining the last house above the shingle beach to starboard and the point in centre of bay to port as there is a rock awash at L.W. lying halfway between shingle beach and bay point and about 100 yd. off-shore. Beware of the dangerous submerged wreck between the point and the awash rock.

Quite exposed to the southward, and should only be used as a temporary anchorage. If desired, a pilot for the Sound of Harris may be engaged here.

Better anchorage may be had in a small pool, Poll an Tighmhail just within the N.E. entrance, sheltered by the Vallay islets (see sketch plan). An off-white scar on E. side of Vallay Island helps to identify anchorage. There are three channels into the pool: Sea, Island and Bay and the last-named is that recommended.

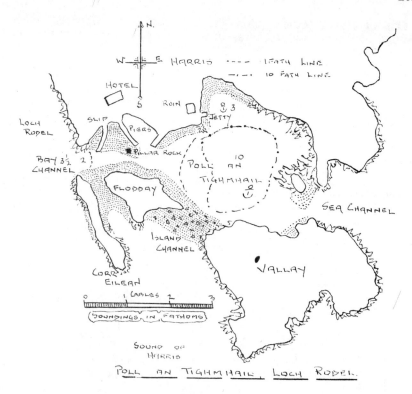

POLL AN TIGHMHAIL, LOCH RODEL.

There is under 1 ft. of water in this channel at L.W. and around 13 ft. at H.W. At the end of it there is a pillar rock surmounted by a perch and when the top of the rock is awash there is 12 ft. in the channel. Coming in keep towards N. end of Corr Eilean and steer for a point about 20 ft. S. of pillar rock and from there make towards centre of pool. Between the pecked lines in sketch there is less than 1 ft. at L.W. (bottom soft mud) but in the area marked by pecked and dotted line there are 8 to 10 fath. A recommended anchoring position is in S. side of pool when W. point of Vallay just closes the point in Harris at S.W. entrance to Loch Rodel (S. anchor in sketch). Anchorage can be had in 3 fath. in N. of pool off jetty (N. anchor in sketch) but swinging room is very restricted and a kedge is necessary.

Good anchorage for small yachts in 1¾ to 3 fath. can be had behind a rock which dries 7 ft. in N.E. corner of pool. It is reported free from swell and there are ring bolts on the rock and at N. end of islet at pool end of Sea Channel.

The Sea Channel dries at L.W. springs and it is very narrow and shallows with boulders extend from the N. shore to beyond mid-channel, and are very dangerous as they cover about half flood or earlier.

The Island Channel has least water in it (dries 4 ft.) and the bottom is very uneven with boulders.

Perfect shelter and beside a good hotel.

Stores—P.O. and stores at Leverburgh. Hotel. Petrol. **Water**—At houses.

Obb of Harris (Leverburgh)—The approach is as described under "Sound of Harris" and anchorage can be had on either side of the pier in 2 to 3 fath.

Be careful not to go too far past the pier, as it is shoal; but in place shown on the plan of Sound of Harris one is clear of steamers coming to the pier.

Stores—Shop. P.O. Tel. Petrol. Calor Gas. **Water**—At pier. **Const.** —4 hr. 35 m. Dover. Sp. 12½ ft., Np. 9½ ft.

Ensay—Anchorage in 1¼ fath. in centre of the bay opposite deserted mansion house. Sheltered from N.W. through S. to E. Approach from Sgeir Voulinish taking care that tide does not set the yacht off her course.

The rocks on the N. side of bay project far into bay and this must be noted when anchoring.

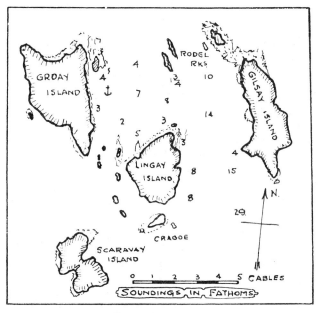

GROAY ANCHORAGE

Groay Anchorage (see plan)—A group of four islands and a number of smaller islets, lies in the centre of the southern entrance to the Sound of Harris. These are called the Groay Islands, and behind them there is splendidly sheltered anchorage in 4 fath.

The entrance is easy and clean, if the passage between Gilsay and Lingay Islands is taken. Reported to be very subject to swell and reported subject to scend in most winds.

Stores—Rodel.

Basin of Vaccacy (see plan)—The Harmetray Islands are a group of islands lying off the N.E. end of North Uist, at the southern side of the entrance to the Sound of Harris, and in the bay formed between Harmetray Island, which is the largest and most E'ly of the group, and Vaccacy Island which lies behind it, there is perfect shelter and anchorage in 4 fath.

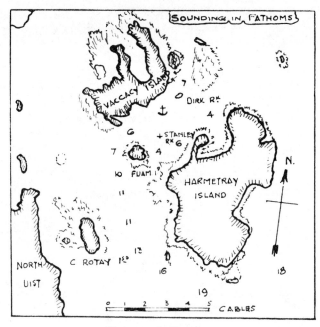

VACCACY ANCHORAGE

The entrance is not difficult if the channel to the W. of Harmetray Island and that between Fuam and Vaccacy Islands is taken. There are two rocks in the bay, Stanley Rock, which has 8 ft. over it at L.W. and Dirk Rock which dries 4 ft.

There is also a very snug anchorage for small yachts in 3 fath. in the bay on the N. side of Harmetray Island, known as Acarsaid Mor. Reported (1963) as uncomfortable in heavy N'ly weather. Holding ground poor owing to thick seaweed.

Good anchorage, too, S. of Stanley Rock between Fuam and Harmetray but on no account should the passage between Fuam and Harmetray be attempted.

Stores—None. **Water**—Small freshwater loch on Harmetray Island. **Const.** —4 hr. 35 m. Dover. Sp. 11½ ft., Np. 8½ ft.

NORTH UIST
Charts 2825 and 3674

North Uist is the island directly S. of the Sound of Harris. The eastern coastline extends about 8½ miles from Leac Lee, at the S. side of the sound, to Flodday Islands, which are the first of the islands between North Uist and Benbecula.

The coast is free of dangers beyond ½ cable off-shore. Two and a half miles below Leac Lee is Weaver Pt., the northern point of the entrance to Loch Maddy. On it is shown a wht. fl. lt. ev. 3 sec., 3½ miles further down is the entrance to Loch Eport, and it is a further 3 miles to the Flodday Islands.

Loch Maddy and Loch Eport are the only places to anchor on this coast.

LOCH MADDY
Chart 2825. C.C.C.S.C. 34

Weaver Pt. is the N. point of the entrance, and off it lies Maddy Beg, an islet 15 ft. high. Leac Maddy is the S. point of the entrance, which is 8 cables across. Off the outer or E. side of this point lies Maddy More, and off the inner part of it lies Glas More on which is gp. (2) fl. wht. lt. ev. 6 sec. In strong winds and adverse tides the seas outside are very bad.

Entering from the S. side, Maddy More is steep-to on its outer side and Leac Maddy has rocks off it $\frac{1}{2}$ cable. Glas More lies $1\frac{3}{4}$ cables off the S. shore and has rocks off its W. side for 1 cable, but the channel between it and the shore is clean.

A group of four islets, the Fahore and Ree Lee islets, lie $\frac{3}{4}$ mile further in, and the S. shore is clean till approaching them. These islets are practically joined together at L.W. The point on the S. shore opposite the islets,

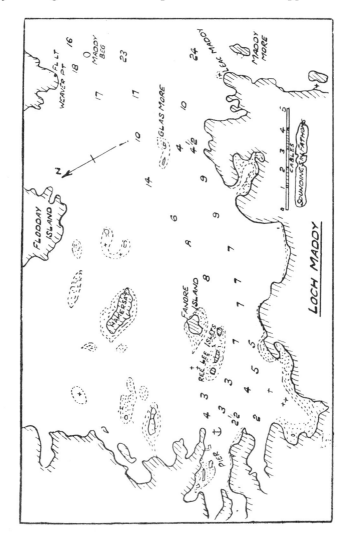

shoals out fully ½ cable, and near mid-channel should be taken. Give the islets a berth to starboard of 1 cable and anchor in 3 to 4 fath. beyond them, off the pier, which will be seen on the S. side of the point opposite.

A reflector beacon 4 ft. high has been established on Camaird Pt., S. of the pier and also on mainland and islands on either side of channel from Maddy Mor to pier.

The bottom is soft mud, and the holding ground not very good.

Stores—Shops. Half-holiday—Tuesdays. P.O. Tel. Hotel. Petrol. Calor Gas. **Water**—On pier inside gate on left side. Ferry to Uig in Skye. **Const.** —4 hr. 45 m. Dover. Sp. 13¾ ft., Np. 10½ ft.

There are some good anchorages to the northward, but access to them all is difficult.

Loch Partan—A perfectly sheltered lagoon in the N.E. corner. Rounding Weaver's Pt., turn N.W. and proceed up Loch Partan channel between the mainland and Flodday Island. Keep mid-channel. Halfway up McKay Rock (covers) lies about 1 cable off-shore on the E. side. The channel narrows at its northern end and shoal water extends fully 1 cable on both hands. Once clear of Flodday, steer for Lowlander's Pt. ahead. Keep in mid-channel between Lowlander's Pt. and the islets to the S.W. of it and hold on to the centre of lagoon, then turn to starboard and proceed up Loch Partan, keeping on the S. side of mid-channel and making to pass S. of the islet (joined to the N. shore at L.W.). It is dangerous to anchor to the W. of this islet as the bay is foul with rocks. Proceed through the channel between this islet and the S. shore and anchor about 1½ cables inside the inner loch keeping towards the S. shore.

Sponish Harbour—Pass through channel between Flodday Island and the islet Little Glas (11 ft.) to the S. of Flodday, giving both shores a fair berth. Immediately you are clear of the channel, haul over to the N. to avoid a dangerous reef, Long Rock, which lies W. of Little Glas. Steer to pass S. of Feramas Island (the next island W. of Flodday), giving the shore a good berth, then keep right up centre of channel between Feramas and the islands to the S. of it. Anchor in 3 fath. when the channel N. of Feramas begins to open up, taking care to avoid a 2 ft. rock that lies in the middle of the channel about halfway between Feramas and the islets W. of it. It is about 1½ cables W. of the N. end of Feramas and slightly to the S. of the line of the N. shore of Feramas.

Charles Harbour—The most difficult of access, owing to many reefs and rocks on either hand of entry. It would be best to make this anchorage at L.W. when some of the reefs show. Pass midway between Hamersay and Fahore (see plan). Passing to W. of both, turn to N.W. and head for a farm lying to S. of Sponish House (a conspicuous 3-storey house). Anchor in 3 fath. on this line about 2 cables off-shore. There are bad reefs to the N. of this line (some of which dry) and to the S. of it shoal water extends in places off the islets for as much as 2 cables.

Orinsay—Perfect shelter may be obtained in the narrow channel behind Orinsay, entering about half-flood from Charles Harbour with careful use of Chart 2825. The channel is narrow and only about 6 ft. deep, so that yachts should moor, but the bottom is soft mud and a vessel can sink in without listing. If necessary one can go alongside the pier which dries out. Very convenient for shops, etc.

Valoquie—An anchorage easy to make but rather exposed to the N., lies S. of Valoquie Island about 4 cables S.E. of the steamer pier. This anchorage should not be made at H.W. as the wreck of a steamer lies on the E. side of the channel and just covers. When the wreck can be seen enter from about due N. and in settled weather anchor N. of it in about 2 fath. but if any swell works in yachts may pass close W. of it and go down the middle of the bay, which shoals slowly from 10 ft. to 7 ft., soft mud. No stores and the house is empty.

LOCH EPORT
C.C.C.S.C. 38

Loch Eport is the next loch, $2\frac{1}{2}$ miles S. of Loch Maddy and the coast between is clean. The entrance is about $\frac{1}{2}$ mile long and, for most of its length, less than 1 cable wide. In the outer and wider part of the entrance there are some bad rocks, Bo Lea and Bo Carrach, but they are easily avoided by keeping N. of the centre line when approaching the narrows.

Clearing the narrows, which are generally steep-to, wide bays open up both to N. and S. The latter is encumbered with rocks and is not recommended. The former affords splendid shelter but there are a number of rocks and reefs running from the inner end of the narrows (N. shore) to nearly halfway across its mouth. The outer rock, Sgeir na Iolla, dries 12 ft. and just N. of it is another which dries 5 ft. Once these rocks are safely astern turn up centre of bay and anchor in 2 to 3 fath. off E. shore. The W. side of the bay is very foul. Holding ground reported not good owing to heavy growth of seaweed.

West of the bays the loch narrows again and Skart Rocks (a group of small islets) lie right in the centre of fairway. Leave these to starboard giving them a fair berth. Two cables further on lies Ship Rock (about 10 ft. high and surmounted by a small cairn). Keep mid-channel between Ship Rock and S. shore. A further 2 cables on is One Stone Rock marked by a perch (reported missing 1953). This is an extensive reef. Once it is passed either hold the S. shore to avoid McMillan Rock (dries 2 ft.) and a shoal patch to the E. of it and carry on till the loch narrows at the tidal islet, Ferguson Island, off the N. shore, or turn to starboard and make for Eiln. Trenoi (3 cables N.W. of One Stone Rock) giving it a berth of about 1 cable; hold N. side of mid-loch till within 2 cables of Wether Is. (the next islet to W.) then cross over to S. side of loch till Ferguson Island is reached. Good anchorage off N. shore W. of Ferguson Island in 2 to 3 fath.

North Trefick Island, about $\frac{1}{2}$ mile from head of loch, is marked by a cairn and S. Trefick by two cairns and Stewart Is. 1 cable W. of Treficks has a cairn. Do not go beyond Red Calf Is. at head of loch.

BENBECULA
Chart 3168

The first of the islands below Loch Eport are the Flodday Islands, and then Benbecula, and this whole E. coast should be given a wide berth of about 1 mile. From Flodday Beg, the northern island, down to Loch Skiport in South Uist, is about 10 miles, and the coast between is greatly broken up and has many outlying dangers. It is a bewildering maze of islets, rocks and inlets. With the chart quoted, some of the anchorages are accessible. The tide runs strongly in the sounds between the islands and anchorages can be uncomfortable sometimes as a consequence.

Anchorages

Flodday Sound—The sound runs behind Flodday More and Beg between these islands and Hamary Island, Ronay, and N. Uist, and the anchorage is either between Hamary and Flodday More or in the bay in N. Uist due N. of the E. end of Hamary both in 3 fath. The latter is reported as the less subject to tide. The approach is made S. of Flodday More and there is no difficulty if the Flodday More shore is held. Going to the N. anchorage keep mid-channel between Hamary and the islets S.W. of Flodday Beg. There are channels N. and S. of Flodday Beg but both are reef encumbered with many sunken rocks.

Kalin. Loch nan Ceall—In the sound between Ronay and Grimsay. There are some bad rocks, Bo More, Bo Carrack, Bo na Traghad in entrance to loch, but by keeping between 1 and 1½ cables off the Ronay shore they are all avoided. Keep the Ronay shore and turn into sound when that opens up and anchor in centre of loch in 1½ to 2 fath. when the conspicuous cottage N. of Kalin village opens up (this is **not** the conspicuous cottage marked on the chart just N. of St. Michael's Pt., the W. point of entrance to the sound). There is anchorage off Kalin village but approach is difficult and it is badly subject to tide. Anchorage reported free of tide N. of Garbh Eilean Mor in Bagh Clann Neill but local knowledge is necessary to make it.

Stores—Shop at Baymore, 1 mile. P.O

Coming along this coast, the principal dangers to avoid are Ritchie Rock, with 3 ft over it, off the S. end of Ronay Isle, and Bo Grianamol, with 7 ft. on it, lying N.E. of Wiay Island.

Peter's Port—At the S.E. corner of the Benbecula group is Wiay, an island 2 miles long and 330 ft. high. At the very S.E. tip lie N. Dusgeir, a small group of rocks and S. Dusgeir, an isolated rock, both about 2 cables off-shore, and 3 cables apart. Round these, and steer due W. (true) from S. Dusgeir for 4 cables to clear Red Rock, a group drying 4 ft., running out on the starboard side. Then steer up the fairway with Wiay to starboard and a row of islands and rocks to port. Pass Cleit nan Luch,

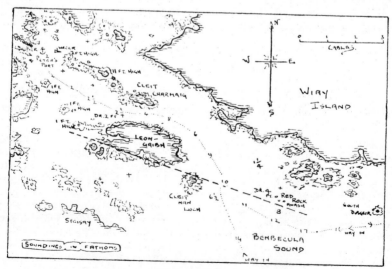

PETER'S PORT

a small steep islet, and Leongaibh, 3 cables long and 50 ft. high; and then turn about 4 pt. to port between Leongaibh and Cleit Charmaig, another small steep island the next in the row. Turn a little to starboard round Cleit Charmaig and carry on for the pier which will be seen 4 cables ahead, keeping the row of rocks almost 1 cable to starboard. Anchor opposite the pier in 2 fath. To the N.E. of this line, about the "R'S" in "PETER'S" on the plan in Chart 3168, lies a wreck covering at 2 hr. flood, presenting a steel knife-edge most dangerous to any vessel. For this reason the alternative way in, keeping Cleit Charmaig and the rest of the row of rocks to port, should not be taken.

If approaching from the S., aim N. by W. (mag.) from the Luirsay Islands, 3 miles N. of Ushinish Light, for a point rather W. of the 305 ft. summit at the extreme S.W. end of Wiay, keeping well clear of Wiay until Cleit an Luch and Red Rock (if showing) are identified, then carry on as above. Perfect shelter.

Stores—Shop and bus 2 miles along the road to the westward.

SOUTH UIST
Charts 3674, 1796 and 3168

South Uist lies to the S. of the Benbecula group. It extends for about 15 miles and has three lochs, Loch Skiport at the N., Loch Eynort and Loch Boisdale at the S. There are also in the extreme N. two little known havens, Loch Sheilavaig, which affords excellent shelter and is not difficult of access, and Loch Carnan, of which an enlarged plan appears on Chart 3168.

Just S. of Loch Skiport lies Ushinish Pt., showing a sectored light fl. W.R. 20 sec., 176 ft. (U), nominal range of 19 mile in white sector 193° through W. to 356° and of 15 miles in red sector 356° to 013°. Five miles further on is Loch Eynort and the coast thus far is clear if given a reasonable offing.

Loch Boisdale lies 3 miles below Loch Eynort and between the two lochs lie Stuley Isle, close to the shore, with some islets off it. They should be given a fair berth. At the S. side of the entrance to Loch Boisdale lies Calavay Island, on the E. side of which a beacon shows a fl. lt. red and wht. sectors, ev. 3 sec. It shows white in the N.E. where the water is clean, and red over MacKenzie Rock, and the water south of it. MacKenzie Rock lies 1 mile S.E. of the light and has 10 ft. over it at L.W. A red buoy is moored ½ cable to the eastward of it. Clan Ewan Rock, which dries 3 ft., lies about 7 cables S. of this buoy and 2½ cables off-shore.

Between this and Ru Melvich, the southern point of South Uist, there are no real dangers.

Loch Sheilavaig—Charts 2750 and 3168. Loch Sheilavaig (pronounced Shellaveg) lies W. of the two Luirsay Islands, which form the N. point of the entrance to Loch Skiport and lie 3 miles N. of Ushinish Lt. Ho. If approaching from the S., pass round these islands and two others close W. of them, giving them a moderate berth and leaving to starboard Grey Island, a double island shaped like a dumb-bell and lying 3 cables to the N. On passing the fourth island the entrance to the loch will be seen opening to the S.W. between this island and Eiln. Phadruig, a much smaller but bold island lying 1 cable to the westward. Steer halfway between the two islands for Canmore Island which looks like a peninsula jutting out from the S.E. shore nearly 4 cables away. Give this island a

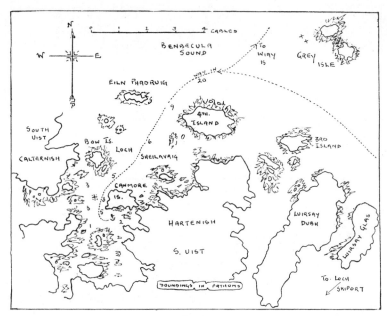

LOCH SHEILAVAIG

berth of 40 or 50 yd. to clear the shore and also a rock (said to be 5 ft. deep) lying 100 yd. from its west H.W. mark. Round Canmore Island and anchor S. of it in 2 fath., mud.

Coming from the N., from the N.E. corner of Wiay, aim S.W. (mag.) for 2 cables W. of Grey Isle when the entrance to Loch Sheilavaig will be seen dead ahead. Excellent shelter and good holding ground.

Stores—none.

Loch Carnan (Chart 3168)—Approaching from the S., steer as for Loch Sheilavaig (above), but keep N. of Eiln. Phadruig, then close the shore of South Uist and follow it N.W. keeping about 100 yd. off H.W. mark to avoid a dangerous line of rocks and reefs lying 2 to 3 cables to north-ward. The anchorage is rather deep, 6 to 7 fath., but 2 cables past the pier and oil tanks a depth of 4 fath. may be found in a bight, the N.W. side of which is formed by a small island.

Entrance from the N. is more difficult as there is a confusing maze of islands and rocks between S. Uist and Benbecula. If this route is taken it should be at L.W., as all isolated rocks are then exposed. From S. Dusgeir (see Peter's Port above) steer W. (mag.) across the sound nearly 2 miles for Gasay, the largest island, green, 40 ft. high, and 2 cables in length. On a reef close N. of Gasay is a prominent perch with a square top, and on an islet 1 cable to the N. is a similar perch with a spherical top. Steer between the perches and along the fairway towards the pier and tanks, and when less than 1 cable from them curve round to starboard and anchor in bight described above.

For the approach from the N. a lit buoyed channel has been established. The first buoy laid in deep water about 1 mile S.S.E. of Wiay Is., is a red and wht. can showing a fl. red lt. ev. 5 sec. The second, 1 mile W. of the first, is to be left to port going W. and it lies just N. of Grey Isle and

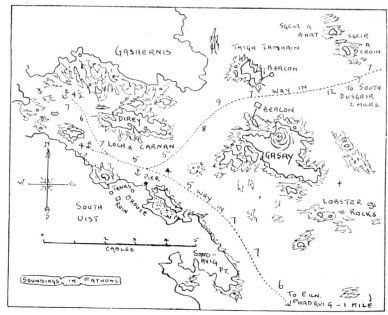

LOCH CARNAN

shows a fl. red lt. ev. 3 sec. Half a mile further W. there are two buoys, the N. of which (blk. con.) shows a fl. wht. lt. ev. 2¾ sec. and the S. a fl. red lt. ev. 2 sec. Pass between these two buoys. In the channel between Taigh Iamhain and Gasay is a red can buoy showing a fl. red lt. ev. sec. Pass close N. and W. of this and close W. of the next red can buoy (fl. red lt. ev. 6 sec.) lying 1½ cables further to the S.S.W. Two cables further to the S.S.W. is a blk. con. buoy showing a wht. fl. lt. ev. sec. Pass close E. of this. On the S. shore are two leading lights (quick fl. red) on a line of 220° which gives the channel between the last two buoys mentioned above and on to the anchorage off the pier and tanks.

LOCH SKIPORT
Chart 2750. C.C.S.C. 35

Loch Skiport lies 2 miles N. of Ushinish Pt. The entrance is about 6 cables wide, and a course for the road (conspicuous) above the disused pier leads right up centre of channel. Off the southern shore at the entrance lies Ornish Island, and between it and Ornish Pt. on the S. shore are several islets and rocks. To the W. of Ornish Island, and also off the southern shore, lies Shillay Beg, and connected to its N. end, Shillay More Island and, just past this island, MacCormack Bay opens out on the N. shore. Beyond this the loch narrows to less than 1 cable, leading into the Linnhe Arm, which runs inland for about 1 mile. **Const.** —4 hr. 58 m. Dover.

There are several good anchorages on the S. shore and in the Linnhe Arm, but the S. shore is reported foul with weed in places. The chart quoted is necessary if using them. Three in the outer part of the loch can be made with the plan, but note that the rock shown 1½ cables N.W. of Wizard Isle in the plan only shows at L.W. and is not an islet.

Stores—None. **Water**—Burns. Bus service to Benbecula airport passes crossroads 3½ miles up road. Telephone kiosk ¼ mile up Linnhe Arm.

McCormack Bay—This bay lies on the N. shore 1 mile within the entrance. Entering the loch by the N. side of Ornish Island and the Shillay Island, there are no dangers. The islands are clean within 50 yds., and also the N. shore. The W. point of the entrance to McCormack Bay has a reef running out 50 yd., and another similar reef about halfway up on the same side, but otherwise the shores are perfectly clean. At the top it takes a bend to the eastward at right angles and narrows. This branch is called Mannoch Arm. Anchorage can be had in 3 fath., at the head of the bay, or in 2 fath. just within the entrance to Mannoch Arm, both perfectly sheltered. Sp. 12¾ ft., Np. 9½ ft. But reported as being subject to severe squalls in S'ly weather and holding ground poor.

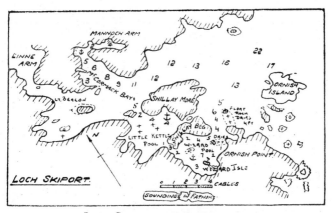

LOCH SKIPORT AND ANCHORAGES

Little Kettle Pool—This land-locked anchorage lies on the W. side of Shillay More. Enter round the N. side of the island, keeping it well aboard until reaching the anchorage marked on the plan. There are 2 fath. at L.W. in the channel at the entrance, and anchorage is in 3 to 4 fath., avoiding the rocks in the pool.

Wizard Pool—A land-locked anchorage S. of Shillay Beg. Entry can be made either through the Kettle Pool and the channel S. of Shillay Beg, in which there is a least depth of 1 fath., or by the channel E. of Shillay Beg. If making in by the E. channel keep Wizard Is. (see plan) just open of the E. point of Shillay Beg until lagoon opens out, then steer to starboard to avoid a reef ending with a rock that dries, that runs in a N.W'ly direction from Ornish Pt. towards Shillay Beg. This line of approach clears Float Rock (dries 4 ft.) lying N. of Ornish Pt. The E. point of Shillay Beg must be given a fair berth. Anchor where shown in the plan, passing mid-way between Wizard Isle and the rock which dries about 1 ft. to the N.W. of it. This anchorage is preferable to Kettle Pool, as the soundings are less and it is less subject to heavy gusts in bad weather.

Water—Burn.

LOCH EYNORT
Charts 1795 and 1796. C.C.C.S.C. 35

Loch Eynort lies 5 miles below Ushinish Pt. The outer part is about 6 cables wide and about 1½ miles long, when there are narrows where the passages are only about 50 yd. wide and where the tide runs strongly between 5 and 7 knots. About 1 mile within the entrance, ½ cable off

Coilenish Pt., lies Bo Coilenish, a rock which is awash at L.W.O.S. and forms the only danger along the N. shore. The S. shore, however, must be given a berth of quite 2 cables, as there are several outlying rocks. Eiln. Eallan and two other islets connected to the shore at L.W. lie 7 cables within the entrance, on the S. shore, and in Cearcdal Bay, a clean bay just beyond them, anchorage can be had in 2 to 4 fath., or in the bay on the N. shore just outside the narrows, in similar depths. This bay is also clean but the loch is exposed to the E. and S.E. swell, and is not particularly recommended. Sp. 12 ft.

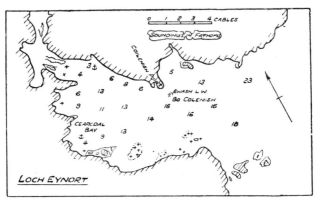

LOCH EYNORT

To go up into Inner Loch it is necessary to pass through two narrow channels. The first is in the N.W. corner of outer loch, between Struthan Beg (the N. shore) and a tidal islet on the S. shore but a long drying reef, Bo Dearg, in the centre reduces the channel to about 50 yd. The chart gives a leading line for this channel—a cottage on shore beyond in line with a 114 ft. hill lying to the N.W.—but the cottage is now a ruin and difficult to locate. Hold the Struthan Beg shore going through but as soon as loch begins to open out veer to port to avoid a rock lying off the Struthan Beg shore. The second narrows, Strue Beg, are equally narrow and to get through the W. side must be kept aboard. Inside, anchorage can be had in any of the bays except that to N.E. which is shallow and has a rock encumbered approach. The best are: the one immediately to E. of N. end of second narrows. Hold either shore going in to avoid a rock dead in centre of narrows. Anchorage is in 2 fath. Bagh Lathach. In 2½ fath. in centre of first bay on N. shore W. of narrows. West of Bagh Lathach the loch narrows and mid-channel must be kept as both shores are foul, particularly the N. one. West of these narrows a large drying reef, Sgeir na Ortireach, lies in the fairway with rocks between it and the N. shore. Hold down towards, but not too close, to S. shore (keep in second quarter of width of loch from S. shore). Near the southern extremity of Sgeir Ortireach there is a boulder which is reported as only covering at H.W. Sp. Good anchorage in 2 to 3 fath. in centre of bay to port and also in 1½ fath, in next bay on N. shore off the cottage under the 114 ft. hill but if making the latter there are bad rocks extending from both shores across the entrance and approach must be made up centre of bay.

LOCH BOISDALE

Chart 618 (see plan). C.C.C.S.C. 38

Loch Boisdale lies 3 miles below Loch Eynort. The entrance is ½ mile wide between the northern point and Calvay Island, which lies off the S. shore at the entrance. The loch runs inland for about 2 miles. Approaching from the N., there are no dangers, but if coming from the S., Clan Ewan Rock, which dries 3 ft., and McKenzie Rock, must be avoided, and the red buoy marking the latter left to port (see South Uist). It is reported that there is a strip of poor holding ground right down the centre of the harbour so let go close either to line of reef or to island. In a S.E'ly gale swell can reach right up to pier.

The fl. lt. on the E. end of Calvay Island shows red over these dangers and white over the clear water to the northward, then red again over foul ground to W. of light.

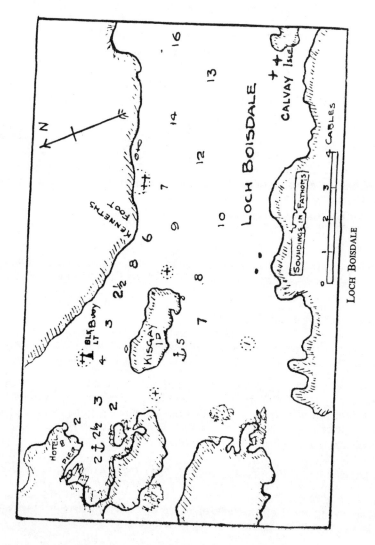

Kisgay Island lies in the centre, 1 mile within the entrance, and divides the loch. Anchorage can be had in 4 fath. fairly close to the S.W. side of Kisgay Island, the entrance being quite clear. By the N. side of the island is the entrance to Boisdale harbour. Kisgay Rock, which dries 2½ ft., lies 1 cable off the S.E. end of Kisgay Island, but Kenneth's Foot, the point on the N. shore opposite to it, is steep-to.

Just a little eastward of Kenneth's Foot there are some rocks ½ cable off-shore, but mid-channel is clear. A large bight runs in to the N., just past the Island of Kisgay and in the centre of it is a blk. con. buoy showing a wht. fl. lt. ev. 6 sec., marking Sgeir Rock. Leaving this to starboard, continue up the harbour and anchor in 2 fath. off the pier. Do not go far into the harbour. There is a pole marking the end of a reef there, and space is limited for swinging. In bad weather the S. anchorage shown on the plan is safer.

Stores—Shops (early closing—Tuesdays). P.O. Tel. Hotel. Petrol. **Water**—Tap at pier. **Const.** —5 hr. 03 m. Dover. Sp. 12¾ ft., Np. 9½ ft.

SOUND OF BARRA (Eastern Side)
Charts 3674, 1796 and 2770 (best)
(see also Sound of Barra, Western Side)
C.C.C.S.C. 39 and 40

Note—Soundings on Chart 2770 are in **feet** and the true meridian is slewed to the left.

The Sound of Barra lies between South Uist and Barra Island, and is about 6 miles wide. Eriskay Island lies at the N.E. side, just round Ru Melvish, the S. point of South Uist, and off Barra, on the other side, lies the Hellisay group, consisting from E. to W. of Gighay, Hellisay, Flodday, Fuiay, and numerous islets. Within the sound, on its W. side, lies Fuday Island.

There are a good many rocks and shoals which cover, but one or two good anchorages may be made with Chart 3674.

Anchorages

Outer and Inner Otter Vore—These anchorages lie behind the Hellisay group and are protected from the N. and W. by Fuday Island and Barra. Coming in from the E., keep towards Binch Rock buoy, a red and wht. ringed sp. buoy moored 1 cable S.E. of a rock with 11 ft., lying between Eriskay and the Hellisay group.

The channels on either side are clean, but keep clear of the S. end of Eriskay. Haul in round the N. end of Gighay and Hellisay Islands, keeping 1 cable off, and anchor off their N. side in 5 fath. If wishing to enter the Inner Otter Vore, which lies between the rocks off the N.W. end of Hellisay and Barra Island, give the patch a wide berth and pass between Grianameal, the northern islet of the patch, and Fuday Island. Grianameal must be given a berth of over 2 cables and under ½ mile. A 10 ft. patch lies ½ mile N.E. of this islet, and further off still, patches with 7 ft. and 6 ft.

Anchor in 4 to 6 fath. behind the patch of rocks lying between Grianameal and Hellisay.

Sgeirishun—To the W. of Rough Lingay (the island W. of Hellisay). Enter round the S. end of Rough Lingay, keeping to the Rough Lingay side of mid-channel to avoid the rocks N. of James Is. and anchor in middle of lagoon. Entrance can be made by the N. of Rough Lingay, but there are several rocks and reefs to be avoided.

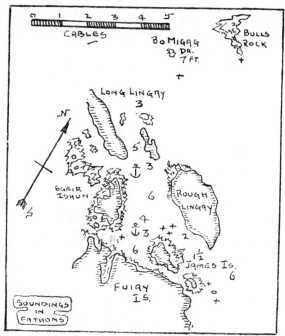

SGEIRISHUN ANCHORAGE

Hellisay—Between Hellisay and Gighay. A perfect anchorage for small craft, but rather encumbered with rocks. There is 12 ft. in N. entrance, and the dangers can be seen as the bottom is white sand and the water is clear. The plan shows way in better than any written description. Follow the lines of soundings and anchor in places shown. More swinging room in N.E. bay. This anchorage has not been surveyed officially and is blank on the charts, but members report favourably upon it.

The entrance is very narrow, tortuous, and difficult to locate as the pool beyond the entrance narrows and cannot be seen from seaward. But a cairn at the northern entrance has been painted white and this can be seen from outside the entrance.

Passage right through the channel is possible with care. The S. entrance has its western half blocked by a rock spit under water. The flood sets into (and ebb out of) both entrances at same time. Strongly for the first $1\frac{1}{2}$ hr. of flood.

Big Harbour, Eriskay (see plan)—There is a land-locked anchorage on the S.E. side of Eriskay Island, suitable for small yachts with auxiliary power, but difficult to enter. Rounding Ru Melvich, keep well off this point and towards Hartimeal Islet, which lies 6 cables to the S.W. Leave this islet well to port as it is foul, particularly off its E. and S.W. ends, and make for the harbour, the water being clean. On entering, hug the N. shore of Grey Pt. very close, not more than 20 yd. off, until on a line joining N. and S. points of entrance (the one N.N.E. of 2 fath. sounding in sketch and the one beside the 3 fath. sounding), then bear off to starboard to pass mid-way between the rock in mid-channel marked with a beacon (covers at about $\frac{3}{4}$ flood) and the S. shore. If rock is not showing, hold the S. shore about 20 yd. off until the bight S. of the $2\frac{1}{4}$ fath. soundings

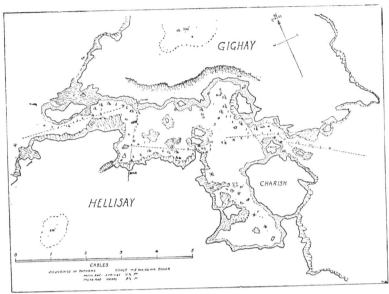

HELLISAY ANCHORAGE

is reached then bear to starboard, thereafter in both cases keep in mid-channel. If approaching from the S., give Stack Islet and the rocks off the S. end of Eriskay a wide berth.

The passage between Grey Pt. and the rock N. of it is not nearly as wide as is indicated in the sketch plan.

Stores—On N. side of island, 2 miles by cart track. P.O. Tel. **Water**—Burn beside black-roofed shed, S. side of bay. Sp. $11\frac{1}{2}$ ft., Np. $8\frac{1}{2}$ ft. **Const.** —5 hr. 03 m. Dover.

North Harbour, Barra (C.C.C.S.C. 39)—This harbour lies between the islands of Flodday and Fuiay, and Barra. Entering from the direction of Binch Rock buoy, and giving the shores of the islands a berth of 1 cable to starboard, there are no dangers up to the anchorage in 5 fath. off the N.W. end of Fuiay Island. Beatson's Shoal, which has a least depth of 8 ft., lies $4\frac{1}{2}$ cables S.S.W. of Flodday Island. If approaching from the southward, the E. coast of Barra must be given a wide berth, keeping well clear of Curachan Rock, 35 ft. high, before turning into the harbour. There are submerged rocks for $\frac{1}{2}$ mile to the N.E. of this rock

If entering the inner harbour, Chart 2770 is necessary.

Note—The soundings on this chart are in **feet.**

The best anchorage is further in than the two anchorages marked on this chart. On the S.E. end of the point dividing the western and eastern arms of the inner harbour is a prominent group of galvanised sheds (which show up well from seawards) with a pier immediately beneath them in the western arm. The anchorage is $2\frac{1}{2}$ cables beyond this pier, past the widest part of the western arm abreast of some cottages to the N. Good holding ground with soft mud in 2 fath. The tall chimney and the inn shown on the chart no longer exist.

Stores—At Castlebay. P.O. and telephone beside cottages. Buses to Castlebay. Air service from Tragh More, 2 miles to the N.

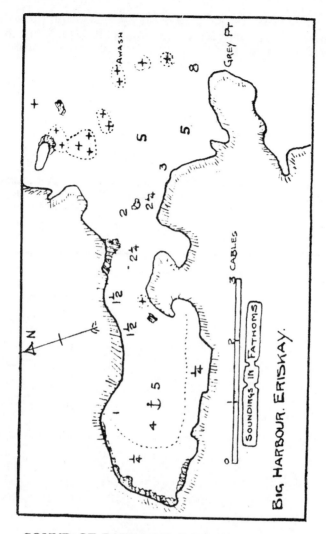

SOUND OF BARRA TO BERNERA ISLAND
Charts 3674 and 1796

The principal islands in the remainder of the chain of the Outer Hebrides from the Sound of Barra southwards are Barra, Vatersay, Muldoanich, Saundray, Pabbay, Mingulay, and Bernera at the extreme S.W. end, a distance of some 17 miles.

On the highest part of Bernera, Barra Head lighthouse shows a wht. lt., bright 30 sec., eclipsed 30 sec.

The E. side of this coast, from the sound to Muldoanich Island should be given a berth of about 2 miles, unless making for Castle Bay or Vatersay Bay, which will be described presently.

There are some dangerous rocks lying off the shore in the 5 miles to Muldoanich, which lies 1½ miles S. of Barra, and is the most E'ly of the outlying islands. Two miles E. by N. of Muldoanich lies Bo Vich Chuan, a rock with 4 ft. on it at L.W. It is marked by a blk. con. buoy on its S. side, showing a wht. fl. ev. 6 sec.

Coming S. from the Sound of Barra, the outer rock off the S.E. point of the entrance to N. Harbour is Curachan, 32 ft. high. It has rocks off its N.E. end for ½ mile. It is necessary to be well outside of line between this rock and Bo Vich Chuan buoy to clear all the dangers.

From Muldoanich to Bernera Island, a distance of about 10 miles, there are no dangers except from the exposed nature of this part of the Sea of the Hebrides.

The only good anchorages in this part of the Hebrides are Castle Bay, Barra, and Vatersay Bay. The latter is best entered by the S. side of Muldoanich.

Anchorages

Castle Bay, Barra. Chart 1144 (see plan)—Entering, come between Bo Vich Chuan buoy and Muldoanich Island, and leave the red buoy, N. of the island, close to port, as a reef lies N.E. of it. The beacon marking this reef is partly carried away (shows at half tide). The buoy shows a gp. (2) wht. fl. lt. ev. 12 sec.

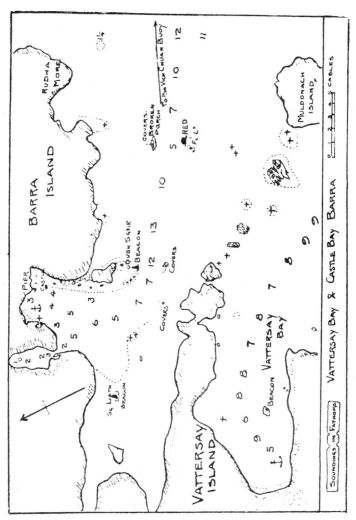

After passing the buoy, make for Dubh Sgeir beacon, and leave it close to starboard, but do not turn up the harbour until the pier shows clear to the left of the castle, because of the rocks just past the beacon. The beacon shows a wht. fl. lt. ev. 2 sec. If beating, this passage requires great care.

The anchorage is in the centre of the head of the bay, in 3 to 4 fath., N.W. of the castle, which stands on a small islet. Between the castle and the shore and to the E. the water is foul A good anchorage is further westward under the projecting rock opposite to the pier as this is well clear of the ferries.

Behind the castle there are usually a number of fishing boats anchored. On Sgeir Liath, a reef to the W., in the passage between Barra and Vatersay, a beacon shows a wht. fl. lt. ev. 3 sec. and two beacons, each showing a fix. red lt., are situated N.W. and N.E. of it (near Ru Glass on Barra). These give a leading line for the approach to the Dubh Sgeir light when coming through Vatersay Sound from the W. and should not be used when to the eastward of that light. Both lights are on a frame white tower and the E. (lower) beacon has a red triangle pointing upwards while a similar triangle on the W. (higher) beacon points downwards. There is another anchorage in Loch Kentagavel, a small loch off the W. side of Castle Bay, but its entrance is only a few yards wide and only possible at slack H.W., and good local knowledge is essential. **Const.** —5 hr. 03 m. Dover. Sp. 11½ ft., Np. 7 ft.

Stores—Shops. Tel. Hotel. Petrol. Calor Gas. **Water**—At pier. Steamer connection thrice weekly.

Vatersay Bay, Barra. Chart 1144 (see plan)—The entrance is to the S. Muldoanich Island and is clear water. The S. shore is shallow and the end of a spit is marked by a beacon. Anchorage at head of bay in 5 to 6 fath.

In sketch of Vatersay Bay and Castle Bay an island is shown close off peninsula dividing bays. This is incorrect. There **is** a small islet further off peninsula with beyond that again a larger island (the biggest of the group). To go from Vatersay Bay to Castle Bay without going round Muldoanich Island pass about 30 ft. west of this largest island and steer 030° (mag.) until on the line of Dubh Sgeir bn. and the red buoy then turn into Castle Bay.

In S.E. to S.W. winds Castle Bay anchorage can be uncomfortable but, under these conditions, shelter can be found in Cormaig Bay on N. side of Vatersay (see plan of Vatersay Sound).

Access is as follows: Pass between first bn. on Rudha Glas and Sgeir Liath keeping in mid-channel and continue on this course until second bn. on Barra shore is abeam (this bn. has a telegraph cable marker beside it). At this point turn due S. aiming for a knoll on the E'ly slope of Heishival More. This course clears the rock off the N.E. corner of Orosay Island and the shoal water to W. of Sgeir Liath. Anchor in 2 to 4 fath. in bay but do not go further up than W. side of Orosay Island.

VATERSAY SOUND
Chart 1144

This narrow sound which separates the island of Barra from Vatersay Island can only be used by small vessels under calm conditions. This applies particularly when making a passage from W. to E. Weather conditions and tide can give heavy disturbance at both ends of sound but particularly so off the W. entrance.

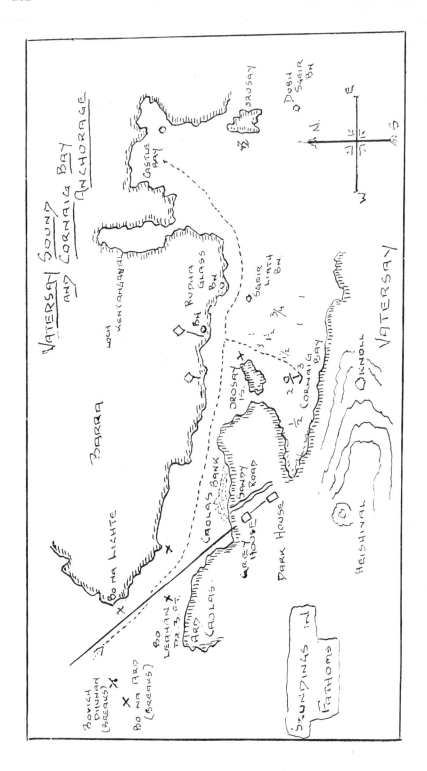

VATERSAY SOUND AND CORNAIG BAY ANCHORAGE

Approaching from Castlebay, the light on Sgeir Liath must be left to port and a mid-channel course steered until Rudha Feudail is reached. Thereafter follow the chart carefully and keep mid-channel till W. entrance is approached. Here tend towards the N. shore to avoid banks to southward but at the same time take care to give Rock Bo na Lichte on the N. shore a reasonable berth.

Even in calm weather any swell breaks heavily both over the banks to southward and over Bo na Lichte.

The W. entrance is about ¾ cable wide and tide floods from W. at 3 knots Sp. **Const.** −6 hr. 0 m. Dover.

For leading marks and lights in sound, see above under Castle Bay.

Approaching from the W. the entrance is only 2 cables wide owing to Bo na Lichte, a rock about ½ cable off Barra shore, and Bovich Dhunan 2 cables W. of it and Bo Lehan off Ard Caolas (S. point of entrance).

On approaching the entrance is very vague but a leading line through the passage is as follows: There are two houses on Vatersay, one on the shore grey in colour, and one further up the hill black in colour and these in line lead clear. A conspicuous white sandy road runs down the hill just E. of them.

Once inside the entrance veer to N. shore to avoid Bo Leahan but, as channel narrows, return to mid-channel to avoid rock on Barra shore which is further out than chart shows. Thereafter hold mid-channel and pass between bn. on Sgeir Liath and bn. N.N.E. of it.

Attention is drawn to caution given below in second paragraph under heading "Outer Hebrides, Western Side".

OUTER HEBRIDES (Western Side)

The western side of the Outer Hebrides is one of the most exposed coasts in Britain, and an element of risk is necessarily associated with its navigation. Lights and buoys are conspicuous by their absence, but fogs seldom occur, and the tidal streams are moderate. Nevertheless, some yachtsmen have been fascinated by the charm of exploring these wild coasts. It is advisable to have a full stock of large-scale charts, and a well manned yacht of not less than 10 tons, with auxiliary power.

It **must** be noted that if there is heavy W'ly weather or if a W'ly swell is running outside **very heavy** and dangerous seas can be expected at the western end of all the channels leading through to the W.

BERNERA ISLAND TO SOUND OF BARRA
Chart 1796

This coast consists of a scattered group of islands, the principal being Bernera, Mingulay, Pabbay, Saundray, Vatersay, and Barra, with sounds of the same name forming passages through, and affording no shelter from W'ly winds. There are no outlying dangers which cannot be seen, if the islands are given a reasonable berth.

SOUND OF BARRA
Chart 2770

The eastern approaches are described under Sound of Barra, Eastern Side. After passing between Stack Islands and Gighay Island, continue on a W'ly course till the E. end of Fuday Is. bears about N.N.W., then steer N.N.W. passing Fuday Is. about 1 cable off, until the two Kate beacons (of white stone) on Fiaray Is. are in line bearing W.N.W. Then proceed on that line through Drover Channel until the W. end of Fuday bears S.; alter course to N. until the S. end of Lungay Is. is in line with the summit of Ben Scrien on Eriskay Is. bearing E. by S. ½S. Then proceed to sea on a W. by N. ¼N. course, through the Temple Channel, which lies between the Temple and Inner Temple Rocks which have least depths of 8 ft. and 7 ft. respectively. Keep on this line till Fiaray is 2 miles astern, before turning N. so as to give the Washington Reefs a wide berth. There is a trigonometric cairn on the summit of Fiaray. Deeper draft vessels can use the Washington Channel 1 mile further N.

Coming in from the W., keep well off-shore until the channel is identified (see view D, on Chart 2770) and, if visibility is poor, it is better to approach from the Barra side where the shore is cleaner. The flood tide sets into the sound from both ends, and the ebb runs out, and the tidal streams are moderate except in Drover Channel, where they run 3 to 4 knots.

SOUND OF BARRA TO SOUND OF HARRIS
Charts 2474, 1796 and 3674

The W. coasts of South Uist and Benbecula are low-lying and shoal water extends over 1 mile out. There is no shelter, and as the appearance of the low points is rather deceptive, the coast should be given a wide berth of several miles. The land at parts is so low that the houses seen from some miles out appear to be sticking out of the sea.

The coast of North Uist is higher, with many outlying rocks and islands.

The group of Monach Islands, about 30 miles N. of the Sound of Barra, is marked by a disused lighthouse on Shillay Island, and is low-lying so that the lighthouse can be seen long before the islands. Approaching from the S., there are no outlying dangers except Bo Ruag, a rock which lies some 4 miles S. of the Sound of Monach, and dries 4 ft. There are many rocks and shoals in the sound, and it is better to pass to the West, giving the island a berth of 5 cables to avoid the rocks on its western side, and keeping inside the Huskeiran Rocks which lie about 1 mile to the N.W. The S. end of these rocks always shows. When through, steer for Causameal Is., leaving Deasgeir to starboard and the Mid Dureberg shoals to port, and off Causameal a course can be laid to clear Griminish Pt. The Haskeir Islands lie off this point about 7 miles to the N.W.

From Griminish Pt. the island of Pabbay off the Sound of Harris will be easily recognised, appearing as a very flat cone, and it should be passed on the outer side, between the island and Shillay Island. A sunken rock, Bo Lea, lies 3½ miles E. by N. ½N. of Griminish Pt.

Coming S. round Griminish Pt., the Sound of Causameal can be used, between Causameal and Ardarnar Pt. Pass about 2 to 3 cables off the point, inside the shallow patch, and avoid confusing Charlotte Rocks with Deasgeir if the former are showing. Pass to the S. of Deasgeir and make for the lighthouse on Shillay Island.

Anchorages

Monach Isles—Safe anchorages available from all winds.

Shillay—Good shelter from winds S.W. to N.W. in 3 to 4 fath. off Lighthouse Pier at S.E. corner of Island of Shillay. Approach from north using two beacons on the Eternal Isles as lead in marks (231° T). Under no circumstances approach anchorage using S. channel.

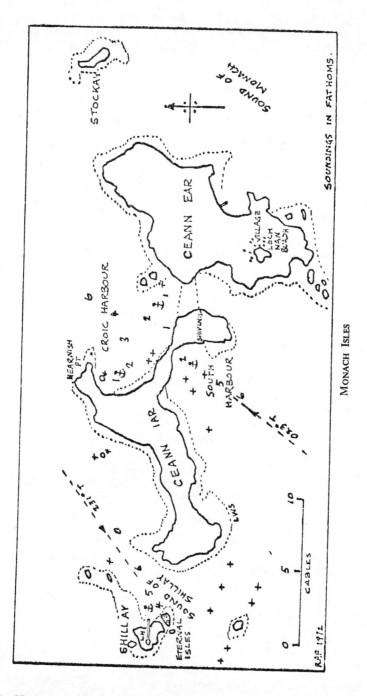

Croic Harbour—Good shelter from E. winds through S. to N. The anchorages are on the W. side of the bay and the S.E. corner in one to two fathoms. On entry keep Hearnish point which is foul, 2 cables to starboard. Beware of lobster pots.

South Harbour—Good shelter from all N'ly winds may be had, provided there is no S'ly scend which may make it uncomfortable. This anchorage should be approached keeping the skerry S. of Shillay at least 5 cables to port and the middle of sandy beach to W. of Shivinish, bearing 023° T.

General—All rocks shown are visible at low water either as such or as patches of kelp. Yachts are advised to avoid the Sound of Monach and E. side of island, due to numerous reefs of which no detailed chart is available.

Stores—No stores are available but water may be had from Loch Nan Buadh. This should be sterilised as island cattle use it. There is an R.T. telephone connected to the Rocket Range on South Uist, located in the old village schoolhouse. **Const.** —5 hr. 04 m. Dover. Sp. 12 ft., Np. 8 ft.

Pabbay Island—Temporary anchorage can be had on the E. and S. sides of Pabbay in 5 to 3 fath., taking care to avoid the reef on its eastern side, and the shoal water to the southward.

North Sand Bay—Temporary anchorage in E'ly winds in North Sand Bay on the Harris shore 1 mile S. of Cape Difficulty. Anchor well offshore in 3 to 4 fath., just S. of Ru na Temple, a point with a ruined building, at the N. end of the neck of land connecting the high land behind Cape Difficulty with the Harris mainland.

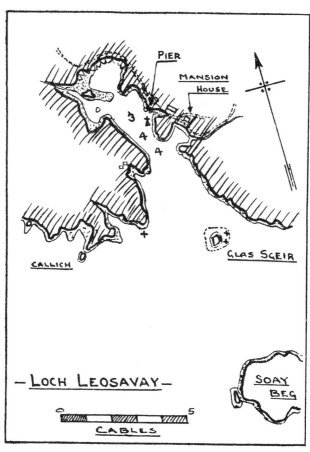

SOUND OF HARRIS—Chart 2642
(see Sound of Harris, Eastern Side)
SOUND OF HARRIS TO WEST LOCH TARBERT
Charts 2841 and 2720

Proceeding northward from the Sound of Harris, after rounding Toe Head, West Loch Tarbert opens out, with Taransay Island in the centre. The loch may be entered on either side of Taransay, the N. side being the clearer. Toe Head and the summit of Coppay Island in line leads into the Sound of Taransay, and clears the Middle Bo patch and the rock Bo Usbig. Then keep mid-sound and avoid the sandy spit on each side of the narrows, and from there the S. shores of the loch is clear to the head. The N. shore has several outlying islands and groups of rocks showing above water, but they are easily avoided by the use of Chart 2841.

Anchorages

East of Taransay Island in 4 fath., to the N. of Corran Rath spit.

At the head of the loch, off Tarbert, in 5 fath., well sheltered.

On the N. shore of the loch, three small lochs provide good anchorage—Lochs Leosavay, Meavag, and Bun Abhuinn Eadar.

Loch Leosavay (see plan)—The approaches are clear except for a small islet, Glas Sgeir, with a cement cairn on top, which lies off the E. side of the entrance. The shores are clean, except for a rock close in on the western side. An iron beacon marks a rock off the mansion house on the eastern shore at the narrows. Anchor off the stone quay in 3 fath. to the N.W. of the beacon. There are two "haystack shaped" beacons, one on Glas Sgeir (mentioned above) and one on the hill immediately above the mansion house which help in identifying the loch.

Loch Meavag (see plan)—If approaching from the W., the rocks Bo Haranis off the entrance must be watched. The loch is narrow, and dries out at the head for some distance. Anchor in 2 fath. off a house on the eastern shore about halfway up. Reported to be subject to swell in heavy S.W.'lies

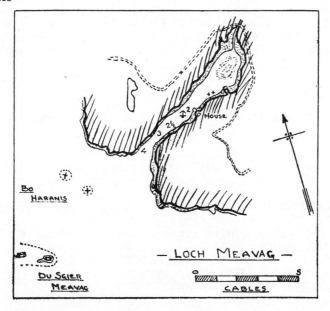

— LOCH MEAVAG —

Loch Bun Abhuinn Eadar (see plan)—The Duisker Rocks lie directly off the entrance, and may be avoided by keeping to either shore. The N. arm is probably the best. Anchorage in 2 fath., to the S. of the wrecked pier.
Stores—Shops. P.O. **Water**—At Tarbert, at the head of the main loch.

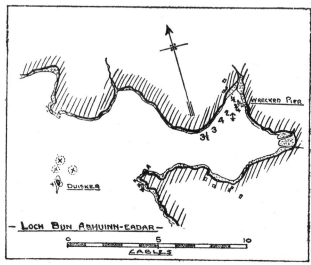

LOCH BUN ABHUINN EADAR

WEST LOCH TARBERT TO LOCH RESORT—Chart 2841

Proceeding out of West Loch Tarbert, give the N. shore a wide berth to avoid the numerous groups of rocks, Taransay Glorigs and Hushinish Glorigs, which have one or more parts above water, and the more dangerous Bo More and Old Rocks which cover. Gasgeir and Gasgeir Beg islets lie about 5 miles off-shore, and may be passed on the inner side. The W. coast of Scarba Island must be given a berth of at least 1 mile, as it is very foul, and there is a perfect nest of rocks, Du Sgeiran, 1 to 2 miles to the N. of it. The clearest entrance to Loch Resort is from the N. round Mealastay Island, but with careful navigation it can be entered between the Du Sgeiran Rocks and Kearstay Island. A reef which dries 6 ft., extends 1½ cables N.N.W. from the northern end of Kearstay. The Sound of Scarba, between the island and the mainland, is only navigable towards H.W., as there is a spit connecting the island with the mainland. The shores of Loch Resort are clean, and sheltered anchorage can be had towards the head. The squalls in strong winds are very fierce.

Anchorages

Loch Hamanavy—In 6 fath. at head of loch, also in bay on S. side, 1 mile from entrance, in 3 fath., but the latter is reported to be foul with lost moorings. Well sheltered. Entering, avoid Bo Thoreuil by keeping close to the shore at the mouth of Loch Healasavay.

Head of Loch Resort—Towards the head, close in-shore on S. side Anchor off the mouth of the burn in 4 fath. at the widest part of the loch, about 2½ miles from the entrance. There are some boulders on the shore, which cover at H.W.

Scarba—On E. side of Scarba Island inside Flodday Island, in 3 fath.
Eilean Mealastay—Shelter from W'ly winds in 3 fath. behind the island.
Stores—None. **Water**—At burns.

LOCH RESORT TO BUTT OF LEWIS—Chart 2720

This stretch of 45 miles of wild and forbidding coast provides little shelter except in the magnificent inlet of Loch Roag, divided by the islands of Bernera, which is almost unsurpassed for the amount of exploring which can be done in a small yacht.

Loch Roag lies about 20 miles N. of Loch Resort, and there are no outlying dangers if the coast be given a berth of about 1 mile. The mouth of the loch is about 5 miles across, with numerous outlying rocky islets, and the northern point, Aird Laimisheader, shows a wht. lt. giving a fl. of 2 sec. ev. 12 sec. This resembles a cottage high up rather than a lt. bn.

The Flannan Isles (Chart 3331), 20 miles off-shore to the N.W., show a wht. gp. fl. lt. (2) ev. 30 sec. (temporarily altered to fl. wht. lt. ev. 1 sec).

From Loch Roag to the Butt of Lewis, a distance of 25 miles, there is no good shelter. The lighthouse on the Butt of Lewis shows a wht. fl. ev. 20 sec. Fog siren 2 blasts of 4 sec. each ev. 90 sec.

FLANNAN ISLANDS—Chart 3331

The bight formed by Eil. Mor to the W. and Eil. Tighe to the E. affords shelter from winds from E. through S. to W. The bottom is rock and the holding ground poor, particularly on the W. side. A tripping line is essential. Subject to swell. Temporary anchorage also in guts between the islands of western group.

LOCH ROAG—Charts 3422 and 2720

The islands of Bernera divide this loch into E. and W. Loch Roag, and there is a passage possible for a small yacht between Little and Great Bernera Islands through Bernera harbour, but it must be taken towards H.W. and with careful chartwork. There is a least depth of 3 ft. at L.W.O.S. in the channel. A bridge joins Great Bernera to Lewis and at it there is a shop of sorts. (Petrol can be obtained.) Sp. 12½ ft., Np. 8 ft. Calor Gas.

The standing stones at Callernish, near the head of the loch, are the most interesting (and complete) in Britain. It is possible to anchor just below the main stone circle, behind the very small islands shown on the lower right-hand corner of Chart 3422. The stones are just off the right margin of the chart.

P.O. and telephone ½ mile S.E. of standing stones.

Anchorages

There are many anchorages in this labyrinth of bays and islands, which may easily be picked off the chart.

Loch Carloway—Near the N. entrance to E. Loch Roag, inside Aird Laimisheader lighthouse. A beacon marks the Tin Rocks, and the anchorage is off the pier in 4 fath., rather exposed to the W. Small craft can get shelter further in.

Stores—At village and vans. Petrol pump on Stornoway road, 1¼ miles from pier.

Bernera Harbour—A snug anchorage between Little and Great Bernera Islands. Coming in from the E., keep generally to the Little Bernera shore, leaving the beacon to starboard, and anchor in the basin which opens out at this spot in 4 fath. Avoid the shallow W. end, and the rock towards the S. side.

It is possible to leave the anchorage by the W. passage towards H.W. There is a least depth of 3 ft. in mid-channel at L.W.O.S.

K

ST. KILDA
Charts 1144 and 2720

The St. Kilda group consists of four islands and three stacks, and lies 42 miles W.N.W. from Shillay Islands, at the other end of the Sound of Harris (see Sound of Harris, Eastern Side).

If the visibility is good, the group comes into view when about halfway across, shaped like a full-rigged sailing-ship, but when nearer the islands and stacks are seen separately.

Village Bay, facing towards the S.E., is free from hidden dangers. Dun Island forms the S. side of the bay, which is about 1 mile wide. The anchorage is in 3 fath., about 1½ cables off the concrete landing jetty below the church and manse in the N.E. corner, with good holding ground and hard sandy bottom.

If the wind is between S. and E., the full Atlantic swell sets into the bay, and it is essential to clear out. A lee can be had anywhere off the shores round the island, which are clear outside of 1 cable, but unless in Glen Bay, a small bay on the N. side, there is no place to anchor. In this bay it is possible to anchor within a stone's throw of the beach, but a little further out it deepens to about 20 fath. The bottom is hard and rocky, and the anchor is liable to get lost, unless buoyed. It is only a temporary anchorage in S'ly or E'ly winds and MUST be vacated if winds go anything N. of W.

Water can be had at both sides of the island, from spring wells near the landing places. No stores can be obtained. There is a good element of risk in going out to St. Kilda, as the changes in weather are sometimes sudden.

After years of being deserted, St. Kilda is now under control of the Armed Forces and a detachment is stationed on the island and a number of roads and buildings have been constructed.

PART VIII

ISLE OF MAN

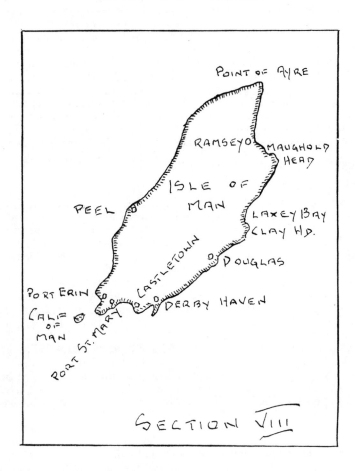

ADMIRALTY CHARTS

NUMBER	TITLE
*45	Clogher Head to Burrow Head
2094	Isle of Man
*1826	Burrow Head to Liverpool
2696	Douglas Bay

CLYDE CRUISING CLUB SKETCH CHARTS

*41	Firth of Clyde to Belfast and I.O.M.

* Used in previous sections

GENERAL

The passage to the Isle of Man from the Clyde is not difficult, and can be made by comparatively small craft in settled weather by easy stages, viz., to Lamlash, the mouth of Loch Ryan and Port Patrick (see Part I).

The oversea distance from the Mull of Galloway to Ayre Pt., the N. end of the Isle of Man, is only 21 miles. The tides on this passage are peculiar and require careful study. The flood tide coming round the N. of Ireland from the W. divides to the S. of Ailsa Craig, one part flowing northward up the Clyde and the other curving round and flowing southward down the Irish Channel. This part meets the main flood coming up the Irish Sea, about the middle of the Isle of Man off Contrary Head, and the flood stream divides again and flows round the N. and S. ends of the island, re-uniting again on the E. side of Maughold Head. The tidal stream is much stronger on the S. and E. sides of the island than on the W. and also runs strongly at Ayre Pt. A branch of the flood tide sets round Mull of Galloway, N. into Luce Bay and E. into the Solway Firth, causing a great race off the Mull of Galloway. The tide runs here at 6 knots Sp., with overfalls. Small craft can avoid this race by keeping a few miles to the westward.

Leaving Portpatrick, which should be done on the last of the ebb, or the first of the flood, steer a S'ly course approximately parallel with the land for 15 miles, to Mull of Galloway, passing about 5 miles to the westward, which will keep clear of the worst of the race, then steer a S.E. course for the Point of Ayre, a distance of 24 miles. There is a lighthouse on the Point of Ayre showing a lt. fl. wht. and red alternately, each flash 8 sec., eclipse 22 sec., ev. 30 sec. Fog siren 3 low blasts $2\frac{1}{2}$ sec. in quick succession ev. 90 sec. There is also a **low** wht. fl. lt. ev. 3 sec. on the extreme end of the point, which is steep-to with shingle beach. On the outer end of the jetty, which lies about 4 cables E. of Ayre Pt. high light, there is a gp. (2) fl. wht. lt. ev. 12 sec. Visible 8 miles. Three-quarters of a mile off the shore to the S.E. of Ayre Pt. is the White Stone Bank with $1\frac{1}{4}$ fath., marked by a red can buoy on its S.W. edge, showing a wht. gp. (2) fl. lt. ev. 10 sec., and a bell rung by the motion of the buoy. To the S.E. lies the Bahama Bank about 3 miles off the coast marked on its S.E. end by a bell and light buoy, red and wht. horizontal bands, showing a gp. fl. wht. lt., 2 fl. of $\frac{1}{2}$ sec. during $2\frac{1}{2}$ sec. ev. 10 sec., and about halfway down its western edge by a red and wht. pillar buoy. This bank lies N.W. and S.E. and is about 3 miles long, the most shoal portion being $\frac{3}{4}$ fath. at the S.E. end. Between this bank and Ramsey there is a green wreck buoy, showing a gp. fl. green lt. The buoy lies to the N.E. of the wreck.

The distance from the Point of Ayre to Douglas is 19 miles with no other outlying dangers. There is a lighthouse on Maughold Head, showing 3 quick fl. ev. 30 sec. Fog siren, 1 blast of 7 sec. ev. 90 sec.

The lighthouse on Douglas Head, S. of the harbour entrance, shows wht. gp. fl. 6 quick fl. during 15 sec., eclipse 15 sec., ev. 30 sec. Fog horn, 1 blast $3\frac{1}{2}$ sec. during 10 sec.

If bound for Peel, proceed as before to 5 miles W. of Mull of Galloway, then steer a course S. $\frac{1}{2}$E. for 25 miles to Peel Harbour. There is a small fix. wht. lt. on the end of the breakwater, and a red and wht. fix. lt. on the pier to the E. There are $1\frac{1}{4}$ fath. alongside the breakwater for two-thirds of its length.

Proceeding S. from Peel the coast is bold and rocky for 19 miles to Port Erin at the S. end of the island. On the S. end lies the Calf of Man, an island about 1 mile long and ¾ mile wide, separated from the mainland by the Calf Sound, which is obstructed by a rocky islet—Kitterland Is., and a sunken rock, to the W. ,Thousla Rock, marked by a red beacon. The clear passage through is ¾ cable wide and course should not be altered until clear passage between Calf of Man shows up. The tide runs at 3½ knots. (See plan on Chart 2094.)

A lighthouse on Calf of Man (obscured 190° to 274°) shows a fl. wht. ev. 15 sec. and gives a Tyfon fog signal of one 2½ sec. blast ev. 45 sec.

Half a mile S.W. of the Calf of Man lies the Chicken Rock, with a lighthouse showing wht. lt. fl. 2½ to 5 sec. ev. 20 sec. Fog horn gives 1 blast of 2 sec. ev. 60 sec.

The flood tide runs at 4 knots to E. round the Chicken Rock and there is a considerable race in strong winds. Small craft can pass between the rock and the Calf Island in fine weather to avoid this race.

From Chicken Rock to Langness Pt., a distance of 7½ miles, there are no dangers except in-shore,,which are described in the anchorages of Port St. Mary and Castletown.

Langness Pt. has some outying rocks and should be given a reasonable berth. The lighthouse on the point shows a wht. gp. (2) fl. lt. ev. 30 sec· Fog siren two 2¾ sec. blasts ev. min.

The tide runs round Langness Pt. at 5 knots and creates a race in strong winds.

From Langness Pt. to Douglas Head, a distance of 8 miles, there are no outlying dangers except Baltic Rock at St. Anne's Head, about 2 cables off-shore, covered at half-flood. The tide is strong along this coast and the passage should be made on the flood if possible.

From Peel to Point of Ayre, a distance of 17 miles, the shore is free from dangers, except the Craig Rock, with 2 fath. of water over it, which lies 2½ miles N.E. ½N. of Peel breakwater. The southern half of this distance is bold and rocky, and the northern half low and sandy with a few scattered hills.

MANX HARBOUR DUES

Partly as a result of the CCC's representations the Isle of Man Harbour Board has granted some concessions to visiting pleasure vessels. For some years there has been a slight lack of harmony between the authorities and the yachtsmen who sail to the Isle of Man on the question of charges.

Yachts racing to, from, or around the island are exempt from dues for 48 hours either side of the event.

Cruising yachts under 25 ft. staying less than 24 hours will only pay 50p, and those over 25 ft. £1, which is less than half the normal tariff for yachts of this type, usually calculated on the size of the vessel.

It has been made clear that the normal charges apply, and that these are concessionary charges until March 31, 1974, when no doubt further application will be made.

Anchorages

Douglas—On the E. side of the island is the best sheltered anchorage, where a yacht can lie afloat at low water, but when the wind is in the S.E. a bad swell sets into the harbour and makes it very uncomfortable.

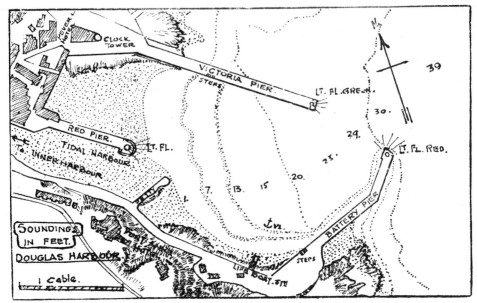

DOUGLAS HARBOUR

Approaching Douglas harbour, keep lighthouse on Battery Pier W. to clear Conister Outer Rocks, which have 13 to 18 ft. at low water.

There is a red fix. lt. and fog whistle, 1 blast ev. 20 sec., when steamers are expected, on Battery Pier, and a green fix. lt. on Victoria Pier.

In W'ly winds, keep to Battery Pier side, as the squalls are sometimes very heavy off Douglas Head.

Enter between the piers and steer for lifeboat station on port hand (see plan). Anchor in 2 to 3 fath., keeping jetty open of Red Pier with fix. wht. lt., and taking position from yachts moored there. When anchored, take stern line to mooring buoys or lay out a kedge.

Land on Victoria Pier above ferry steps or at Battery Pier at ferry steps of lifeboat slip.

The inner harbour dries out at L.W. and has 2 to 3 fath. Sp. and 1½ fath. Np., at high water. There is a swing bridge at inner end of Red Pier which is opened as required from half-flood to half-ebb.

The Red Pier extends much further than is shown in sketch plan and a light is shown on outer end of jetty.

Stores—Shops. Hotels. P.O. Tel. **Water**—At ferry house on Victoria Pier or hydrant on Battery Pier steps. Taps at lifeboat house and harbour board depot. Steamers to Fleetwood, Liverpool and Ardrossan.

Douglas Bay—Anchorage can be had at N. end in 6 to 7 fath. Sheltered from N.E. to S.W. through W.

Stores—In Douglas. **Water**—At hydrants on esplanade. Sp. 22¼ ft., Np. 17½ ft. **Const.** +0 hr. 11 m. Dover.

Garwick Bay—Just N. of Clay Pt. Anchor off cottage at head of beach. Sheltered from N. through W. to S.

Laxey Harbour—A small-boat harbour in Laxey Bay (N. of Garwick Bay) where a yacht can dry out alongside. Enter 2 hr. either side of H.W. keeping close to starboard three beacons marking a breakwater, then turn to port into harbour proper. Care required as there are usually many small local craft moored therein.

Ramsey (see plan on Chart 2094)—Bay lies 5½ miles S. of Ayre Pt., and sheltered anchorage can be had in winds from N.N.W. to S.W. through W. Anchor in 3 fath. N. of Queen's Pier, which has 2 fix. red lts., vertical, at each end, with Marina Villas and red beacon (Carrick Rock) in line, and keeping clear of entrance. Carrick Rock lies S. of pier and is marked by a beacon, 10 ft. high, with red cage on top.

The inner harbour dries out and has 17 ft. Sp. and 12 ft. Np. at H.W. The entrance is 100 ft. wide between the two piers. The N. pier has 1 fix. green lt. and the S. pier 1 fix. red lt. Entering harbour keep S. pier close to, as after half-flood the tide runs to the N. With head winds power is necessary, or trackers from shore. Moor alongside quay wall at the S. end of the harbour, close up to and below, the swing bridge. Three buoys available for visiting yachts have been laid inside the head of the iron (or Queen's) pier.

Stores—Shops. Hotels. P.O. Tel. Calor Gas. **Water**—At hydrants on quay. Sp. 20¾ ft., Np. 17½ ft. **Const.** +0 hr. 10 m. Dover.

Rail and bus connections to Douglas.

Peel (see plan on Chart 2094)—On the W. side of the island, When approaching from the S., Peel Castle will be seen on St. Patrick's Isle, and the harbour is on the N.E. side of the castle. When past the castle, the harbour and breakwater will come in view, on the N. side of the island. There is a wht. fix. lt. at the E. end of the breakwater. On the E. pier end there is a red and wht. lt. fixed. Red over shoal at castle side, white to entrance and red again over shoal waters at E. pier, obscured to shore.

A groyne runs out E. by N. from the E. pier and has a fix. red lt. on the outer end.

Dredging alongside breakwater allows vessels to tie up and remain afloat.

Anchor close to the outer end of the breakwater in 1½ fath. Sheltered from N.W. to E. through S. When the wind is in the N.E. a heavy swell comes in.

The inner harbour dries out and has 2½ fath. Sp., 1½ Np. at H.W. The entrance is between E. pier and small jetty on castle side; moor alongside quay.

Stores—Shops. Hotels. P.O. Tel. **Water**—Hydrant on quay. Sp. 18½ ft., Np. 14 ft. **Const.** +0 hr. 08 m. Dover.

Rail to Douglas and Ramsey.

Port Erin (see plan on Chart 2094)—A bay at the S.W. end of the island, easily picked out by the Milner Tower which stands on Bradda Head at its northern side. Leading line is given by two red fix. lts. at head of bay on E.S.E. bearing.

A ruined breakwater, 1½ cables long, runs out from the southern shore, marked by a blk. con. buoy on its outer end. The bay shoals gradually to a sandy beach. Anchor in 3½ fath. off the lifeboat slipway on the S.

shore, behind the ruins of the breakwater. A small pier with fix. green
lt. at end further in provides a landing place, but the beach behind it
dries out at L.W. The bay provides shelter in winds from N. to S.S.W.
through E., but is exposed to W'ly winds.

Stores—Shops. P.O. Tel. Hotels. **Water**—At lifeboat house. Train and
bus connections to Douglas.

Port St. Mary— (see plan on Chart 2094)—At S. end of the island on
the W. side, a breakwater 1½ cables long, runs out from the S. side of the
bay with an occ. red lt. on its outer end. The Carrick Rock, marked by a
blk. bn. exhibiting a quick fl. red lt. lies in the centre of the bay and
should be left to starboard on entering.

Ledges extend 2 cables S.E. from breakwater to Kallow Pt. and to
clear these and all dangers keep Chicken Rock Lt. Ho. in sight until the
fix. red lt. on the inner harbour and the occ. red lt. on breakwater are in
line then steer directly for them. Give the end of the breakwater a berth
of ½ cable to clear a shallow patch to E. The bay is sheltered in winds
from N.E. to S.W. through W. Anchor about 1 cable off the end of the
breakwater in 2 to 3 fath. Small craft can find shelter in S'ly winds just
behind the end of the breakwater in 6 to 7 ft. of water. The inner harbour,
with a fix. red lt. on pier end, dries out at L.W.

Dredging allows quite large yachts to lie afloat alongside the breakwater
as far as the second lot of steps. Small craft up to 4 ft. 6 in. draft as far
as third lot of steps. Holding ground in bay is reported as poor owing to
thick seaweed.

The Isle of Man Y.C. have provided two mooring buoys (one inside the
outer jetty and one to N. of the inner harbour) for the use of visitors who
are welcomed at the clubhouse.

Stores—Shops. P.O. Tel. Hotels. **Water**—Hydrant at inner end of
breakwater. Train and bus connections to Douglas and Port Erin.

Castletown Bay (see plan on Chart 2094)—On the S.E. end of the
island at Langness Pt. W. of Langness Pt. is Castletown Bay which provides shelter in winds from N.W. to S.E. through N. The E. side is foul
and should not be approached too closely. On the W. side are the
Lheeahrio Rocks covered at H.W. and marked on the S.E. side by a red
can buoy. Anchor about 2 cables E. or S.E. of this buoy in 6 to 7 faths.

The harbour, which has a fix. red lt. on the S. pier, dries out at L.W.,
and can only be reached in the dinghy from halfflood to half-ebb, avoiding
the Seal Rock on port hand going in, and the sunken rock, Boe Norris,
on the starboard hand. Steps at pier end.

Stores—Shops. P.O. Tel. Hotels. Half-holiday—Thursdays. Calor Gas.
Water—At houses. Train and bus connections to Douglas.

Derby Haven—Lies N.E. of Langness Pt. and provides shelter in winds
from W. and S.W. when Castletown Bay would be untenable. A fix. green
lt. is shown from S. end of breakwater. Anchor in centre of bay in 1½ to 2
fath. about 1 cable outside lt. The bay dries out for about 2½ cables at the
head. Exposed only to N.E.

Stores—Castletown, 1¼ miles distant.

PART IX

NORTH-EAST COAST
OF IRELAND

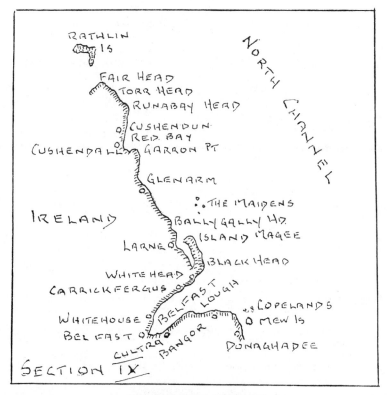

ADMIRALTY CHARTS

GROUP I

NUMBER	TITLE
*1577	Western Approaches to Firth of Clyde
*45	Clogher Head to Burrow Head
46	Ailsa Craig to Bloody Foreland (with plan of Maidens)
*2199	North Channel—North Part.
*2198	North Channel—South part.

GROUP II

1753	Belfast Lough
1237	Larne Lough and Approaches. Larne Harbour
3709	Copeland Islands and Donaghadee Sound

CLYDE CRUISING CLUB SKETCH CHARTS

*41	Firth of Clyde to Belfast and I.O.M.

* Used in previous sections

GENERAL

Anyone wishing to cruise in Irish waters are advised to obtain a copy of the Irish Cruising Club's handbook.

The passage from Lamlash to the N. of Ireland can be undertaken by small yachts and presents no great difficulties, but the prevailing winds are S., S.W., and W., which set up a fair sea, especially S. of Corsewall Pt. and near the Irish coast, where the tides are stronger, varying from 2 to $3\frac{1}{2}$ knots in places. In the N. channel, between the Mull of Cantyre and Fair Head, the flood stream flows S. down the Irish coast at $3\frac{1}{2}$ knots, and 4 knots off the Maidens and Hunter Rock. Between Isles of Muck and the Maidens the flood tide flows at $2\frac{3}{4}$ knots S. There is an eddy inshore on the flood at half-tide off Larne, extending to Blackhead, about $1\frac{1}{2}$ miles off-shore. This eddy meets the North-going stream and causes a race off Skernaghan Pt. About $\frac{1}{2}$ mile off the Isle of Muck is the Race of Muck, where the tide increases in velocity to 6 knots.

The flood tide flows S. from Blackhead and divides at Grey Pt. on the S. shore of Belfast Lough, part filling up the Lough, and part flowing E. past Bangor to the South Briggs at the rate of $\frac{1}{2}$ knot, and increasing to 5 knots in Donaghadee Sound.

East of Mew Island is a race extending about $1\frac{1}{2}$ miles N. of the island, and is caused by the true ebb meeting the counter tide from $3\frac{1}{2}$ hr. to 6 hr. after H.W. at Belfast.

The Ram Race, extending 2 miles S. of Mew Island on its eastern side, is caused by the flood tide meeting the stream from S. of the Copelands, which lasts from $2\frac{1}{2}$ hr. before to $\frac{1}{2}$ hr. after H.W. at Belfast.

It will be seen from the foregoing that the best passage for small boats is from Lamlash to Loch Ryan. The sea distance is $22\frac{1}{2}$ miles from Lady Bay (see Part I, under Loch Ryan Anchorages).

From Corsewall Pt., steer W. by S. $\frac{3}{4}$S. to Blackhead, a distance of 23 miles. In clear weather, Blackhead stands out high and bold, and the land N. of it showing up the entrance to Belfast Lough. On Blackhead is a lighthouse, standing high up, 1 wht. fl. lt. $\frac{1}{2}$ sec. ev. 3 sec. Fog signal, explosive, one report every 5 min.

There are no outlying dangers in this passage and tides are normal.

In the passage from Campbeltown to Belfast Lough, the tides have to be considered and, naturally, in unsettled weather, these will cause steep seas. Leaving the Cantyre shore, the first outlying danger is the Paterson Rock, off Sanda, which is marked by a red bell buoy, with staff and cage. Giving this rock a wide berth, steer a course S.W. by S. $\frac{1}{2}$S. to clear the Highland Rock and the Maidens, a group of rocks which lie $6\frac{1}{2}$ miles N.E. of Larne. Highland Rock is marked by a red perch; N.E. extreme of the Maidens and E. of the rock a blk. con. lt. buoy, wht. fl. ev. 3 sec. Automatic whistle. The Maidens are marked by a wht. tower with red belt in centre, on East Rock, 1 wht. gp. (3) fl. in quick succession, ev. 20 sec., vis. 15 miles.

An auxiliary red fl. lt. ev. 3 sec. is shown from the Maidens Lt. Ho. in a sector marking the Russel and Highland Rocks. There is a bad tide race off the E. side of the group, and the tide sets across the rocks at about 4 knots, making very broken water, extending about $\frac{3}{4}$ mile S.W. These rocks should be given a wide berth to the E. Hunter Rock, with 4 ft. of water on it, lies off the entrance to Larne Harbour and is marked by a con. blk. buoy, with staff and globe, on the N.E. side, and a blk. con. bell gas buoy showing two wht. fl. ev. 10 sec., on the W. side of the rock The Farris Pt. Lt. Ho. at Larne Lough throws a red sector over these rocks, and white elsewhere. The tide sets over Hunter Rock at $3\frac{1}{2}$ knots and it should be given a wide berth.

In the vicinity of Hunter Rock there exists abnormal magnetic variation and, if steering by compass, great care must be taken and position checked by marks or lights, if visible.

When approaching the Antrim coast, Blackhead stands out clear, but care must be taken not to mistake the headland for the Gobbins, an outstanding headland $2\frac{1}{2}$ miles N., which stands out from the shore, when going S. The distance from Paterson Rock to Blackhead is $31\frac{1}{2}$ miles and allowance must be made for tides.

Very small craft are recommended to proceed from Loch Ryan to Portpatrick (which see), and wait for good weather to cross to Belfast Lough —a distance of about 18 miles. Course W. by S.

BELFAST LOUGH
Chart 1753

Entering the Lough from Blackhead, the coast is high and bold. Several unmarked rocks lie close in-shore between Blackhead and Whitehead, but off Whitehead lies the North Briggs Reef, marked by a blk. con. buoy showing a short wht. fl. ev. 4 sec., and about 6 cables southward of this buoy there is a green con. buoy showing a gp. (3) fl. green lt. ev. 10 sec. marking a wreck in-shore of buoy. From here to Carrickfergus the shore is shoal and should not be approached too near.

About $1\frac{1}{2}$ miles S.E. of Carrickfergus there is a lit pilot vessel and here is the beginning of the buoyed channel to Belfast Harbour dredged to 30 ft. Black con, or pile lt. buoys with odd numbers starting from seaward and showing wht. lts. on N. and W. side, and on S. and E. side red can buoys or pile lts. (even numbers) showing gp. fl. red lts. except No. 2 at start of channel which shows an int. quick red fl. Except for the channel the Lough W. of buoys 9 and 10 shoals badly. The yellow buoys in Lough are yacht racing marks.

Across the Lough about S.W. of Carrickfergus is Cultra, the headquarters of the R.N. of I. Y.C. The shore is very shoal. Grey Pt. lies about 3 miles E. of Cultra where the flood tide divides going E. and W. From Grey Pt. to Bangor is $1\frac{1}{2}$ miles, and the shore is shoal and foul close in and should be given a wide berth. Bangor is the headquarters of the Royal Ulster Y.C. On the E. side of Bangor Bay is Luke's Pt., with outlying rocks unmarked. Ballyhome Bay has a long sandy beach and is shoal. The South Briggs Rocks lie E. of Groomsport Bay and are marked by a red can buoy, showing 2 red fl. ev. 10 sec. Between the shore and the South Briggs buoy, the passage is foul with rocks. There is little tide in the Lough, about 1 knot at most. Sp. 11 ft., Np. $9\frac{3}{4}$ ft.

Anchorages

Whitehead lies 1 mile S.W. of Blackhead and is exposed from N.E. through S. to S.W. The anchorage off the village is not good, and there is a 3 ft. rock 2 cables off the shore, and another rock awash about 1 cable N.E. of Whitehead. The best anchorage is W. of the North Briggs buoy, S.W. of Clogham Pt. This point is very foul and should be given a wide berth, after passing the buoy. Approach the bay from S.W. and anchor about 2 cables off concrete railway embankment in 2 to $2\frac{1}{2}$ fath.

Stores—At Whitehead, 1 mile away. No road except along shore or railway lines. Shops. Tel. P.O. Hotel at Whitehead. **Water**—None. Train and bus to Belfast.

Carrickfergus—On the N. shore of the Lough, lies 5½ miles to the W. of Blackhead. There is a good harbour accessible at all states of tide. The entrance is between two piers. There are two fix. red lts. on the E. pier and one on the W. pier. The anchorage is 2 cables S. by E. of the harbour in 2 fath.

Exposed from E. to S.W. through S. Off the harbour lies the Carrickfergus Bank. There is 8 ft. of water over this bank at L.W. In strong E. winds the shallow water sets up a steep sea over the bank. The Pilot Service for Belfast Lough operates from this harbour and the Harbour Master controls berthing.

Dredging to make the harbour an all deep water one is reported as being under way. If making fast at quay do **not** secure alongside the Pilot Vessels and the quay on the port hand is frequently occupied by ships. The channel (1 fath. at L.W.) to the quay on the starboard hand is very narrow—on entering harbour turn sharp to starboard.

Sp. 11 ft., Np. 9¾ ft.

Stores—At Carrickfergus. Hotel. P.O. Shops. **Water**—At hydrants on pier end. Train and bus to Belfast.

Cultra—Lies on the S. side of the Lough, S.W. by S. of Carrickfergus. The shore is very shoal, and the anchorage is 5 or 6 cables off the shore at the Royal North of Ireland Yacht clubhouse (which can be easily distinguished as a long two-storey building with a flagpole in front) in 2½ to 3 fath., beside other yachts and moorings there. In strong N'ly winds the anchorage is very uncomfortable, when it is better to run across to Carrickfergus. Exposed E. to N.W. through N. Sp. 11 ft., Np. 9¾ ft.

Stores—Shops. P.O. Tel. Hotel at Hollywood, 1 mile W. **Water**—At R.N.I.Y. clubhouse. Train and bus to Belfast.

Bangor—On the S. side of the Lough, due S. of Blackhead and 5 miles E. of Cultra. There is a pier on the N.E. corner of the bay with 2 fix. red lts., one at each outer angle; also a small harbour with two piers. On the central pier is a fix. red lt. with green sector. There is less than 6 ft. at L.W. and only small draft boats can lie in shelter. Steamers discharge coal at this pier. Opposite the harbour is the bathing station, and anchorage can be had there in 2 to 3 fath., not too close in. There is another anchorage between the Royal Ulster Yacht Club and the pier in 4 fath., about 1¼ cables off-shore. These anchorages are exposed to the N. and E. and a big sea runs in here, making the anchorage untenable in strong winds. It is better to get out and run for Carrickfergus or Cultra. To the E. of this pier there is a reef running out parallel with the shore.

Const. +0 hr. 12 m. Dover. Sp. 12 ft., Np. 10 ft.

Stores—Shops. Hotels. P.O. Tel. Petrol. Amusements. **Water**—At harbour and bathing station. Calor Gas.

Ballyhome Bay—Lies ½ mile to the eastward of Bangor, but care must be taken to clear outlying rocks lying about 2½ cables off Luke's Pt., at the W. side of Ballyhome Bay. This bay has a long sandy beach about ¾ mile long, and shoals badly to the head. Temporary anchorage can be had in 2 to 3 fath. about 1½ cables off-shore, near the yacht slip. Exposed N.W. to E. through N. The E. side of the bay is foul.

Shelter from E'ly winds can be obtained opposite the most N'ly large stone house on E. side of bay. If entering from E., give Ballymarcormich Pt. a wide berth as it is very foul. When most N'ly house on E. side is bearing E., head in-shore until Blackhead on opposite side of Belfast Lough is **just open** from spit at N.E. end of bay.

Anchor in 2 fath. directly opposite the stone dyke which is conspicuous at the N. end of the house.

Stores—Shops at Ballyhome and Bangor. **Water**—At yacht slip.

Belfast Harbour (Spencer Basin)—In very bad weather with wind from the E. the harbour is the only shelter in the Lough. The dredged channel is well buoyed. (For approach channel, see Belfast Lough).

At the head the channel is divided into three by E. and W. Twin Islands, Herdman Channel branching off to the right, and Musgrave Channel to the left. Hold straight on, between the islands, passing a shipbuilding yard on starboard hand then the end of Millwater Basin. Immediately above Millwater Basin is Spencer Basin. Steer to starboard into Spencer Basin, leaving the two vertical red lights on the W. pierhead to port, and tie up near the entrance with Dock Master's sanction. Calor Gas.

COPELAND ISLANDS AND DONAGHADEE SOUND
Chart 3709

In the passage from Bangor to Donaghadee there are many outlying rocks but they are all marked. The South Briggs lie 3 miles E. by N. of Bangor, and are marked by a red can buoy, showing 2 red fl. ev. 10 sec., lying $\frac{1}{2}$ mile off-shore, and should be left on the starboard hand. Coming S. the shore is foul for about 2 cables with fairly high land behind. The tides are very irregular and attain a speed of 5 knots in places. Great care is necessary to avoid being carried on to the reefs in light winds. The N'ly stream begins 2 hr. after L.W. and runs for 8 hr. through the sound. Between Great Copeland Island and the mainland, the passage is very foul with rocks and reefs, but it is well buoyed. Red Rock, lying to the southward of Great Copeland Island, about 1 cable off, should be given a wide berth. On the mainland, about the middle of the sound—at Foreland Pt. —is an outlying reef of rocks, marked by a red iron perch, with a cage on top, and $3\frac{1}{2}$ cables S. is a second red perch, but between them are several outlying rocks, and this shore should be given a wide berth if beating. Foreland Spit lies about 2 cables N.N.E. $\frac{1}{2}$E., and is marked by a red can buoy, red fl. lt. ev. $2\frac{1}{2}$ sec. on its N. side, and this buoy should be taken on the **starboard** hand going S. Two and a half cables S.E. of the Foreland Spit lies Deputy Reef, a group of rocks marked on its S. side by a con. blk. buoy, with wht. fl. lt. ev. 2 sec., which should be left to **port** going S. Magic Rocks lie N.E. of this buoy. Governor Rocks, marked by a red can buoy, red fl. ev. $2\frac{1}{2}$ sec., lying $1\frac{1}{2}$ cables W. of Deputy Reef. This buoy should be left on the **starboard** hand going S. There is foul ground about 1 cable N. of N. pier of Donaghadee harbour.

Outside the S. pier is the Wee Scotchman Rock and reef, marked by a red perch fairly close in-shore.

Copeland Sound between Great Copeland Island and Mew Island is strewn with rocks and shoals, marked only on the E. side by a red buoy. This passage should not be used.

K 3

Mew Island—On the N.E. corner of Mew Island is the lighthouse (black with one wht. band) having 1 wht. gp. fl. lt., 4 fl. ev. 30 sec., eclipse $4\frac{8}{10}$ sec. between each group. During the interval between each group, weak reflections may be observed. Fog diaphone gives a group of 4 short blasts in 6 sec., then silent 24 sec. Off the lighthouse there are overfalls on the ebb tide which runs at 4 knots, extending about 1 mile N. of Mew Island. This race is occasioned by true ebb meeting counter tide from $3\frac{1}{2}$ hr. to 6 hr. after H.W. at Belfast. East of Mew Island there is a race from $2\frac{1}{4}$ hr. before to $\frac{1}{2}$ hr. after H.W. at Belfast. In unsettled weather this part should be avoided by keeping about $1\frac{1}{2}$ miles to the E.

Donaghadee (see plan on Chart 3709)—There is a lighthouse on the end of the S. pier, showing an occ. wht. lt. (2 sec.) ev. 4 sec. Entering the harbour at night, keep the light bearing S.W. $\frac{1}{4}$S.

Enter between piers in centre and anchor in 9 or 10 ft. (at L.W.) near S. pier and run stern warp to quay.

In N.E. winds a swell comes in and makes the anchorage uncomfortable. Landing steps on S. pier. The N. pier does not reach the shore at H.W. Sp. $12\frac{3}{4}$ ft., Np. 11 ft.

Stores—Hotels. Shops. P.O. Tel. Amusements. Calor Gas. **Water**—At pierhead. Train and bus service to Belfast.

BELFAST LOUGH, BLACKHEAD TO FAIR HEAD AND RATHLIN ISLAND
Chart 1577

The coastline from Blackhead North on the E. side of Island Magee is bold and steep-to, with no outlying dangers until the Isle of Muck, $4\frac{1}{2}$ miles N. of Blackhead. This island lies $1\frac{1}{2}$ cables off-shore and is connected to it by a spit which dries at L.W. The E. side of the island is clean, but there are rocks $\frac{1}{2}$ cable off the northern end. There is a bad race off its E. side, extending about $\frac{1}{4}$ mile to the E., which can be easily avoided. At Skernaghan Pt. and about $\frac{1}{2}$ cable off it is a rock which shows above water. Brown's Bay lies between Skernaghan Pt. and Barr Pt., which has a lattice iron beacon painted red, and fog gun report ev. 20 sec. This bay is clean but shoals at the head for about 2 cables.

About 5 cables S.W. of Barr Pt. is Farris Pt., with a lighthouse showing a wht. fix. lt. with red sector. Red over Hunter Rock and Barr Pt. and wht. elsewhere. Between these two points is Farris Bay, clean 1 cable off-shore, and shoal at the head. Farris Pt. is the E'ly point of entrance to Larne Lough. Off Barr Pt. the flood runs 9 hr. to the eastward and at half-tide and close in-shore is an eddy. Hunter Rock and the Maidens lie off the coast here and are described above. On the western side of the entrance to Larne Lough is Sandy Pt., marked by Chaine Tower, showing occ. lt., bright 3 sec., eclipse 2 sec., ev. 5 sec., wht. over fairway, red to shore, obscured from N.E. through N. to the shore, Lying $1\frac{1}{2}$ cables E. by N. of Chaine Tower is a blk. buoy with fl. red lt. ev. $2\frac{1}{2}$ sec., marking a spit, which should be left to starboard entering the Lough.

Going N. of Larne, the shores are bold and steep-to, and there are no outlying dangers at more than $\frac{1}{2}$ cable off-shore. From Ballygalley S. to Blackhead, there is an eddy at half-tide; off Ballygalley Head the tide runs at $2\frac{3}{4}$ knots. About $8\frac{1}{2}$ miles N. of Larne is Path Head, the southern end of Glenarm Bay. This headland is conspicuous by a cliff face about 500 ft. high. The bay is clean. From Glenarm to Carnlough is $1\frac{1}{2}$ miles. From here to Red Bay is 8½ miles. The coast is very high and steep-to with a very high headland at Garron Pt., the extreme E. of Red Bay. On the N.E. side of the point there is a rock awash, about 1 cable off-shore, otherwise the bay is clean. An R.N.L.I. I.R.B. operates from Cushendall during the summer months. There is a fl. 10 sec. 32 ft. 5 Mile light on the pier at Waterfoot.

From Red Bay to Cushedun Bay, a distance of 4 miles, the land is high and the shore steep-to, and the bay is clear of obstruction.

The coastline N. to Tor Pt. and Fair Head is high and steep-to with no outlying rocks, at a reasonable distance off-shore, but the tides become very strong, from Tor Pt. N. to Fair Head, running at 5 to 6 knots, with overfalls and tide rips extending about 1 mile off-shore and should be carefully avoided in unsettled weather. The flood stream flows S. along this coast at 3 knots, and at the protruding headlands increases to about 5 knots. The flood stream runs from 5¾ after to ¾ hr. before H.W. Dover, and at Fair Head spring tides run at 6 knots 1 hr. after commencement of East-going stream.

Rathlin Island (Rue Pt.) lies 2½ miles N. of Fair Head. The flood tide runs S.E. through the Sound at from 5 to 6 knots and starts 5 hr. before H.W. Dover. The ebb or N.W. stream begins at H.W. Dover. The E'ly side of the Sound is free from outlying rocks, but great care is necessary in selecting the weather, as the seas can be very bad owing to the strong tides. There is no lighthouse on Fair Head, which is a bold headland dropping sheer into the sea.

Rue Pt., the S.E. point of Rathlin, has a lighthouse octagonal concrete tower, with blk. and wht. bands, showing a wht. double fl. lt. 2 fl. of ½ sec. each ev. 5 sec. The E. shore of Rathlin Island is rugged and should not be approached too close, on account of eddies. At the N.E. corner is Altcarry Head, with a lighthouse, showing a gp. fl. lt. On the W. side is a lighthouse, showing a fl. lt. red ev. 5 sec.

Anchorages
LARNE LOUGH—Chart 1237

The entrance to Larne Lough is between Farris Pt. and Sandy Pt. on its W. side. Chaine Tower off Sandy Pt. shows occ. lt. bright 3 sec., eclipse 2 sec., ev. 5 sec., wht. over fairway and red to shore obscured N.E. through N. to the shore. There is a blk. buoy lying 1½ cables E. by N. of Chaine Tower, showing a red fl. lt. ev. 2½ sec. marking a spit. This buoy should be left to starboard on entering and the centre of the channel kept, and then holding over towards the railway pier, which has 2 red lts. at each end of pier. These are leading lights and should be kept in line when entering at night until close on the first one, then sheer to port towards a beacon showing a fix. wht. lt. to avoid the extension built to the pier beyond the second light. The flood tide runs at 3½ knots. The anchorage is about 2 cables S.W. and not inside a line of the piers and opposite Olderfleet Castle in 16 ft. of water, but this anchorage is in the tideway. On the E. shore opposite Olderfleet Castle there is a power station, and a pier, with a row of mooring buoys off it, has been built.

Steps at railway pier. The upper part of the Lough is very shoal, except a narrow channel about 1½ cables wide for 1 mile further up on the E. side. The remainder practically dries out (see chart).

Const. +0 hr. 08 m. Dover. Sp. 8¾ ft., Np. 8¼ ft.

Stores—Shops. P.O. Tel. Hotels. Petrol. Calor Gas. **Water**—At railway pier.

Brown's Bay—1½ miles E. of Larne. A very pleasant anchorage with no tidal disturbances. Exposed to N.

Glenarm Bay—Temporary anchorage in off-shore winds in 5 fath. off old quay. Inside quay there is about 18 in. of water. One fix. wht. lt. is shown on the quay only when steamers are expected.

Sp. 11 ft., Np. 9 ft.

Stores—Shops. P.O. Tel. **Water**—At pier end.

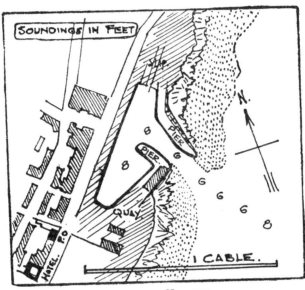

CARNLOUGH HARBOUR

Carnlough (Chart 2199)—Temporary anchorage can be had in the bay off the harbour entrance in about 3 fath. in off-shore winds.

There is a small harbour with about 8 ft. of water, 6 ft. at bar, on the N.W. side of the bay. The entrance is between two piers facing about S.E. and has a very narrow entrance (see plan). The harbour is about ¾ cable long and ¼ cable wide, so great care is necessary. When entering boats must tow in or go slow under power and tie up as there is no room to manoeuvre. On the outside of the S. pier the shore is shoal and the centre of the gut must be kept. Enter with a bearing of N.W. ¼N. on three painted houses. They can be distinguished by a flagpole at the E. end and a factory chimney at the W. end. (A pilot can be got if wanted.) From the middle of March to September, there is a fix. red lt. on the S. pier from half-flood to half-ebb and on the N.E. pier a wht. fix. lt. There are also 2 fix. green lts., 60 yd. apart, leading lights shown occasionally from half-flood to half-ebb. In this harbour steamers load limestone, and it is necessary to keep all sails covered.

It is reported (1964) that owing to the suspension of limestone shipments dredging, too, has been suspended and silting is taking place and depths shown in the sketch are much reduced, and leading lights meantime discontinued.

Const. +0 hr. 20 m. Dover.

Stores—Shops. Tel. P.O. Hotel. **Water**—At hydrant on quay. Nearest railway line, Larne.

Red Bay—Good anchorage can be had in off-shore winds close in at the village of Waterfoot or off the pier in 3 to 4 fath. to escape the tide. There is a small pier running out to the S. Behind the pier there is a depth of 7 ft. at L.W. alongside, but is subject to E'ly swell. When the winds are S.W., heavy squalls strike this bay and are sometimes very fierce.

Stores—Shop. P.O. Tel. **Water**—At village.

Cushendun Bay—Temporary anchorage in settled weather in off-shore winds in 2 to 5 fath. Anchor off the conspicuous white hotel and not N. of the centre of bay as, besides some rocks 2½ cables off-shore, there is a submerged rock in the northern half.

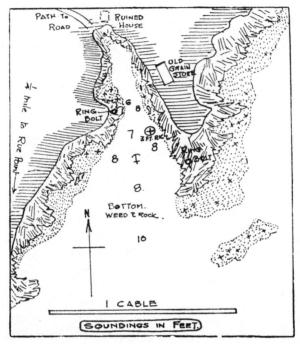

RATHLIN REFUGE

Rathlin Island, Ushet Port (Refuge)—Ushet Port, about ¼ mile N. of Rue Pt., on the E. shore, is a small gut in the rocks with about 6 to 8 ft. at L.W. This refuge is about 500 ft. long and about 150 ft. wide, and is not recommended as an anchorage, but is only given as a refuge. It is sheltered from all winds except S.

There is a 3 ft. rock on the E. side, halfway up. On each side are ring bolts on the rocks to make fast to, as there is little room to swing (see plan). On the W. side are some rocks and weed. The head of the gut is full of decaying seawrack and smells horribly. This port was used long ago for unloading grain, but is now disused. The strong tides outside make the time of H.W. and L.W. irregular. The rise is about 3 to 4 ft.

Stores—Shop at Church Bay, 2½ miles W. **Water**—At tank at lighthouse.

Church Bay—Very exposed and not recommended as an anchorage.

U

GLOSSARY OF GAELIC TERMS

Aber	-	- Confluence of rivers.
Abhainn, Avon		- A river.
Acarsaid	-	- Anchorage.
Ailean, Aline		- A meadow or green spot.
Aird, Ard		- A promontory.
Aros	-	- River mouth.
Ach, Auch		- A field.
Ban, Bahn		- White.
Ban	-	- A woman.
Beg, Beag		- Little.
Beith	-	- Birch.
Bodach	-	- An old man.
Bo, Bogha		- A sunken rock.
Bun	-	- A river mouth.
Breac	-	- Speckled.
Bruaich	-	- A brae.
Bhuide, Buidhe		- Yellow.
Cailleach	-	- An old woman.
Camus	-	- A bay.
Caol, Caolas		- A strait.
Carr	-	- Rough ground.
Ceann, Chinn		- A head.
Clach	-	- A stone.
Coir, Coire		- A corrie
Con, Choin		- A dog.
Creag, Craig		- A cliff.
Darach	-	- Oak.
Dearg	-	- Red.
Dun	-	- A castle.
Dhu, Dubh		- Black.
Druim	-	- A ridge.
Each	-	- A horse.
Eilean	-	- An island.
Ear	-	- East.
Fraoich	-	- Heather.
Gabhar, Gobhar		- A goat.

Gal, Gall	-	- A stranger.
Gamhainn, Gamhna		- A stirk.
Garbh	-	- Rough.
Glas, Ghlas		- Gray or green.
Gorm, Ghorm		- Green or blue.
Inver	-	- River mouth.
Ken, Kin (Ceann)		- A head.
Kil (Cille)	-	- A Church.
Kyle (Caol)		- A narrow strait.
Leac	-	- A stony slope.
Leathann	-	- Broad.
Liath	-	- Grey.
Maol, Maoile		- A bare top.
Mara	-	- The Sea.
Meall	-	- A round hill.
Mor, Mhor		- Large.
Ob, Oban	-	- A bay.
Poll, Puill	-	- A pool.
Righ	-	- A king.
Ron, Roin		- A seal.
Ruadh	-	- Red.
Ru, Rudha		- A point.
Sgeir	-	- A sea rock.
Sguir, Sgurr		- A rocky peak.
Sron, Strone		- A nose, or point.
Sruth	-	- A current.
Tarbet, Tarbert		- A narrow isthmus.
Tigh	-	- A house.
Tioram	-	- Dry.
Tober, Tobar		- A well.
Traigh	-	- A sand beach.
Uamh, Uamha		- A cave.
Uig	-	- A hollow or bay.

APPENDIX

To find the times of High and Low Water at any port

To find the times of H.W. take the times of H.W. for the reference standard port from the daily prediction tables (Admiralty Tide Tables or one of the almanacs) and add (or subtract) the tidal constant for the port taken from this appendix. To find the times of L.W. add (or subtract) 6 hr. 12 m. to the times of H.W. The tidal constants given in this appendix are referred to the standard ports given in the Admiralty Tide Tables. If the reference ports given in the almanacs are different from these the appropriate time difference constants can be found as shown in the following example.

To find the times of H. and L.W. at Loch Inver on 1st July, 1972

Times of H.W. at Stornoway (almanac ref. port)	10 35	22 53

Time difference Loch Inver/Ullapool (from appendix) −0 05. Time difference Stornoway/Ullapool (from appendix) −0 10, i.e. time difference Ullapool/Stornoway +0 10. Net difference

Loch Inver/Ullapool −0 05 + 0 10	= + 0 05	+ 0 05
Times of H.W. at Loch Inver	10 40	22 58
Subtract 6 hr. 12 m.	− 6 12	− 6 12
Times of L.W. at Loch Inver	04 28	16 46

TIME AND HEIGHT DIFFERENCES FOR TIDAL PREDICTIONS

(Reproduced from Admiralty Tide Tables with the sanction of the Controller, H.M. Stationery Office, and of the Hydrographer of the Navy.)

Notes: * denotes no data available.
In the Sound of Jura, S. of Loch Crinan, the rise of tide occurs mainly during the $3\frac{1}{2}$ hours following low water, and the fall during the $3\frac{1}{2}$ hours following high water. At other times the changes in level are usually small and irregular. At Port Ellen weather conditions have a marked effect on sea level, S'ly and E'ly gales raising the level up to 3 feet; at neaps the tide is sometimes diurnal, while the range is negligible. At Machrinhanish springs occur when it neaps at Port Ellen.

Standard Ports		Height in ft.	
Secondary Ports	Average time difference H.W.	Differences	
		M.H.W.S.	M.L.W.S.
Ullapool		15·4	0·8
Kyle of Tongue	+0 50	— 0·4	*
Rispond (Loch Eriboll)	+0 35	— 1·2	+ 0·5
Kyle of Durness	+0 30	— 0·7	+ 1·0
Cape Wrath	+0 25	— 0·4	*
Stornoway	—0 10	— 1·3	— 0·1
Loch Shell	—0 16	— 1·2	0
E. Loch Tarbert	—0 39	— 0·8	— 0·1
Loch Maddy	—0 39	— 1·0	— 0·1
Loch Skiport	—0 52	— 1·9	— 0·6
Loch Boisdale	—0 54	— 1·8	— 0·1
Barra (N. Bay)	—0 57	— 2·8	— 0·2
Barra Head	—1 04	— 3·3	*
Shillay	—1 03	— 2·6	— 0·5
Uachdair	—0 49	— 3·1	— 0·2
Leverburgh	—0 40	— 1·4	+ 0·2
W. Loch Tarbert	—0 53	— 3·2	*
Bernera Harbour	—0 26	— 2·9	— 0·7
Village Bay (St. Kilda)	—0 55	— 5·8	— 0·6
Flannan Isles	—0 31	— 4·1	— 0·7
Rockall	—2 36	— 9·0	*
Loch Bervie	+0 20	— 1·1	+ 0·1
Loch Laxford	+0 15	— 1·5	— 0·7
Badcall Bay	+0 05	— 0·5	+ 1·0
Loch Nedd	0	— 0·4	+ 0·2
Loch Inver	—0 05	— 0·6	+ 0·2
Tanera More	—0 05	— 0·3	+ 0·2
Mellon Charles (Loch Ewe)	—0 10	+ 0·2	+ 0·2

Standard Ports					Height in ft.	
Secondary Ports				Average time difference H.W.	Differences	
					M.H.W.S.	M.L.W.S.
Ullapool	....	....	....		15·5	0·8
Gairloch	....	....	....	−0 20	+ 0·4	0
Shiledaig	....	....	....	−0 20	+ 1·7	+ 0·2
Plockton	....	....	....	−0 20	+ 1·5	+ 0·6
Broadford Bay	....			−0 25	+ 0·3	− 0·3
Portree	....	....		−0 25	+ 0·2	− 0·2
Uig Bay (Loch Snizort)		....	....	−0 37	+ 0·6	+ 0·6
Loch Dunvegan	....			−0 47	− 0·4	− 0·3
Loch Harport	....			−0 55	− 1·0	− 0·6
Camus nan Gall (Soay)		....		−0 40	− 1·5	*
Kyle of Lochalsh	....		·¹	−0 20	− 0·6	− 1·4
Glenelg Bay	....	....		−0 50	+ 0·4	+ 1·3
Loch Hourn	....	....	....	−1 07	+ 1·1	+ 1·7
Inverie Bay	....	....	....	−1 03	− 0·3	+ 0·1
Mallaig	....			−0 57	− 0·9	− 0·3
Bay of Laig (Eigg)		....		−1 05	− 1·6	− 0·6
Loch Moidart	....			−1 12	− 1·2	− 0·4
Loch Eatharna (Coll)		....		−1 09	− 1·6	*
Scarinish (Tiree)	....			−1 22	− 3·4	− 1·4
Carsaig Bay (Mull)	....			−1 37	− 3·0	+ 0·1
Iona	....	....	....	−1 35	− 2·8	+ 0·4
Bunessan	....	....	....	−1 42	− 1·4	+ 1·3
Ulva Sound	....	....	....	−1 40	− 1·7	+ 0·6
Salen (L. Sunart)	....			−1 27	− 0·9	+ 0·7
Scalasaig (Colonsay)		....	....	−1 40	− 3·4	+ 0·1
Glengarrisdale Bay (Jura)		....	....	−1 37	− 4·5	0
Oban	....	....	....		11·3	0·9
Tobermory	....	....	....	+0 10	+ 2·0	+ 0·1
Loch Aline	....	....	....	+0 12	+ 2·8	*
Corran	....	....	....	+0 07	+ 1·7	+ 0·1
Corpach	....	....	....	+0 22	+ 1·5	*
Loch Eil Head	....			+0 46	*	*
Loch Leven Head	....			+0 45	*	*
Port Appin	....	....		−0 05	+ 1·1	+ 0·5
Dunstaffnage Bay	....			−0 10	0	0
Bonawe	....	....		+2 25	− 5·7	*
Seil Sound	....	....		−0 25	− 3·0	+ 0·2
Rubha A'Mhail	....			−0 10	0	+ 0·3
Ardnave Point	....			−0 12	− 0·9	− 0·2
Orsay Island	....	....		−1 10	− 4·8	− 1·0
Port Ellen	....	....	{ Neap	−5 30	− 8·7	0
			{ Spring	−0 50		
Port Askaig	....	....	....	−0 50	− 4·8	+ 0·3
Craighouse	....	....	{ Neap	−4 30	+ 8·0	− 0·1
			{ Spring	−1 30		
Loch Beag	....	....	....	−0 57	− 4·0	− 0·1

Standard Ports					Height in ft.	
Secondary Ports			Average time difference H.W.		Differences	
					M.H.W.S.	M.L.W.S.
Oban					11·3	0·9
Charsaig Bay			−0 52		− 5·7	− 0·2
Gigha Sound .... { Neap			−4 50		− 7·8	− 0·1
{ Spring			−2 10			
Machrihanish .... { Neap			−5 20		Mean range 1·6 ft.	
{ Spring			−3 50			
Greenock					10·8	0·7
Southend (Kintyre)			−0 30		− 4·0	0
Sanda Island			−0 40		− 2·9	*
Campbeltown			−0 32		− 1·9	− 0·2
E. Loch Tarbert			−0 05		+ 0·1	+ 1·4
Inveraray			+0 11		+ 0·2	+ 0·2
Millport			−0 15		+ 0·5	+ 1·0
Rothesay Bay			−0 11		− 0·3	− 0·3
Wemyss Bay			−0 05		+ 0·2	+ 0·8
Coulport			−0 05		+ 0·5	+ 0·3
Lochgoilhead			+0 15		− 0·2	0
Arrochar			−0 05		+ 0·2	+ 0·2
Rhu Pier			−0 05		+ 0·3	+ 0·6
Shandon			−0 05		+ 0·4	+ 0·4
Garelochhead			0		+ 0·4	+ 0·3
Helensburgh			0		+ 0·4	+ 0·5
Port Glasgow			+0 08		+ 0·5	+ 0·1
Bowling			+0 24		+ 0·8	− 0·5
Brodick Bay			0		+ 0·7	+ 1·5
Lamlash			−0 26		− 1·7	*
Ardrossan			−0 20		− 1·6	− 0·8
Irvine			−0 20		− 1·8	− 0·8
Troon			−0 20		− 1·7	− 0·8
Ayr			−0 20		− 1·3	+ 0·4
Girvan			−0 33		− 0·6	+ 0·7
Stranraer			−0 20		− 1·6	−0 ·6
Liverpool					29·0	1·5
Portpatrick			+0 22		−16·5	− 0·3
Drummore			+0 25		−10·9	− 0·4
Isle of Whithorn			+0 20		− 7·0	− 0·5
Garlieston			+0 20		− 7·8	*
Kirkcudbright Bay			+0 15		− 5·9	− 0·3
Abbey Head			+0 20		− 3·7	*
Hestan Islet			+0 25		− 2·0	+ 1·1
Peel			−0 04		−11·0	+ 0·2
Ramsey			+0 04		− 6·2	0
Douglas			−0 04		− 6·2	+ 1·2
Calf Sound			+0 05		− 9·9	− 0·5

Standard Ports		Height in ft.	
Secondary Ports	Average time difference H.W.	Differences	
		M.H.W.S.	M.L.W.S.
Belfast		11·4	1·4
Donaghadee	+0 20	+ 1·7	+ 0·2
Carrickfergus	+0 05	— 0·9	— 0·3
Larne	+0 02	— 2·2	0
Red Bay	+0 06	— 6·3	— 0·8

TABLES OF DISTANCES

TABLE I. CLYDE ESTUARY UPPER SECTION
Distances given in miles.

	Fairlie Pier	Towmont End	Bogany Point Buoy	Toward Point Buoy	Skelmorlie Bell Buoy	Gantocks Light	Cloch Light House	Strone Point Buoy	Kempoch Point	Rosneath Patch N. Buoy	Rosneath Point Buoy	Rosneath Narrows
Fairlie Pier		2.1	7.5	7.0	6.4	11.0	11.1	13.3	13.5	14.8	16.1	18.1
Towmont End	2.1		5.4	4.9	4.3	9.0	9.2	11.1	11.6	12.9	14.2	16.2
Bogany Point Buoy	7.5	5.4		1.3	3.2	7.0	7.7	9.3	10.1	11.4	12.7	14.7
Toward Point Buoy	7.0	4.9	1.3		1.9	5.7	6.4	8.0	8.8	10.1	11.4	13.4
Skelmorlie Bell Buoy	6.4	4.3	3.2	1.9		4.7	5.2	7.0	7.6	8.9	10.2	12.2
Gantocks Light	11.0	9.0	7.0	5.7	4.7		1.2	2.3	3.6	4.9	6.2	8.2
Cloch Light House	11.1	9.2	7.7	6.4	5.2	1.2		2.1	2.4	3.7	5.0	7.0
Strone Point Buoy	13.3	11.1	9.3	8.0	7.0	2.3	2.1		2.9	3.7	5.0	7.0
Kempoch Point	13.5	11.6	10.1	8.8	7.6	3.6	2.4	2.9		1.3	2.6	4.6
Rosneath Patch N. Buoy	14.8	12.9	11.4	10.1	8.9	4.9	3.7	3.7	1.3		1.3	3.3
Rosneath Point Buoy	16.1	14.2	12.7	11.4	10.2	6.2	5.0	5.0	2.6	1.3		2.0
Rosneath Narrows	18.1	16.2	14.7	13.4	12.2	8.2	7.0	7.0	4.6	3.3	2.0	

TABLE 2. CLYDE ESTUARY — FAIRLIE TO THE KYLES OF BUTE
Distances given in miles.

	Fairlie Pier	Tan Spit Buoy	Garroch Heads	Bogany Point Buoy	Toward Point Buoy	Ardmaleish Buoy	Colintraive Pier	Ormidale Pier	Buttock of Bute	Carry Buoy	Ardlamont Buoy	Inchmarnock South End
Fairlie Pier		3.5	6.5	7.5	7.0	10.3	13.8	16.5	15.1	17.2	19.2	12.2
Tan Spit Buoy	3.5		3.0	7.0	7.0	9.8	13.3	16.0	14.6	13.7	11.7	8.7
Garroch Heads	6.5	3.0		8.6	9.0	11.4	14.9	17.6	16.2	10.7	8.7	5.7
Bogany Point Buoy	7.5	7.0	8.6		1.3	2.8	6.6	9.3	7.9	12.9	14.9	17.9
Toward Point Buoy	7.0	7.0	9.0	1.3		3.8	7.3	10.0	8.6	13.6	15.6	18.6
Ardmaleish Buoy	10.3	9.8	11.4	2.8	3.8		3.5	6.2	4.8	9.8	11.8	14.8
Colintraive Pier	13.8	13.3	14.9	6.6	7.3	3.5		2.7	1.3	6.3	8.3	11.3
Ormidale Pier	16.5	16.0	17.6	9.3	10.0	6.2	2.7		1.6	6.6	8.6	11.6
Buttock of Bute	15.1	14.6	16.2	7.9	8.6	4.8	1.3	1.6		5.0	7.0	10.0
Carry Buoy	17.2	13.7	10.7	12.9	13.6	9.8	6.3	6.6	5.0		2.0	5.0
Ardlamont Buoy	19.2	11.7	8.7	14.9	15.6	11.8	8.3	8.6	7.0	2.0		3.0
Inchmarnock South End	12.2	8.7	5.7	17.9	18.6	14.8	11.3	11.6	10.0	5.0	3.0	

TABLES OF DISTANCES

CLYDE ESTUARY LOWER SECTION — TABLE 3 — Distances given in Miles

	Fairlie Pier	Gull Point	Garroch Heads	Holy Isle N. End	Ailsa Craig	Pladda Lt. House	Inchmarnock S. End	Cock of Arran	Ardlamont Buoy	Skipness Point	Skate Island
Fairlie Pier	X	4.7	6.5	15.9	32.7	23.3	12.2	14.9	15.2	17.0	18.8
Gull Point	4.7	X	2.8	11.2	25.0	18.6	8.5	10.2	10.5	12.3	14.1
Garroch Heads	6.5	2.8	X	11.0	28.2	18.8	5.7	7.6	8.7	10.5	12.3
Holy Isle N. End	15.9	11.2	11.0	X	18.2	9.6	X	X	X	X	X
Ailsa Craig	32.7	25.0	28.2	18.2	X	10.0	X	X	X	X	X
Pladda Lt. House	23.3	18.6	18.8	9.6	10.0	X	X	X	X	X	X
Inchmarnock S. End	12.2	8.5	5.7	X	X	X	X	4.4	3.0	5.7	6.6
Cock of Arran	14.9	10.2	7.6	X	X	X	4.4	X	6.2	3.2	7.4
Ardlamont Buoy	15.2	10.5	8.7	X	X	X	3.0	6.2	X	6.0	4.1
Skipness Point	17.0	12.3	10.5	X	X	X	5.7	3.2	6.0	X	5.5
Skate Island	18.8	14.1	12.3	X	X	X	6.6	7.4	4.1	5.5	X

TABLE 4 — KILBRENNAN SOUND AND LOCH FYNE — Distances given in Miles

	Skate Island	East Loch Tarbert	Ardrishaig Lt. Ho.	Otter Spit Beacon	Paddy Rock	Inverary	Skipness Pt. Buoy	Carradale Buoy	Davaar Lt. House	Pladda Lt. House	Sanda Is. N. Beacon	Ailsa Craig
Skate Island	X	3.3	11.1	10.6	17.8	27.8	5.5	17.4	26.4	X	X	X
East Loch Tarbert	3.3	X	9.0	9.0	16.2	26.2	8.2	20.1	29.1	X	X	X
Ardrishaig Lt. Ho.	11.1	9.0	X	3.6	10.8	20.8	16.3	28.2	37.2	X	X	X
Otter Spit Beacon	10.6	9.0	3.6	X	7.2	17.2	16.0	27.9	36.9	X	X	X
Paddy Rock	17.8	16.2	10.8	7.2	X	10.0	23.2	35.1	44.1	X	X	X
Inverary	27.8	26.2	20.8	17.2	10.0	X	33.2	45.1	54.1	X	X	X
Skipness Pt. Buoy	5.5	8.2	16.3	16.0	23.2	33.2	X	11.9	20.9	X	X	X
Carradale Buoy	17.4	20.1	28.2	27.9	35.1	45.1	11.9	X	9.0	16.0	18.6	22.5
Davaar Lt. House	26.4	29.1	37.2	36.9	44.1	54.1	20.9	9.0	X	14.4	11.0	18.4
Pladda Lt. House	X	X	X	X	X	X	X	16.0	14.4	X	18.0	10.0
Sanda Is. N. Beacon	X	X	X	X	X	X	X	18.6	11.0	18.0	X	15.9
Ailsa Craig	X	X	X	X	X	X	X	22.5	18.4	10.0	15.9	X

TABLES OF DISTANCES

TABLE 5 ROUND THE MULL TO CRINAN AND AILSA CRAIG TO BELFAST. DISTANCES GIVEN IN MILES.	SANDA IS. N. BEACON	DEAS POINT	MULL OF CANTYRE LT. HO.	CARA IS. S. END	McARTHUR HEAD	McCORMAIG ISLES	TAYVALLICH	DORUS MOR	CRINAN	AILSA CRAIG	CORSEWELL POINT	BELFAST ROADS
SANDA IS. N. BEACON		5.7	8.5	27.5	37.0	44.5	54.5	59.3	59.0	15.9	22.3	39.0
DEAS POINT	5.7		2.8	21.8	31.3	38.8	48.8	54.6	54.3	21.6	27.6	38.6
MULL OF CANTYRE LT. HO.	8.5	2.8		19.0	28.5	36.0	46.0	50.8	50.5	24.4	29.9	40.2
CARA IS. S. END	27.5	21.8	19.0		12.0	17.0	27.0	31.8	31.5			
McARTHUR HEAD	37.0	31.3	28.5	12.0		13.0	23.0	27.4	27.1			
McCORMAIG ISLES	44.5	38.8	36.0	17.0	13.0		10.0	14.8	14.5			
TAYVALLICH	54.5	48.8	46.0	27.0	23.0	10.0		24.8	24.5			
DORUS MOR	59.3	54.6	50.8	31.8	27.4	14.8	24.8		3.0			
CRINAN	59.0	54.3	50.5	31.5	27.1	14.5	24.5	3.0				
AILSA CRAIG	15.9	21.6	24.4								14.6	42.5
CORSEWELL POINT	22.3	27.6	29.9							14.6		19.0
BELFAST ROADS	39.0	38.6	40.2							42.5	19.0	

TABLE 6 CRINAN TO LOCH ALINE AND TOBERMORY VIA FLADDA LT. HOUSE AND VIA CURN SOUND DISTANCES IN MILES	CRINAN	FLADDA LT. HOUSE	3 CABLES W. OF S. END SHEEP IS.	EASDALE PT. VIA FLADDA SD.	LADY ROCK	DUART POINT	GREY ISLE	ARDTORNISH PT.	LOCH ALINE FERRY PIER	GREEN ISLE	TOBERMORY PIER
CRINAN		10.6	14.4	13.7	23.2	24.4	27.6	29.6	30.7	34.7	42.4
FLADDA LT. HOUSE	10.6		3.8	3.1	12.6	13.8	17.0	19.0	20.1	24.1	31.8
3 CABLES W. & S. END SHEEP IS.	14.4	3.8		1.2	8.8	10.0	13.2	15.2	16.3	20.3	28.0
EASDALE PT. VIA FLADDA SD.	13.7	3.1	1.2		10.0	11.2	14.4	16.2	17.5	21.5	29.2
LADY ROCK	23.2	12.6	8.8	10.0		1.2	4.3	6.3	7.4	11.5	19.2
DUART POINT	24.4	13.8	10.0	11.2	1.2		3.2	5.2	6.3	10.3	18.0
GREY ISLE	27.6	17.0	13.2	14.4	4.3	3.2		2.0	3.1	7.1	14.8
ARDTORNISH POINT	29.6	19.0	15.2	16.4	6.3	5.2	2.0		1.1	5.1	12.6
LOCH ALINE FERRY PIER	30.7	20.1	16.3	17.5	7.4	6.3	3.1	1.1		4.5	12.2
GREEN ISLE	34.7	24	20.3	21.5	11.5	10.3	7.1	5.1	4.5		7.8
TOBERMORY PIER	42.4	31.8	28.0	29.2	19.2	18.0	14.8	12.6	12.2	7.8	

TABLES OF DISTANCES

TABLE 7 EASDALE POINT TO FORT WILLIAM VIA LYNNS OF LORNE AND MORVEN DISTANCES GIVEN IN MILES	EASDALE POINT	LOCH SPELVE S.W.CORNER	PUILLADOBHRAIN	S.ENTRANCE KERRERA SD.	N.ENTRANCE KERRERA SD.	DUNSTAFFNAGE	PORT APPIN LIGHT VIA LYNN OF LORNE	LISMORE LT.HO.	PORT RAMSAY VIA LYNN OF MORVEN	CULCHENNA SPIT BUOY	PORT AN DUN	CORRAN NARROWS	FORT WILLIAM PIER
EASDALE POINT	✕	9.4	4.9	6.6	10.4	13.6	18.8	10.5	19.0	28.3	31.7	34.1	41.3
LOCH SPELVE S.W. CORNER	9.4	✕	8.7	8.6	11.2	14.0	18.0	9.0	17.5	27.2	30.6	33.0	40.2
PUILLADOBHRAIN	4.9	8.7	✕	2.8	6.6	9.8	15.0	7.8	16.3	24.5	27.9	30.3	37.5
S.ENTRANCE KERRERA SD	6.6	8.6	2.8	✕	3.8	7.0	12.2	8.2	16.7	21.7	25.1	27.5	34.7
N.ENTRANCE KERRERA SD	10.4	11.2	6.6	3.8	✕	3.2	8.4	4.4	12.8	17.9	21.3	23.7	30.9
DUNSTAFFNAGE	13.6	14.0	9.8	7.0	3.2	✕	7.6	6.0	14.5	17.1	20.5	22.9	30.1
PORT APPIN LT. VIA LYNN OF LORNE	18.8	18.0	15.0	12.2	8.4	7.6	✕	10.0	1.8	9.5	12.9	15.1	22.3
LISMORE LT. HO.	10.5	9.0	7.8	8.2	4.4	6.0	10.0	✕	8.5	18.9	22.3	24.7	31.9
PORT RAMSAY VIA LYNN OF MORVEN	19.0	17.5	16.3	16.7	12.8	14.5	18	8.5	✕	10.4	13.8	16.2	23.4
CULCHENNA SPIT BUOY	28.3	27.2	24.5	21.7	17.9	17.1	9.5	18.9	10.4	✕	3.4	2.4	9.6
PORT AN DUN	31.7	30.6	27.9	25.1	21.3	20.5	12.9	22.3	13.8	3.4	✕	5.8	13.0
CORRAN NARROWS	34.1	33.0	30.3	27.5	23.7	22.9	15.1	24.7	16.2	2.4	5.8	✕	7.2
FORT WILLIAM PIER	41.3	40.2	37.5	34.7	30.9	30.1	22.3	31.9	23.4	9.6	13.0	7.2	✕

TABLE 8 FROM TOBERMORY AND FROM FLADDA LT.HO. TO THE WEST COAST OF MULL DISTANCES GIVEN IN MILES	TOBERMORY PIER	DRUMBUY	ARDNAMURCHAN LT.HO.	CALIACH POINT	LUNGA, TRESHNISH ISLES	GOMETRA HARBOUR	ULVA SOUND, S.ENTRY	INCH KENNETH	BULL HOLE	FLADDA LT.HO.	ARINAGOUR	GOTT BAY
TOBERMORY PIER	✕	5.0	9.8	11.0	18.6	22.7	25.4	25.0	29.8	✕	17.2	27.8
DRUMBUY	5.0	✕	12.2	14.4	22.0	26.1	29.8	29.4	33.2		20.2	31.8
ARDNAMURCHAN LT.HO.	9.8	12.2	✕	8.5	16.1	20.2	23.9	23.5	27.3		11.8	25.0
CALIACH POINT	11.0	14.4	8.5	✕	7.6	11.7	15.4	15.0	18.8		6.8	17.3
LUNGA, TRESHNISH ISLES	18.6	22.0	16.1	7.6	✕	6.2	10.5	10.2	10.3		8.5	14.2
GOMETRA HARBOUR	22.7	26.1	20.2	11.7	6.2	✕	6.2	5.6	9.6		13.5	18.8
ULVA SOUND, S.ENTRY	25.4	29.8	23.9	15.4	10.5	6.2	✕	2.0	12.0		18.3	23.7
INCH KENNETH	25.0	29.4	23.5	15.0	10.2	5.6	9.6	✕	11.3		18.0	23.4
BULL HOLE	29.8	33.2	27.3	18.8	10.3	9.6	12.0	11.3	✕	29.0	18.4	18.8
FLADDA LT. HO.									29.0	✕		
ARINAGOUR	17.2	20.2	11.8	6.8	8.5	13.5	18.3	18.0	18.4	✕	✕	12.6
GOTT BAY	27.8	31.8	25.0	17.3	14.2	18.8	23.7	23.4	18.8		12.6	✕

TABLES OF DISTANCES

TABLE 9
TOBERMORY TO KYLE AKIN AND TO CANNA
DISTANCES GIVEN IN MILES

	Tobermory Pier	Ardnamurchan Lt. Ho.	Bo Faskadale Buoy	Eigg Harbour	So. of Sleat Beacon (Sleat Point)	Mallaig	Isle Ornsay Harbour	Inverie Bay (Scottis)	Kyle Rhea Lt. Ho.	Ob Totaig	Kyle Akin Lt. Ho.	Canna Harbour
Tobermory Pier		9.8	15.8	18.8	29.8	31.8	39.8	35.4	47.7	53.0	52.8	31.3
Ardnamurchan Lt. Ho.	9.8		6.0	9.0	20.0	22.0	30.0	26.6	37.9	43.2	43.0	22.5
Bo Faskadale Buoy	15.8	6.0		3.6	14.0	16.0	24.0	20.6	31.9	37.2	37.0	
Eigg Harbour	18.8	9.0	3.6		9.2	13.3	21.5	17.4	28.9	34.2	34.0	19.7
So. of Sleat Beacon	29.8	20.0	14.0	9.2		6.8	13.0	10.8	18.5	24.2	24.0	16.2
Mallaig	31.8	22.0	16.0	13.3	6.8		9.7	4.0	17.2	23.5	23.3	23.0
Isle Ornsay Harbour	39.8	30.0	24.0	21.5	13.0	9.7		12.3	7.9	13.2	13.0	29.2
Inverie Bay (Scottis)	35.4	26.6	20.6	17.4	10.8	4.0	12.3		15.7	21.0	20.6	27.0
Kyle Rhea Lt. Ho.	47.7	37.9	31.4	28.9	18.5	17.2	7.9	15.7		5.3	5.1	37.7
Ob Totaig	53.0	43.2	37.2	34.2	24.2	23.5	13.2	21.0	5.3		7.0	42.4
Kyle Akin Lt. Ho.	52.8	43.0	37.0	34.0	24.0	23.3	13.0	20.8	5.1	7.0		42.2
Canna Harbour	31.3	22.5		19.7	16.2	23.0	29.2	27.0	37.7	42.4	42.2	

TABLE 10
KYLE AKIN TO THE NORTH AND TO SKYE
DISTANCES GIVEN IN MILES.

	Kyle Akin Lt. Ho.	Ayre Point Lt. Raasay	Portree Pier	Acarsaid Mor, S. Rona	Ru Hunish	Vaternish Point	Dunvegan Pier	Plockton	Rudha na Fearn, Loch Torridon	Badachro, Loch Gairloch	Ru Re	Aultbea	Greenstone Point	Tanera Mor, Summer Is.
Kyle Akin Lt. Ho.		10.3	18.9	18.7	35.0	45.8	56.8	7.3	20.8	31.0	36.8	45.8	44.1	55.6
Ayre Point Lt. Raasay	10.3		8.6	13.2	28.5	39.3	50.3	13.0	17.0	27.2	32.5	41.5	39.8	51.3
Portree Pier	18.9	8.6		10.6	24.0	34.8	45.8	21.6	19.4	25.0	30.0	39.0	37.3	48.8
Acarsaid Mor, S. Rona	18.7	13.2	10.6		17.3	28.1	39.1	14.8	9.2	16.8	21.6	30.6	28.9	40.4
Ru Hunish	35.0	28.5	24.0	17.3		10.8	21.8	34.5	19.0	20.6	20.0	29.0	27.3	38.8
Vaternish Point	45.8	39.3	34.8	28.1	10.8		11.0	45.3	29.6	31.4	30.8	39.6	38.1	49.6
Dunvegan Pier	56.8	50.3	45.8	39.1	21.8	11.0		57.1	40.8	42.4	41.8	50.6	49.1	61.6
Plockton	7.3	13.0	21.6	19.8	34.5	45.3	57.1		21.8	31.5	38.7	47.7	46.0	57.5
Rudha na Fearn, L. Torridon	20.8	17.0	19.4	9.2	19.0	29.8	40.8	21.8		10.5	17.0	26.0	24.3	35.8
Badachro, Gairloch	31.0	27.2	25.0	16.8	20.6	31.4	42.4	31.5	10.5		12.0	21.0	19.3	30.8
Ru Re	36.8	32.5	30.0	21.6	20.0	30.8	41.8	38.7	17.0	12.0		9.0	7.3	18.8
Aultbea	45.8	41.5	39.0	30.6	29.0	39.8	50.8	47.7	26.0	21.0	9.0		7.5	19.0
Greenstone Point	44.1	39.8	37.3	28.9	27.3	38.1	49.1	46.0	24.3	19.3	7.3	7.5		11.5
Tanera Mor, Summer Is.	55.6	51.3	48.8	40.4	38.8	49.6	61.6	57.5	35.8	30.8	18.8	19.0	11.5	

TABLES OF DISTANCES

TABLE 11 — THE OUTER HEBRIDES — Distances given in Miles	CANNA HARBOUR	DUNVEGAN PIER	CASTLE BAY, BARRA	BIG HARBOUR, ERISKAY	CALVA IS. LT., L.BOISDALE	WIZARD POOL, L.SKIPORT	LOCH EPORT ENTRANCE	WEAVER PT., L.MADDY	LOCH RODEL	SCALPAY IS. LT., HARRIS	LOCH MARNVEG, L.ERISORT	STORNOWAY
CANNA HARBOUR	✕	39.0	36.5	28.0	26.5	31.0	37.0	40.0	46.0	51.0	74.0	79.0
DUNVEGAN PIER	39.0	✕	52.0	40.0	34.0	27.5	19.0	20.0	21.0	24.5	43.0	48.0
CASTLE BAY, BARRA	36.5	52.0	✕	12.5	20.0	32.0	44.0	47.0	56.0	65.0	87.0	92.0
BIG HARBOUR, ERISKAY	28.0	40.0	12.5	✕	8.5	20.5	33.0	36.0	45.0	54.0	76.0	81.0
CALVA IS. LT., LOCH BOISDALE	26.5	34.0	20.0	8.5	✕	13.0	27.0	30.0	39.0	48.0	70.0	75.0
WIZARD POOL, L.SKIPORT	31.0	27.5	32.0	20.5	13.0	✕	15.0	18.0	27.0	36.0	58.0	63.0
LOCH EPORT ENTRANCE	37.0	19.0	44.0	33.0	27.0	15.0	✕	3.5	13.0	22.0	44.0	49.0
WEAVER PT., L.MADDY	40.0	20.0	47.0	36.0	30.0	18.0	3.5	✕	10.0	19.0	41.0	46.0
LOCH RODEL	46.0	21.0	56.0	45.0	39.0	27.0	13.0	10.0	✕	12.0	34.0	39.0
SCALPAY IS. LT. HARRIS	51.0	24.5	65.0	54.0	48.0	36.0	22.0	19.0	12.0	✕	22.0	27.0
LOCH MARNVEG, LOCH ERISORT	74.0	43.0	87.0	76.0	70.0	58.0	44.0	41.0	34.0	22.0	✕	7.0
STORNOWAY	79.0	48.0	92.0	81.0	75.0	63.0	49.0	46.0	39.0	27.0	7.0	✕

INDEX

INDEX—*Continued*

INDEX—*Continued*

INDEX—*Continued*

INDEX—*Continued*

I N D E X—*Continued*

INDEX—*Continued*

I N D E X—*Continued*

INDEX—*Continued*

INDEX—*Continued*

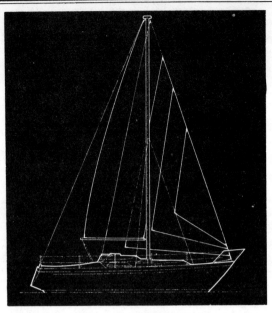
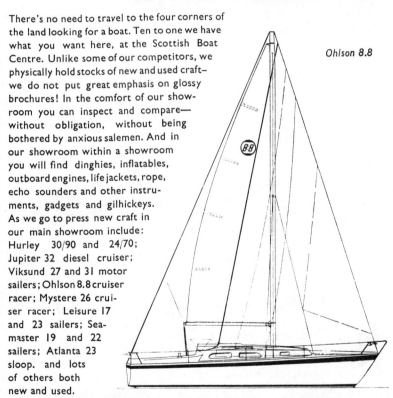
L

Commercial and Colour Printers

Printers and Publishers
of the
Sailing Directions

Gilmour & Lawrence Ltd.

Clydeway Industrial Centre
8 Elliot Place, Glasgow G3 8EL
Telephone 041-221 2228

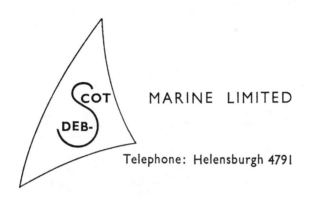

SCOT DEB- MARINE LIMITED

Telephone: Helensburgh 4791

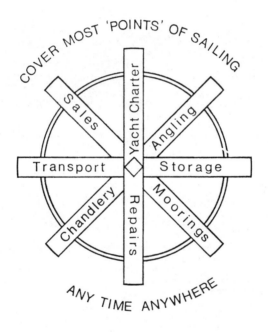

COVER MOST 'POINTS' OF SAILING

Yacht Charter

Sales

Angling

Transport

Storage

Chandlery

Repairs

Moorings

ANY TIME ANYWHERE

MᶜWILLIAM SAILMAKERS

Spinner   *Aquila of Down*

Our Company was set up in 1973 to produce top quality yacht sails concentrating on the Celtic fringe you might say.

Personnel

Our small team is energetic and flexible. My own background is sufficiently varied to give me an objective viewpoint and valuable combination of skills. It includes professional qualifications in engineering and aeronautics, and a thoroughly international sailmaking training, I cut all our sails myself and supervise their construction throughout.

Performance plus Service

Performance plus service is our constant aim and, to this end I spent twenty weekends racing with customers last season. We set up a temporary sail loft at Rothesay to look after you during the 1973 Clyde International Regatta.

Whilst at Rothesay I raced on 'BILLYCAN', a Norlin 34 which chose eleven of her thirteen sails from us after a critical weekend's match racing in Ballads off Gourock the previous winter. 'BILLYCAN' won her Class on the Feeder Race, won the Middle Distance Race and Class A2 overall. Two other yachts using our sail exclusively also won their Classes overall—'SKULMARTIN' (Hustler 30, Class B) and 'MUFFIN' (Ruffian 23, Quarter Ton).

Down in the Irish Sea, our sails won both R.O.R.C. races, every Class in the Round the Isle of Man Race, and every Class in the 1973 I.S.O.R.A. Points Championship.

LIMITED

Scampi	North Channel 29	Hustler 35
Tearaway	*Garland of Howth* (now *Blackwater*)	*Andromeda*

Cruising

In case you think it's all racing, our sails have been examined in detail by Laurent Giles & Partners, and selected for a world-wide cruising yacht they have designed. Seven of our Radial-Head and Starcut spinnakers were taken on the Round-the-World Race.

Our deliveries are always on time—we can deliver a sail to Glasgow Airport in four hours from our loft. I spent twenty days in Scotland last season personally looking after customers and this year has joined a light aircraft syndicate which will speed up communications.

Contact

If you want to talk sails or sailing, do give me a ring—evenings are quietest and the lines are clearer, Alternatively I can call while in Scotland if you drop me a note. In any case ring 832200 next time you are in Crosshaven—cruising or racing, you will be WELCOME!

McWILLIAM SAILMAKERS LIMITED

CROSSHAVEN   CORK
TEL. CORK (021) 832200

Clyde Cruising Club

OTHER PUBLICATIONS

Sketch Charts of the West Coast of Scotland
and North Channel

The 1974 Edition contains 50 revised charts
Cost £4.40 plus postage and packing

Club Log Book cost £1 plus postage
and packing

THE WHISKY RUN

Series of articles on the West Coast of Scotland
Cost 40p plus postage and packing

Available from the Honorary Secretary's Office

S.V. Carrick
Clyde Street Glasgow G1 4LN

Tel. 041–552 2783

A complete finance service for purchase & improvement of small craft

Should you require finance to purchase your next craft or to replace suits of sails, install navigational equipment or make other improvements, take advantage of the competitive terms offered by Forward Trust. Forward Trust is a member of the Midland Bank Group and is the finance company that has enjoyed a long association with the cruising and sailing world. Terms for marine mortgages are particularly attractive and you may qualify for tax relief on the interest paid. And if you should die before the payments are completed, your family is fully protected under our Family Protection Plan. Full information about Marine Finance through Forward Trust is available from any Forward Trust branch (see your telephone directory)

ft Forward Trust (Scotland) Ltd.

Ashley House, 181/195 West George Street,
Glasgow C2. Tel: 041-221 8981
Forward Trust (Scotland Ltd.)
Associated with Clydesdale Bank
is a member of the Midland Bank Group.

Open all the year round

CAIRNBAAN

Lochgilphead, Argyll

Telephone Lochgilphead 2488

Oil-fired central heating
throughout. Razor sockets,
radio and intercom in every
bedroom

Excellent Cuisine

Fully Licensed

CRINAN HOTEL

Argyll

Telephone Crinan 235

Suites or bedrooms with
private bathrooms.
Spacious lounges and modern restaurant
overlooking Loch Crinan.
Beatifully appointed cocktail bar
adjoining sun lounge.
Central Heating.
Fully Licensed.
A.A. R.A.C. R.S.A.C.

Both Hotels overlook Crinan Canal

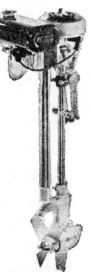

now there are five

SCOTTISH MARINE CENTRES

caledonian yacht services ltd

116 HOPE STREET GLASGOW G2 6PS SCOTLAND

Yacht Brokers

Agents in Scotland and Northern Ireland for Camper and Nicholsons

Transatlantic

A new name in sailing wear from old hands at the game

Transatlantic is an exciting new range of sailing wear from Edward Macbean - famous for waterproof clothing for almost 100 years.
(Old salts swear by Macbean's PVC Weatherbar range in Vinco 27).
Transatlantic is made in Winskyn - the new wonder material Winskyn is 100% waterproof. It is tough, but with sufficient stretch to improve comfort and it 'breathes'
- No perspiration or condensation problems.
Leading yachtsmen and sailors have already tried, tested and suggested some of the design features of Transatlantic sailing wear.
* Seams 100% waterproofed
Stitched and electronically welded
* Heavy duty nylon zips
* Adjustable storm cuffs
* Velcro fastening pockets
* Non-corrosive studs
* Highly resistant to oils, grease, petrol, scuffs and abrasions.

CLYDE DIVISION RNR
130 Whitefield Road,
Glasgow G51 2SA

∿∿∿

Right in the heart of Glasgow

Naval know-how for over 70 years

Recommended for all Sailing men

∿∿∿

Telephone: 041-427 2421

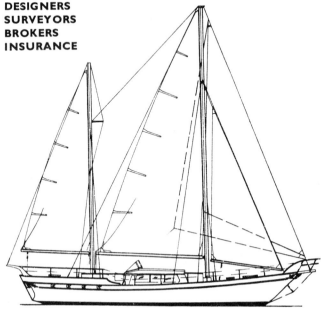

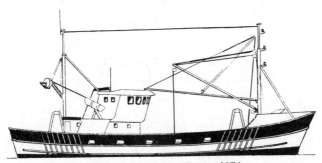

Welcome to

MACDONALD ARMS HOTEL
Tobermory

Telephones: 2011 (Office) and 2076 (Visitors)

Resident Proprietors:— Bert and Mona Hall

Lounge and Public Bars

★

Dining Rooms—*late meals*

★

Supper Room

★

Baths and Showers *usually available*

★

Clothes drying facilities

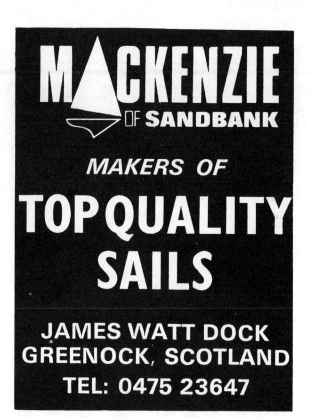
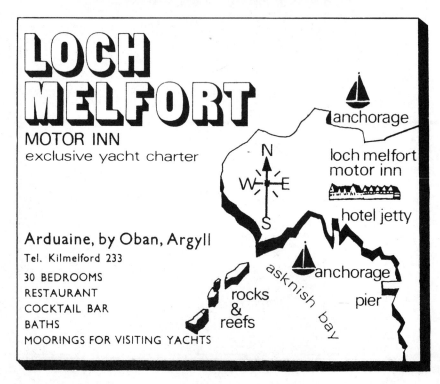